People's Power

Latin American Perspectives Series

Ronald H. Chilcote, Series Editor

People's Power

Cuba's Experience with
Representative Government

Peter Roman

Westview Press
A Member of the Perseus Books Group

Latin American Perspectives

Copyright © 1999 by Westview Press, A Member of the Perseus Books Group

Published in 1999 in the United States of America by Westview Press, 5500 Central Avenue, Boulder, Colorado 80301-2877, and in the United Kingdom by Westview Press, 12 Hid's Copse Road, Cumnor Hill, Oxford OX2 9JJ

Library of Congress Cataloging-in-Publication Data
Roman, Peter, 1941-
  People's power: Cuba's experience with representative government / Peter Roman.
    p.   cm. — (Latin American perspectives)
  Includes bibliographical references and index.
  ISBN 0-8133-3586-8 (hc)
  1. Representative government and representation—Cuba.   I. Title.
II. Series.
JL1013.R66   1999
320.47291—dc21   98-55919
                                                                      CIP

The paper used in this publication meets the requirements of the American National Standard for Permanence of Paper for Printed Library Materials Z39.48-1984.

10   9   8   7   6   5   4   3   2   1

I wish to dedicate this book to Daniel Morales and Carlos Walfrido Rodríguez. Both have been municipal assembly delegates from Playa, and dedicated and selfless public servants in the best sense of the term. They represent the best socialism can create, and they helped in creating the best in socialism. It is because of people like Carlos and Daniel that socialism can work. Both went out of their way and did all they could for many years to help me in every way possible to complete this book, not just because of friendship, but also because both want the true story of Cuban local government to be told.

Contents

Acronyms

ANAP   (*Asociación Nacional de Agricultores Pequeños*, National
          Association of Small Farmers)
CDR   (*Comités de la Defensa de la Revolución*, Committees for the
          Defense of the Revolution)
CEA   (Centro de Estudios sobre América)
CEN   (*Comisión Electoral Nacional*, National Electoral
          Commission)
CETSS   (*Comité Estalal de Trabajo y Seguridad Social*, State
          Committee on Work and Social Security)
CIERI   (Center of Information and Study on Interamerican
          Relations)
CTC   (*Central de Trabajadores de Cuba*, Federation of Cuban
          Workers)
ECUSE   (Cuban Service Enterprise)
FEEM   (*Federación de Estudiantes de Estudios Medios*, Federation of
          High School Students)
FEU   (*Federación de Estudiantes Universitarios*, University Students
          Federation)
FMC   (*Federación de Mujeres Cubanas*, Federation of Cuban
          Women)
INIFAT   (Institute of Fundamental Investigations on Tropical
          Agriculture)
JUCEIs   (*Juntas de Coordinación, Ejecución e Inspección*, Coordination,
          Operations and Inspection Boards)
JUCEPLAN (*Junta Central de Planificación*, Central Planning Board)
MINCIN   (*Ministro de Comercio Interno*, Ministry of Domestic Trade)
OLPP   (*Organos Locales del Poder Popular*, Local Organs of People's
          Power)
OPP   (*Organos del Poder Popular*, Organs of People's Power)
PCC   (*Partido Comunista de Cuba*, Cuban Communist Party)
SDPE   (*Sistema de Dirección y Planificación de la Economía*, System
          for Direction and Planning of the Economy)
UJC   (*Unión de Jovenes Comunistas*, Union of Young Communists)

Acknowledgments

The research on which this book is based was supported in part by grants from the City University of New York PSC/CUNY Research Foundation and the CUNY/Caribbean Exchange Program at Hunter College, as well as by support from Hostos Community College of the City University of New York.

I received valuable help and guidance from Cuban scholars at the Centro de Estudios sobre América (CEA), especially from Haroldo Dilla Alfonso and Juan Valdés Paz, who read early drafts and made substantial suggestions for the focus of my research. Also helpful were Alfredo Prieto, Luis Suárez, and Aurelio Alonso. Especially important was the full assistance and cooperation I received from Cuban municipal assembly delegates (including officers), most of all Carlos Walfrido Rodríguez, Daniel Morales, and Roberto Díaz Vence of Playa; Raquel García and Omar Torres of Cienfuegos; and Mario García and Felix Gómez of Bauta. They facilitated my entry into all aspects of Cuban municipal government, which made this study possible. Also providing access and information were National Assembly Presidents Juan Escalona and Ricardo Alarcón, as well as Arcardio Pérez, who worked for the National Assembly. Hector Igarza of Prensa Latina helped me by informing me of and getting me to important events.

Those in the United States who helped me significantly include Roger Owen, professor emeritus at Queens College, who was the person most responsible for assisting and encouraging me in my efforts in writing the manuscript; Rogelio Batista and Cristina Piñyero, former students of mine at Hostos Community College, who transcribed the tapes; Barbara Metzger, who edited the original manuscript (the many changes she suggested made the manuscript more coherent and readable); Margaret Ritchie, who did the final copyediting; Jill Hamberg, who provided me with valuable material for the study; and Nanette Díaz and Mildred Carrero, the secretaries for the Behavioral/Social Sciences Department at Hostos Community College, who helped me considerably by printing, copying, and mailing my manuscripts. Gail Lindenberg, my wife and partner, was the main person with whom I discussed all aspects and ideas found in this book.

Introduction

"We know everything, or almost, about electoral systems or the workings of parliaments in capitalist states. We know nothing, or practically nothing, about electoral systems or the workings of the largest decision-making bodies in socialist states."[1] This study attempts to partially redress this neglect, pointed out by Norberto Bobbio, by examining local representative government in socialist Cuba.

Cuban local representative government since 1976 has been characterized by (1) representation of a population, not divided into antagonistic classes, by municipal assembly delegates, nominated by their constituents and elected in competitive elections, who are socially and economically indistinguishable from the electorate and for the most part not professional politicians; (2) an electorate that nominates, elects, closely identifies with, and has personal contact with its municipal delegates; (3) municipal delegates who do not have legislative powers but are directly accountable to their constituents, their main functions being to resolve community problems and to serve as a conduit for constituents' concerns; and (4) an important role for the electorate through its elected representatives in forming, determining, developing, and monitoring local and national economic plans and budgets, and in checking all economic activity located in the municipality.

To elucidate the origins of these characteristics, I begin by exploring the democratic theories based on the convergence of civil and political societies and the *mandat impératif* (instructed delegate model) in Rousseau, Marx, and Lenin and the emergence and application of these theories in the Paris Commune of 1871, the soviets of 1905 and 1917, the first constitutions of the Soviet Union, and the Soviet Union until the mid–1970s. I go on to examine the development of the Cuban *Organos del Poder Popular* (Organs of People's Power—OPP) within the parameters of the 1976 Constitution, with special emphasis on the relevance of these theoretical concepts for the municipal assemblies within the *Organos Locales del Poder Popular* (Local Organs of People's Power—OLPP). Included are the changes brought by the 1992 Constitution and Electoral Law. Finally, I present the results of a detailed investigation of how these theories have been put into practice in Cuba by examining the electoral system, the municipal delegates account-ability sessions, and the *consejos populares* (people's councils).

I chose for close examination four municipalities with distinctive charac-teristics with respect to geography and type of location, size, and population; type of constituency; and the local economic activity. Playa, in the City of Havana Province, is mostly urban, has a mixed constituency of professionals and white- and blue-collar workers, and contains marginal neighborhoods as well as those that were formerly working-, middle-, and upper-class. It con-tains various industries, including fishing, a large beer factory, and major tourist hotels. Bauta, in Havana Province about ten miles from Havana, is agricultural, but its main economic activity is a huge textile factory. Many who live in Bauta work in the City of Havana. Cienfuegos, in Cienfuegos Province, about two hundred miles southeast of Havana on Cuba's south coast, is a major urban, industrial, and agricultural center and an important ocean port. Its population is heavily dominated by industrial workers who belong to strong unions. Palmira, about fifteen miles north of Cienfuegos, also in the Cienfuegos Province, is dominated by sugarcane cultivation and refining, and its small population is mostly rural.

The study on which this book is based began in 1986 with the fifth leg-islative session of the Cuban municipal assemblies. The fieldwork was done in Cuba from 1986 to 1998. I was there for the municipal elections in Octo-ber 1986, for nine months from September 1987 to June 1988, and re-turned in December 1988, May 1989, and February 1992.[2] I traveled to Cuba in February 1993 for the elections for provincial assemblies and the National Assembly, in February 1994 to attend the workers' parliaments,[3] in May 1996 to study the *consejos populares,* and in January 1998 for the provincial assembly and National Assembly elections.

In the tradition established during the Paris Commune of 1871 and of the soviets of 1905 and 1917, the Cuban OPP consist of governing institutions whose purpose is to represent the interests of the proletariat and its allies (peasants, professionals, and others). The economic and social composition of the elected members, especially municipal delegates, closely corresponds to that of the Cuban population, within which there is far greater equality than, for instance, in the population of the other countries in Latin Ameri-can. The wage difference between the lowest- and highest-paid workers, as calculated by Swedish economist Claes Brundenius, is about four to one, and this gap is further reduced when free and subsidized benefits available to all are taken into account.[4] In 1986, the population with the lowest 40 per-cent of income received 26 percent of the total income, whereas the highest 5 percent received 10.1 percent of the total.[5] Since the legalization of the U.S. dollar in 1993, the increasing number of Cubans who receive remit-tances in dollars from relatives and other sources abroad has resulted in an increase in income inequality.[6]

Eligible voters, those citizens over sixteen years old who live within the electoral district, excluding prisoners and those declared mentally incompetent, freely nominate and elect their municipal delegates by secret ballot, in competitive elections.. There must be between two and eight candidates, and the delegate must win a majority of the votes. If one candidate fails to win a majority of the votes cast in an electoral district, a second round of elections is held. Each municipal delegate represents an electoral district of about a thousand voters (fewer in rural areas, more in some urban ones) for a term of two and a half years. Municipal delegates must reside in their electoral districts. In place of electoral campaigns the biographies of the candidates are posted in the neighborhoods. Under the 1976 Constitution, the municipal assembly delegates elected the provincial assembly delegates every two and a half years and the National Assembly deputies every five years; under the 1992 Constitution, provincial delegates and National Assembly deputies are directly elected by the Cuban people every five years.

Representative government in Cuba has three levels—the municipal assemblies, the provincial assemblies, and the National Assembly. The lower bodies are directly subordinate to the higher ones. Each of these levels is responsible for supervising the economic and social activities under its direct control and, to some degree, all the economic and social activities within its territory; thus the Cuban parliaments have potentially far broader scope than their capitalist counterparts. Only the National Assembly has legislative powers.

Because of the absence of private property and profound social class divisions or differences, parliamentary debates and decision making in Cuba are different from those in capitalist representative systems, which are more often characterized by political and class antagonisms, in which one side wins at the expense of the other. In Cuba, prior to voting, an attempt is made to resolve and include wherever possible the concerns expressed by the delegates during the discussions and debates of the assemblies' plenary sessions and commissions. I witnessed only a few divided votes (only in municipal assembly sessions): Most were unanimous. Unanimity can also be considered a part of the heritage of Rousseau's general will, as well as of the practice in the former Soviet Union, the stress being on unity, harmony, and consensus. Cuban political commentator Julio García Luis perceives the goal of the system as being "to secure political unity and efficient management of the society by the only way possible: the systematic search for consensus through communication, dialogue, information, persuasion and the permanent contact between representatives and the represented."[7]

The municipal assembly analyzes, discusses, supervises, monitors, inspects, and controls the social, economic, judicial, and political affairs of the municipality. It selects managers for local enterprises and entities such as public health clinics and schools, and it helps formulate and approves the municipal economic plan and budget. It also monitors the performance of enterprises, including industries and services, under provincial and national subordination located within the municipality. The assembly meets in ordinary session twice a year and in special session about four times a year.

The municipal assembly has commissions composed of delegates and citizen volunteers with expertise, for areas such as education, public health, and economic affairs. These commissions investigate, inspect, issue written reports to the assembly, and review citizen complaints and suggestions *(planteamientos)* made to the delegates. In 1989, the *consejos populares*—groups of delegates of approximately fifteen contiguous electoral districts within a municipality—were created in the City of Havana in an effort to make the government more accessible to the population. By 1993, these *consejos populares* were spread throughout the entire country.

Municipal assembly delegates are the access point and main link between the people and their government. Among the delegates' most important tasks is to fulfill the mandates of the electorate by attempting to resolve issues raised by their constituents either in person or at biannual neighborhood accountability sessions. Delegates are also responsible for coordinating projects in their electoral districts and for solving problems that may surface. They participate in municipal assembly work commission meetings, conduct on-site inspections and interviews, and write reports. They attend the sessions of their municipal assembly and various seminars to share experiences and to educate the delegates (for example, to explain the economic planning process).

The provincial assembly controls and directs the state economic enterprises and social and service entities directly subordinate to the provincial government and helps monitor economic and social activities that are subordinate to the national government but lie within the province. The provincial assembly also formulates and approves provincial economic plans and budgets. It holds two regular sessions and several extraordinary sessions per year. It also aids, inspects, monitors, and coordinates the work of the municipal assemblies in the province. Because it works with the municipalities of the province, providing assistance when requested, it is one connecting point between the municipalities and the national government. Its commissions work with provincial enterprises and entities and receive from the municipalities the complaints and suggestions citizens make to their delegates, which correspond to the commissions' areas of responsibility. The commissions monitor the resolution of these concerns and visit the citizens who have raised them. They also coordinate areas of municipal concerns within the province.

The National Assembly controls, inspects, and monitors the national government ministries and state organs, including the national judiciary and the attorney general's office, and the OLPP, primarily the provincial assemblies. National Assembly deputies elect, in noncompetitive elections, which seem to be pro forma, the president, the vice president, and the secretary of the

National Assembly and the Council of State, and they ratify the membership of the Council of Ministers and the leadership of both councils. The president of both councils during the time of my study was Fidel Castro. Deputies debate and vote on proposed laws, reports, and the commentaries and critiques made by National Assembly commissions on each report and each piece of proposed legislation. The Assembly discusses and approves at each session the reports of one province and one government ministry, and of the attorney general and the judiciary branch. It votes to approve the national economic plan and budget and the reports of the Council of State, which represents the assembly between sessions, and the Council of Ministers.

The major part of the duties of most deputies consists of serving on the National Assembly commissions. These commissions investigate and prepare commentaries on reports and proposed laws to be debated during the National Assembly sessions and write their own reports. Their role is mainly consultative and investigative; rather than approve or oppose proposals, they mainly help formulate and modify them.

The role of the Cuban Communist Party (PCC) is essentially political leadership. It sets national priorities and long-term goals for the whole society, including the government. It initiates, directs, and encourages the spread of socialist consciousness and behavior; it monitors and assists the OPP in carrying out their representative and governmental functions; it reviews legislation prior to submission to the National Assembly; and it names and/or approves personnel who fall under the nomenclature system (the right to designate high government officials). According to my research, the party does not propose, nominate, or in any other way interfere in the selection of candidates for municipal assembly delegates. Up to the mid–1980s, in some instances, neighborhood party nuclei did informally propose individuals for nomination, but they never had the authority to nominate. According to what I was able to determine, this practice did not represent the norm. Of course, party members, like others, may still attempt informal influence on local nominations, but not in an official capacity. Whereas previously the party did have a prescribed role in the selection of candidates for municipal and provincial assembly leadership positions, provincial assembly delegates, and National Assembly deputies, with the electoral changes passed in 1992 the party no longer is officially represented on candidacy commissions at any level, nor does it have any formal role in proposing and nominating candidates for provincial assembly delegates and National Assembly deputies.

Neither the collapse of socialism in Europe and the Soviet Union nor the steep decline of the Cuban economy with the onset of the "special period" beginning in 1990 has altered the general thrust of my findings. According to Howard French of the *New York Times*, prior to this economic crisis,

Cuba was "one of Latin America's healthiest and most affluent countries."[8] Johanna McGeary and Cathy Booth, writing in *Time*, similarly found that "Cubans look back on the time before 1989 as a Golden Age, when the system brought them a standard of living better than most Caribbean nations and roughly equal for every citizen."[9] Thus much of my fieldwork before 1990 took place in what could be considered relatively "normal" circumstances.

The main emphasis of this study is not on high government and party officials, but on the elected municipal assembly delegates, who also make up close to half those elected to the provincial assemblies and the National Assembly. Although the importance of President Fidel Castro and other national Cuban political leaders is evident, it is also clear that they alone are not and cannot be responsible for the functioning of the system. Cuban sources, including newspapers, officials, and intellectuals, are taken seriously, and their arguments are not dismissed out of hand but are given a full hearing.

While all political systems are subject to change, the focus of this study is on the existing socialist government in Cuba, and it does not presume the necessity or likelihood of transition, as does some of the recent scholarship on Cuba.[10] Furthermore, since the definition of *democracy* is elusive, varying according to the settings and political circumstances, no claims are made as to whether Cuba is or is not a democracy. For example, China's 1998 experiment with competitive village elections, comparable to those held in Cuba since 1976 in a similar political context, has been referred to in the U.S. press as "rudimentary democracy" and "the beginning of liberalization."[11] Cuba, on the other hand, continues to be cited as a dictatorship whose leaders promise "no constructive change for Cuba" and have no "evident taste for democracy."[12]

My main objectives in examining this system are to understand the Cuban local parliamentary system as a product of socialist theory, history, and economics, and to determine to what extent it has been an effective instrument for political participation in governing and in providing input for local and national policy. Within these parameters, this study seeks to determine to what extent and in what manner Cuban citizens identify with the political system and their municipal delegates, whether these elected representatives are legitimately chosen by and representative of their constituents, and whether they are bound by their constituents' mandates. Ultimately, I am concerned about evaluating whether a local parliamentary system can be considered legitimate, representative, and effective in the absence of oppositional politics, electoral campaigns, and a multiparty system.

The general outline and objectives of my study were approved by and the initial introductions to the government bodies I planned to investigate were arranged by the National Assembly. However, the decisions as to what to study and whom to interview were mine alone. I was permitted to do the fieldwork as I saw fit without interference from the Cuban government or the PCC. I did seek and receive assistance when I needed it. The principal help I was given in organizing and conducting my study came from locally elected assembly leaders and other municipal delegates. I conducted most of the interviews and attended meetings, seminars, inspections, and assembly sessions alone. The exceptions were the initial interviews and events, when I was accompanied for purposes of being introduced, and a few of the interviews of high government and party officials, for which being accompanied seemed to be more a question of protocol. Since I am fluent in Spanish, I did not need an interpreter. I also benefited greatly from the support and suggestions of Cuban scholars who formerly worked at the *Centro de Estudios sobre América* (CEA) in Havana. I have had close contact with them during my stays in Cuba, and they have offered me valuable assistance and suggestions and provided me with important publications.

I had the opportunity to attend neighborhood nomination meetings for municipal delegates, as well as neighborhood meetings at which votes were taken to initiate the process for delegate recall. During municipal elections, I visited various polling places and interviewed voters there. During the provincial assembly and National Assembly election campaigns, I attended rallies and encounters between candidates and constituents. I also observed accountability sessions between municipal delegates and constituents, meetings between delegates and representatives of governmental entities, seminars for municipal delegates, visits by delegates to constituents' homes, sessions of municipal and provincial assemblies, meetings of municipal assembly executive committees, meetings and activities of the assembly commissions of the three levels of the OPP, and a meeting of a municipal candidacy commission to decide on candidates for provincial delegates. I interviewed constituents; municipal and provincial assembly delegates and National Assembly deputies; members of municipal and provincial assembly executive committees; the president, the vice president, the secretary, and the commission presidents of the National Assembly; the minister of education; local, provincial, and national Communist Party officials; and local, provincial, and national economic planning directors. During twelve days in 1996, I accompanied the president of a *consejo popular* in his daily activities.

During my nine-month stay in 1987–1988, I lived with my family in an apartment in the centrally located Vedado section of Havana. (During later visits, I stayed at hotels and at the homes of municipal delegates.) My daughter attended nursery school, and we received medical attention mainly at the local public health clinic. We purchased our fruits and vegetables at the local market *(agromercado)* and our bread at the local bakery *(panadería)*. We owned an automobile, and the hitchhikers I picked up provided me with some of my most interesting discussions. We became close friends of a number of the people whom we met. This integration into Cuban life enabled me to gain important insights into the political system from a variety of perspectives.

Notes

1. Norberto Bobbio, *Which Socialism? Marxism, Socialism and Democracy* (Richard Bellamy, ed.), (Worcester: Polity Press, 1987), p. 33.

2. Peter Roman, "Representative Government in Socialist Cuba," *Latin American Perspectives*, Issue 76, Vol. 20, No. 1 (Winter 1993), pp. 7–27.

3. Peter Roman, "Workers' Parliaments in Cuba," *Latin American Perspectives*, Issue 87, Vol. 22, No. 4 (Fall 1995) pp. 43–58.

4. Claes Brundenius, "Cuba: Redistribution and Growth with Equity," in Sandor Halebsky and John M Kirk (eds.), *Cuba: Twenty-five Years of Revolution, 1959–1984* (New York: Praeger Publishers, 1985), pp. 203–204.

5. Andrew Zimbalist and Claes Brundenius, *The Cuban Economy: Measurement and Analysis of Socialist Performance* (Baltimore: Johns Hopkins University Press, 1989).

6. James C. McKinley, Jr., "In Cuba's New Dual Economy, Have-Nots Far Exceed Haves," *New York Times*, January 11, 1999, pp. A–1, A–6.

7. Julio García Luis, "La soberanía reside en el pueblo," *Trabajadores*, January 5, 1998, p. 3 (my translation).

8. Howard W. French, "43,412 Stricken Cubans, and Not a Single Answer," *New York Times*, June 15, 1993, p. A–4.

9. Johanna McGeary and Cathy Booth, "Cuba Alone," *Time*, Vol. 142, No. 24 (December 6, 1993), p. 45

10. Miguel Angel Centeno and Mauricio Font, *Towards a New Cuba? Legacies of a Revolution* (Boulder: Lynne Rienner, 1997).

11. Philip Caputo, "The Wei That Wasn't," *New York Times Magazine*, June 21, 1998, p. 29; Thomas L. Friedman, "Here Comes the Sun," *New York Times*, March 14, 1998, p. A–17.

12. "After Fidel Castro," *New York Times*, February 4, 1998, p. A–22.

1

Early Theories of Socialist Representative Government

As Stephen White, John Gardner, and George Schopflin have pointed out, communist states "have a democratic theory of their own which, in line with Marxist and indeed with some earlier theories of democracy, places more emphasis upon the content of democracy than upon its form, and upon the socio-economic rights of citizens rather than upon their formal independence of state power."[1]

Just as the study of Locke, Hobbes, and Montesquieu is indispensable for an understanding of the formation and logic of the capitalist system of representative government, the works of Rousseau, Marx, and Lenin, among others, are essential to the understanding of the origins and logic of the structures and practices of socialist representative government, including that of Cuba. The theory relating democratic government to economic equality, the merging of civil and political societies, political participation, and the *mandat impératif* can be traced directly to Rousseau. Marx and Lenin built on this foundation.

Also of significance with regard to the development of the theory of representative government under socialism and to the formation of socialist governmental structures and practices are certain historical events and models, the most important of which are the Paris Commune of 1871, the Russian soviets of 1905 and 1917, the Russian Revolution itself, and the period immediately following (especially those of the first constitutions) and the evolution of the Soviet Union (especially after the death of Stalin). Just as most formal state systems are derived from existing ones, the Cuban organs of People's Power were patterned after existing socialist representative systems, with the Soviet system of the 1970s serving as the basic model.

However, socialist representative government has been neither necessarily fixed nor stagnant and, within its historical context, has been subject like any

other system to evolution, development, and change. Innovations introduced during and after the Cuban institutionalization process of the early
1970s departed from the existing Soviet model by including competitive
elections for municipal delegates, with candidates proposed and nominated
by the constituents rather than by the Communist Party, and with the requirement that local delegates reside in their electoral districts and be directly accountable to their constituents at all times.

In the eighteenth and nineteenth centuries, the theories of Rousseau,
Marx, and Engels and the experience of the 1871 Paris Commune most influenced the path socialist representative government was to take.

Rousseau

The French philosopher Jean-Jacques Rousseau, while not a socialist, represented an important break with liberal political theorists, including Hobbes,
Locke, and Montesquieu,[2] and in this sense, he was an important predecessor to the Marxian critique of bourgeois society. The Italian Marxist philosopher Lucio Colletti wrote, "In an age in which all the most advanced
thinkers were interpreters of the rights and reasons of rising bourgeois society, its prosperity and industry (and in France struggled to give this new society adequate political forms), the critique of 'civil society' in the *Discourse*
irretrievably isolated Rousseau from his contemporaries, and made his
thought appear absurd and paradoxical to them."[3]

Rousseau's writings had a powerful though unacknowledged influence on
Marx's theory. Colletti went so far as to say that with regard to specifically
"political" theory, "Marx and Lenin have added nothing to Rousseau, except for the analysis (which is of course important) of the 'economic bases'
for the withering away of the state."[4] He added that Fidel Castro is reported
to have told a French reporter that he considered Rousseau to be his teacher
and that he had carried the *Social Contract* with him during the struggle
against Fulgencio Batista. Colletti concluded, "I do not think that Castro
disowned this last statement when he added, 'that since then, he has preferred reading Marx's *Capital.*'"[5]

Rousseau argued, as did Marx and Engels later, that private property was
the source of inequality in society. The British historian Eric Hobsbawm
considers Rousseau's concept of equality the precursor of the modern communist movement:

> First, the view that social equality must rest on common ownership of wealth
> and central regulation of all productive labour is a natural extension of
> Rousseau's argument. Second, and more important, the political influence of
> Rousseau's egalitarianism on the Jacobean left, out of which the first modern
> communist movements emerged, is undeniable. . . . The communism whose ac-
> quaintance Marx and Engels first made had *equality* as its central slogan; and

Rousseau was its most influential theorist. Inasmuch as socialism and communism in the early 1840s were French—as they largely were—a Rousseauist egalitarianism was one of the original components.[6]

Rousseau's theory of equality was a precursor of the socialist concept of political equality in that its essence is the absence of profound economic and social divisions and differences among the electorate. Rousseau rejected the liberal concept of equality under the law, a notion that overlooks the economic and social inequalities that abounds in civil society. This paradox of legal equality but economic inequality foreshadowed the early Marx's contention that the separation of civil society and the state in capitalist society made truly representative government a fiction.[7] Rousseau rejected inequality based on class and status but recognized the social importance of individuals' merits:

> I conceive that there are two kinds of inequality among the human species; one which I call natural or physical, because it is established by nature, and consists in a difference of age, health, bodily strength, and the qualities of the mind or of the soul; and another, which may be called moral or political inequality, because it depends on a kind of convention, and is established, or at least authorized, by the consent of men. This latter consists of the different privileges which some men enjoy to the prejudice of others; such as that of being more rich, more honoured, more powerful or even in a position to exact obedience.[8]

In his "Letters Written from the Mountains," he deplored the existence of

> people who abound in wealth on the one hand, and the most abject and low on the other. Is it in these extremes, where the one doth his utmost to buy, and the other to sell himself, that we are to expect the love of justice and the laws? They are the causes of the state's degeneracy. The rich have the law in their pockets, and the poor choose bread rather than liberty.[9]

Galvano della Volpe called Rousseau's concept of equality "egalitarian freedom" or "anti-leveling egalitarian society."[10] For him, Rousseauian equality acquired its concrete meaning, resolution, and historical continuity and development in Marx, Engels, and Lenin:

> The double aspect, the two souls, of modern liberty and democracy are *civil* (political) liberty initiated by parliamentary, or political, democracy and expounded theoretically by Locke, Montesquieu, Kant, Humboldt, and Constant; and *egalitarian* (social) liberty, instituted by socialist democracy, and expounded theoretically in the first instance by Rousseau and then, more or less explicitly, by Marx, Engels and Lenin. . . . It means the *right* of *every human* being to *social* recognition of his *personal* capacities and potentialities. . . . This contrasting of the *two souls* of modern democracy, of the two modern demands for liberty, means in political terms, in the last resort, the comparison of liberal-

ism, or the political system of liberty without equality or (social) justice, with socialism, or the political system of social justice, or justice for all (egalitarian liberty in its full development).[11]

Della Volpe argued that this conception of egalitarianism theorems resolves itself in Marx's concepts of class struggle, abolition of classes, and proletarian emancipation and egalitarianism as presented in the "Critique of the Gotha Programme," Engels's "Anti-Dühring," and Lenin's "State and Revolution."[12] Colletti, however, pointed out that whereas Rousseau argued that society should recognize natural differences, Marx's position was that society should suppress the disadvantages and privileges that result from individual attributes.[13]

Rousseau attributed civil inequality to societal factors. In "A Discourse on the Origin of Inequality," he wrote:

> The first man who, having enclosed a piece of ground, bethought himself of saying "This is mine," and found people simple enough to believe him, was the real founder of civil society. From how many crimes, wars, and murders, from how many horrors and misfortunes might not any one have saved mankind, by pulling up the stakes, or filling up the ditch, and crying to his fellows: "Beware of listening to this impostor; you are undone if you once forget that the fruits of the earth belong to us all, and the earth itself to nobody."[14]

He believed that equality and egalitarian liberty could be realized only through politics. Thus, in his view, the responsibility for the resolution of inequality lay with society, rather than, for example, with God, or the individual: "The ethical task of the triumph of good over evil is therefore necessarily identified with the political task of the transformation of society."[15] Rousseau's concept of freedom, similarly, was not the liberal concept of freedom from or against society but a freedom to be realized together with equality "in and through" society [16] with "the creation of a new moral and social order."[17]

Another characteristic of modern socialist government that can be traced back to Rousseau is the importance given to achieving unity and consensus. His emphasis on the relation of consensus to democratic society has been cited in the Cuban newspaper *Trabajadores* in connection with the consensus at the time of the 1959 Revolution and during the February 1993 elections for National Assembly deputies and provincial assembly delegates. "Unity by consensus is a primary value of substantial democracy. Rousseau, in his Origin of the Inequality of Mankind, asserted: 'If there is no common destiny, there is no fruitful living together with others.'"[18] For Rousseau the capacity to carry out necessary political tasks presupposed a sufficiently authoritative and unitary society to "prevent any centrifugal movement by individuals and classes who may be parasitic and exploitative of man."[19] According to the historian J. L. Talmon, Rousseau considered "partial interests the greatest enemy of social harmony."[20] Colletti added that for Rousseau, the individual could be fully realized only as part of the whole society: "Society is a true 'society' when it is the expression of the 'general will,' or a real socialization, a real common interest."[21]

Knowing the general will leads to unity and unanimity. Talmon referred to the eighteenth-century concept of democracy, "whose postulates were unity and unanimity. . . . This expectation of unanimity was only natural in an age which, starting with the idea of the natural order, declared war on all privileges and inequalities."[22] Rousseau, in "The Social Contract," equated the general will with both unanimity and the realization of freedom: "The more concert reigns in the assemblies, that is, the nearer opinion approaches unanimity, the greater the dominance of the general will."[23] Those who oppose the general will oppose their own freedom: "The constant will of all the members of the State is the general will; by virtue of it they are citizens and free."[24]

Rousseau's theory of the general will in contradistinction to particular wills reappeared in the young Marx's discussion of the democratic state liberated from the rule of special interests[25] and subsequently has been manifested in the emphasis on harmony and pressure for conformity and unanimity in parliamentary votes in both Cuba and the former Soviet Union. Rousseau's theory of the legislator as the representative of the leadership directing society to the general will is brought to fruition in the concept of the vanguard party as developer of socialist consciousness and formulator of society's goals under socialism.

Rousseau's influence is also manifested in Cuba's stress on active citizen involvement in local civic affairs and close relation between delegates and constituencies. For Rousseau, the evolution of the new type of citizen was to be achieved through political participation: "There is nothing that Rousseau insists on more than the active and ceaseless participation of the people and of every citizen in the affairs of the State. The State is near ruin, says Rousseau, when the citizen is too indifferent to attend a public meeting."[26] The conditions for political participation were identified by Rousseau as "first, a very small State, where the people may easily be got together and where each citizen can with ease know all the rest. . . . Next, a large measure of equality in rank and fortune, without which equality of rights and authority cannot long subsist."[27] According to Richard Fralin, Rousseau "was convinced that civic virtue was doomed among a people who habitually limited their participation in communal life to the occasional election of representatives."[28]

Rousseau's theory implies a strong identification of the people and their representatives, recognizing the necessity "for the representatives to be mingled with the body of the people."[29] He stressed the need for unity, respect, and identity of interests between the governors and the governed,[30] writing,

"I would have wished to be born in a country where the sovereign and the people could have only one and the same interest."[31]

Rousseau's aim was for society to resume the sovereign power that liberal theory had relegated to the political sphere and thus to foster the unity of civil society and government. To this end, Rousseau argued for a unitary form of government and for the mandate system (*mandat impératif*), both of which exist in Cuba. According to Colletti:

> This resumption signifying in fact the suppression of the division between civil "society" and civil "government" or "civil" society and "political" society . . . is expressed on the one hand in the unification (against the "division of powers") of government and parliament, of executive and legislature; and on the other, in their "common reduction" to mere "commissions" or "working" functions, which society not only requires some of its members to do (in the same way as with all other work functions), but which are carried out on behalf of and under the direct control of the mandators (the theory of the *mandat impératif*) who retain full power to effect their immediate "recall."[32]

The mandate system, characterized by formal instructions by constituents to their elected representatives, including the right of recall, is what makes Rousseau's direct democracy attainable. The deputies must be the agents of their constituents. Because sovereignty cannot be represented, "The deputies of the people . . . are not and cannot be its representatives: they are merely its stewards."[33] Returning to Rousseau's teachings in his own *General Theory of Law and the State*, Hans Kelson included as part of the definition of the concept of the legislative *mandat impératif* that "it is necessary that the representative be legally obliged to execute the will of the represented and the fulfillment of this obligation be legally guaranteed."[34]

Soviet social scientist V. F. Kotok traced the roots of the *mandat impératif*, or "instructed delegate" model, which he called the most distinctive element of socialist representative government, to the *Estates General* in late medieval France.[35] Representatives were agents of the estates—clergy, nobility, or bourgeoisie—and were held accountable for expressing the views of those estates.[36] According to Fralin, "in much of eighteenth-century Europe some form of mandate system was prevalent."[37] The "instructed delegate" model was used in the Revolutionary Commune installed by the Jacobeans in Paris in 1792. The historian Oskar Anweiler wrote of the Jacobean Commune, "The Paris sections were expressions of a direct radical democracy; the delegates chosen by universal suffrage were held permanently answerable and could be recalled. Though modified by immediate political and strategic needs, direct democracy as embodied in the Commune nevertheless remained the central principle of a continuing revolutionary tradition."[38] Bakunin carried forward this tradition: "He suggested the formation of revolutionary committees with representatives from the barricades, the streets, and the city districts, who would be given binding mandates, held accountable to the masses, and subject to recall."[39]

Commenting on Article 80 of the 1976 Cuban Constitution, which states that National Assembly deputies should not receive personal privileges or economic benefits that would separate them from the people, Cuban constitutional scholar Fernando Alvarez Tabio referred to the deputies' activities as determined by the "*mandato imperativo*" of the electorate and quoted Couthon, the Jacobean member of the 1793 French Convention: "The national interest, the justice owed to the people and the sacred principle of equality, do not permit that a distinction be established between a representative of the nation and any other citizen."[40]

Rousseau's clearest statements accepting the *mandat impératif* system and the need to hold deputies accountable to their constituents are found in his "Considérations sur le gouvernement de Pologne": "After all, it is not to express their own private sentiments, but to declare the will of the nation, that the nation sends deputies to the diet."[41] The right of voters to recall their political rulers is set forth in "The Social Contract": The people "can set them up and pull them down when it likes."[42]

Thus, because according to this theory the deputies' personal views are not really relevant, Rousseau presaged the practice in Cuban local elections of having voters' decisions based not on campaign promises, but on the candidates' personal histories. C. E. Vaughan suggested that for Rousseau, "trustworthiness in the lower grades of the public service is to be the sole qualification for election to the Diet."[43] In "Letters Written from the Mountains," Rousseau wrote that when voting for candidates for political office, citizens should consider the following criteria among the most important: "Those who, by long experience, are well versed in publick affairs; those who, despising the false luster of ambition, choose no higher rank but that of citizens; lastly, those who, having had no other views but the good of their country and the support of the laws, have justly deserved the esteem of the publick, and the confidence of their equals."[44] He advocated the right of citizens to meet with their political leaders in order to restrain them and to air grievances. Rousseau called this the "right of representation" *(droit de représentation)*,[45] foreshadowing the Cuban accountability sessions between municipal delegates and constituents.

The "Letters Written from the Mountains" contain an analysis of the government in Geneva, where, according to Rousseau, the edict of 1707 gave citizens the right to air grievances to their magistrates: "And thus the remonstrances of a citizen, or of any number of them together, is only a declaration of their opinion upon a matter that properly concerns them."[46] Remonstrances might relate to two objects: "One is the making some alteration in the law; the other is, the reparation of some transgression of the law."[47] Rousseau concluded that "the government should be administered by a few, but the inspection of that government belongs to many."[48]

This right of representation, as described by Rousseau, concerned "not the act of legislation . . . but of the administration of the laws. . . . By this article alone, your government, otherwise subject to many considerable defects, becomes the best that ever existed."[49] Thus, in Vaughan's opinion, for Rousseau the right of representation was fundamental: "Rightly understood, it is the cornerstone of the liberties of the citizens."[50] Fralin argued that this right was consistent with "The Social Contract" and that Rousseau saw the right of representation "even in the limited sense of a device for bringing charges of maladministration against the government, as an effective means of ensuring popular sovereignty."[51]

Marx and Engels

Much of what Marx wrote regarding representative government, especially in 1843–1844, appears to have been influenced by Rousseau's ideas on equality, the unity of civil and political society, and the importance of the political realm. Colletti traced to Rousseau Marx's "critique of parliamentarism, the theory of popular delegacy and even the idea of the state's disappearance."[52] In his later writings, such as "The Civil War in France," Marx continued these themes. Along with Engels, he contributed concepts related to class struggle and class rule through the dictatorship of the proletariat and communism as society's goal that Della Volpe regards as Rousseau's "egalitarian liberty in its full development."[53] But neither Marx nor Engels produced a fully developed theory of socialist politics. Hobsbawm outlined some of the implications of this lack:

> Since they refused to speculate about the details of the coming socialist society and its arrangements, or even about the details of the transitional period after the revolution, they left their successors little more than a very few general principles with which to confront it. Thus they provided no concrete guidance of practical use on such problems as the nature of the socialization of the economy or the arrangements for planning it. . . . Instead, they placed the action of the movement firmly in the context of historical development.[54]

Hal Draper pointed to Marx and Engels's "struggle to give democratic forms a new *social* (class) content, above all by pushing them to the democratic extreme of popular control from below, which in turn entailed extending the application of democratic forms out of the merely political sphere into the organization of the whole society."[55] Hobsbawm agreed with this premise: "The transitional proletarian state, whatever functions it maintained, must eliminate the separation between the people and government as a special set of governors."[56]

Draper explained that the concept of democracy as employed by Marx, especially in his early critique of Hegel, must be placed in the context of the Enlightenment tradition and the use of the concept "democracy" in the first half of the nineteenth century, a period heavily influenced by traditions stemming from ancient Greece. Marx was influenced by the then prevalent tendency to fuse the political and the social, to give more importance to the social content than to governmental structures, and to emphasize social equality. "The people, the *demos*, might directly participate in the regime or might merely have great weight in it in some sense (including a demagogic sense) without reference to forms of participation."[57] Richard Hunt also argued that Marx's political model closely resembled that of Periclean Athens, especially regarding the emphasis upon widespread citizen participation and nonprofessional politicians.[58] Cuban leader Fidel Castro has also associated the Cuban concept of political democracy with the idea of Athenian democracy, minus the exclusion from politics of slaves, women, and foreigners, but more in terms of the absence of the political fragmentation, abstentionism, and violence found in varying degrees in capitalist democracies.[59]

Like Rousseau's, the young Marx's criticism of the separation of civil and political society (or the state) in bourgeois democracy was based upon political equality, with the absence of social and economic equality. It was through the French Revolution that "*class distinctions* in civil society became merely *social* differences in private life of no significance in political life. This accomplished the separation of political life and civil society."[60] In "The Jewish Question," Marx stressed the disunity of civil society "fragmented into private interests competing against each other."[61] Thus the general will emanating from political society in bourgeois democracies sanctified and legitimized the social inequality and disunity within them.[62]

In terms of forms of representative government, the separation between civil and political society is manifested by the isolation and separation of the delegates from the electors. "The deputies of civil society are a society which is not connected to its electors by any 'instruction' or commission," wrote Marx. "They have authority as the representatives of *public* affairs, whereas in reality they represent *particular* interests."[63]

Hobsbawm noted that "Marx envisaged a system of democracy in which participation and representation would no longer be distinct."[64] Yet, according to Christopher Pierson, "in characterizing democracy as the unity of civil and political life, Marx sought to avoid the classic conundrum of how all the people individually should take part in deliberating and deciding on political matters of general concern."[65] As had Rousseau, Marx found part of the answer to the problem of truly representative government in the *mandat im-*

pératif, where representatives are instructed by and bound to their electors. Representation becomes a *working* rather than a *political* function, and the resultant legislature is representative in a functional sense in that "it is characteristic or typical of the people in general."[66] In Cuba the goal is to have the National Assembly be representative of all sectors of society. In Marx's words:

> The legislature is representative only in the sense that *every* function is representative. For example, a cobbler is my representative in so far as he satisfies a social need, just as every definite form of social activity, because it is a species activity, represents only the species. That is to say, it represents a determination of my own being just as every man is representative of other men. In this sense he is a representative not by virtue of another thing which he represents but by virtue of what he *is* and *does*.[67]

In 1843, Marx went beyond Rousseau by introducing socialism as the only basis upon which "true democracy" could be achieved. Only through socialism, he wrote, could the separation between civil and political societies be resolved in modern democracies. Later that year, he added the proletariat as the main agent of radical social change. Hunt, commenting on Marx's association of socialism with a democratic political system, argued that "formal democracy without socialism was for Marx not *worthless* but *inadequate*."[68] According to Colletti, Marx viewed the separation between parliament and society as ceasing when "society is an organism of solidarity and homogeneous interests, and the distinct 'political' sphere vanishes along with the division between governors and governed. This means that politics becomes *the administration of things*, or simply another branch of social production."[69]

Marx's notion of working-class rule in a socialist society became the basis for his concept of the dictatorship of the proletariat. From his concept of the state under socialism as no longer an external body dominating society, he derived the theory of the depoliticization of state functions or, in other words, the withering away of the state. Ralph Miliband summed up the meaning of dictatorship of the proletariat as understood by Marx and Engels as "*both* a statement of the class character of the political power *and* a description of the political power itself."[70]

In contemporary Cuba, the nonantagonistic, nonoppositional characteristic of the delegate elections and the parliamentary debates could be categorized within Marx's concept of the depoliticization of the political sphere. Marx's espousal of eliminating the separation between political and civil society is manifested in Cuba in that most elected representatives are not professional politicians and continue working in their regular jobs, and in that close, personal, and social class ties link municipal delegates, who are mainly from the working class, to their constituents.

The dictatorship of the proletariat excludes not parliamentary government, but bourgeois parliamentary government. Both Marx and Engels identified the Paris Commune of 1871, which was based on elected representatives, as an example of the dictatorship of the proletariat.[71] According to the Brazilian sociologist Theotonio dos Santos, "For Marx the State is by definition a dictatorship in the service of a particular class, even if that State is administered in a democratic way."[72]

The essence of Marx's theory of the dictatorship of the proletariat was that whatever the constitutional form or governmental mechanism adopted, the main question was the class content or social basis of political power. As Draper put it, "*How far down in the social scale, in the hands of what class or class stratum, was political power expected to reside?* This was the link between the class struggle and often technical sounding questions of constitutional forms."[73] For Marx, government was to be associated with what he called the "immense working majority";[74] the entire class (or people) was to be involved in governing itself.[75]

Socialist economic reorganization "determines the centralising and coercive structure he [Marx] had in mind,"[76] according to Neil Harding. Referring to the appeal of dictatorship of the proletariat, Harding argued:

> It was undoubtedly its tough-minded content, its promise to end exploitation and charge retribution upon the capitalists, that provided the basis of the appeal of Marxism to the industrial workers. This Marxism was addressed not to humanity as a whole, nor to the fiction of "society" (and in this it distinguished itself from all species of Utopianism), but to the oppressed and poor and exploited. It was a programme of *their* redemption. Its emphases and objectives were class-exclusive and were attainable only through the economic and political expropriation of the bourgeoisie.[77]

In Marx's theory, the abolition of private property, to be accomplished under proletarian rule, would make possible the elimination not only of the separation of state and civil societies but also of the gulf between governors and the governed, as the governors would no longer represent private interests as opposed to public ones. The abolition of private property would create the conditions for the disappearance of the state as a separate political element dominant over and antagonistic to civil society, as there would no longer be private interests to defend against the public. As Marx and Engels wrote in the *Manifesto of the Communist Party,* "When, in the course of development, class distinctions have disappeared, and all production has been concentrated in the hands of a vast association of the whole nation, the public power will lose its political character. Political power, properly so called, is merely the organised power of one class for oppressing another."[78]

The ultimate disappearance of what was known as the state would be part of the lengthy process of the development of communist society. To be sure, during the transition period, "the new workers' power *is* a type of state. *It is a state-which-is-in-the-process-of-becoming-a-nonstate.*"[79] Public or social functions and authority would continue "analogous to present-day state functions."[80] But these statelike functions would gradually be transformed as private interests were no longer pitted against each other nor against the public interest. In addition, the legislature and the judiciary would be deprofessionalized. This new type of state "would cease to exist as a separate institution standing over society and run by professionals; public business would become the part-time or short-term activity of ordinary citizens."[81] It would no longer constitute "a special organism separated from society through division of labour."[82]

For Marx, elections would no longer be antagonistic, and elected delegates would be subject to recall by their constituents. To a degree, his "Conspectus of Bakunin's *Statism and Anarchy*" anticipates the nonpolitical nature of the Cuban municipal elections: "The character of the election does not depend on this name, but on the economic foundation, the economic situation of the voters, and as soon as the functions have ceased to be political ones, there exists 1) no government function, 2) the distribution of the general functions has become a business matter, that gives no one domination, 3) election has nothing of its present political character."[83]

The 1871 Paris Commune

Marx and Engels's notion of the dictatorship of the proletariat found its concrete expression in the Paris Commune of 1871. In the words of the French historian Henri Lefebvre, "This utopia, this alleged myth, became fact and life for a few days. In this sense the Commune became the very idea of the revolution, understood not as an abstract ideal, but as the concrete idea of liberty."[84] Beyond the example it set as the first working-class government, the Paris Commune had an important influence on the political thought of Marx and Lenin and the popular acceptance of Marxist theory, and on the forms of governmental organization of the Russian Revolution[85] and subsequently the Cuban Revolution. "The experience of the Commune," wrote Eugene Schulkind, "foreshadows similar (not identical) forms of workers' power."[86] According to the German historian Arthur Rosenberg:

> The work of Marx on the Civil War of 1871 has an extraordinary historical significance; for by this bold step Marx annexed the memory of the Commune. It is only since then that Marxism has possessed a revolutionary tradition in the eyes of mankind. By 1870 Marx had already acquired a reputation as an outstanding theoretician of the labour movement, but the general public knew nothing of the political and revolutionary activity of the Marxists. It is only since Marx's resolute public defence of the Commune in 1871, with which he

drew upon himself the entire indignation of bourgeois society, that he achieved his aim of identifying his International and the Commune in the public mind. . . . The Paris Commune as interpreted by Marx exerted an extraordinary influence on the development of Russia.[87]

Foreshadowing the working-class background and status of most Cuban municipal delegates, according to Schulkind, "The Paris Commune was to represent the first general rejection in history of the belief that ordinary workers are not equipped to govern."[88] The Parisian working class was able to establish its own government because of events clearly beyond its control, and although working-class activities, ideology, and politics were on the rise in Paris, the creation of the Commune was to a great extent spontaneous and improvised.[89] The more radical and militant Parisian republican groups in the years before the Commune espoused the notion of a *république démocratique et sociale*, including the social emancipation of the working class.[90] As class polarization escalated, there developed a preoccupation with improving living and working conditions, social as well as political equality, and "a conscious underlying effort to give a political voice to the working class."[91]

The French National Assembly, elected in February 1871, was very reactionary, as was reflected in the newly formed government led by Louis Adolphe Thiers. The Prussian army had defeated the French and partially surrounded Paris, thus shutting down much of the city's economy and creating widespread hardship. One of the few remaining sources of employment was the well-armed Paris national guard, which had become a workers' militia with elected officers and a central committee. The national guard was hated by the wealthy Parisian bourgeoisie.[92] The National Assembly proceeded to threaten the livelihood of the working and lower middle classes in Paris by demanding immediate payment of rents and commercial bills that had been suspended during the Prussian siege, and by suspending the daily pay of the national guard.[93] Rosenberg related what followed:

> On March 18, 1871 the Thiers government ordered the regular troops to remove the artillery of the National Guard. The Central Committee was not prepared for this moment, just as in general it had no definite policy during those decisive days. Nevertheless the people spontaneously opposed the removal of their cannon. A revolt developed. The government troops refused to fire on their brothers. Now the National Guard had not only retained its cannon but was suddenly in possession of the capital. The government together with its officials and the remainder of its troops evacuated Paris.[94]

The central committee of the national guard, which was the only authority left in Paris capable of administering the city, took control and immediately called for elections. On March 28, the "Commune of Paris" was elected. Of

485,000 registered voters, 229,000 turned out—a surprising number given that many, especially among the upper and middle classes, had fled the city, leaving behind mainly workers, shopkeepers, less important civil servants, the sick and aged, and some writers and artists.[95] According to G. D. H. Cole:

> Quite a number of moderate Liberals and Radicals were elected, mainly from the middle-class areas; but these either did not take their seats or soon withdrew. The rest were a mixture of well known Radicals, including many journalists, members of the Central Committee of the National Guard, Blanquists, and Jacobeans from the revolutionary clubs, and working-class members and a few others connected with the International.[96]

Class polarization increased with the bielections held on April 16, 1871, to fill the seats left vacant by the more moderate delegates who withdrew. Voter participation in the non-working-class areas dropped. In the general atmosphere of radical social change, the conviction grew within the working class that the Commune had come to represent it.[97] Although the majority of the elected delegates were not working-class, most were in sympathy with working-class demands. Half of the thirty-six Commune leaders identified were less than thirty-two years old, and the delegates of this new generation were mainly trade union leaders and included a wood carver, a joiner, a skilled mechanic, a painter, and a jewelry worker.[98]

Marx understood, as he wrote in 1881, that "the majority of the Commune was in no sense socialist, nor could it be."[99] In fact, during the two months it existed its main task was to fight for survival. When defeat came at the hands of the French government forces with Bismarck's assistance, a slaughter ensued. Estimates of the number of Parisians killed during and after the fighting exceed forty-three thousand. Of the twenty thousand tried and condemned by the regular courts, the vast majority were manual workers.[100] Marx compared the wholesale slaughter, torturing of prisoners, and hunt for concealed leaders to "the times of Sulla and the two Triumvirates of Rome."[101] Rosenberg gave the following account:

> It is apparent that the so-called republican government of France employed the imperial military machine in order to render the workers of Paris and the real republicans innocuous. A true slaughter was organized among the insurgents and even among the non-combatant population. The number of dead in Paris amounted to at least twenty thousand. In addition thousands of Parisian workers were thrown into prisons and concentration camps or were forced to flee. The defeat of the Commune was accompanied by the physical destruction of the proletarian and republican vanguard of France. To find another example of such a horrible defeat of the working classes one must go back to the Peasant War of 1525.[102]

Among the clear lessons of the Paris Commune for future proletarian uprisings were the need to grasp and prepare for the temper of the class enemy and the total unacceptability to the capitalist ruling class of a working-class government, which apparently the Cubans have taken seriously with regard to the United States. As Gordon Lewis summed it up, "Nothing tells more about the bestial depths to which a ruling class on the defensive will descend than the brutal savagery of the Commune's enemies of every political complexion."[103]

The significance of the Paris Commune for Marx and Engels was, as Shlomo Avineri argued, a model for the future based more on the potentialities of its institutions than on the actual, concrete arrangements.[104] As a government, however brief, of and by the working class, the Commune became for Marx tangible evidence of the possibilities for his concepts of representative government, the dictatorship of the proletariat, and the end of the state. According to Monty Johnstone, Marx found in the Commune

> a thorough-going participatory democracy, combining direct democracy at the base with the election at regional and national levels of delegates operating under continuous control and briefing from below. Such forms were necessary for the adequate expression and safeguarding of the class character of the new transitional regime, which would begin to transcend the divorce between state and civil society that Marx had deplored as early as 1843, and to prepare the way for a classless and stateless society.[105]

According to Paul Bellis, "With the advent of the Commune, the working class was to achieve, albeit temporarily, the historical role as a universal class which Marx had attributed to it in his earlier writings."[106] Schulkind concluded that for Marx, Engels, and Lenin, the Commune was "an embryonic dictatorship of the proletariat in so far as it was directed towards serving the needs of the working class and implementing the direct democratic participation of that class."[107] The working class remained hegemonic, but it was also openly acknowledged by the middle class and peasants as "the only class capable of social initiative."[108]

Marx also regarded the Commune as having the potentiality of overcoming the bourgeois separation between civil and political societies, private and public interests, and giving the individual "a real sense of participation and control—a real identification of his will with that of the community."[109] Overcoming these divisions was possible because the working class did not possess private property or represent private interests, and thus, under its class rule, "the public functions would cease to be a private property bestowed by a central government upon its tools."[110]

According to the historian Bertell Ollman, Marx believed that people in the government had no important interests that conflicted with those of the class from which they came and therefore that the elected leaders of the proletarian dictatorship would want to represent the workers appropriately.[111] Marx wrote, "Never [were] delegates fuller representing the masses from which they had sprung. To the objection of the outsiders that they were unknown—in point of fact they were known to the working classes, but no old stagers, no men illustrious by the infamies of their past, by their chase after self and place—they proudly answered 'So were the 12 Apostles' and they answered by their deeds."[112]

Marx praised the Commune for paying its members only ordinary workers' wages, thus keeping them at the economic level of their constituents and preventing them from becoming a privileged sector separated from those constituents. This leveling and demystification of political work was a reaction to the careerism and the secrecy associated with political leadership, fostering the notion of a trained caste representing a higher class that the people had to obey. The Commune, for Marx, also made it clear that ordinary working people were by no means incapable of managing affairs of state:

> When plain working men for the first time dared to infringe upon the Governmental privilege of their 'natural superiors,' and, under circumstances of unexampled difficulty, performed their work modestly, conscientiously, and efficiently . . . the old world writhed in convulsions of rage at the sight of the Red Flag, the symbol of the Republic of Labour, floating over the Hotel de Ville.[113]

The lesson Marx drew from the Commune, confirming theory set forth in his earlier writings, was that the proletariat had to destroy and replace the structures and institutions of the bourgeois state: "The working class cannot simply lay hold of the ready-made State machinery, and wield it for its own purposes."[114] This perception had wide ramifications for future socialist governments and was clearly understood by the leaders of the Cuban Revolution. Since Thiers had removed the superstructure of the French state from Paris and the privileged classes had left the city, the Communards had the opportunity to construct a new type of state. "The Commune," according to Engels, "was no longer a state in the proper sense of the word."[115] Marx argued that "as the state machinery and parliamentarism are not the real life of the ruling classes, but only the organised general organs of their dominion, the political guarantees and forms and expressions of the old order of things, so the Commune is not the social movement of the working class and therefore of a general regeneration of mankind, but the organised means of action."[116] As a result of the Commune experience, Marx and Engels came to view the dictatorship of the proletariat and the disappearance of the state as part of the same process of the transition to socialism rather than as two distinct stages.[117]

Marx counterposed the type of representative government linked to the bourgeoisie and characterized by separation of powers, to the commune state, which combined executive, administrative, judicial, and legislative functions. According to Rosenberg:

> The normal bourgeois-liberal state is characterized by a separation of powers; the legislative, the executive, and the judicial departments are separated strictly from each other. The purpose of this arrangement is to impose restrictions on

parliament, since it is the chief representative of popular sentiment. The administrative and judicial apparatus must be as independent of parliament as possible so that the radical advances which arise among the electorate can be defeated by the resistance of the bureaucracy and the judges.[118]

Marx wrote that "the Commune was to be a working, not a parliamentary, body, executive and legislative at the same time."[119] Thus the Commune was responsible for all administration, including the daily functioning of the departments overseen by its commissions and also economic activities and planning. For example, Marx criticized the Commune for not having expropriated the Bank of France.[120] According to Theodore H. Friedgut, this unitary model also "serves as the basis for the view that the representative organs must act primarily as a link between the executive and the citizenry, expediting administration rather than concentrating on legislative functions."[121] This is also a description of the functions of the Cuban municipal assemblies, which have no legislative role.

In analyzing the Paris Commune, Marx returned to the theme of the *mandat impératif*, which gave the working class in the Commune the means to impose its collective will. "A Commune had been elected by universal suffrage," wrote Evans, "a body of delegates rather than representatives."[122] Marx connected the instructed-delegate model with a system including indirect elections and recall elections:

> In a rough sketch of national organisation which the Commune had no time to develop, it states clearly that the Commune was to be the political form of even the smallest country hamlet. . . . The rural communes of every district were to administer their common affairs by an assembly of delegates in the central town, and these district assemblies were again to send deputies to the National Delegation in Paris, each delegate to be at any time revocable and bound by the *mandat impératif* (formal instructions) of his constituents.[123]

For Marx indirect elections meant giving importance to local organs, since they were responsible for electing the delegates to the higher bodies.[124] If the working class electors were to "make a 'mistake', which in this context could only refer to the faulty character of an individual office holder, it will be quickly rectified through the instrument of the recall."[125]

Marx's treatment of the defeat of the Commune was also to influence later socialist practice. The strength and viciousness of the class enemy had been underestimated. The Commune's military preparation was inadequate, and the national guard, instead of seizing the initiative and marching on Versailles, relinquished its power too soon by immediately calling for elections. According to Marx:

> In destroying the existing conditions of oppression by transferring all the means of labor to the productive laborer, and thereby compelling every able-bodied

individual to work for a living, the only base for class rule and oppression would be removed. But before such a change could be effected a proletarian dictature [Fr. dictatorship] would become necessary, and the first condition of that was a proletarian army. The working classes would have to conquer the right to emancipate themselves on the battlefield. The task of the International was to organize and combine the forces of labor for the coming struggle.[126]

Conclusion

The need for a working-class party was to become a central question for Marx and Engels after the defeat of the Commune.[127] From the perspectives of the political thought of Rousseau and of Marx and Engels and the experience of the Paris Commune, the most important contributions to the development of modern socialist political practice, and thus the Cuban OPP, can be summarized as follows: (1) the definition of equality as economic and social as well as political, (2) the unity of political and civil society, (3) representative government based on the *mandat impératif*, (4) rule and control by the working class, (5) the necessity of a new state structure, and (6) the emergence of the nonpolitical state.

Notes

1. Stephen White, John Gardner, and George Schopflin, *Communist Political Systems: An Introduction*, 2d edition (London: Macmillan Education, 1987), pp. 223–224.

2. C. E. Vaughan, *The Political Writings of Jean Jacques Rousseau*, Vol. 2 (New York: Wiley, 1962), p. 185. See also Richard Fralin, *Rousseau and Representation: A Study of the Development of His Concept of Political Institutions* (New York: Columbia University Press, 1978), pp. 20, 77, 133–134.

3. Lucio Colletti, *From Rousseau to Lenin: Studies in Ideology and Society* (London: New Left Books, 1972), pp. 169–170.

4. Ibid., p. 185.

5. Ibid., pp. 143–144.

6. Eric J Hobsbawm, "Marx, Engels and Pre-Marxian Socialism," in Eric J. Hobsbawm (ed.), *The History of Marxism*, Vol. 1, *Marxism in Marx's Day* (Bloomington: Indiana University Press, 1982), p. 5.

7. Karl Marx, "Critique of Hegel's Doctrine of the State," in Karl Marx, *Early Writings* (New York: Vintage Books, 1975), pp. 180–198.

8. Jean Jacques Rousseau, "A Discourse on the Origin of Inequality," in Jean Jacques Rousseau, *The Social Contract and Discourses* (G. D. H. Cole, trans.) (New York: Dutton, 1950), p. 196.

9. Jean-Jacques Rousseau, "Letters Written from the Mountains," in *The Miscellaneous Works of Mr. J. J. Rousseau*, Vol. 4 (New York: Burt Franklin, 1972), p. 330.

10. Galvano della Volpe, *Rousseau and Marx and Other Writings* (London: Lawrence and Wishart, 1976), p. 43; Rousseau, "The Social Contract," in Rousseau, *The Social Contract and Discourses*, pp. 13–16.

11. della Volpe, *Rousseau and Marx*, pp. 109–110.

12. Ibid., pp. 96, 150.

13. Colletti, *From Rousseau to Lenin*, p 192.

14. Rousseau, "Discourse on the Origin of Inequality," pp. 234–235; Colletti, *From Rousseau to Lenin*, pp. 154–155.

15. Colletti, *From Rousseau to Lenin*, p. 144.

16. Ibid., p. 151.

17. Ibid., p. 152.

18. Renato Recio, "Cuba: integrar la democracia al patrimonio revolucionario," *Trabajadores*, July 7, 1993, p. 2 (my translation).

19. Della Volpe, *Rousseau and Marx*, p. 143.

20. J. L. Talmon, *The Origins of Totalitarian Democracy* (New York: Norton, 1970), p. 45.

21. Colletti, *From Rousseau to Lenin*, pp. 173, 184.

22. Ibid., p. 44.

23. Rousseau, "The Social Contract," p. 104.

24. Ibid., p. 106.

25. Alfred G Meyer, *Leninism* (New York: Praeger, 1971), p. 58.

26. Talmon, *The Origins*, p. 47.

27. Rousseau, "The Social Contract," pp. 65–66.

28. Fralin, *Rousseau and Representation*, p. 127.

29. Della Volpe, *Rousseau and Marx*, p. 55.

30. Fralin, *Rousseau and Representation*, pp. 30, 51; Jean Jacques Rousseau, "A Discourse on Political Economy," in Rousseau, *The Social Contract and Discourses*, pp. 294–301.

31. Rousseau, "Dédicace," cited in Fralin, *Rousseau and Representation*, p. 53.

32. Colletti, *From Rousseau to Lenin*, p. 184.

33. Rousseau, "The Social Contract," p. 94.

34. Cited in Colletti, *From Rousseau to Lenin*, pp. 186–187.

35. Jeffrey W Hahn, *Soviet Grassroots: Citizen Participation in Local Soviet Government* (Princeton: Princeton University Press, 1988), p. 133.

36. Fralin, *Rousseau and Representation*, pp. 16–17.

37. Ibid., p. 2.

38. Oskar Anweiler, *The Soviets: The Russian Workers, Peasants, and Soldiers Councils, 1905–1921* (New York: Random House, 1974), p. 7.

39. Ibid., p. 10.

40. Fernando Alvarez Tabio, *Comentarios a la Constitución Socialista* (Havana: Ciencias Sociales, 1985), p. 280–281 (my translation).

41. Quoted in Fralin, *Rousseau and Representation*, p. 184. See also Jean Jacques Rousseau, "Considérations sur le gouvernement de Pologne," in Vaughan, *The Political Writings*, pp. 460, 385–386.

42. Rousseau, "The Social Contract," pp. 99–100.

43. Vaughan, *The Political Writings*, p. 388.

44. Rousseau, "Letters Written from the Mountains," p. 341.

45. Ibid., pp. 209–342; Fralin, *Rousseau and Representation*, pp. 112, 151–164; Vaughan, *The Political Writings*, pp. 179–181.

46. Rousseau, "Letters Written from the Mountains," p. 259.

47. Ibid., p. 260.

48. Ibid., p. 332.

49. Ibid., p. 257.

50. Vaughan, *The Political Writings*, p. 180.

51. Fralin, *Rousseau and Representation*, p. 158.

52. Lucio Colletti, "Introduction," in Marx, *Early Writings*, p. 46.

53. Della Volpe, *Rousseau and Marx*, p. 110.

54. Eric J. Hobsbawm, "Marx, Engels, and Politics," in Hobsbawm, *History of Marxism*, pp. 257–258.

55. Hal Draper, *Karl Marx's Theory of Revolution*, Vol. 1, *State and Bureaucracy* (New York: Monthly Review Press, 1977), p. 310.

56. Hobsbawm, "Marx, Engels," p. 257.

57. Draper, *Karl Marx's Theory*, p. 85; see also Colletti, "Introduction," p. 41.

58. Richard N. Hunt, *The Political Ideas of Marx and Engels: Marxism and Totalitarian Democracy, 1880–1850*, Vol. 1 (Pittsburgh: University of Pittsburgh Press, 1974), pp. 83–84.

59. Julio García Luis, "La soberanía reside en el pueblo," *Trabajadores*, January 5, 1998, p. 3.

60. Marx, "Critique of Hegel's Doctrine," p. 146.

61. Colletti, "Introduction," p. 35.

62. Ibid., pp. 36–37.

63. Marx, "Critique of Hegel's Doctrine," p. 194.

64. Hobsbawm, "Marx, Engels," p. 230.

65. Christopher Pierson, *Marxist Theory and Democratic Politics* (Cambridge: Polity Press, 1986), p. 15.

66. Ibid., p. 16.

67. Marx, "Critique of Hegel's Doctrine," pp. 189–190.

68. Hunt, *The Political Ideas*, p. 69; see also Ralph Miliband, *The State in Capitalist Society* (New York: Basic Books, 1969), pp. 265–277.

69. Colletti, "Introduction," p. 44.

70. Ralph Miliband, "Marx and the State," in Ralph Miliband and John Saville (eds.), *The Socialist Register, 1965* (New York: Monthly Review Press, 1965), p. 289.

71. Hunt, *The Political Ideas*, pp. 308–309; see also Miliband, "Marx and the State," p. 291.

72. Theotonio dos Santos, "Socialism: Ideal and Historical Practice," in Milos Nicolic (ed.), *Socialism on the Threshold of the 21st Century* (London: Verso, 1985), p. 185.

73. Draper, *Karl Marx's Theory*, p. 308.

74. Michael Evans, "Karl Marx and the Concept of Political Participation," in Geraint Parry (ed.), *Participation in Politics* (Totowa, N.J.: Rowman and Littlefield, 1972), p. 138.

75. Hal Draper, *Karl Marx's Theory of Revolution*, Vol. 3, *The "Dictatorship of the Proletariat"* (New York: Monthly Review Press, 1986), p. 116.

76. Neil Harding, "Socialism, Society, and the Organic Labour State," in Neil Harding (ed.), *The State in Socialist Society* (Albany: SUNY Press, 1984), p. 8.

77. Ibid., p. 13.

78. Karl Marx and Frederick Engels, "Manifesto of the Communist Party," in Karl Marx and Frederick Engels, *Selected Works* (New York: International Publishers, 1968), p. 53.

79. Hal Draper, "The Death of the State in Marx and Engels," in Ralph Miliband and John Saville (eds.), *The Socialist Register 1970* (London: Merlin Press, 1970), p. 302.

80. Karl Marx, "Critique of the Gotha Programme," in Marx and Engels, *Selected Works*, p. 332.

81. Hunt, *The Political Ideas*, pp. 80, 81.

82. Marx, "Critique of the Gotha Programme," p. 332.

83. Karl Marx, "Conspectus of Bakunin's *Statism and Anarchy*," in David Fernbach (ed.), *Karl Marx, Political Writings*, Vol. 3, *The First International and After* (New York: Random House, 1974), p. 336.

84. Henri Lefebvre, "The Commune and the Nature of Revolution," in Jeffry Kaplow (ed.), *Western Civilization: Mainstream Readings and Radical Critiques*, Vol. 2, *From the French Revolution to the Present* (New York: Knopf, 1973), p. 221.

85. Ibid., p. 225.

86. Eugene Schulkind, "Introduction," in Eugene Schulkind (ed.), *The Paris Commune of 1871: The View from the Left* (New York: Grove Press, 1974), p. 53.

87. Arthur Rosenberg, *Democracy and Socialism* (Beacon: Boston, 1965), pp. 204–205.

88. Schulkind, "Introduction," p. 31.

89. Ibid., p. 35.

90. Ibid., p. 39.

91. Ibid., p. 45.

92. Rosenberg, *Democracy and Socialism*, pp. 191–192.

93. Schulkind, "Introduction," pp. 40–41.

94. Rosenberg, *Democracy and Socialism*, p. 198.

95. G. D. H. Cole, *A History of Socialism*, Vol. 2, *Socialist Thought Marxism and Anarchism, 1850–1890* (London: Macmillan, 1954), p. 169.

96. Ibid., p. 147.

97. Schulkind, "Introduction," p. 43.

98. Cole, *A History*, pp. 148–154.

99. Karl Marx, "Letter to Domela Nieuwenhuis, February 22, 1881," in Karl Marx and Friedreich Engels, *Correspondence 1846–1895* (New York: International Publishers, 1935), p. 387.

100. Cole, *A History*, p. 157.

101. Karl Marx, "The Civil War in France," in Hal Draper (ed.), *Karl Marx and Friedreich Engels: Writings on the Paris Commune* (New York: Monthly Review Press, 1971), p. 91.

102. Rosenberg, *Democracy and Socialism*, p. 202.

103. Gordon Lewis, "The Paris Commune Then and Now," *Monthly Review*, Vol. 28, No. 6 (November 1968), pp. 89–90.

104. Shlomo Avineri, quoted in Paul Bellis, *Marxism and the USSR: The Theory of the Proletarian Dictatorship and the Marxist Analysis of Soviet Society* (Atlantic Highlands: Humanities Press, 1979), p. 7.

105. Monty Johnstone, "The Paris Commune and Marx's Conception of the Dictatorship of the Proletariat," *Massachusetts Review*, Vol. 12, No. 3 (Summer, 1971), p. 458.

106. Bellis, *Marxism and the USSR*, p. 12.

107. Schulkind, "Introduction," p. 54.

108. Ibid., p. 78.

109. Harding, "Socialism, Society," p. 6.

110. Marx, "The Civil War," p. 200.

111. Bertell Ollman, "Marx's Vision of Communism: A Reconstruction," *Critique*, No. 8 (Summer 1977), p. 17.

112. Marx, "The Civil War," pp. 147–148.

113. Ibid., pp. 77–78.

114. Ibid., p. 70.

115. Engels, "Letter to A. Betel, March 18, 1875," in Draper (ed.), *Karl Marx and Friedreich Engels*, p. 231.

116. Marx, "The Civil War," p. 154.

117. Bellis, *Marxism and the USSR*, p. 14.

118. Rosenberg, *Democracy and Socialism*, p. 200.

119. Marx, "The Civil War," p. 73.

120. Ibid., p. 77; see also Marx, "Letter to Domela Nieuwenhuis," p. 387.

121. Theodore H Friedgut, *Political Participation in the USSR* (Princeton: Princeton University Press, 1979), p. 35.

122. Evans, "Karl Marx," p. 140.

123. Marx, "The Civil War," p. 74.

124. Johnstone, "The Paris Commune," p. 462; Evans, "Karl Marx," p. 141.

125. Ollman, "Marx's Vision," p. 17.

126. Karl Marx, speech at the International's anniversary banquet in London, September 24 or 25, 1871, in Draper, *Karl Marx and Friedreich Engels*, p. 225; see also Marx, "Letter to Liebnecht," p. 220; Marx, "Letter to Kugelmann," p. 221.

127. Johnstone, "The Paris Commune," pp. 452, 461.

2

Lenin and the Socialist State

Lenin adapted and applied Marx and Engels's theories on the socialist state to the Russian setting, especially those theses derived from the Paris Commune of 1871. His theories and political activities were also profoundly influenced by the events and outcomes of the Russian revolutionary process that were shaped by the demands of the Russian proletariat. The 1905 and 1917 soviets were examples of workers developing their own political structures and mechanisms, influenced by past events and theory, but relatively free of outside direction and domination. The major characteristics of the communal type of government that emerged—its working-class composition and identity of the governed with their representatives, and the *mandat impératif*—continued during the immediate postrevolutionary period and subsequently influenced the Soviet Union after Stalin and, in turn, the OLPP in Cuba.

The Soviets

After the Paris Commune, "conciliar" or "communal" forms of government did not again become an important part of Marxist thought until the formation of the 1905 soviets. But neither did this theme completely disappear, because, as Miliband noted, "councils are in one form or another a recurring and spontaneous manifestation of popular power in history."[1]

During the meetings in 1873 and 1874 of the rival workers' international that sought to replace Marx's largely defunct International, debates commonly involved the characteristics of the "commune" state along the lines of the 1871 Paris Commune, as well as theories involving the development of a workers' state. Among the points agreed upon, according to Cole, was that "the local Commune would itself be responsible for the conduct of local public services, would own the land and probably the main capital installations, and would be the foundation on which all larger structures of public administration and control would rest."[2] It was agreed that there would have to be a federation with elected federal representatives. Workers would "play an active part in the Commune by direct legislation or referendum as well as by choosing delegates and giving them imperative instructions (the *mandat impératif*) and recalling them at will."[3]

The soviets of 1905 were not created by Marxist parties, although Marxist groups and individuals were influential in the operation. A basic initial characteristic that linked them to the Paris Commune of 1871 was that they were composed of and representative of the working class.

The British scholar Ronald Hill describes the 1905 and 1917 soviets as "strike committees to coordinate the revolutionary activity of the working class," which were "the spontaneous creations of the working class itself."[4] According to Oskar Anweiler, "As self-governing bodies of Russian workers and as committees serving the revolutionary struggle, the soviets of 1905 were new, having traits which were specifically Russian but also useful outside Russia and typical of revolutionary and sociopolitical conditions later repeated elsewhere."[5]

In Russia toward the end of the nineteenth century, the term *soviets,* or *workers' councils,* first referred to temporary elected strike committees of factory workers who negotiated with employers or the state. The massacre in front of the Winter Palace in St. Petersburg on January 9, 1905, set in motion disorders and strikes in the subsequent months, together with the formation of workers' soviets of a more permanent and political nature. Two commissions, one under Senator Shidlovsky were established in St. Petersburg to determine the causes of and to find solutions for workers' dissatisfactions. For Anweiler, "The real significance of the Shidlovsky Commission lay in another area: by electing deputies in the factories, it prepared the way for the soviets to represent the metropolitan working class."[6]

During the 1905 strikes, workers elected committees to negotiate with management. However, when strikes spread to several factories, workers' elected committees likewise became more extensive, even citywide. As Anweiler noted, "Whenever such a strike committee . . . turned into a permanent elected delegation with much broader aims, then we have before us a council (soviet) of workers deputies."[7] In May 1905, the first of such bodies appeared in the textile center of Ivanovo-Voznesensk, northeast of Moscow. More than one hundred deputies constituted the Ivanovo-Voznesensk Authorized Council (Soviet), representing forty thousand workers from several factories. The elected presidium negotiated for economic conditions and political rights and participated in the conduct of local affairs. According to Hahn, "Although the soviet was disbanded on July 18 . . . , the former deputies continued to speak for the workers, and the idea of the soviet attracted attention in other parts of the country."[8] In the weeks that followed, similar soviets were organized in nearly all the Russian industrial centers.[9]

The Moscow Soviet, organized during this period, became the first citywide representative of the area's entire workforce, recognized not only by the factory owners but also by the government.[10]

The Petersburg Soviet of Workers' Deputies, constituted in October 1905 to lead the general strike, lasted fifty days, became the most important soviet of this period, and served as the model for soviets elsewhere in Russia at that time. Later it would serve as the prototype of the 1917 Petrograd Soviet of Workers' and Soldiers' Deputies and thus provide a model for the Soviet government following the October 1917 Revolution.[11] Its formation cannot be directly attributed to any political party or movement. This soviet began with elected plant representatives and was strongly influenced both by the earlier Moscow Soviet and by Menshevik propaganda for revolutionary self-government. Its 550 delegates were elected by 250,000 workers from factories, workshops, and trade unions. The Mensheviks, the Bolsheviks, and the Social Revolutionaries, all left-wing parties, were the main political groups represented. The Petersburg Soviet developed a formal organizational structure and a newspaper (the predecessor of *Itsvestiya* of 1917).[12] Mainly under the leadership of Leon Trotsky, it went on to become a "workers' parliament" unprecedented in history, and a militant revolutionary political organ. According to Anweiler, "General election of deputies in factories, with the possibility of their continuing accountability and recall at any time, gave the workers the feeling of genuine and effective participation in an organ elected by them."[13]

Following the tradition of the *mandat impératif,* the elected deputies of the 1905 soviets received mandates from their electors in factory workers' collectives prior to election, and these mandates became the basis for the soviets' activities and actions. Furthermore, deputies were obliged to report back on their activities to their constituents.[14] In 1905, the striking workers at the Ivanovo-Voznesensk textile factory presented a list of twenty-six demands to the delegates elected to their soviet.[15] A directive from the 1905 Moscow Soviet, for example, noted, "The deputies are obliged to frequently render accounts of their conduct, for which purpose they must organize general and local workers' assemblies."[16] This system of mandates and reporting to constituents can be considered a direct historical link to the Soviet mandate system, and to the Cuban system of citizen *planteamientos* and municipal delegates' accountability sessions with their constituents—which are also called rendering accounts *(rendición de cuenta)*—as were provisions for recall of deputies, which were also part of the electoral process and were included in the official rules of some of the soviets.[17]

In another historical precedent connecting the Cuban OPP to the original soviets' structure, the soviets of 1905 organized working commissions and executive organs, among these commissions on finance and the distribution of food and other supplies. Executive committees were elected by the deputies to handle daily affairs. Many of their activities concerned workers' immediate social and economic problems, and according to Anweiler, "This conferred on the soviet its prestige and authority in the eyes of the masses."[18]

These soviets were disbanded by the government after the defeat of the Revolution of 1905, and the leaders of the Petersburg Soviet, including Trotsky, were arrested. Trotsky's conduct of the legal defense helped give lasting prestige to the soviets.[19] Anweiler summed up their legacy:

> In the soviets the Russian workers created an instrument of democratic self-government, well-suited to represent the revolutionary demands of the oppressed masses. . . . The significance of the 1905 soviets can be compared to that of the Paris Commune of 1871. Both gained historical importance primarily from later events: the Paris Commune from its inclusion in the theory of the state articulated by Marx and later by Lenin; the soviets of 1905 as precursors of the 1917 soviets. From the combination of the two—the interpretation of the Commune by Marx and Lenin and the soviets—emerged the theory and practice of the Bolshevik soviet system.[20]

In a similar vein, V. Koldáiev wrote that the soviets' experience "served as a starting point for Lenin for the subsequent elaboration of the theory of the Soviets as the form the state would take under the dictatorship of the proletariat."[21]

The new Russian parliament, known as the Duma, which was one of the achievements of the 1905 Revolution, was described by the historian Alexander Rabinowitch as "the pale copy of a Western-style parliament that had been established in tsarist Russia following the revolution of 1905."[22] It certainly did not represent the entire population. "The Fourth Duma," continued Rabinowitch, "in session in 1917, had been elected in 1912 under regulations that excluded the bulk of the population from the franchise."[23] Similarly, according to E. H. Carr, the Russian Provisional Government established after the February Revolution of 1917 was drawn from the bourgeoisie and the official class. Workers in Petrograd in March 1917, once again excluded from sharing power, created the Petrograd Soviet of Workers' Deputies without central direction from political parties. Again the underlying and defining characteristic was its working-class representation and composition. This new soviet was modeled after the 1905 Petersburg Soviet, elected by factory workers, and included among its representatives Mensheviks, Bolsheviks, and Social Revolutionaries.[24] Rabinowitch provided an account of what followed:

> In the spring and summer of 1917, soviets were established in each of the districts of Petrograd, and, concomitantly, similar institutions of grass roots democracy came into being in cities, towns, and villages throughout Russia. In

May an All-Russian Congress of Peasants' Soviets was convened in Petrograd, and in June representatives of workers' and soldiers' soviets gathered in the capital for their first nationwide congress. These national conventions formed permanent All-Russian Executive Committees (the Central Executive Committee of the All-Russian Congress of Soviets of Workers' and Soldiers' Deputies and the Executive Committee of the All-Russian Congress of Peasants' Deputies), which, taken together, were numerically more representative and, by virtue of the loyalty that they commanded among factory workers, peasants, and particularly soldiers, potentially more powerful than the Provisional Government.[25]

The soviets' decision early in 1917 not to join the Provisional Government was crucial in bringing about a system of "dual power." The soviets derived authority, legitimacy, and strength from the support of the workers, peasants, and soldiers, who strongly and closely identified with them and believed that they rather than the Provisional Government defended their interests, since the soviet deputies came from their ranks.

Political scientist and Lenin scholar Marcel Liebman compared the Soviet Executive Committee and the Provisional Committee of the Duma in early March 1917: "What a difference in atmosphere there was between the two! On the Soviet side everything was in feverish turmoil, in revolutionary disorder, and there were many signs of poverty among those assembled there. But as one passed into the part of the palace assigned to the Duma, one seemed to step into a different world."[26]

In August 1917, General L. Kornilov led a failed right-wing coup attempt that radicalized the soviets and enhanced their popularity among the masses.[27] In a profusion of letters, resolutions, and political declarations, workers and soldiers from the main factories and garrisons of the Petrograd Soviet, as well as from the regional soviets, opposed any collaboration with the bourgeoisie and the Provisional Government and became more insistent on preserving and solidifying the class nature of the soviets. The Petrograd Soviet was called upon to assume political power. For example, workers in the huge Putilov factory declared that "the future government has to be composed solely of representatives of the revolutionary classes," and the employees of the Novo-Admiralteisky shipbuilding plant resolved that "state power must not remain in the hands of the counterrevolutionary bourgeoisie a minute longer."[28] According to Hahn, although the Provisional Government was the official governing body from February to October 1917, real power lay with the Petrograd Soviet, which not only controlled workers' and soldiers' activities but also had a de facto veto over government decisions.[29] During the course of 1917, the soviets all over Russia began to replace the local parliaments and gradually took over the functions of a collapsing central government and the local bureaucracies.[30] The minister of war of the Provisional Government admitted that the Soviet of Workers' and Soldiers' Deputies had the real power.[31]

The practical, daily activity of the soviets was in the hands of the elected executive committee, which reported to the plenary for approval. Much of the work of the soviets was performed by commissions. Continuing the tradition of the Paris Commune, professional politicians were transformed from a highly paid privileged stratum to workers paid at workers' wages, and all elected delegates were subject to immediate recall. The soviets combined executive and legislative functions, favoring a unitary system rather than one of checks and balances.[32] The relation of the local soviets to the higher provincial and national bodies was through indirect elections in which the lower bodies elected delegates to the higher ones, as was the case in Cuba prior to 1992. In the tradition of Rousseau and Marx, and resembling the elections held under the Cuban OPP, partisan politics was absent from local soviet elections during 1917:

> Even more than in Petrograd and Moscow, provincial soviets were politically undifferentiated during the early weeks and months of the revolution: party lines were blurred, and most deputies were unaffiliated or altogether apolitical. The workers elected first of all people they knew, without examining their specific political orientation. Usually it was enough if a candidate could identify himself as a "revolutionary," without needing a party card to prove it.[33]

Authority was seen as originating from the direct initiative of the masses (*mandat impératif*) rather than from a representative body.[34] An example of the importance given to citizen mandates can be found in the Congress of Soviets held in late October 1917, when Lenin announced the Land Decree. This decree was followed by a special appendix entitled "Concerning the Land" that advocated giving land to the peasants rather than following the socialist preference for nationalization because, according to Liebman, it was responsive to the 242 mandates presented by local peasants' assemblies, incorporating "all the instructions the peasant electors had given their representatives at the first Congress of Peasants' Soviets."[35]

The most vivid example of the influence of popular demands during 1917 was the rejection and overthrow by insurrection of the Provisional Government at the end of October. This insurrection was preceded by the increased involvement in public affairs by workers, soldiers, and peasants, who became influential in determining the course of events. Participation by the proletariat was accompanied by a growing national acceptance of and identification with the rule of the soviets. Liebman described the role of the masses in this period:

> The whole of October was, in Petrograd and in the provinces alike, a period of ceaseless political activity: the soviets of the various regions assembled in conferences and congresses. . . . In October, 1917 the permanent revolution took concrete form in a permanent debate. And if the masses took no direct part in the insurrection, this was, in the last analysis, because there was no need for

them to do so. . . . The workers, sailors and soldiers who patrolled the streets of Petrograd in October 1917, occupied strategic points and stormed the Winter Palace, were *carrying out a mandate* the existence of which was proved by the numberless demonstrations and resolutions, frequent elections, and the thousand-and-one ways that the will of the masses found to express itself. In other words, Lenin's tactic of insurrection, while adding something new to socialist practice, was itself fundamentally inspired by socialist practice.[36]

The October Revolution resulted in the defeat of the Provisional Government, and at each level of government, the existing soviets replaced the former governmental structures and personnel. The basic character of the soviet system was for the most part retained in the first provisional documents and then codified in the first constitution presented and approved in Russia in July 1918. Although the role, power, and importance of the soviets diminished substantially, especially in relation to the Soviet Communist Party, their basic structure remained unchanged in the constitutions of 1923, 1936, and 1977. Goran Therborn described the unfolding of this transfer of power to the soviets:

> In Russia, the act of insurrection was presented by the Bolsheviks not to a ritualized parliament, packed with dignitaries and intellectuals who had progressed in the school of bourgeois law and journalism, but to a tumultuous meeting of workers', peasants', and soldiers' deputies in Petrograd. Local risings throughout the vast territory of Russia involved not party putsches but the seizure of power by broad masses, who proceeded to replace the lofty old city dumas and village councils with new, popular soviet organs.[37]

After the October Revolution, local soviets patterned after the existing ones spread over all of Russia. In towns, they operated with elected deputies; in rural areas, by direct democracy. The soviets assumed both legislative and administrative powers.[38] However, the need soon arose for some regularity in their composition and procedure, which Carr pointed out were "loose and informal assemblies without clearly defined functions . . . created under no fixed or uniform rules."[39] Furthermore, "The very spontaneity of the movement which had created Soviets in factory and village up and down the country meant that their independent acts were irregular, uncoordinated and disruptive of orderly administration."[40]

The first decree of the Soviet Central Executive Committee regarding deputies, drafted by Lenin, instituted the right of recall. In January 1918, what was called the Provisional Soviet Organization spelled out some basic rules for running the soviets, including rules regarding the election of the presidium and the executive committee and their functions, and required that the presidium "render an account of its activity to the executive committee and to the entire Soviet, who have the right to recall them and to replace them at any time and period." On committees of the soviets, it provided for the possible inclusion of "learned persons with the privilege of a consulting vote." Also included was the *mandat impératif* and recall: "If a member of the Soviet deviates from the instructions of his constituents [they] have a right to recall him and elect another in his place."[41] Hahn reported, however, that voter mandates "were apparently used only sporadically in the period following the Revolution of 1917, and they received scant attention in the legislation on the soviets."[42]

Later in January, "The Organization of Local Self-Government," a second provisional government document published in the *Gazette of the Provisional Workers' and Peasants' Government,* gave the local soviets power over the administrative, economic, financial, and educational institutions in their jurisdictions, with the stipulation that "their decrees must be of a character corresponding with the decrees and laws of the larger Soviet organs and the decrees of the Central power."[43] The "Rights and Duties of Local Soviets" requirement that the soviets "render a report to the central Soviet Government regarding all measures undertaken by them and important local events"[44] was similar to the requirement to render accounts *(rendición de cuenta)* between and within branches of the Cuban OPP.[45]

The executive committee of the fourth All-Russian Congress of Soviets created a commission to draft a constitution in April 1918. According to Carr, the principal leaders of the October Revolution, including Lenin, did not participate in drafting this document, their attention being directed principally toward ensuring the survival of the regime. In July, the draft constitution was submitted to the central committee of the Bolshevik Party and then to the fifth All-Russian Congress of Soviets.[46] This new constitution, approved in July 1918, removed the provisional status of the new government. "The new constitution," wrote Carr, "did not so much create new forms of government as register and regularize those which were in course of being established by uncoordinated initiative in the aftermath of the revolutionary upheaval."[47] Along the same lines, Carr continued:

> The peculiarity of the Soviet structure lay in the fact that it was built up around Soviets which had already taken shape and acquired some degree of organization before they became constitutional organs of state power. It was emphasized again and again that the constitution merely registered forms spontaneously evolved by the masses themselves. In the words of the *rapporteur* to the fifth All-Russian Congress of Soviets, it "was realized in practice long before it was written down on paper."[48]

Lenin himself called attention to the derivation of the new soviet governmental institutions from the soviets created by the Russian masses during the revolutionary process:

> Had not the popular creative spirit of the Russian revolution, which had gone through the great experience of the year 1905, given rise to the Soviets as early

as February 1917, they could not under any circumstances have assumed power in October, because success depended entirely upon the existence of available organisational forms of a movement embracing millions. The Soviets were the available form . . . and all we had to do was pass a few decrees, and transform the power of the Soviets from the embryonic state in which it existed in the first months of the revolution into the legally recognised form which had become established in the Russian—i.e., into the Russian Soviet Republic. The Republic was born at one stroke; it was born so easily because in February, 1917, the masses had created the Soviets even before any party had managed to proclaim this slogan.[49]

The 1918 Constitution essentially clarified, codified, and attempted to impose the existing Soviet structure uniformly. The relationship between the local, regional soviets and the All-Russian Congress of Soviets remained the same, with the addition that all soviet functions, including budgets, were brought under regional and then central control or review. The system of indirect elections whereby local soviets elected the representatives for the higher bodies was also retained, as was the combination of legislative and executive functions, rejecting the separation-of-power concept in favor of the unitary state. The role of the executive committee was to carry out governmental duties between sessions of the soviet.[50] The right of recall was included. The soviets' standing committees emerged from the seventh Congress of Soviets in 1919 to control the parallel administrative organ. Besides deputies, their membership included representatives from factory committees and trade unions and, a little later, volunteers from the public.[51]

The Dictatorship of the Proletariat

By 1917, Lenin had identified the soviets as descendants of the 1871 Paris Commune and as the basic state institution under socialism. He also understood that they were creations of the proletariat as part of the revolutionary process in Russia and had virtually replaced the old regime:

> The Russian revolution has created the Soviets. No bourgeois country in the world has or can have such state institutions. No socialist revolution can be operative with any other state power than this. The Soviets must take power not for the purpose of building an ordinary bourgeois republic, nor the purpose of making a direct transition to socialism. This cannot be. What, then, is the purpose? The Soviets must take power in order to make the first concrete steps towards this transition, steps that can and should be made.[52]

One of Lenin's most important theoretical contributions regarding the socialist state was advancing Marxist political theory based on the soviets. He rejected the principal contemporary Russian Marxist theorists' support of a bourgeois rather than a socialist revolution and their consigning the socialist movement mainly to defending workers' rights and interests under capitalism. According to Umberto Cerroni,

> Lenin understands that in Russia there is a historical vacuum that only the proletariat could fill. . . . On this basis arises the understanding of the soviets as the political form of conduct particular to the Russian revolution—as *controlled representative organs* that constitute the authentic revolutionary alternative to the various state Dumas and, indeed, the bridge whereby the democratic revolution [of February] is to mature and move toward the socialist revolution [of October].[53]

Lenin's major theoretical study of the state under socialism, *The State and Revolution,* completed in 1917 just before the October Revolution, was aimed at "correcting" Marx's study of the Paris Commune and "reexamining it on the basis of the experience of the soviets."[54] His understanding of the economic, political, and social crises in Russia led him to regard socialism as historically necessary and possible, and to understand the necessity of gaining working-class support and establishing the Bolshevik Party as its leader and the soviets as the vehicle for insurrection and proletarian government. After the Bolsheviks won the leadership in the majority of the soviets, "All power to the soviets"[55] became the slogan for the insurrection and the basis for shaping the new proletarian state. In contrast, the Western Marxist movements of the time simply attempted to copy the soviets without a theory of an alternative state.[56]

Given the decline in importance of the soviets relative to the Communist Party after the civil war in 1921 and the establishment of one-party rule, "The State and Revolution" may seem a utopian work. Attilio Chitarin called it "neither a book of political agitation at an 'everyday' level, therefore linked to the specific problems of the revolution in Russia, nor an abstract academic essay [but] a theoretical book considered and written as a contribution to the definition of the future socialist world revolution."[57] In it, Lenin described Marxism as essentially extending "the recognition of the class struggle to the recognition of the *dictatorship of the proletariat,*"[58] and he clearly equated the dictatorship of the proletariat with the soviets, calling on the proletariat to fight "for a democratic republic after the type of the [Paris] Commune, or a republic of Soviets of Workers' and Soldiers' Deputies, for the revolutionary dictatorship of the proletariat."[59]

Lenin's concept of the dictatorship of the proletariat and of power to the soviets as its derivative encompassed and built on the political theories of Rousseau and the early Marx, including equality, the general will, the *mandat impératif,* the close identity between governed and governors, the merging of civil and political society, and working-class rule. Goran Therborn summarized as follows:

> The concept of the dictatorship of the proletariat, then, refers to two fundamental theses. First, the idea that *the very form of organization of the state is a*

materialization of a particular mode of class rule. Secondly, in consequence of the first, that *the socialist state of the working class must have a specific form of organization.* The term "the dictatorship of the proletariat" is used by Marx, Engels and Lenin as synonymous both with "rule of the proletariat" and with the particular form of state that expresses this rule.[60]

Lenin regarded the soviets as a new state apparatus that could "elevate, train, educate, and lead the *entire vast mass* of these [oppressed] classes, which has up to now stood completely outside of political life and history."[61] Lenin demanded "an immediate break with the prejudiced view that only the rich, or officials chosen from rich families are capable of *administering* the state, of performing the ordinary, everyday work of administration."[62] This link to the Russian proletariat separated Lenin and the Bolsheviks from the more moderate Mensheviks. According to Liebman, "Social-Democracy with which Lenin was severing all ties had too easily resigned itself to accepting as inevitable the inferiority of the working class."[63] Because it was the Russian masses who pushed the Bolshevik Party to take power, Liebman concluded, "How could Lenin have remained unaffected by this upsurge of the masses themselves—these 'elemental,' 'dark' forces, condemned by the moderate socialists, which for Lenin constituted the driving force of the revolution?"[64]

The proletariat was becoming more radical and, through the work of the Bolsheviks, more political—succeeding, in Liebman's words, "in breaking through the innumerable forms of conservative conditioning."[65] All over Russia, discussions, debates, and demonstrations continually took place, and there was intense participation in the committees that sprang up in almost every sector with the intention of taking part in running public affairs. The creation of the soviets was part of this process. Liebman concluded, "The model of Soviet democracy and, still more, the model for the direct democracy that we see depicted in 'The State and Revolution' was found by the spectacle presented by revolutionary Russia."[66]

By September 1917, the Russian proletariat had begun to influence, accept, and identify with the Bolsheviks as its own party and had made it the majority party in the principal soviets and especially in the local ones. "When, through frequent elections and the genuine revocability of mandates, identification between the masses and some deliberative and executive body became closer and closer, Bolshevism made itself felt by the numerical strength of its representation and the acceptance of its overall policy."[67] This widespread support of the Bolsheviks and the socialist revolution by the popular classes was demonstrated in the taking of the Winter Palace in October 1917 and even more at the end of 1918 in the "very hard, long and fierce civil war."[68]

Cerroni summed up Lenin's concept of direct democracy as "democracy controlled from below,"[69] and Carr traced it to Rousseau's discussion of di-

rect democracy in the *Social Contract*.[70] A few days after the October Revolution, Lenin appealed to the workers: "Remember that now *you yourselves*
are at the helm of state."[71] In "The State and Revolution" he wrote, "We
shall reduce the role of state officials to that of simply carrying out our instructions as responsible, revocable, modestly paid 'foremen and accoun-
tants.'"[72] He criticized Eduard Bernstein's rejection of binding mandates
and unpaid officials.[73]

In Lenin's theory of socialist society during the transition to communism,
the elimination of private property and private interests and of antagonistic
social classes includes Marx's concept of the reconciliation and merging of
civil and political society. When the working people participate in and administer the government, he argued, it ceases to be composed of "the special
institutions of a privileged minority."[74] When working people perform them,
governmental functions "will finally die out as the *special* functions of a special section of the population."[75] Referring specifically to representative government according to the model of the Paris Commune, Lenin wrote, "Representative institutions remain, but there is *no* parliamentarism here as a
special system, as the division of labour between the legislative and the executive, as a privileged position for the deputies."[76] Cerroni concluded, "'The
State and Revolution' proposes an alternative based . . . on the direct participation of the producers . . . in the 'reabsorption'—as [Antonio] Gramsci
called it—of political functions into civil activities."[77]

According to Colletti, the basic theme of "The State and Revolution" is
"the destruction of the diaphragm that separates the working classes from
power"[78] and its replacement by new institutions built and run by the working class. This replacement entails not only a new class in power but also a
new type of power: "For Lenin the socialist revolution has to destroy the old
state because it must destroy *the difference between governors and governed itself.*"[79]

In the same vein, Lenin stressed the close identification of the people with
the soviets, which provided "a bond with the people so intimate, so indissol-
uble, so easily verifiable and renewable, that nothing even remotely like it existed in the previous state apparatus."[80] Writing in April 1918, he said:

> Even in the most democratic capitalist republics in the world, the poor never re-
> gard the bourgeois parliament as "their" institution. But the Soviets are "theirs"
> and not alien institutions to the mass of workers and peasants. . . . It is the
> closeness of the Soviets to the "people," to the working people, that creates the
> special forms of recall and other means of control from below which must be
> most zealously developed now.[81]

Lenin's main premise in "The State and Revolution" and other writings of
this period was the impossibility of a socialist revolution without a definitive
break with the existing bourgeois state structure. In opposing the "oppor-

tunism" of Bernstein and Karl Kautsky, who in this period put forth the argument that the proletariat need only take control of the bourgeois parliamentary state, Lenin insisted that the class struggle did not end with the taking of power but continued with the dictatorship of the proletariat, whose initial task was the destruction of the old state apparatus.[82] Cerroni summarized Lenin's argument:

> In substance, Lenin wants to demonstrate in "The State and Revolution" that universal suffrage does not change the nature of the bourgeois State and that bourgeois representative democracy should be surpassed by direct democracy of the socialist State . . . , because the representative State founded on universal suffrage continues being always a political force that, as such, presupposes the impossibility of direct and equal political access in a society which continues being . . . atomized and privatized by the capitalist relations of production.[83]

Lenin rejected the more prevalent interpretation of Marxism at the time, which concentrated on economic factors such as exploitation and the ownership of the means of production, and made political theory an integral part of his understanding of society and revolution. In his view, *"Communism is Soviet power plus the electrification of the whole country,"*[84] with *Soviet* referring to the political sphere and *electrification* to the economic. Socialism meant transforming the relations of production to eliminate capitalist exploitation of the proletariat, but these economic changes were necessarily tied to and made possible only by the transformation of bourgeois representative government to a soviet government.[85] Lenin suggested that only a strong, popularly based government of a soviet type would be capable of instituting needed economic measures to initiate and foster socialism and mobilizing the support of the masses to defeat capitalist resistance.[86] According to Neil Harding, "In this optimistic, highly theorised prospectus it seemed that, at last, the freedom and self-activity of the Commune form could be reconciled with a planned and regulated administration of things."[87]

The theory of the unsuitability to socialist society of institutions inherited from capitalist society can be applied both to the disbanding of the Russian Constituent Assembly in 1918 in favor of a government based on the soviets, and to the unwillingness to reinstate the 1940 Cuban Constitution after the triumph of the Cuban Revolution in 1959, despite promises to do so by the Cuban 26th of July Movement. During the months preceding the October Revolution, the Bolsheviks and their supporters called for elections and the convening of the Constituent Assembly, which had been promised by the Provisional Government but repeatedly delayed.

In both cases, the commitment was not kept because the leadership believed it would result in a government organization that retained the prerevolutionary state structure and class domination, which in turn would have meant forsaking the essence of the revolution and the demands of the popular classes, which were among its strongest supporters. The elements that opposed the economic and social goals associated with these popular classes were not to be permitted to use the state apparatus to regain power.

According to the Brazilian sociologists Vania Bambirra and Theotonio dos Santos, "This is one of the innumerable manifestations of Leninist flexibility. The slogan that in one period represents a progressive demand, is no longer so in a subsequent stage and, therefore should be dropped."[88] Lenin offered the following explanation:

> The demand for the convocation of a Constituent Assembly was a perfectly legitimate part of the programme of revolutionary Social-Democracy, because in a bourgeois republic the Constituent Assembly represents the highest form of democracy. . . . For the transition from the bourgeois to the socialist system, for the dictatorship of the proletariat, the Republic of Soviets (of Workers', Soldiers' and Peasants' Deputies) is not only a higher type of democratic institution (as compared with the usual bourgeois republic crowned by a Constituent Assembly), but is the only form capable of securing the most painless transition to socialism.[89]

Although the Bolshevik Party had been calling for the Constituent Assembly, it had also called for all power to the soviets, and the two were incompatible. By the time of the revolutionary takeover, the decision to follow the latter was made clear. On October 25, 1917, the day of the insurrection, Lenin declared "the establishment of Soviet power"[90] and proclaimed socialism as the goal of the revolution.[91] As interpreted by Lenin in the "Theses on the Constituent Assembly," the democratic revolution was superseded by the proletarian socialist revolution, and thus the Constituent Assembly became an anachronism.[92] Therefore, according to Carr, "After October 1917 nobody could undo what had been done or force the revolution back into a bourgeois democratic mold."[93] Carr argued that to have acted differently would have meant abandoning the socialist revolution carried out in the name of and based on the soviets.

In the elections for the Constituent Assembly in November 1917, the Bolsheviks won 25 percent of the seats, but in the context of a proletarian revolution, this small percentage included the majority of the seats from urban Petrograd, Moscow, and other large industrial cities. The Social Revolutionary Party won a majority, but the election lists did not reflect the split in that party prior to the elections. Its left wing, which was closer to the Bolsheviks and supported soviet rule, was underrepresented in the Constituent Assembly.[94] The Kadets and Mensheviks did very poorly.

At the beginning of January 1918, Lenin drafted the first constitutional declaration, known as the "Declaration of Rights of the Working and Exploited People," to be presented for approval to the Constituent Assembly. It begins, "The Constituent Assembly resolves: 1. Russia is hereby proclaimed a Republic of Soviets of Workers', Soldiers' and Peasants' Deputies. All power, centrally and locally, is vested in these Soviets."[95] It defined the task of the Constituent Assembly as writing a constitution based on Soviet power—"establishing the fundamental principles of the socialist reconstruction of society" and "of a federation of Soviet Republics of Russia."[96]

On January 18, 1918, the Constituent Assembly rejected this declaration and declared itself the highest power in the land. On January 19, the central executive committee of the All-Russian Soviet disbanded the Constituent Assembly, and it never met again. The decree approved by the central executive committee stated:

> The working classes learned by experience that the old bourgeois parliamentary system had outlived its purpose and was absolutely incompatible with the aim of achieving socialism. . . . To relinquish the sovereign power of the Soviets, to relinquish the Soviet Republic won by the people, for the sake of the bourgeois parliamentary system and the Constituent Assembly, would now be a step backwards and would cause the collapse of the October workers' and peasants' revolution.[97]

There was little public reaction to the closure, and even supporters of the Constituent Assembly blamed the timid moderates more than the Bolsheviks.[98] Carr concluded, "It was one more demonstration of the lack of any solid basis, or any broad support, in Russia, for the institutions and principles of bourgeois democracy."[99] Even the State Duma declared in May 1917 that the peasants had no opinion or ideas about the Constituent Assembly.[100] Anweiler also argued that the Russian workers and peasants more closely identified with the soviets than with the Constituent Assembly:

> The masses of peasants and workers, who never quite ceased to view the Constituent Assembly as a distant and abstract concept, tended to prefer the practical measures of the new rulers to the paper resolutions of an assembly backed by no real power. . . . Russia had little or no tradition of local democratic self-government or of a national parliament, so that the new revolutionary bodies of workers', soldiers', and peasants' Soviets could easily be established in their place. . . . The masses regarded them as "their" organs, and could not have been mobilized against them.[101]

Finally, the disbanding of the Constituent Assembly occurred at the time when counterrevolutionary forces were beginning to organize for insurrection against the new government, and the Bolsheviks felt that the Constituent Assembly could provide legal cover.[102] Furthermore, the Constituent Assembly would have been dominated by the moderate socialists who had opposed the October insurrection and thus had lost popular support. It was unlikely that the Bolsheviks would renounce the power that they had seized in favor of these politicians and their class.[103]

In the last analysis, the issue of the Constituent Assembly goes beyond a particular historical period and must be understood in the context of revolutionary theory. Liebman wrote:

> Finally, the question "Soviets or Constituent Assembly?" transcends the historical and geographical limitations in which we have hitherto considered it, for it is not confined either to the year 1917 or to Russia. When we think of the great social clashes of modern times, we observe, in France and Germany as in Russia, that the revolutionary dynamic has always been blocked by the paralysing or braking force of the election mechanism, even in its democratic form of universal suffrage. This happened in 1848 in Paris, when the proletariat attacked in the streets and the bourgeoisie answered with rifle-fire and with votes. This happened in 1871, too, when the National Assembly was able, in the face of the Commune, to boast of a democratic legitimacy that the workers of Paris did not have: *they* were not representatives of the nation's sovereign will.[104]

One-Party Rule and Centralization

Lenin's concept of the role of the Communist Party and its relationship to state power and, more particularly, to the soviets led to one-party control in the post-Stalin Soviet Union and in those regimes modeled after the Soviet Union, including Cuba. The period from the start of the civil war in 1918 until Lenin's death in 1924 was one of reduced emphasis on the soviets as instruments of self-government, the transfer of effective power to the Communist Party, the elimination of opposition parties, and the centralization of political and economic control.

The development of a centralized one-party dictatorship in the Soviet Union, supposedly acting in the interests of the working classes in the name of socialism, must be analyzed in the context of class warfare, foreign threats and invasions, poverty and the need for economic growth, and the specific historical experiences of the Russian Revolution. Boris Kagarlitsky finds no theoretical justification for one-party rule:

> Here it has to be made clear that not only in the works of Lenin but even in the official manuals of "Marxism-Leninism" we fail to find a developed justification for the one-party system. Even fervent Stalinists cannot bring themselves to assert that the one-party system is a "law" or principle of socialism. This is only implied, hinted at, when they talk of the leading role of the Party (but the leading role of one party does not rule out the existence of others).[105]

In the new Soviet state, the road to one-party rule began with the closure of the Constituent Assembly because, according to Carr, "It made irrevocable the breach between the Bolsheviks and the socialist parties."[106] Because, except for the Left Social Revolutionaries, the socialist parties refused to recognize the sovereignty of the soviets, they became, in effect, counterrevolutionaries in relationship to the dominant revolutionary power. Subsequently the Bolshevik Party tried and failed to form a coalition cabinet including all the socialist parties. The Left Social Revolutionaries at first joined the Council of People's Commissars but later withdrew because of their opposition to the separate peace with Germany. By the time the fifth All-Russian Congress of Soviets had approved the new constitution in July 1918, the Left Social Revolutionaries had been expelled and outlawed. By November 1918, there was only a bare minimum of non-Bolshevik delegates in the All-Russian Congress of Soviets.[107] Carr concluded, "The growth of the one-party state and the impact of the civil war, which for the next two years put the survival of the republic in almost daily jeopardy, destroyed the optimistic foundations on which the constitution had been built. . . . The needs of the army in the field and of security at home created an atmosphere inimical to constitutional niceties."[108] Although excluded from the government, opposition parties continued to exist legally for two more years provided they did not support the civil war and were not openly counterrevolutionary. The Mensheviks, for example, had offices in Moscow, held conferences, issued news sheets and proclamations, and won seats in local soviet elections. The All-Russian Congress of Soviets in December 1920 was the last to admit, without voting rights, Menshevik and Social Revolutionary delegates.[109]

By March 1921, the civil war had ended, leaving tremendous losses and destruction. Widespread discontent was symbolized by the Kronstadt mutiny of March 1921. By the summer of 1921, independent parties in Soviet Russia no longer existed. Differences of opinion were now concentrated within the Bolshevik Party, and even these ceased to be tolerated.[110] After the Mensheviks were repressed in 1921, the final blow to organized opposition came with the trial for treason of the Social Revolutionary leaders in 1922. Carr claimed that this was not a show trial or a sham because "evidence was brought against the defendants of acts which under any system of government would have been criminal."[111]

What is significant from a theoretical perspective—and relevant to an understanding of the one-party state in socialist Cuba—is Carr's viewpoint that the development of the Soviet one-party state can be grasped only in the historical context of class struggle and the opposing parties' antagonism toward the nature and survival of the revolutionary Soviet state. The demise of legal opposition cannot be attributed solely to the actions of one party: "If it was true that the Bolshevik regime was not prepared after the first few months to tolerate an organized opposition, it was equally true that no opposition party was prepared to remain within legal limits. The premise of dictatorship was common to both sides of the argument."[112]

With the elimination of opposition parties, political debate was replaced by technical discussions on how best to achieve goals and policies determined by the party: how to overcome economic problems and achieve economic growth in the period of transition to socialism, and how to strive toward the long-term goals of a communist society. "Democracy therefore," according to Harding, "in the sense of great controversy between competing political parties, was irrelevant."[113] This deemphasis of the "political" characteristics of the proletarian state flows from Marx's perception of the withering away of the state and Lenin's description in the same vein in "The State and Revolution" of the state being transformed "into something which is no longer the state proper."[114] It thus serves as one premise for comprehending the absence of "politics" in Cuban election campaigns and parliamentary debates.

Lenin, in his report to the eighth All-Russian Congress of Soviets, held in December 1920, stressed the overriding need for economic development. To achieve this goal, he included the necessity for the dictatorship of the proletariat to resort to compulsion and persuasion, the need to educate the workers and peasants, and the need for more technical experts to lead the discussions in the Soviet Congress: "This marks the beginning of that very happy time when politics will recede into the background. . . and engineers and agronomists will do most of the talking. . . . Henceforth, less politics will be the best politics."[115]

The centralization of political power and the transference of political power from the soviets to the Communist Party occurred during the course of the five years following the October 1917 Revolution. The concept of "democratic centralism" originally applied to party organization and was only later extended to the state. In 1905, Lenin's main theme was, according to Michael Waller, "an appeal to *implant* democratic procedures where they had not hitherto existed."[116] This goal included making the local party organizations the principal party units and ensuring that higher-level bodies would be subject to election, accountability, and recall by lower bodies—a relationship that, as we have seen, also characterized the various levels of the 1871 Paris Commune and the 1905 soviets. Furthermore, in 1906, even in the context of armed insurrection, Lenin had called for full and universal freedom to discuss and to criticize before an action was decided upon and, in order to achieve unity of action, a closing of the ranks and suspension of criticism after a decision by the Central Committee.[117] Waller pointed out that from 1905 on, there was a significant commitment to democratic accountability and open discussion in Bolshevik Party politics:

> The political practices of the Bolsheviks were guided until some four years after the revolution of 1917 by a principle which combined an insistence on organisational cohesion with an element of democracy which existed in fact and not merely in the aspiration. Elections were held to the extent which circumstances allowed, issues were freely debated at congresses and in the party's press, and votes were freely taken.[118]

After the defeat of the 1905 Revolution and the triumph of the counter-revolution in 1907, Lenin also began stressing the authoritarian and centralist aspects of the theory of democratic centralism. By the time he wrote "The State and Revolution" in 1917, he was arguing that "Marx was a centralist" and defining democratic centralism in economic terms as "transferring the privately-owned railways, factories, land and so on to the *entire* nation."[119]

The role of the PCC in Cuba in relation to the OPP has been subject to debate and was modified and reduced with the 1992 Constitution and Electoral Law. In 1905, Lenin also posed the question of "how to divide, and how to combine, the tasks of the Soviet and those of the Russian Social-Democratic Party."[120] Together with the trend toward centralized political power after the October Revolution, the problem of the relations of the party to the soviets again became an issue. Lenin wanted the party to be concerned with three main activities: (1) the organization and education of the working class, (2) the selection of administrative personnel of the state, and (3) ensuring the political coordination of state institutions.[121] At one point, Lenin "urged a clear specification and demarcation of the respective spheres of each and proposed that the organs of the state be given much greater autonomy and freedom from Party interference. . . . If the Party and state machines were to be kept separate then the party itself could act as the agency of criticism and benefit from pressing for the remedying of popular grievances against the bureaucracy."[122] But by the autumn of 1918, power and control were centralized in both the soviet and the party structure, and the functions of the party and the state were merged, with the former increasingly dominant over the latter.

The basis for future centralization of state power lay in part in the structure set forth in the first constitution. The makers of that constitution had assigned a large share of the power to the All-Russian Congress of Soviets and, between sessions, to the Congress's central executive committee. At first, the local soviets had great autonomy, but because of the civil war and other factors, their power had rapidly disintegrated by the autumn of 1918, and the Bolshevik Party had assumed effective political control. According to Liebman, "Until then the power of the soviets, especially on the local plane, had been almost undivided, and in any case greater than that of the Bolshevik Party."[123] A resolution adopted by the Eighth Party Congress in March 1919, formulating the relations between the party and the state, concluded that the Russian Communist Party should control the politics and the work of the soviets. Grigory Zinoviev, in remarks preceding the vote on this resolution, identified the role of the party as that of deciding "fundamental questions of policy, international and domestic."[124] Another important function of the Bolshevik Party in relation to the state was the power of "nomenclature"—the right to name people to important positions. Rudolf

Bahro explained Lenin's reasoning as follows: "Lenin was particularly decisive in rejecting all attacks on the policy of nomination, the installation of
important party, state and trade-union functionaries from above. Abandoning this would be to give up the leading role of the party, he said, and that in
turn would spell the defeat of Soviet power."[125]

By 1922, Lenin was expressing some dissatisfaction with the lack of separation between the party and the government and was accepting some of the
blame for it. Speaking at the Eleventh Party Congress, he said, "The relations between the Party and the Soviet government bodies are not what they
ought to be."[126] Referring specifically to the Council of People's Commissars and the All-Russian Congress's central executive committee, he called
for more serious work by these bodies to raise the prestige of the government in relation to the party.[127]

After the October 1917 Revolution and the legalization of the Bolshevik
Party, the concept of democratic centralism was interpreted for both party
and government along lines resembling the organization of the soviets.
There was also new emphasis on centralism. A resolution passed at the Com-
intern's second congress in 1920 stated that "the main principle of democratic centralism is that of the higher cell being elected by the lower cell, the absolute binding force of all directions of a higher cell for a cell subordinate to
it."[128]

The interpretation of democratic centralism that defined the relationship
of local soviets to the central authorities was "dual subordination." In 1922,
local soviet executive committees were made accountable to the local soviet
congresses and to the higher-level soviets and also to the central governmental ministries. Lenin defended this subordination to central organs by arguing that "legality must be one" throughout the country.[129] "Dual subordination" was included in the 1976 Cuban Constitution, but removed in the
1992 version.

The Soviets After Stalin

Political life as it had been known before virtually ceased in the USSR with
the consolidation of Stalin's rule in the late 1920s. Between 1929 and 1935,
the Supreme Soviet met only once, and it neither discussed nor approved the
five-year plans that brought drastic social and economic changes.[130] The
1936 Constitution formalized the centralization of state power and, at least
on paper, was the basic document, with later amendments, upon which the
Cuban OPP were founded. It included dual subordination, deputies' obligation to report to their constituents, susceptibility to recall, and the soviets
meeting in formal session only four to six times a year.[131] Beginning with the
Twentieth Party Congress in 1956, where Khrushchev denounced Stalin, a
series of new laws, Communist Party resolutions, and debates regarding revi-

talizing and strengthening the soviets also profoundly influenced the 1976 Cuban Constitution and culminated in the Soviet Constitution of 1977. According to Friedgut, Khrushchev's design was to reconcile centralism with mass participation by enhancing the responsibility of the local soviets. The goal was to improve economic planning, production, distribution, communication, and the flow of information without creating independent sources of power.[132] The de-Stalinization process was also an attempt "to close the gap between the regime and its citizens" and to return "the soviets to some part of their originally conceived role as popular organs of rule."[133]

After Stalin's death, the Central Committee of the Communist Party issued a document in 1957 called "On Improving the Activity of the Soviets and Strengthening Their Links with the Masses," which called for deputies to "know the needs, demands and mood of the masses, regularly meet their electors and receive them, study attentively the needs and complaints of the population and help to deal with them."[134] It also called for making executive committees and administrators accountable to local soviets, enhancing the economic capacity of the soviets and their committees and deputies, and eliminating needless party meddling and interference in the soviets. According to Hahn, this document "is rightly considered a turning point in the revival of interest in promoting citizen participation in local government."[135] Resolutions of party congresses held in 1966 and 1971 reiterated these points, and in 1971, they were included in new legislation that defined the rights and obligations of local soviets.[136]

The intent to revitalize the soviets was influenced by Marx's and Lenin's theories on the commune and on the merging of civil and political societies—"the activity of the soviets represents an attempt to promote the closeness of regime and citizens, the creation of face-to-face politics in which civil society and political society, community and regime, can merge"[137]— and patterned after the early soviets of the Russian Revolution.

The depoliticized nomination and election process in the post-Stalin Soviet Union was also derived from the early years of the soviet state. In 1922, the Bolshevik leader M. Kalinin stated that "elections do not involve the transfer of power from one social group to another. . . . there are only changes in personnel, the selection of superior, practical and organizational forces."[138] In a similar vein, the Soviet writer Boris Strashun noted that even in the case of competitive elections, "Individual competition does not imply the existence of political opposition, the competition of political programs. Competition between candidates means competition of their personal qualities,"[139] anticipating the Cuban municipal elections, which, while competitive, do not allow political campaigning and presentations of policy alternatives by the candidates.

There were also significant differences from the Cuban system. In the Soviet Union, local deputies were nominated in their workplaces, except for

army units and villages, where the community participated, with the nominations usually determined in advance by the party.[140] The usual practice was
to nominate a single candidate for each elected position. The candidate did
not have to live in the electoral district, and this may be one reason that in
the Soviet Union, few citizens knew, could name, or had much contact with
their local deputies.[141] In Cuba, municipal delegate candidates must reside
in their election district and are nominated by the constituents in neighborhood meetings, and the elections are competitive. Changes instituted in the
late 1980s under *perestroika* included nominations by neighborhood residents, with less intervention by the party, and competitive elections, which
are reported to have made soviet deputies more responsive to the electorate.[142] It was still not a requirement, however, for local deputies to reside
in their voting districts.

The Cuban system was influenced by voter mandates to local deputies,
which were revived after Stalin's death and inserted by popular demand as
Article 102 in the 1977 Soviet Constitution.[143] The procedures instituted
for citizens' complaints to deputies or directly to their soviets were presented
in decrees and party resolutions as "an institutional reflection of the ideological imperatives implicit in the communal model of direct democracy: workers must control those who administer."[144] Hahn referred to the "imperative" character of voter mandates in the USSR: "Deputies must try to do
what their constituents have demanded, or if there are good reasons why
they cannot, they must explain these publicly."[145] Recall of elected representatives by their electors was tied to failure to carry out voters' instructions,
and Soviet theorists held that it was the possibility of recall that ultimately
gave voter mandates their imperative character.[146]

Stephen Sternheimer classified the various types of voter mandates as an
essential element of the participatory model of the Soviet state, because they
provided the government with essential information from the bottom up.
Voter mandates allow the government to

> assess citizen satisfaction or discontent with state polities, particularly with re-
> spect to items of social consumption (for example, housing transportation, pub-
> lic services) as well as the small matters (*melochi*) of everyday life. From the per-
> spective of communications, the model suggests secondarily that channels
> formerly used exclusively or primarily for social mobilization purposes (for ex-
> ample, mandates issued to city soviet deputies . . .) have taken on a new func-
> tion, that is, the transmission upward of large amounts of unadulterated data on
> social conditions which flow freely to lower- and middle-level government and
> party officials.[147]

One could draw the conclusion from this participatory model that direct
inputs by Soviet citizens primarily pertained to local issues that "directly
touch the citizen's daily life," what Seweryn Bialer called "low politics" and

distinguished from the larger societal issues of "high politics."[148] (This, to be sure, is not to say that citizen mandates did not have an important influence on larger societal issues.)

Emphasis was placed in the Soviet Union, and was also followed up in Cuba, on consensus politics and the merging of local or particular interests in determining the general interest. Anatoli Bezúglov argued that the deputy should be guided not only by his or her own constituents but also by the will of the national electorate.[149] This argument is based, according to Friedgut, on a rejection of "contentious mobilizing of conflicting interests. Instead of contest, Soviet theorists propose consensual participation based on a common understanding of a socially optimal allocation of resources."[150] Hahn pointed out that "whatever conflicts do exist are thrashed out beforehand and presented to the public as consensus opinion."[151]

Election campaigns gave the voters a chance to present mandates to the candidates. Friedgut explained the procedure as follows:

> At election times a more socialized form of demand articulation exists in the form of what are known as "imperative voters" mandates. To qualify as a mandate, a request must reflect a general social need, be presented formally at an election meeting, and be adopted by a majority vote of those present as a special resolution. If such requests are considered to be indicative of a "general will," they are written in the election meeting protocol as a recognized mandate and presented as such to the local soviet.[152]

Mandates were also presented twice a year to deputies during general meetings with constituents. At these meetings, deputies also informed the community of their work and of the work of the relevant soviet. Political scientists in the Soviet Union considered these meetings, together with the preelection meetings, "an institutional expression of the theory of direct democracy."[153]

Citizens brought issues of a more individual nature (known as proposals, declarations, and complaints in the Soviet Union and as *quejas* in Cuba) directly to the local soviet executive committee mainly by means of interviews and letters and were expected to receive an answer within a month.[154] During regular office hours, local deputies also received mandates, which usually involved personal matters such as the need for housing. Both of the practices are mirrored in the Cuban OLPP.

The process of resolving mandates in the Soviet Union was the same as for *planteamientos* in Cuba. Deputies, upon receiving a mandate, were expected to intercede with relevant authorities to resolve the issues. According to Friedgut, "The deputy's status gives him access to local decision makers and administrators that is not available to the ordinary citizen."[155] If mandates could not be resolved at the level of the local soviet, they were sent to higher levels.[156] Citizens not satisfied with the response at the local level could appeal to higher authorities.[157] If necessary, local soviet standing and executive committees assisted the deputies, by finding resources to implement mandates or by pressuring administrators to act.[158] Deputies also organized voluntary labor in the voting district to help complete projects that had originated in mandates. Citizen mandates were included where necessary or possible by the soviets in formulating the economic plan and budget at the appropriate level.[159]

The precursors of the soviets' standing committees had appeared in the years immediately following the revolution. According to Friedgut:

> Following a decision of the Seventh Congress of Soviets of the RSFSR in 1919, "sections" composed of deputies, members of factory committees, and trade union administrators were set up in each soviet to parallel the administrative departments of the local soviets. A little later activists from the public were mobilized to take part in the activities of these sections. . . . The sections were chiefly concerned with control of the administrative organs and mobilization of the public.[160]

Cuban OPP commissions at the three levels are similar to those that existed in the Soviet Union. Soviet standing committees, according to White, Gardner, and Schöpflin, were intended to "provide a means of investigating matters of public concern as well as of checking upon the performance of government and discussing the annual economic plan and state budget."[161] Their duties included overseeing administrative agencies and economic enterprises (whose functions the committees paralleled) within the soviet's jurisdiction and assisting the executive committee and the soviet with the implementation of policy.[162] Standing committees were also directly involved with citizens concerning their registered complaints.[163] Besides deputies, standing committees also had unpaid volunteers from the community as members, known as *activ*, mainly persons employed in the area, or with knowledge of the committee's concerns. Besides being a channel for citizen participation, such voluntary work mobilized and made use of the public's knowledge and experience.[164]

The most powerful committee of the local soviet (corresponding to the council of administrators in the Cuban OLPP) was the executive committee, elected by the deputies. The officers of the executive committee were full-time employees of the soviet. Most of the rest of the deputies were not professional politicians and continued in their regular jobs. The executive committee reported on its activities and decisions to the soviet and to the executive committee of the next higher soviet. The executive committee met and carried on the business of the soviet between sessions. It tended to dominate the local soviet because it controlled the local government activity and the work of the deputies. It prepared the agenda for sessions of the soviet, appointed and coordinated the work of the standing committees, helped the deputies with their tasks including resolving citizen mandates, submitted nominations and removals of directors and administrators for approval by the soviet, and directly handled citizens' letters, complaints, and requests.[165]

The deputies' groups, similar to the *consejos populares* in the Cuban municipal assembly structure, had been set up in local soviets in the first years after the revolution and were revived in the 1950s to help deputies from contiguous areas (ranging in number from three to thirty) to solve common problems, to implement soviet decisions and policies, and to transmit citizens' requests and concerns to the soviets and help resolve them.[166] The deputies' groups also brought government closer to the people. According to Friedgut, "The deputies group or council, accepting its role as administrator along with its representative role, constitutes a significant extension of the apparatus of the soviet into the community, both for the citizens and for the paid full-time administrators. . . . It has the advantage of close contact with the citizen."[167]

The national parliament was the least effective and responsive of the elected representative bodies. According to White, Gardner, and Schöpflin, the formal sessions of the Supreme Soviet were mainly "for the explanation of government policy to deputies and to the country at large."[168] However, they did attribute importance to the standing commissions: "All in all the expansion in the number and authority of the standing commissions is perhaps the most significant development to have occurred in Soviet legislative politics over the last couple of decades and it is the respect in which the 'rubber stamp' stereotype is most obviously inadequate."[169] Standing commissions investigated government performance, made recommendations, and proposed amendments to legislation. While commissions had the right in both cases to initiate legislation, this was more in name than in substance.[170]

Hill attributed to Soviet scholars the view differentiating the role of the Communist Party and the state, allocating "*policy-making, leadership and general supervision* to the party, with the functions of *legislation and policy application*, and to some extent *information-gathering*, being assigned to the state."[171]. Furthermore, Soviet scholars argued, "The party, with all the authority conferred by the *ideology*, defines the parameters of policy for building communism; that policy is then made law by the state, with the legal authority vested in the soviets by the Constitution."[172]

The influence of the party in relation to the state went beyond persuasion. The policy decisions of the Communist Party were obligatory for state organs. With regard to legislation, the party organs participated in formulating bills and reviewed and revised them prior to submission.[173] Furthermore, foreign policy and especially international crises involved direct party decisions.[174]

The party's monitoring of the performance of state bodies and their members was not necessarily designed to be inhibiting; rather it was concerned with attendance at meetings and attending to constituents' needs. According to Friedgut, party decisions served "as a spur to encourage the soviets to improve their effectiveness and overcome some of their weaknesses."[175] Friedgut also cited the party's role in supplying the "core of activists" for the soviets as well as its role as coordinator among state bodies: "Clearly, in the clash of conflicting goals and the demands that surround Soviet economic and administrative bodies, the local party secretary has the advantage of being a step above the competition and thus able to bring together the various agencies whose efforts must be coordinated to effect any change, large or small."[176]

Hahn's conclusion regarding local soviets, which also holds for Cuba, was that "for most issues resolved by local government the need for party authority simply does not arise. Only when there are jurisdictional disputes between governmental and non-governmental agencies, or within the bureaucracy, would the party committee be likely to get directly involved."[177] However, besides the similarities, there were also major differences with the PCC's role in Cuba. In the Soviet Union, the party picked and/or approved the candidates for deputies at all levels, as well as for all parliamentary leadership positions. Even after *perestroika*, the first secretary of the local party unit was a member of the executive committee or even president of the local soviet.

Conclusion

Many of the characteristics of the Cuban OPP were derived from the commune system as developed and implemented by the workers in the 1905 and 1917 soviets, which in turn provided the pattern for how the soviets functioned in the Soviet Union. Besides leading the revolution, Lenin contributed by incorporating and emphasizing these practices within and as complementary to Marx's political theory. Also setting the parameters for the Cuban state were his contributions regarding the need to destroy the old regime and the role of the Communist Party vis-à-vis the soviets. The most immediate and direct influences shaping the OPP came from the Soviet Union in the post-Stalin era, with, however, significant differences in Cuba at the municipal level, most notably in nominations and elections and the party's role in this process.

Notes

1. Ralph Miliband, *Marxism and Politics* (New York: Oxford University Press, 1977), p. 134.
2. G. D. H. Cole, *History of Socialism*, Vol. 2, *Socialist Thought Marxism and Anarchism, 1850–1890* (London: Macmillan, 1954), pp. 294–295.

3. Ibid., p. 205.

4. Ronald J Hill, "The 'All-People's State' and 'Developed Socialism,'" in Neil Harding (ed.), *The State in Socialist Society* (Albany: State University of New York Press, 1984), p. 105.

5. Oskar Anweiler, *The Soviets: The Russian Workers, Peasants, and Soldiers Councils, 1905–1921* (New York: Random House, 1974), p. 20.

6. Ibid., pp. 36–37.

7. Ibid., p. 39.

8. Jeffrey W. Hahn, *Soviet Grassroots: Citizen Participation in Local Soviet Government* (Princeton: Princeton University Press, 1988), p. 56.

9. E. H. Carr, *The Bolshevik Revolution, 1917–1923*, Vol. 1 (Baltimore: Penguin Books, 1966), pp. 58–59.

10. Anweiler, *The Soviets*, p. 42.

11. Hahn, *Soviet Grassroots*, pp. 56–57.

12. Carr, *The Bolshevik Revolution*, p. 59.

13. Anweiler, *The Soviets*, p. 52.

14. V. Koldáiev, "Creación y desarrollo de los soviets," in M. Shafir et al., *Los Soviets, Organos del Poder Popular* (Moscow: Progreso, 1979), p. 29 (my translation); see also Theodore H. Friedgut, *Political Participation in the USSR* (Princeton: Princeton University Press, 1979), p. 103.

15. Hahn, *Soviet Grassroots*, p. 138.

16. Quoted in Koldáiev, "Creación y desarrollo," p. 29.

17. Ibid., pp. 29–30.

18. Anweiler, *The Soviets*, p. 58.

19. Carr, *The Bolshevik Revolution*, p. 59.

20. Ibid., p. 64.

21. Koldáiev, "Creación y desarrollo," p. 32.

22. Alexander Rabinowitch, *The Bolsheviks Come to Power: The Revolution of 1917 in Petrograd* (New York: Norton, 1976), p. xxii.

23. Ibid.

24. Carr, *The Bolshevik Revolution*, p. 81.

25. Rabinowitch, *The Bolsheviks*, pp. xxii-xxiii.

26. Marcel Liebman, *The Russian Revolution* (New York: Random House, 1970), p. 117.

27. Rabinowitch, *The Bolsheviks*, p. 166.

28. Ibid., pp. 154–157.

29. Hahn, *Soviet Grassroots*, p. 58.

30. Anweiler, *The Soviets*, p. 112.

31. Quoted in Liebman, *The Russian Revolution*, p. 114.

32. Anweiler, *The Soviets*, pp. 158–159.

33. Ibid., p. 115.

34. Ibid., p. 158

35. Liebman, *The Russian Revolution*, p. 282; see also Friedgut, *Political Participation*, p. 103.

36. Marcel Liebman, *Leninism Under Lenin* (London: Jonathan Cape, 1975), p. 180.

37. Goran Therborn, *What Does the Ruling Class Do When It Rules? State Apparatuses and State Power Under Feudalism, Capitalism, and Socialism* (London: Verso, 1980), p. 108.

38. Liebman, *Leninism Under Lenin*, p. 218.

39. Carr, *The Bolshevik Revolution*, p. 140.

40. Ibid., p. 141.

41. James H. Meisel and Edward S. Kozera (eds.), *Materials for the Study of the Soviet System: State and Party Constitutions, Laws, Decrees, Decisions and Official Statements of the Leaders in Translation*, 2d edition (Ann Arbor, Mich.: George Wahr, 1953), pp. 50–51.

42. Hahn, *Soviet Grassroots*, p. 138.

43. Ibid., pp. 52–53.

44. Ibid., p. 54.

45. Koldáiev, "Creación y desarrollo," pp. 36–37.

46. Carr, *The Bolshevik Revolution*, pp. 134–135.

47. Ibid., p. 134.

48. Ibid., p. 140.

49. V. I. Lenin, "Political Report of the Central Committee, Seventh Congress of the R.C.P.(B.)," in V. I. Lenin, *Selected Works*, Vol. 2 (New York: International Publishers, 1967), pp. 575–576.

50. Carr, *The Bolshevik Revolution*, pp. 134–159.

51. Friedgut, *Political Participation*, pp. 188–189.

52. V. I. Lenin, "The Seventh (April) All-Russia Conference of the R.S.D.L.P.(B.)," in Lenin, *Selected Works*, Vol. 2, p. 74.

53. Umberto Cerroni, *Teoría política y socialismo* (Mexico: Era, 1976), p. 108 (my translation).

54. Ibid., p. 109.

55. V. I. Lenin, "Letter to the Bolshevik Comrades Attending the Congress of Soviets of the Northern Region," in Lenin, *Selected Works*, Vol. 2, p. 430.

56. Cerroni, *Teoría política*, p. 109.

57. Attilio Chitarin, "Problemas de la transición del capitalismo al socialismo en la URSS," in Paul Sweezy et al., *Teoría del proceso de transición* (Buenos Aires: Siglo XXI, 1973), p. 128 (my translation).

58. V. I. Lenin, "The State and Revolution," in Lenin, *Selected Works*, Vol. 2, p. 292.

59. Ibid., p. 359. Also see V. I. Lenin, "Letter to American Workers," in Lenin, *Selected Works*, Vol. 3, p. 26.

60. Goran Therborn, *Ruling Class*, p. 25.

61. V. I. Lenin, "Can the Bolsheviks Retain State Power?" in Lenin, *Selected Works*, Vol. 2, p. 395.

62. Ibid., p. 404; see also V. I. Lenin, "How to Organize Competition," in Lenin, *Selected Works*, Vol. 2, p. 513.

63. Liebman, *Leninism Under Lenin*, p. 195.

64. Ibid., p. 201.

65. Ibid., p. 208.

66. Ibid., p. 202.

67. Ibid., p. 208.

68. Cerroni, *Teoría Política*, p. 128.

69. Ibid., p. 129.

70. Carr, *The Bolshevik Revolution*, p. 249.

71. V. I. Lenin, "To the Population," in Lenin, *Selected Works*, Vol. 2, p. 482.

72. Lenin, "The State and Revolution," p. 303.

73. Ibid., p. 357.

74. Ibid., p. 298.

75. Ibid., p. 304.

76. Ibid., p. 302.

77. Cerroni, *Teoría Política*, p. 134.

78. Colletti, *From Rousseau to Lenin: Studies in Ideology and Society* (London: New Left Books, 1972), p. 221.

79. Ibid., p. 222.

80. Lenin, "Can the Bolsheviks?" p. 395.

81. V. I. Lenin, "The Immediate Tasks of the Soviet Government," in Lenin, *Selected Works*, Vol. 2, p. 678.

82. Lenin, "The State and Revolution," p. 271.

83. Cerroni, *Teoría política*, p. 126.

84. V. I. Lenin, "Eighth All-Russian Congress of Soviets," in Lenin, *Selected Works*, Vol. 3, p. 512.

85. Cerroni, *Teoría política*, p. 131.

86. Rabinowitch, *The Bolsheviks*, p. 172.

87. Neil Harding, "Socialism, Society, and the Organic Labour State," in Neil Harding (ed.), *The State in Socialist Society* (Albany: State University of New York Press, 1984), p. 20.

88. Vania Bambirra and Theotonio dos Santos, *La estrategia y la táctica socialista de Marx y Engels a Lenin*, Vol. 2 (Mexico: Era, 1981), p. 135 (my translation).

89. V. I. Lenin, "Theses on the Constituent Assembly," in Lenin, *Selected Works*, Vol. 2, p. 408.

90. V. I. Lenin, "To the Citizens of Russia," in Lenin, *Selected Works*, Vol. 2, p. 451.

91. Carr, *The Bolshevik Revolution*, p. 116.

92. Ibid., pp. 124–125.

93. Ibid., pp. 131–132.

94. Anweiler, *The Soviets*, p. 216.

95. V. I. Lenin, "Declaration of Rights of the Working and Exploited People," in Lenin, *Selected Works*, Vol. 2, p. 520.

96. Ibid., p. 522.

97. V. I. Lenin, "Draft Decree on the Dissolution of the Constituent Assembly," *Selected Works*, Vol. 2, pp. 523–524.

98. Liebman, *The Russian Revolution*, p. 319; see also Carr, *The Bolshevik Revolution*, pp. 129–130.

99. Carr, *The Bolshevik Revolution*, p. 130.

100. Christopher Hill, *Lenin and the Russian Revolution* (Harmondsworth: Penguin Books, 1971), p. 97.

101. Anweiler, *The Soviets*, p. 218.

102. Carr, *The Bolshevik Revolution*, p. 122.

103. Liebman, *The Russian Revolution*, p. 319.

104. Liebman, *Leninism Under Lenin*, p. 236.

105. Boris Kagarlitsky, *The Thinking Reed: Intellectuals and the Soviet State 1917 to the Present* (New York: Verso, 1988), p. 258.

106. Carr, *The Bolshevik Revolution*, p. 124.

107. Liebman, *The Russian Revolution*, p. 321.

108. Carr, *The Bolshevik Revolution*, p. 159.

109. Ibid., pp. 179–183.

110. Ibid., pp. 184–185.

111. Ibid., p. 190.

112. Ibid.

113. Neil Harding, *Lenin's Political Thought*, Vol. 2, *Theory and Practice in the Socialist Revolution* (London: Macmillan, 1981), p. 303.

114. Lenin, "The State and Revolution," p. 298.

115. V. I. Lenin, "Report on the Work of the Council of People's Commissars, Eighth All Russian Congress of Soviets," in Lenin, *Selected Works*, Vol. 3, pp. 495, 498, 510.

116. Michael Waller, *Democratic Centralism: An Historical Commentary* (New York: St. Martin's Press, 1981), p. 45.

117. Marcel Liebman, "Lenin in 1905," *Monthly Review*, Vol. 21, No. 11 (April, 1970), pp. 62–63.

118. Waller, *Democratic Centralism*, p. 30.

119. Lenin, "The State and Revolution," p. 306.

120. Quoted in Ralph Miliband, *Marxism and Politics* (New York: Oxford University Press, 1977), p. 138

121. Liebman, *Leninism Under Lenin*, pp. 280–281.

122. Quoted in Harding, *Lenin's Political Thought*, Vol. 2, p. 296.

123. Liebman, *Leninism Under Lenin*, p. 229.

124. Carr, *The Bolshevik Revolution*, p. 225.

125. Rudolf Bahro, *The Alternative in Eastern Europe* (London: Verso, 1981), p. 110.

126. Lenin, "Political Report, Eleventh Congress of the R.C.P.(B.)," in Lenin, *Selected Works*, Vol. 3, p. 708.

127. Ibid., pp. 708–710. Also see Liebman, *Leninism Under Lenin*, p. 281.

128. Quoted in Waller, *Democratic Centralism*, p. 44.

129. Carr, *The Bolshevik Revolution*, pp. 223–225.

130. Harding, "Socialism, Society," p. 43.

131. Hahn, *Soviet Grassroots*, p. 67.

132. Friedgut, *Political Participation*, pp. 41–44.

133. Ibid., p. 157.

134. Quoted in Ronald J Hill, "The Development of Soviet Local Government since Stalin's Death," in Everett M. Jacobs, *Soviet Local Politics and Government* (London: George Allen and Unwin, 1983), p. 19.

135. Hahn, *Soviet Grassroots*, pp. 68–70.

136. Ronald J Hill, "Recent Developments in Soviet Local Government," *Community Development Journal*, Vol. 7 (1972), pp. 169–175.

137. Friedgut, *Political Participation*, p. 322.

138. Quoted in Victor Zaslavsky and Robert J Brym, "The Structure of Power and the Function of Soviet Local Elections," in Jacobs, *Soviet Local Politics*, p. 75.

139. Quoted in ibid., p. 71.

140. Hahn, *Soviet Grassroots*, pp. 100–102.

141. Ibid., pp. 189, 194; see also Theodore H. Friedgut, "The Soviet Citizen's Perception of Local Government," in Jacobs, *Soviet Local Politics*, p. 125; Ronald J. Hill, *Soviet Politics, Political Science and Reform* (New York: M. E. Sharpe, 1980), pp. 45–46; and Hill, "The Development of Soviet Local Government Since Stalin's Death," in Hill, *Soviet Politics*, p. 32.

142. David K Shipler, "The Politics of Neighborhood," *New Yorker,* June 3, 1991, pp. 45, 62.

143. Ibid., p. 139; see also Donald E. Schulz, "Political Participation in Communist Systems: The Conceptual Approach," in Donald E. Schulz and Jan S. Adams (eds.), *Political Participation in Communist Countries* (New York: Pergamon Press, 1981), pp. 11–12; and L. G. Churchward, "Public Participation in the USSR," in Jacobs, *Soviet Local Politics*, p. 44.

144. Hahn, *Soviet Grassroots*, p. 159.

145. Ibid., p. 137.

146. Ibid., pp. 181–182; see also Churchward, "Political Participation," p. 43.

147. Stephen Sternheimer, "Communications and Power in Soviet Urban Politics," in Jacobs, *Soviet Local Politics*, p. 138.

148. Quoted in Hahn, *Soviet Grassroots*, p. 263.

149. Anatoli Bezúglov, *El diputado soviético: Estatuto Jurídico* (Moscow: Progreso, 1976), pp. 40–42.

150. Friedgut, *Political Participation*, p. 50.

151. Hahn, *Soviet Grassroots*, p. 284.

152. Friedgut, *Political Participation*, p. 102.

153. Hahn, *Soviet Grassroots*, p. 149.

154. Sternheimer, "Communications and Power," p. 145.

155. Friedgut, *Political Participation*, p. 155.

156. Churchward, "Public Participation," p. 44; see also Bezúglov, *El diputado sovitico*, p. 130.

157. Hahn, *Soviet Grassroots*, p. 162.

158. Ibid., pp. 146–147; see also Bezúglov, *El diputado soviético*, p. 138.

159. M. Shafir and O. Kutafin, "La Constitución de la URSS acerca de los Soviets de Diputados Populares y las Normas de su Elección," in Shafir et al., *Los Soviets*, pp. 106–107; see also Bezúglov, *El diputado soviético*, pp. 128–129, 133–134; and Hahn, *Soviet Grassroots*, pp. 143–145.

160. Friedgut, *Political Participation*, pp. 188–189.

161. Stephen White, John Gardner, and George Schöpflin, *Communist Political Systems: An Introduction*, 2d edition (London: Macmillan Education, 1987), p. 84.

162. Hahn, *Soviet Grassroots*, pp. 228, 230.

163. Friedgut, *Political Participation*, p. 229; see also Hahn, *Soviet Grassroots*, p. 237.

164. Friedgut, *Political Participation*, p. 197.

165. B. Chernov, "Organos Locales de Poder y Administración del Estado en la URSS," in Shafir et al., *Los Soviets*, pp. 285–295; see also Hahn, *Soviet Grassroots*, pp. 246–249.

166. Hahn, *Soviet Grassroots*, pp. 163–164, 204; see also Chernov, "Organos Locales," pp. 281–284.

167. Friedgut, *Political Participation*, pp. 210–211.

168. White, Gardner, and Schöpflin, *Communist Political Systems*, p. 91.

169. Ibid., p. 93.

170. Ibid.

171. Hill, *Soviet Politics*, p. 120.

172. Ibid., p. 122.

173. Ibid., p. 123.

174. Archie Brown, "Political Power and the Soviet State: Western and Soviet Perspectives," in Harding, *The State in Socialist Society*, p. 80.

175. Friedgut, *Political Participation*, p. 53.

176. Ibid., p. 54; see also Hill, "The Development of Soviet Local Government," p. 29.

177. Hahn, *Soviet Grassroots*, p. 259.

3

The Organs of People's Power: An Overview

During the period between the triumph of the Cuban Revolution in 1959 and the inauguration of the Organs of People's Power in 1976, Cuba experimented with a series of provisional governmental structures. The 1976 Cuban Constitution, which included the establishment of the new governmental institutions, was not a radical break in the political course of the Cuban Revolution but a formalization, revitalization, strengthening, and restructuring of past practices and tendencies, with, however, new emphasis on decentralization. That the prior governmental structures served as a training ground for many who would later be in leadership positions in the OPP is a further element of continuity in the institutionalization process. Citizen participation and the strong and close identification of the people with their government, which had evolved as the political underpinnings of the revolutionary state, were now to take on, in the words of then First Deputy Prime Minister Raúl Castro, "a regular, systematic and institutionalized form."[1] In July 1992, the National Assembly passed the Constitutional Reform Law, and in October 1992, it passed a new electoral law. To some extent, the changes are a rejection of copying *(copismo)*, defined as "the transposition of the institutional soviet system and of its ideological forms."[2] The constitutional changes made in 1992, however, maintained the basic structure of the OPP.

Revolutionary Government in the Early Years

Fidel Castro and his adherents moved into an institutional vacuum when they defeated the old regime in Cuba in 1959. According to Carollee Bengelsdorf, the enemy was weak, with no coherent ruling class, no party structure, and no ideology, a circumstance that helps explain the lack of per-

manent political structure in the beginning of the revolutionary government.[3] Bengelsdorf quoted sociologist Maurice Zeitlin to the effect that
given the criminality, corruption, and brutality of Batista's rule, "Nothing—
not the Congress, not the constitution, not electoral politics, not the judiciary, nor any political party or trade union—remained undenigrated and respected."[4] Cuban leader Fidel Castro interpreted the provisional nature of
the government at that time: "We had to seize revolutionary power; we had
to begin to make the Revolution. And, the only way to do that was by taking
the state and establishing a revolutionary government."[5] He spelled out the
reasons for the provisional nature of the government:

> Of course, historically, many social movements have been characterized by first
> of all drawing up a supreme law, a constitution. The result is that during the
> process that constitution becomes a kind of inviolable taboo; it becomes an in-
> efficient intellectual creation, unable to conform to reality. Our Revolution did
> not wish, for example, to start off by creating in the abstract, and, through that
> abstract creation, establish an "impressive" so-called socialist constitution.
> . . . In the light of present experience, and looking back over the immense dark-
> ness of our past ignorance, we see with absolute clarity how many errors in con-
> cept, how many unintelligible things, how many unrealistic ideas and abstrac-
> tions a thousand leagues from reality such a constitution would have involved.[6]

Castro's brother, Raúl, further explained why the provisional government
in the initial stages of the Cuban Revolution had lacked representative institutions, pointing to the need at the time for rapid and profound changes,
the requirement for quick and decisive action to confront external threats
and internal counterrevolutionary activities, and the lack of sufficient material resources, which, taken together, could have prevented representative
bodies from fulfilling their tasks and thus have discredited them. He concluded:

> In the first years of the Revolution we were not equipped to face the task of set-
> ting up representative institutions. At the time we did not have a strong party,
> the mass organizations were not sufficiently developed. . . . To all these factors,
> we should add a certain lack of experience and understanding on the part of
> many of us regarding the importance of these representative institutions and the
> role which they are to play.[7]

In response to a question on the process of destroying the old bourgeois
state and building the socialist state, Fidel Castro stressed the ad hoc nature
of the government in the initial stages following the 1959 triumph of the
Cuban Revolution: "There wasn't any classical legislative power, no judicial
power or anything else left, because all that disappeared on January 1
[1959], with the collapse of the Batista regime. A de facto revolutionary
government was established, and the laws were enacted by decree."[8] William

LeoGrande characterized the first years after the revolutionary takeover as a kind of "guerrilla administration" structured much as the war had been waged: unorganized, chaotic, with little formal control.[9]

The period prior to the mid–1970s featured numerous participatory channels as well as concrete advances for most citizens as a consequence of measures favoring equality and social justice. Cuban social scientist Haroldo Dilla identifies Cuban political practice of this period with the Marxist theory of merging civil and political societies: "The Revolution was able to overcome definitively the 'deceptive separation' between economics and politics—the main key of the liberal dogma."[10] Cuban Minister of Culture Armando Hart linked "politics" in the preinstitutionalization period to participation in organizing production, "insuring an ever more conscientious, an ever more enthusiastic and an ever more effective participation of the masses . . . in that production and that social life."[11]

According to LeoGrande, the concept of "direct democracy" that predominated in Cuba in the 1960s was based on a definition of political participation as supportive activity by the majority of the citizenry. This support was manifested through public mobilizations to implement policies that served the interests of the people and the national goals identified by the leadership. Responsiveness to the people's needs was to be ensured by "a direct, informal, and non-institutional relationship between the people and their leaders."[12] This concept of direct democracy as a concept and goal, was announced by Fidel Castro soon after taking power: "This democracy . . . has found its expression, directly, in the intimate union and identification of the government and the people."[13]

Dilla regarded the practice of direct democracy in Cuba during this period as part of the development of a new political culture that linked popular participation to the military defense of the revolution and of national sovereignty, and to mobilizations to promote economic development. This identification with the Cuban Revolution, in turn, made possible articulation of "the active consensus of the majority of the population with regard to the process of changes . . . which provided the Cuban leadership with a great capacity to call upon the masses, reinforced by a style of permanent contact with the masses . . . with the invaluable resource of the charismatic personality and political ability of Fidel Castro."[14]

This concept of direct democracy has also included, throughout the history of the Cuban Revolution, consultation with the population on important laws through work centers, mass organizations, and military units, described by Castro as "a situation in which all the people are the lawmakers!"[15] An example of such popular consultation was the Law on Loafing, which "was discussed by more than three million people in 115,00 assemblies."[16] In the mid–1970s, the Family Code and the new constitution were similarly discussed at meetings with the Cuban population.[17] The practice continued after the establishment of the OPP. Regarding the Labor Code, according to Gail Lindenberg, "The most important proposed changes were discussed among the 2 million+ members of the *Central de Trabajadores de Cuba* (Cuban Workers Federation or CTC) before approval by the National Assembly in 1984."[18] Prior to the Fourth Party Congress in October 1991, grassroots meetings were held in all parts of the island as forums for citizens to propose topics and resolutions for this congress.[19] In all these examples, some changes were incorporated as a result of consultations with the Cuban people.

The first attempt to establish local government, the *Juntas de Coordinación, Ejecución e Inspección* (Coordination, Operations and Inspection Boards, or JUCEI), lasted from 1961 until 1965. These were composed of representatives from political and mass organizations and from agencies of the central government, whose purpose was to coordinate all the economic and social activities that had come under state control in the first years of the revolutionary government.[20] However, they were almost totally lacking in structure, and in 1966, they were replaced by a system called *Poder Local* (Local Power) that survived until the OPP were instituted in the mid–1970s.

Dilla and Gerardo González assigned great importance to the early development of mass organizations, especially concerning citizen participation, for creating the bases for the OPP:

> The JUCEI and Local Power can be considered institutional antecedents of the present municipal system, but probably much more relevant was the existence of a strong framework of community participation which had its center in a collection of political and mass organizations based on neighborhood, principally the *Comités de la Defensa de la Revolución* (Committees for the Defense of the Revolution or CDR) and the *Federación de Mujeres Cubanas* (Federation of Cuban Women or FMC).[21]

The structures and modes of citizen participation of the OPP were portended in these mass organizations and in the trade unions.[22] For example, in a speech celebrating the twelfth anniversary of the CDR in 1972, Fidel Castro called them "the real foundation on which we can build our democratic superstructure" and said that through them, "more and more of the people will be participating directly in solving their problems."[23] The local rule that LeoGrande described for mass organizations reaching back to the 1960s is similar in structure to what were to become the municipal assemblies:

> Candidates for leadership positions in the mass organizations at the local level are nominated by the membership itself, with the requirement that there must always be at least two candidates for every position. The Communist Party is

prohibited from either nominating or endorsing any candidate. After a discussion of the merits of the candidates, the membership votes (in the trade unions, at least, this vote is by secret ballot). . . . In addition, most national congress delegates are drawn from the base of the organization: local units elect delegates to congresses in the way they elect local leaders.[24]

Whereas Bengelsdorf and Dilla have minimized the importance of the local government structures that preceded the OPP, [25] it was Local Power that provided much of the personnel for the OPP and anticipated many of their practices. According to LeoGrande, "The similarities between People's Power and the abortive Local Power experiment are striking."[26] Julio Carranza, the former national coordinator of Local Power, told me in an interview in 1988 that the development of much of the leadership for the OPP, other state organs, and also the Cuban Communist Party was another one of Local Power's legacies.

The basic objective of Local Power, according to Domingo García Cárdenas, "was to achieve an organic and systematic participation of the general public in state activities."[27] LeoGrande reported that "Local Power had two basic objectives: a significant decentralization of administrative authority enabling local government to be more responsive to local needs and conditions; and a major increase in popular participation in local government. Increased participation was understood to mean both greater popular support in the implementation of policy and greater popular input to policy making."[28] Eleven thousand Local Power delegates were elected from both neighborhoods and work centers. Candidates were nominated directly by the voters present at meetings in the neighborhoods and work centers, without overt interference by the party. (Carranza told me that in a few instances, the party did propose candidates, but these candidates did not always win.) Delegates were elected by a show of hands immediately following the nominations. Every municipality had ten elected delegates, two secretaries, and a president, who was elected by the local nucleus of the PCC.

Following the tradition of the *mandat impératif,* elected delegates were required to meet with constituents every six months in what was called the "Report to the People's Assemblies." As is the current practice under the OLPP, the delegates heard voters' *planteamientos* (concerns, complaints, proposals, and suggestions), answered questions, and reported on the activities of the local government.[29] The semiannual meetings with constituents were also, according to García Cárdenas, "a means of incorporating the population into the realization of the local governments' work, such as the construction of service centers, the cleanup of towns and cities and other measures."[30] Thus delegates had an advisory role as a link between citizens and administrators and had the task of organizing and mobilizing the masses. The Local Power delegates were unpaid volunteers.

Administrative agencies under the municipal Local Power units were in charge of local social services, commerce, and industry. Committees of elected delegates aided and checked on these agencies. Similarly, the regional and provincial units supervised economic activities in their respective areas and the Local Power units below them. At the top was the National Coordinating Board for Local Power, which was not meant to be a national government, had no legislative power, and was not elected. Formal legislative power continued to be exercised by the cabinet.[31]

Local Power rapidly became an administrative unit with few real powers. Some of the regulations with which Local Power operated were written, and some were simply based on practice, emphasizing again Local Power's transitional and provisional nature.[32] In fact, the electoral system was never really sustained. Delegate elections were postponed and then, in 1970, canceled as the country became involved in the massive effort to achieve the ten-million-ton sugar harvest. The semiannual meetings with citizens were also abandoned. While Local Power officially lasted until 1976, according to García Cárdenas it became "just one more administrative agency in the country."[33] Its lack of resources to solve neighborhood problems, the lack of an adequate institutional system, and excessive centralization eliminated any possible development or growth of Local Power.[34]

For Dilla, the period prior to 1976 was characterized by

> an excessive growth of the central state apparatus and the Party and consequently . . . intense bureaucratic centralization. . . . The invasion by the Party into state administrative spheres weakened not only the capacity of the Party to exercise its political leadership role, but also the very efficacy of the administrative body. . . . Popular mobilization was weakened and was directed toward the fulfillment of unreachable economic goals.[35]

Local Power was unable to fulfill the objectives of administrative decentralization and governmental responsiveness. Also contributing to the decline of mass input into decision making was the weakening of the CDR and the FMC, and the CTC practically ceased functioning. Raúl Castro spoke of "an excess of centralization in many areas, when we had inadequate administrative procedures, when there was little understanding of and much confusion about the role and functions of the Party, the state agencies and the mass organizations."[36]

The catalyst for the recognition of the need for profound changes in all sectors of the society was the failure to reach the ten-million-ton goal in the 1970 sugar harvest. The Cuban leadership had staked the reputation of the revolution on reaching this goal. Not only did the harvest fall short of the goal, but the massive effort caused serious disruptions and distortions in other major sectors of the economy, along with excessive centralization and near collapse of governmental channels and other modes of citizen input.

The 1970 harvest was the culmination of a misguided attempt to construct socialism and communism simultaneously, in what Fidel Castro called "a utopian period."[37] Bengelsdorf noted the lack of concern about state institutions, the lack of administrative controls and increasing administrative inefficiency, and the increased use of political criteria for choosing top administrators. Weak political structures collapsed, as did the subculture of local democracy, leaving the party as the only viable structure.[38] She summed up the situation as "the verticalization of political power, the isolation of decision makers at the center and the people beyond the structured periphery."[39]

The leadership recognized the widespread discontent among the population and, beginning in the last half of 1970, attempted to understand its source through discussions in workplaces and other local settings. At the same time, it "began a process of adjusting the system at its most fundamental levels, to speak to the general discontent."[40] This adjustment included the institutionalization and revitalization of mass organizations, with emphasis on creating structures that would give people sufficient control to run many of their own affairs and to voice and resolve dissatisfactions and difficulties.[41] During the May 20, 1970, broadcast address in which Fidel Castro first informed the Cuban people of the impossibility of reaching ten million tons, he placed the blame on the country's leadership: "We can say with absolute certainty that the people didn't lose the battle. . . . The administrative apparatus and the leaders of the Revolution are the ones who lost the battle."[42] In the same speech he referred to the "inefficient managing of the mills"[43] and mentioned the need to strengthen the mass organizations and to redirect the role of the PCC: "The party doesn't administer. It guides, directs, supports and guarantees the fulfillment of the plans of the revolutionary leadership in every area."[44]

In his July 26, 1970, speech Castro again engaged in self-criticism, citing "our inefficiency in the general work of the Revolution" as causing difficulties: "Our enemies say we have problems and in reality our enemies are right. They say there is discontent, and in reality our enemies are right. They say there is irritation, and in reality our enemies are right."[45] As an example of discontent, he cited the high level of absenteeism in truck transportation. He placed the responsibility on the revolutionary leadership and especially on himself. His twice-repeated offer to resign was apparently rejected by the crowds in Havana's Plaza de la Revolución.[46] Later in this speech, he referred to the failure of the local administrations (Local Power) to meet the population's demands because of the lack of proper authority, a problem that would require not just replacing certain individuals but also increasing and institutionalizing the authority of local government: "You cannot hold a man responsible for anything unless he is in a position where he can decide things."[47] More concretely, Castro pointed again to the need to revive the work of the mass organizations and to introduce representatives of a factory's workers into its management. (The PCC, he said, should not be directly involved in management.) Finally, he mentioned the need to create a new political structure to coordinate social production, as the Council of Ministers alone was no longer adequate for this task. He concluded, "We are not offering magic solutions here. We have stated the problems facing us and we have said that only the people, only with the people—and the people's awareness of our problem, the people's information, the determination and will of the people—can those problems be overcome."[48]

In a speech at the celebration of the tenth anniversary of the FMC on August 23, 1970, Castro referred to Lenin's concept of the revolutionary process as a "school of government in which millions of people learn to solve problems and carry out the responsibilities of government."[49] He defined the new, more serious, and more profound phase into which the revolution was entering as one of greater participation by the people in their own affairs and the replacement of old administrative and bureaucratic procedures:

> Administrative procedure could reach a given efficiency, but can never rise above certain levels. Sending a man down from the top to solve a problem involving 15,000 or 20,000 people is not the same thing as the problems of those 15,000 or 20,000 people—problems having to do with their community—being solved by virtue of the decisions of people of that community who are close to the source of those problems![50]

On September 3, 1970, at a CTC meeting, Castro reiterated the need for more local input and his criticism of using only administrative methods. He also mentioned the necessity of a constitution and introduced one of the main features of a new electoral system—the revocability of elected officials by their electors: "We must make it clear that any official can be removed at any time. He can be removed whenever another election is called, so nobody should get the idea that simply because he was elected one day he can spend a year doing just as he damn pleases."[51] Castro further elaborated, on September 28, 1970, on two dominant themes in relation to the institutionalization process: that the PCC should not coincide with or substitute for the government or the mass organizations and that effective mass participation in solving problems depended on invigorating the mass organizations and on decentralization:

> Imagine a bakery in some block that gives services to every neighbor in that block, and an administrative apparatus controlling that bakery from up above. . . . How can the people fail to take an interest in how that bakery operates? How can the people fail to take an interest in whether the administrator is a good administrator or a bad one? . . . How can the people fail to take an interest in the problems of hygiene in that store? And how can they fail to take an interest in the problems of production, absenteeism, amount and quality of the

product? Of course they can't! Can anyone imagine a more effective means for controlling this activity than the masses themselves?[52]

Continuing the theme that local community affairs should be administered by the local community instead of the central government, in December 1970 Castro introduced the Leninist concept of dual subordination. General regulations would come from the center but the administration from the local level. "There is nothing wrong with MINCIN [Ministry of Domestic Trade] running the wholesale distribution and laying down the guidelines for the distribution of goods, but it should be relieved of the job of running a grocery store or even a supermarket."[53]

Decentralized management, based initially on the mass organizations and trade unions, was to be "the starting point" for creating "a really advanced, non-bureaucratic form of social and political life."[54] This institutional development should be given concrete form, he argued, on the basis of socialist theory applied to Cuban reality, just as the Paris Commune and the soviets were—for Marx and Lenin, respectively—the "organizational form created in the Revolution."[55] In Cuba, oversight and control of local administration were to be placed in the hands of popularly elected municipal assemblies.

The Institutionalization Process, 1970–1976

At the meeting of the political bureau and the secretariat of the PCC in August 1970, it was decided to begin systematic studies of how to go about building state institutions.[56] The study of the reforms was carried out by the party's Commission on Juridical Studies, presided over by Blas Roca of the prerevolution Communist Party. By 1972, in response to economic recovery and the strengthening of the mass organizations, this process was accelerated. At the end of that year, the Council of Ministers was restructured with the addition of an executive committee. Carmelo Mesa-Lago saw this as "a step forward in the delegation of power from the prime minister and central coordination."[57] In 1973, the judicial system and the criminal and procedural codes were reformed. According to Mesa-Lago, "The 1973 reform rejected the division of state powers into three branches—executive, legislative and judiciary—as a bourgeois institution. . . . The reform has placed the judicial system hierarchically subordinated to the executive."[58] This concept of unitary government, without division of powers, was retained in the 1976 Constitution. At the same time, the party apparatus was modified, and its role and responsibilities were redefined, especially in relation to the state. The Thirteenth Congress of the CTC, held at the end of 1973, strengthened the Cuban labor unions. The congress resolved that the CTC should once again assume the role of defending workers' rights and give the workers a greater voice in managing the economy.[59]

Preparations were made to organize for the following year a pilot program of the OPP, first in the municipality of Cárdenas in Matanzas Province, and then in the entire province. A team was set up to study local governments in both capitalist and socialist countries. (Local Power leader Julio Carranza, a member of this team, was given the task of studying Detroit's municipal government.) One result of this groundwork was the "Constitution of Organs of People's Power," which became the basic document for the elections in Matanzas in June and July of 1974. In fact, the essential characteristics of what were to become the OPP were already present in this document: direct, competitive popular elections for municipal assembly delegates; indirect elections for higher parliamentary bodies; no campaigning for office; municipal delegates meeting periodically with electors to receive and answer mandates; immediate recall procedures; and delegates as unpaid volunteers.[60]

As reported in the *Wall Street Journal*, the 1974 elections for municipal delegates in the Matanzas Province pilot project were competitive and by secret ballot. Candidates were nominated by neighborhood groups without Communist Party participation or interference. The municipal delegates, in turn, elected delegates to the higher bodies. The elections were viewed by the *Wall Street Journal* as "finally carrying out long-standing promises of democratizing the Castro dictatorship."[61]

The National Coordination of Local Administrations turned over to the OPP all production and service units in the province. Similarly, national ministries, agencies, and institutes turned over control of the schools, health clinics, stores, repair shops, movie theaters, and recreation centers to the appropriate levels of the OPP. The *Wall Street Journal* recognized the importance of the Matanzas elections in putting political and economic power in the hands of Cuban voters, noting the potential increase in economic decentralization and efficiency: "Though democracy is stressed as the dominant feature of Popular Power, increasing of efficiency is perhaps equally important."[62]

On October 24, 1974, a constitutional commission was appointed by the central committee of the Communist Party, consisting of lawyers and constitutional experts from the party, the government, and the mass organizations. It submitted a draft constitution on February 24, 1975. During a two-month period, the draft was discussed throughout the country—in all the cells of the Communist Party, all the workplaces, all the local affiliates of the *Asociación Nacional de Agricultores Pequeños* (National Association of Small Farmers, or ANAP), all the CDR, all local sections of the FMC, and all high school and university students' associations.[63] As a result of the popular debate, some changes were considered and accepted, but the essential structure of the OPP was kept. The First Party Congress approved the new constitution in December 1975, and in a referendum in February 1976, it received over 95 percent approval from Cuban voters. Four chapters of the constitution—7, 8, 9, and 11—deal specifically with the OPP.

The OPP are based on the unitary model taken from the 1871 Paris Commune, in which the parliament was both an executive and a legislative body, and provided administrative oversight for administrative departments and economic activities and planning. In fact, only the Cuban National Assembly was given legislative powers. President Castro reiterated this rejection of the concept of separation of powers: "Here we will not reproduce the famous division of powers of the very famous Montesquieu. . . . Here there is one power, which is the power of the people and the power of the Revolution which performs distinct functions. And these functions are independent, but not independent state organs."[64]

Article 66 spelled out the concept of democratic centralism and included the basic principles developed after the Russian Revolution—such as that all state parliamentary organs are to be elected, that lower bodies are to be accountable to higher ones, that the minority is to be subordinate to the majority, and that the decisions of the higher organs are to be binding on the lower ones.[65] It called for elected representatives to account for their work to their electors, gave the latter the right to recall the former, and emphasized local initiative.[66] Alvarez Tabio pointed out the importance Lenin gave to the union of local and national interests through "firm and secure ties between all parts of the state"[67] and quoted Lenin to the effect that democratic centralism must allow for local initiatives and support a variety of forms, methods, and resources.[68] Under the principle of dual subordination, each local administrative organ was to be subordinate to the local government and to the corresponding central government ministry. For example, the local governments' education departments were to run the primary schools and be answerable to the municipal assemblies and also to the national Ministry of Education with regard to general policy. Again citing Lenin, Alvarez Tabio stated in his commentary that "this system of dual subordination is very important, as it allows combining local interests and the general interests of the state."[69]

With dual subordination and administrative decentralization, the norms, procedures, and methods were still to be set on a national level. Fidel Castro explained this concept in a speech shortly after the Matanzas elections: "We indicated that the state is one, but the state is organized at different levels, and it administers at different levels. Of course, this doesn't mean that the people in every community will be able to do whatever they want with the school, hospital or store. . . . No—for, as we indicated, the state is one, and all activities must be standardized and resemble each other all over the country."[70] (The section on dual subordination was eliminated from Article 68 of the 1992 Cuban Constitution, which corresponds to Article 66 of the 1976 Constitution, in order to strengthen the municipalities, especially in relation to the provincial governments. However, the relationship between local and national administration remained basically unchanged.)

By the middle of 1976, preparations were being made for constituting the OPP throughout the country. On October 10, municipal delegates were elected, and three weeks later, the municipal assemblies met and elected provincial delegates and, two days later, National Assembly deputies. On November 7, the provincial assemblies met, and on December 2, 1976, the National Assembly was constituted.

The First Party Congress also approved resolutions for a new national political and administrative division that became law in July 1976 and for a new economic planning mechanism called the *Sistema de Dirección y Planificación de la Economía* (System for Direction and Planning of the Economy, or SDPE), which was fully implemented in 1979. Under the new political and administrative division, which provided the context in which the OPP and the SDPE were to function, the previous six provinces were divided into fourteen. The City of Havana was made into a separate province. The regional level of government, between the municipalities and the provinces, was eliminated. The previous 407 municipalities were reduced to 169, each divided into from 30 to 200 electoral districts. Each municipality and province was to be governed by a municipal and a provincial assembly, respectively. One of the reasons for eliminating the regional level and making the municipalities larger was to increase the economic importance of the level closest to the voters, allowing for more meaningful local citizen participation. According to Dilla, "The process of centralization which took place in the first years of the Revolution had reduced the municipalities to minimum expressions as far as geographic and demographic attributes and size."[71] The SDPE also "implied considerable advance in decentralization and the application of democratic centralism in the economic direction. . . . The SDPE concedes to the lower and intermediate levels greater possibilities of involvement in drawing up economic plans and budgets."[72]

The Municipal Assembly

The municipal assembly analyzes, discusses, supervises, monitors, inspects, and controls the social, economic, judicial, and political affairs of the municipality. It also ratifies and dismisses administrators for local enterprises and entities (such as stores and polyclinics) and municipal judges. It participates in formulating and overseeing the municipal budget and economic and social plan, which it must approve. It monitors the performance of the municipality's provincial- and national-level enterprises. It complies with and carries out laws and ordinances of the higher levels of state.[73] The municipal assembly has no legislative powers: These lie solely with the National Assembly. The 1992 Constitution gave a broader and more detailed definition of the municipality: "A territorial extension determined by necessary economic and

Municipal Assembly President, Vice President and Secretary, presiding over assembly session in Palmira Municipality.

social relations of its population, and with the capacity to satisfy the minimum local needs."[74]

To coordinate the work of the municipal assembly between sessions, in 1992 the municipal assembly executive committee was replaced by the administrative council . It is led by the assembly president and vice president, who are elected by the assembly and must be delegates. The other members, each of whom is in charge of managing an area, such as health or housing, and the corresponding agencies under the control of the assembly are proposed by the president and ratified by the delegates. They do not have to be elected delegates. The assembly officers and other members of the council of administrators are assembly professionals; that is, unlike the other delegates, they receive their salary from the municipal assembly. No longer are there nonprofessional at-large members, selected from among the delegates, as existed in the former executive committees. Because under the previous system the tendency was for the executive committee to assume the functions of the assembly, the purpose of the change was "the demarcation of the functions of the administrative organ (council of administrators) and the deliberative organ (assembly)."[75] An attempt was made to enhance the assembly delegates' oversight role through the permanent commissions.

The newest structures within the municipal assembly, the *consejos populares*, were given constitutional status in 1992.[76] They are groupings of about ten delegates from contiguous electoral districts, together with representatives from government agencies located in the territory. The *consejo* president and sometimes the vice presidents are full-time assembly professionals, and their constant presence in the neighborhood is meant to strengthen the role of the delegates. The *consejos* monitor economic activities and provide vigilance to control fraud and crime.[77]

Unlike the practice in the former Soviet Union, municipal assembly delegates are directly nominated with no party interference by the voters from the election district they represent and in which they must reside, and they are elected in secret, competitive elections. They serve for two-and-one-half-year terms and may stand for reelection without limit.[78]

Following in the tradition of the Paris Commune of 1871 and of the soviets of 1905 and 1917, the municipal assembly delegates are for the most part working people from humble families. The Cuban people closely identify with and have personal contact with their directly elected municipal representatives, who are socially and economically indistinguishable from the electorate, although the delegates tend to have achieved a higher level of education and also have a higher percentage of party membership.

Most of the municipal delegates I interviewed, including those who were in leadership positions and those who were also provincial delegates and national deputies, were of worker or peasant backgrounds. An important reason for this relative class homogeneity, of course, was the emigration from Cuba of most of the wealthy of Cuba and much of the middle class. That the municipal assembly delegates come mainly from the middle and lower economic and social strata also is a consequence of nominations directly by neighbors in small street meetings, in which those well acquainted in the neighborhood tend to be chosen. It is, furthermore, difficult for those in professions requiring more time and/or travel commitments to serve as directly elected delegates, because of the enormous amount of time required to engage in what is voluntary labor. According to Castro, "Many worthy comrades could not be included in the elections to the Municipal Assembly on account of their activities, of their commitments."[79] As a result, most delegates are not only workers or lower-level professionals but also, because of the small size of the electoral districts, are usually well-known by and strongly representative of their constituencies.

As noted above, and in the tradition of the Paris Commune, except for a few municipal assembly and *consejo popular* leaders, the delegates are not professional politicians—they receive no salary for their work as municipal delegates and continue to work and be paid in their workplaces (the same is true for most provincial delegates and National Assembly deputies) and thus do not form a caste or group separated from the rest of the population. Bengelsdorf explained the reasoning for having nonprofessional representatives who reside in their districts: "It is assumed that if delegates no longer remained at their normal jobs, no longer lived in the neighborhoods they represent, they would be personally removed from their constituencies' needs and problems, and their relationship to these problems would inevitably change, since they would no longer share them."[80]

According to Harnecker, "The delegates elected by the rank and file follow their usual work routines and devote the rest of their time to the jurisdiction's problems and to attending municipal meetings whenever they take place. It is the best method to keep them close to the people and free from becoming bureaucrats."[81] My observations in Cuba support this contention. Municipal delegates were the least likely to act like bureaucrats and give constituents the bureaucratic runaround. The higher one went in the Cuban government, the more bureaucratic was the response.

People are aware of the importance of the delegates and amount of work they do without monetary remuneration or privileges. The personal style of the delegates' work with the community is conducive to a comfortable, even familiar, identification of the constituents with their government and a positive attitude toward the political process. Most residents know who their delegates are, and many are personally acquainted with them, and use the term *delegado* when addressing them. At any moment, citizens may discuss problems, including personal ones, with their delegates, whether in chance encounters in the street or by going to the delegates' homes or offices. This familiar political style seems to me in large measure a consequence of the nonantagonistic and personal nomination and election procedures, the small size of most electoral districts, the emphasis on equality in Cuban society, and the open and public characteristics of neighborhood life and interaction. The style has perhaps also been influenced by the personal manner in which President Fidel Castro relates to the public.

The close relationship between municipal delegates and their constituents and easy access by the latter to the former blurs the distinction between political and social spheres, very much in the tradition of Rousseau and Marx. As I have said elsewhere, "There is a very intimate relationship between the delegate and the elector. Most are on a first name basis with their delegate, know where the delegate lives, and know that he is the one to see if there are problems. . . . I do not know any Cuban . . . who is not personally acquainted with his delegate and does not feel that he can go to the delegate at any time with a problem or suggestion."[82] The small size of the electoral districts and the nomination system contribute to an atmosphere of familiarity and trust. Bard Jorgensen, studying delegate-citizen interaction in the municipality of Nuevitas, observed a "lively relationship between the elected and the electors. We might call it an existing horizontal democracy at the local level."[83] Walking down any street in Santa Fe with Daniel Morales, a municipal delegate and former president of the *consejo popular* in the Santa Fe section of Playa, everyone was on a first name basis with him, and many approached him on the spot with their problems.

A survey of 1,000 Cuban voters conducted by *Bohemia* in 1990 found that when asked whether they knew the name of their municipal delegate, 75.2 percent said yes, 12.9 percent said no, and 11.9 percent said they knew but could not remember it. When asked whether they trusted their delegate, 59.1 percent said yes, 23.3 percent said somewhat, and 17.6 percent said no.[84]

Delegates hold accountability sessions with their constituents twice a year in designated areas within the electoral districts, where they report on their activities and those of the municipal assembly and the *consejo popular*, respond to citizen *planteamientos* raised during the previous session, and hear new *planteamientos*. There are usually between one and four areas, depending on the size of the district. Delegates constantly hear from constituents regarding local administrators, neighborhood services, public transportation, and many other local problems. Delegates also hold office hours once a week where they also hear *planteamientos*, which more often concern individual rather than social problems.

Delegates are responsible for projects and for responding to problems that arise in their electoral districts, especially those raised in *planteamientos* by their constituents. For example, delegates I knew coordinated volunteer workers on Sundays to fix a roof on a local store and build a sidewalk. A delegate in Bauta organized fellow retirees to repair street signs. Delegates also work closely with the mass organizations in the neighborhood, such as the CDR and the FMC, and with the police, the local Communist Party nucleus, and local social workers, family doctors, and health clinic personnel in order to help deal with local social or public health.

The public conceives that their delegates are on call at all hours and for any reason. Many citizens with emergencies or personal problems contact their delegate first. A delegate in Playa who was woken up at 4 A.M. with news of a death in a constituent's family; a delegate in East Havana received a visit at 11 P.M. from a neighbor whose wife had left him, and he told the man he could not get his wife back but he could arrange for his children to attend secondary boarding schools in the countryside. While I was having lunch on a Sunday afternoon at the home of Carlos Walfrido Rodríguez, a delegate in Playa, a constituent came to his house for help in resolving the problem of nonfunctioning toilets in his apartment building. Rodríguez left to arrange help and returned about one half hour later. While president of the Santa Fe *Consejo Popular* Daniel Moales was awakened at 2:30 A.M. by a family who had lost their electrical power. He told me of having received physical threats from a former restaurant administrator who had been dismissed as a result of Daniel's reports of his poor performance. Almost every delegate I spoke with had a similar story, which could help explain delegate burnout resulting in a significant turnover in municipal delegates. By 1998, most of the delegates I had known in 1987 no longer held office because they chose not to run again.

Municipal delegates spend far more time on constituent services than on governing. In a carryover from the Soviet model, the municipal assemblies originally met in ordinary session twice a year (as did the provincial assemblies and the National Assembly), and in special session about four times a year, each session lasting about one day. According to Dilla, this schedule has meant that many important matters were left to be resolved by the assembly leadership because, "without a doubt, this results in sessions which are too limited and insufficient for the exercise of their deliberative and decision making functions."[85] According to the articles of the municipal assemblies' bylaws passed by the Council of State on September 13, 1995, municipal assemblies are now required to meet in ordinary session at least four times a year. However, *Granma* reported that in 1998 over 100 municipal assemblies were not in compliance.[86] Delegates also attend special meetings held, for example, to explain the economic planning process, to review municipal problems in preparation for the accountability sessions with constituents, and to try to resolve remaining *planteamientos* prior to these sessions.

As members of the permanent commissions of the municipal assembly that oversee specific areas, such as health, education, public works, budget and planning, and commerce, delegates make on-site inspections. Each commission is charged with investigating, inspecting, and writing commentaries and critiques on reports presented to the municipal assembly by state organs under the purview of the commission. Municipal assembly commission members and leaders are chosen by assembly leadership, which also sets the agendas. The majority of commission members are delegates, but, as was the practice in the local soviets, there are also volunteer members from the community chosen from among citizens with expertise in the commission's area of concern (e.g., public health workers on the public health commission). The president of each commission, however, is always a delegate.

During an inspection of restaurants in Playa that I attended in May 1988, a delegate from the commerce and gastronomy commission checked the kitchen, food storage areas, and bathrooms for cleanliness; verified that food listed on the menu was being offered; questioned the customers about the quality of the food and service; and reviewed the restaurant's records with its administrator. During an inspection of a dental clinic in Bauta, the commission members toured the building, questioned patients and dentists, and met with the administrators to discuss problems related to service that had come to the commission's attention mainly from constituents' *planteamientos*.

The municipal office of planning and budget is under the control of the municipal assembly, with oversight by the assembly's economic commission chaired by the vice president (who is usually the person in charge of economic affairs for the municipal assembly), and receives inputs mainly from the assembly leadership and the administrative council, and from the administrators and unions of local entities. This office then draws up the municipal economic plan and budget, which must be approved, together with a report from the assembly's economic commission, by the municipal assembly delegates. Citizens' *planteamientos* weigh heavily in investment decisions for the economic plan at all levels.

The commission and assembly debates I reviewed regarding economic plans and budgets on all three levels of the OPP were minimal in content, perhaps reflecting a lack of sufficient knowledge of economic matters or timely information. At one municipal assembly session in Playa, delegates asked the municipal director of the budget to write his report in a style more accessible to them. Even though the most important economic activities are not fully under the control of the municipal assemblies, municipal assemblies are not lacking in power or importance. The major branches of the Cuban economy and economic planning are under provincial and national control, but citizens' suggestions and needs expressed through the municipal assemblies are given serious consideration in the formulation of the provincial and national plans. Municipalities also can and do veto site locations for projects proposed in these plans. Raúl Castro pointed to the importance of local input in his 1974 speech to the Matanzas delegates:

> You must struggle to make possible the fulfillment of the economic plans, technological development in production and services, work discipline, increasing work productivity, and all of that not only in regard to the activities and units which are to be transferred to People's Power, but also in regard to those which are to remain subordinate to the central state agencies from the administrative point of view.[87]

Furthermore, the municipal directors of planning, administrative council members, and municipal assembly commissions monitor performance, plan fulfillment, the labor supply, and the profitability of national and provincial enterprises and entities located in their municipality. The results of their monitoring are periodically reported to the municipal assembly. One reason for the municipality's concern regarding the operations within its boundaries is that it shares in the profits from these firms.

If problems are identified, the one in charge of economic affairs informs both the local administrators and the national authorities. In Palmira, the sugar refineries are run by the central government, but oversight and day-to-day management are done mainly by the municipal assembly. In Bauta, the only complete monitoring of the large Ariguanabo textile plant is done by the municipality. In Playa, the same is true of the beer factory.

Policy with regard to many social services, such as health, education, and transportation, is set at the national level, but the municipal assembly has been responsible for personnel, performance, and problem solving within its territory. During a campaign in 1987 and 1988 to alleviate the shortage of nursery schools in the City of Havana Province, microbrigades composed, in part, of volunteer workers who came after their regular work shifts, working day and night (I visited one work site in Playa in full operation at 10 P.M.) built 104 new nursery schools. The construction was closely coordinated and monitored by professional members of the municipal assembly leadership, who were frequently present at the work site.

Government leaders periodically meet with all the municipal assembly presidents. Also usually present are the provincial assembly presidents, the National Assembly leadership, and the PCC first secretaries. During the meeting held on June 11 and 12, 1998, the presidents heard reports from and participated in exchanges of opinions and experiences with ministers and other officials. The topics discussed included public health, education, control of material resources, administrative discipline, crime, and *planteamientos*. President Castro attended the session on June 12.[88]

By the beginning of 1999 the municipal assemblies were being criticized by National Assembly Vice President Ernesto Suárez for not realizing their potential: "They run the risk of becoming perfunctory, of not being effective, and of violating their legal foundations."[89] The attributes conferred on them by the Constitution and laws surpass what they have achieved in practice. This has been, in part, due to Cuba's economic crisis and, in some cases, to central state organs impeding the efforts of the municipalities. Municipal assembly presidents were also cited. Besides having failed to convene the requisite number of ordinary assembly sessions, some have tended to bring matters of importance to the administrative council instead of the assembly, forgetting that they head the administrative council because they were elected to direct the assembly, and not vice versa.[90]

The 1992 Constitution changed the terms for provincial delegates from two and one half to five years, to correspond with the terms of the National Assembly deputies. The consensus was, however, that the municipal delegates' term should remain two and one half years, since, given the enormous amount of voluntary work involved, especially in the conditions of the economic crisis, serving five years would wear them out. After every election, more than one half of the delegates do not continue serving, and during the term, many delegates quit for various reasons. Thus, extending the term to five years was again being reconsidered as a means of achieving more continuity, improving the quality and stability of the work of the delegates, and increasing, systematizing, and diversifying their preparation.[91]

The Provincial Assembly

Provincial assembly delegates are elected by the people in direct, noncompetitive elections every five years. They represent voters in municipalities or in districts within the larger municipalities. Up to one half of the provincial delegates are also municipal delegates.[92]The provincial assembly controls and directs the state economic enterprises and social and service entities under provincial control and helps monitor those under national control. It formulates and approves provincial economic plans and budgets and assists in, inspects, monitors, and coordinates the work of the province's municipal assemblies. It holds two regular sessions and several extraordinary sessions per year. The president and vice president are elected by the assembly and must be provincial assembly delegates. The president chairs the administrative council, which carries on the work of the assembly between sessions. Its members include the vice president, the secretary, and those in charge of specific areas like public health or education, who are proposed by the president and approved by the delegates, but who do not have to be provincial delegates.

The provincial assembly is much less likely than the municipality to take initiatives and more likely to work with the municipalities of the province, providing assistance when requested. It is the link between the municipalities and the national government. Officers and functionaries of the provincial assembly periodically visit municipalities to inspect, to interview delegates, and to issue reports on the municipal government's activities and needs, including those of the delegates and the bureaus under municipal control. The municipal assembly issues periodic reports to the provincial assembly. Because of the special urban characteristics of City of Havana Province, which is subdivided into several municipalities, its provincial assembly directly controls areas such as transportation and water supply (which in other provinces are under municipal control) and thus necessarily takes more direct initiatives regarding services and economic planning.

Complaints *(quejas)* made by individuals to the municipal governments are monitored by an official at the provincial level, who issues reports listing the complaints by categories and municipalities, and how many have been resolved. Another official issues similar reports on citizen *planteamientos* compiled by municipal delegates. The provincial assemblies help to prepare municipal delegates for their biannual accountability sessions. The members of the provincial assembly administrative organ receive copies of all the *quejas* and *planteamientos* from the municipalities that correspond to their areas of responsibility and, if necessary, work with the municipalities to resolve them, emphasizing those that correspond to the greatest collective needs.

Most provincial delegates belong to commissions similar to those of the municipal assemblies. As is the case with the municipal assembly commissions, some of the members are not delegates. The provincial assembly commissions work with provincial enterprises and entities and monitor proposals received from municipalities that correspond to their areas of responsibility. They also coordinate activities involving several municipalities within the province. For example, in 1988 the education commission of the City of Havana Provincial Assembly visited nursery schools (under municipal control) to check on enrollment and attendance with the goal of making full use of all the schools in the province.

Development of the provincial economic plans and budgets, done by departments under the provincial assembly, consist mainly of assembling, evaluating, and combining the municipal plans and budgets, which are then added to the investments and expenses related specifically to the province. Almost all the discretionary investments below the national level are at the municipal level. The provincial assembly participates in formulating and adjusting municipal plans and budgets and also provides input to the central planning department with regard to needs in the province.[93]

The National Assembly

National Assembly deputies are elected in direct, noncompetitive elections every five years, held concurrently with the provincial delegate elections. Up to one half of the National Assembly deputies are also municipal delegates.[94]

As of 1998, there were 601 National Assembly deputies. There is one deputy for 20,000 voters or fraction over 10,000 in a municipality. The maximum is 5 deputies per municipality or district within the larger municipalities. The minimum number of deputies for each municipality is 2.

As is the case with the municipal assembly delegates, National Assembly deputies and provincial assembly delegates receive no compensation for their work as representatives, with the exception of the National Assembly leadership and its commission officers. National Assembly President Ricardo Alarcón noted this as one of the distinguishing characteristics of the Cuban system. Those selected feel honored but receive "neither salary, emoluments, expenses, nor the whole series of privileges and political plums which in other places are associated with such a political figure."[95]

The National Assembly's charge is to pass laws; to approve the national economic plan and budget and actions taken by the Council of State and the Council of Ministers between sessions; to control, inspect, and monitor the national government ministries and state organs, including the judiciary and the attorney general's office; and to supervise the OLPP, primarily the provincial assemblies. The National Assembly does not set long-range national policy goals (this is considered the role of the party).

Within the OPP only the National Assembly has legislative powers. While individual deputies may propose laws, legislative initiatives have not come from deputies. They have neither the time (since most are not professional politicians, they continue working at their regular jobs) nor the staff nor the necessary support to give them sufficient independence. Thus the National Assembly serves more as a consultative than an initiating body, where proposed legislation is submitted for review, modification, and approval. Legislative proposals have come mainly from ministries and nongovernmental entities such as the CTC (for labor legislation) or the mass organizations. Ministry officials work with the corresponding assembly commission to draft a final version, and the commission formulates a commentary regarding the proposed legislation. Ministry officials then meet with deputies from each province to explain the proposals and answer questions.

During this process, substantial changes are possible as, for example, happened during the discussion of the penal code in the constitutional affairs commission in 1988. During the year prior to submitting and passing the law on forestation in the National Assembly in July 1998, National Assembly commissions, individual deputies, specialists, and officials debated the project. It was discussed with the population in the mountainous areas and in Pinar del Rio Province. As a result, the Ministry of Agriculture had to revise the project several times.[96]

During the plenary sessions, deputies debate and vote on proposed laws, reports, and National Assembly commissions' commentaries and critiques made regarding these reports and proposed legislation. At each regular session the deputies discuss and approve the reports of a province, a government ministry, the attorney general and the judiciary branch. They vote on the national economic plan and budget (once a year) and on the decrees approved by the Council of State (a body that represents the legislature between sessions) and the report of the Council of Ministers.

Up to the mid–1990s, the National Assembly plenary session documents were published and debates were reported with considerable detail in the newspapers. In December 1990 the entire session was televised. For the December 1997 and July 1998 sessions the press printed only the speeches of President Castro, various government ministers, and the president of the permanent commission on global economic affairs. For the Special Assembly session to amend the penal code held in Februrary 1999, *Granma* resumed the practice of publishing portions of the debates.[97]

Regular National Assembly sessions usually last for two days and are held twice a year (special sessions are convened if necessary). Especially given the large number of deputies, this schedule leaves insufficient time for thorough debate and critical contributions on the part of the deputies during the plenary sessions. Deputies told me that because of the time constraints, they are discouraged from intervening at length during the debate (the clear exception being President Castro), and that there is not enough time for serious discussion to be able to understand and to modify legislation. President Castro dominates the discussions in the National Assembly. For example, reviewing the minutes of the July 18 and 19, 1988, sessions, of the 204 times when deputies spoke, 71 were done by Castro. Castro participated in 75 of the 78 dialogues between deputies.

Alarcón's response has been that the bulk of the deputies' work is in the assembly's permanent commissions. The plenary sessions are preceded by commission meetings in Havana and in the territories, and during the rest of the year, commission members engage in exchanges with specialists, institutions, and the public and do studies throughout the country. Therefore, he concluded, "The members of this Parliament, without being professional deputies, dedicated as much time to substantive legislative work as their as their counterparts in other countries."[98]

Not all deputies belong to commissions. During the Fifth Legislature starting in 1998, 290 deputies (48.3 percent of the total) made up the membership of the ten permanent commissions.[99] Many of the *directo* deputies (those who are not also municipal delegates) who have high government positions or other prominent careers have little time to participate in the commissions, unless they serve as commission officers, a circumstance that points to the relative importance of the less prominent deputies, especially the *de base* deputies (those who are also municipal delegates), in carrying out the functions of the National Assembly.

The commissions undertake investigations and report their findings to the National Assembly and prepare commentaries on reports and proposed laws to be debated during the National Assembly sessions. Annual commission agendas are set by the National Assembly presidency. The commission on economic affairs comments on the national economic plan and budget. The constitutional and juridical affairs commission issues commentaries on all proposed legislation to verify that there is no conflict with the Cuban Constitution or existing laws. The commission on the OLPP makes on-site inspections to prepare commentaries on the biannual reports of provincial assemblies to the National Assembly. It also monitors the processes of accountability sessions held by municipal delegates with their constituents. In 1988, I was told by members of this commission that upon visiting mountainous regions of Las Tunas Province, they discovered that those living in isolated areas were not receiving milk, and at their insistence, local dairies were established.

After the July 1998 session, members of the commission on productive activities traveled around the country to gather information on the plans for increasing tobacco and coffee production, the latter having been affected by the drought occurring in Cuba. The deputies also sought to find ways to support people's efforts to produce their own food, and to gather information about the utilization of land set aside for such purposes. The commission members also reviewed the production of construction materials and the application of the law on forests passed in the July 1998 session.[100]

Debates in the National Assembly are characterized by the pursuit of consensus, and votes are almost always unanimous. An article in *Trabajadores* attempts to explain the lack of divided votes in Cuba's National Assembly.

Achieving consensus is attributed to a lack of corporate interests and strug-
gles among competing powerful interest groups. Consensus is defended not
as a false unanimity but as "the confluence of many opinions to arrive at a
unity of action." The heterogeneous composition of the National Assembly
foments a climate of diversity and possibilities of differences of opinions.
Each topic debated in the National Assembly is preceded by analysis in the
assembly commissions, and among sectors of the population, where deputies
do not have to abandon their points of view but rather enrich them with
other perceptions and nuances:

> If as deputy I am in disagreement with determined aspects of a law and I freely
> express my disagreements in various settings before arriving including to the
> National Assembly session, there is debate. But if my opinion is in a minority,
> why afterwards, upon voting for the law as a whole, if I am in agreement with
> its essence, must I vote against my own viewpoint of general acceptance of the
> law in order for others to say that in Cuba there is democracy?

When specific disagreements are sufficiently significant, they merit greater
reflection, and the assembly vote is postponed:

> Why is one obliged to continue that path towards a hasty discussion with the fi-
> nal result determined by a vote, instead of by persuasion of what is better for the
> country? . . . Is it not more important, if the laws really are going to reflect the
> national interests, that there be the greatest accord possible, among all the soci-
> ety's protagonists, of the measures that need to be taken, and that in fact a deci-
> sion not be imposed on a social scale? . . . From my point of view, consensus
> corresponds with our socialist idea of a society where development with fairness
> and transformation with social justice would be possible, trying to reach a har-
> monious combination between collective and individual interests, a possible and
> desirable country where national harmony prevails.[101]

When strong disagreements surface, in some instances proposed legislation
has been withdrawn for further study and modification in order to arrive at
an acceptable compromise. This happened in the late 1980s, for example, after the debate on measures to ensure that divorced husbands would pay al-
imony and child support, and when many deputies found certain aspects of
the penal code too lenient (fines for minor thefts) and others too harsh
(penalties for teenage girls who hide their pregnancy from their families and
subsequently kill their newborns). Judging by the meetings I attended, dissent is more commonly expressed and then resolved within the commissions.

   I was told that prior to the vote in the National Assembly in October
1992 on the Electoral Law, many deputies expressed their reservations in the
halls outside the main chamber about certain parts of the proposed legislation, such as the absence of competitive elections for provincial assembly delegates and National Assembly deputies and the manner of electing municipal

assembly officers. A few deputies questioned these points during the assembly debate, but despite this opposition, no changes were made, and the vote for the new law was unanimous.[102] In the August 4, 1994, National Assembly session debate, some deputies, who were also CTC leaders, objected to a modification in the proposed tax law allowing for an income tax.[103] They were responding to the opposition to this tax expressed in the workers' parliaments held that year.[104] Nevertheless the income tax was included in the legislation, which passed unanimously.[105] During the September 1995 session, opposition to allowing Cubans living in exile to invest in Cuba, expressed during the debate regarding proposed legislation on foreign investments, did not lead to modifications, and the vote in favor was unanimous.[106] Clearly unanimity has not always meant consensus.

The "call" for the Fourth Party Congress held in October 1991 specifically rejected "false, mechanical, and formalistic unanimity."[107] In a 1992 interview, then National Assembly President Juan Escalona told me of the need to end meaningless formal practices, many borrowed from the former Soviet Union, such as the pressure for unanimous votes. When I asked him why all of the National Assembly votes had been unanimous, he responded:

> It is absurd—the country of unanimity. But if you read with care the call for the Fourth Party Congress, you will see that there we recognize that the concept of unanimity which drove us for many years is something which we have overcome. We are conscious that not everyone in the country necessarily thinks like us. To the extent that when you think that a country unanimously thinks like you, you do not do political work, you neglect a series of activities that the party must carry out, because you think that everyone agrees with you. Now, when you realize that you have to maintain the majority that you have through political work and efforts, it is different.

This goal has proved difficult to achieve. National Assembly deputies have told me of pressures they felt to conform, especially at the time of voting. One deputy told me that acquiescence results from feeling intimidated and the fear many have of not being renominated and reelected (a woman deputy who voiced disagreement with aspects of the 1992 Electoral Law during the National Assembly debate was not renominated), and even of being punished (although this has never happened), possibly because the deputies have no independent base of support. There is an underlying apprehension of contradicting, questioning, or demanding responses from Castro, or of continuing to state a point of view to which the leadership objects. During an assembly session in the late 1980s, one deputy attempted to make a minor correction to a point being made by President Castro by adding a necessary word. He was cut off and not allowed to finish, and subsequently he never spoke again in the National Assembly during his tenure (he was not renominated).

Whatever dissent is expressed is more likely to come from *de base* deputies. To a great extent, the *directos* speak when called on by Castro or the assembly president. In a debate during the June 1978 National Assembly session, forty-seven *de base* deputies responded to criticisms made by a government official of municipal delegates' deficiencies in resolving citizen complaints, by blaming instead the lack of resources and the unresponsive administrators.[108]

The lack of debate on the economic plan and budget can furthermore be attributed to the complexity of the material and the fact that deputies had been given only synopses, usually only on the day of the vote, so that they have little time for study or review. The lack of debate on the reports of the Council of State and the Council of Ministers can also be attributed in part to deputies' lack of information; for example, the texts of the decrees listed for approval are not made available to them.

Deputies told me that they vote for proposals even when they have doubts or lack information, citing the "prestige of the leadership." When I questioned Escalona about this response, he said, "Fidel is the leader of the Revolution and there are things that necessarily, while he is here, the people will vote for on the basis of confidence. But there are mechanisms which must be analyzed as to whether or not they will be kept when he is no longer here, and we must create mechanisms which can guide us."

Even though most votes are also unanimous during municipal assembly sessions, there is much less reluctance to express dissent, perhaps because the delegates feel less intimidated and also have a more independent base of voters' support. *De base* deputies told me they give more importance to their role in the municipal assembly and spend more time preparing for its sessions.

With the goal of increasing its importance, the National Assembly has undergone some reform. By the early 1990s, there was widespread recognition of the need to strengthen the National Assembly, which had not fulfilled its role as the supreme state organ either in fact or in public perception. The need to strengthen the National Assembly emerged as a priority during the debates and discussions held among the citizenry prior to the Fourth Party Congress of the PCC in 1991 and was included in the resolutions approved.[109] Following the first direct elections for deputies in February 1993, Alarcón was chosen to be the National Assembly's president, which seemed a clear signal of the increased importance given this body, as he was well known in Cuba, had served as its foreign minister (and continues as an important diplomatic spokesperson), and is a member of the Political Bureau of the PCC. He was reelected by the assembly after the 1998 elections. Escalona told me in 1992 of plans to strengthen the permanent commissions, with the result that commission presidents and other commission officers are now professionals and are no longer linked to the ministries that their commissions supposedly oversee. Prestigious individuals were appointed as presidents of important commissions such as foreign affairs and economic affairs.

Prior to the December 1997 plenary session, the Minister of Economics and Planning and the Minister of Finances and Prices addressed the economic affairs commission regarding the 1998 economic plan and budget, and the vice president of the Cuban Central Bank offered details regarding bank reform. The presentations made to the plenary sessions by the economic affairs commission's president were given equal billing with those of the Minister of Economics and Planning and were published in the PCC newspaper, *Granma*.

Escalona told me that the National Assembly should play a greater role in economic planning. He considered the whole system of planning in terms of specific time frames (one-year plans, five-year plans, etc.) a disastrous inheritance from the earlier socialist countries that has made it impossible for the National Assembly to consider and debate economic matters, and by 1992, indicative economic planning with defined objectives and development programs had replaced central all-inclusive economic planning.[110] Finally, and perhaps most important, Escalona recognized the need to develop political structures and practices in preparation for the time when Fidel Castro is no longer the leader of the Cuban Revolution. Castro's prestige and dominant personality have resulted in national leadership selection procedures—for example, noncompetitive elections for the Council of State and its leadership—which for all practical purposes cannot be changed while he remains the recognized authority.

Whereas prior to 1992 the *directos* among National Assembly deputies and provincial assembly delegates had little contact and were for the most part unknown by the public,[111] Article 84 of the 1992 Constitution requires all representatives to have contact with and be accountable to their constituents.[112] Alarcón called on deputies to hold meetings with their constituents to let their constituents know what they have done for the community, and to engage in more socioeconomic and political work in the territories they represent.[113] In meetings of the newly elected deputies held in each province following the January 11, 1998, election, they expressed the need for more identification and interrelation with their constituents, through scheduled periodic encounters with voters throughout the municipality from which they had been elected, so the deputies could report to the voters regarding their activities and the debates in the National Assembly, and the deputies could learn firsthand the concerns of the citizens. As reported in the Cuban press, some of the deputies also pointed out their need for more and better-quality information as a way of increasing their political efficacy and suggested that meetings be held prior to the plenary sessions, during which the deputies would receive information on domestic and international affairs and could express their doubts and concerns.[114] Reporting on the efficiency assemblies held subsequently in the Fishing Industry Ministry, *Trabajadores* noted the attendance of National Assembly deputies for the purpose of contributing and gaining information and experience.[115]

The Communist Party

The official explanation of the relationship to representative government of a vanguard party was given by Fidel Castro in 1974: The party "regulates and guides society and the state. The party doesn't administer the state. . . . There is a need for the state as an instrument of the revolutionaries to carry out the process leading to socialism and communism."[116]

During that same year, Raúl Castro delineated the roles of the party and the state in more detail. The party

> must never meddle in the daily routine work of the organs of people's power. . . . You must remember that the party is the highest political and ideological authority in the province, but that the maximum state and administrative authority . . . does not rest with the party organs but with the organs of people's power. . . . The party . . . must help coordinate the activities of people's power with other state and mass organizations; control and assist the organs of people's power in selecting and appointing the best personnel for the various administrative posts subordinate to it; to contribute to the education and improvement of personnel; to establish guidelines and make suggestions relating to the organs of people's power in order to improve their work and guarantee the fulfillment of their responsibilities; to help achieve through the party apparatus and its membership, the most successful evolution of those organs. . . . The party can and must make suggestions, proposals, recommendations, it must council and guide the organs of people's power, but must never "hand down decisions," never impose decisions.[117]

He noted that prior to institutionalization, the party had been excessively engaged in state and administrative tasks because separate institutions and mechanisms were lacking: "The establishment of the organs of people's power and their correct functioning will enable the Party to concentrate on and carry out thoroughly its own responsibilities."[118]

The principal role of the Communist Party is supposed to be political rather than administrative. It sets long-range goals for the whole society, including the government, and attempts to stimulate, guide, and promote the development of a socialist society and a populace with socialist consciousness. Its role should be to persuade the people to accept socialism as a goal—to put societal good above individual benefits and be willing to work to achieve this goal. In socialist development, consciousness, to a large extent, should replace the capitalist market and the profit motive in the administration and coordination of production and in the management of labor. Socialist consciousness, although difficult to implant, implement, and spread, is one of the principal elements making socialist transition possible. In Cuba, it is clearly the party whose task it is to create and encourage socialist consciousness and behavior, as its militants are supposedly selected in part on the basis of their consciousness and it encompasses all levels of societal and governmental structure.

Pedro Sáez, member of the PCC Political Bureau and party secretary in Havana Province, attempted to delineate the role of the party in a 1998 meeting with agricultural leaders in the province regarding cronyism and paternalism. The party must exercise oversight and direction *(controlar y dirigir)* over the conduct of work center administrators (who should be models of exemplary conduct) but not supplant their administrative functions.[119]

Dilla noted that in daily life, the separation between the government and the PCC has not always been clear, especially in local politics. His study of four municipalities shows that the PCC was involved in administrative activities, supplanting or cooperating with the government, and that this activity was recognized as being correct and necessary by all those interviewed, including party functionaries. Local government officials looked to the local PCC committee as a strong source for help in resolving local problems, increasing local autonomy, and cutting through bureaucratic bottlenecks.[120]

Rather than antagonism between party and government, there seems to exist a spirit of working together and reaching agreements. LeoGrande explained the Cuban party-state relation in nonconflictive terms: "The Organs of People's Power were never intended to be above the influence and leadership of the Communist Party, and of course they are not. The extent to which the OPP constitutes a real center of decision making rather than a mere formalism will depend upon its ability to operate effectively within the context of party hegemony, rather than against it."[121] Raúl Castro noted that if there was disagreement, for example, between the municipal party leadership and the municipal assembly, agreement to settle the dispute would be taken to the next highest level of both the party and the state.[122]

The municipal assembly leaders I met, most of whom were party militants, were firm with regard to their autonomy in relation to the local party unit. When disagreements did occur that could not be resolved at the municipal level, either the government prevailed or the issue was raised at the provincial level. The local party leader in Cienfuegos told me in 1987 that in the case of a disagreement between the municipal assembly and the party regarding where electrification would take place, the assembly had prevailed. Speaking at a 1988 provincewide seminar for municipal assembly commission members in the City of Havana Province, Jorge Lescano, then first secretary of the Communist Party for the City of Havana, made some criticisms of the work of the commissions. Many delegates publicly disagreed with him, and in the following session of the provincial assembly, he felt it necessary to mollify the delegates by clarifying his remarks.

In relation to the OPP, the role of the party has been greatest in the National Assembly, because that is the only body with legislative powers. While in the past the party approved all proposed legislation in advance, National Assembly President Alarcón told me in an interview in February 1994 that this is no longer the case. The party also has had an important influence on the agendas of the National Assembly, the Council of State, and the commissions and approves the candidates for the National Assembly's president, vice president, and secretary and for the Council of State. Escalona told me that the party would retain the right to select the leadership. It is at the national level of the OPP that the overlap between party and state leadership has been the greatest and the separation between party and government less clear. Escalona explained to me the leadership role of the PCC in relation to the National Assembly:

> You must understand that in a socialist country, in which the party is the highest leadership body—and this we will not change—the party sets the broad outlines of national policy as decided by the party congress. Thus what the legislative body does is transform into laws the decisions of the party congress, and at this point there may, perhaps, be some differences regarding details in the appraisal of these decisions, such as we now see in the discussion of the constitution. We are doing all this according to the recommendations of the party. The National Assembly makes its decisions, and at times, people can disagree about details, but concerning general policy, no.

One important role the party plays in relation to the OPP is to help the delegates and especially the leadership carry out their functions. Party officials try to work with the municipal and provincial assembly leadership in solving problems, both local and national. In Cienfuegos, for example, the first secretary of the municipal party promised at a session of the municipal assembly to help pressure the administrators of enterprises to resolve the remaining *planteamientos.* In Playa, the person in charge of commerce and the president of the commerce commission worked with a special party commission to improve services to the public. Party representatives participated in seminars for delegates in the City of Havana. The party neighborhood nuclei, composed mainly of housewives and retirees, helped local delegates in tasks such as preparation for neighborhood nomination and accountability sessions. Municipal party representatives attend these meetings and evaluate how they have been conducted. The role of the party nuclei in the workplaces of the municipal government is to evaluate professional members of the assembly leadership (most of whom are party militants) and criticize them for poor job performance, such as not attending meetings or failure to attend to constituents' needs, rather than to instruct them how to vote or to administer.

Information on needs and opinions of the people is also transmitted to all levels of the OPP through public opinion polls conducted by the PCC, and through the *estado de opinión,* a monthly report conducted by the municipal party organization on anonymous opinions regarding local issues and candidates for leadership positions, overheard on the street, in markets, and so on by party members. The names, if known, of those whose opinions are quoted are never used.

Because its main purpose is to provide orientation, for the most part the PCC does not instruct local delegates who are party militants how to vote or what to do. As militants, of course, they are bound to the party program and agreements, but these consist mainly of general, long-term policies, strategies, and guidelines and have little relation to the everyday debates, votes, decisions, and work of the municipal assembly delegates. When I asked municipal and provincial delegates who were party militants about resolutions passed at recent local party assemblies, only the municipal assembly presidents (who, prior to 1992, customarily had been members of the municipal party bureau) had even read them. The municipal and provincial delegates I interviewed, including those who were also professional executive committee members, National Assembly deputies, and presidents of National Assembly commissions, all told me that the party does not try to tell them what to do with regard to their governmental role. The party does not act differently toward a delegate who is not a militant, and I observed no measurable differences in attitude and behavior among delegates based solely upon party militancy, which was also the conclusion reached by Dilla, González, and Vincentelli.[123] Dilla, González, and Vincentelli found that although party members are obliged to carry out party resolutions, they rarely have anything to do with how delegates think, vote, or decide on local problems. In their survey of municipal delegates in Santa Cruz del Norte Municipatity, only 17 percent (twenty-five delegates, most of whom were party members and also in leadership positions) said that the PCC sometimes or frequently interposed itself regarding votes or opinions expressed, but mainly regarding only "highly sensitive topics."[124]

Party officers must be granted formal permission by vote of the municipal delegates to speak at a municipal assembly session. In contrast to Soviet practice, party officers may not serve as municipal assembly officers. Other practices regarding party participation vary among municipalities. In Bauta, the second secretary of the municipal party was invited, along with a representative of the municipal CTC, to the executive committee meetings.

Although about 15 percent of the Cuban population belongs to the party, approximately 60 to 70 percent of the municipal delegates are usually party members (after the 1997 elections, 76 percent were party members), not through party manipulation but because they are nominated and elected by their constituents. The percentage of party members may be high because, given the great amount of volunteer work involved in being a delegate, those with the strongest ideological commitment tend to be party members and are among the most likely to accept nomination. Furthermore, nonparty delegates who stand out for their excellent work are likely to be invited to become party members; I observed two such cases in Playa. The percentage of party members among the municipal assembly leadership, the provincial delegates, and the National Assembly deputies had in the past usually been much higher (close to 100 percent) than the percentage of municipal delegates who were party militants. This percentage changed with the direct elections for the National Assembly deputies. After the 1993 and 1998 elections, the percentage of deputies who belonged to the party was a little over 70 percent. Dilla, González, and Vincentelli also denied that the overrepresentation of party members as municipal delegates is either an explicit sign of popular support for the party or a result of the lack of real options for the voters. Rather, they concluded that it follows from the delegates' relatively high level of political-ideological commitment and the greater likelihood of their accepting leadership positions.[125]

With the goal of further reducing the role of the party vis-à-vis the municipal assembly, the Fourth Party Congress in 1991 decided that the municipal assembly president would no longer be a member of the party's municipal bureau and that the party's bureaucracy would be cut in half. The municipal party unit would no longer parallel in structure the municipal assembly administrative unit (e.g., a party person overseeing education corresponding to the municipal assembly professional in charge of education); thus the possibility of interference was sharply reduced. The revised 1992 Constitution brought important changes regarding the role of the PCC in the candidate selection for National Assembly deputies and officers, provincial assembly delegates and officers, and municipal assembly officers. The PCC and the *Unión de Jóvenes Comunistas* (Union of Young Communists or UJC) no longer participate on any of the candidacy commissions, so formal party control is greatly reduced over selection of municipal assembly leadership and of candidates for provincial delegates and National Assembly deputies. These commissions are now headed by CTC representatives and include representatives from the CDR, the FMC, the ANAP, the *Federación de Estudiantes Universitarios* (University Students Federation, or FEU), and the *Federación de Estudiantes de Estudios Medios* (Federation of High School Students, or FEEM). Cuban sociologist Luis Suárez regards this as "an undeniable step forward in eliminating unnecessary intervention by the political party in the popular sovereignty and a new advance toward the theory and practice that avoids having the *Partido Único* [single party] . . . be converted into an electoral party."[126]

The pledges of "free and conscious respect for the leading role that the Communist Party of Cuba plays in our society," along with the pledge "to carry forward the tasks of the construction and development of socialism," were eliminated from the oath of office taken by municipal and provincial delegates and National Assembly deputies. The new oath calls only for respect for the Cuban Constitution and the laws.[127] Furthermore, the PCC is no longer defined as the vanguard of a particular class, but as the vanguard of the Cuban people. The 1992 Constitution also deleted references to a state ideology, and guarantees against religious discrimination were strengthened. The terms *democratic centralism*, *unity of power*, and *dual subordination* were eliminated, but "socialist democracy," the subordination and accountability of lower state organs to higher ones, and the subordination of the minority to the majority were kept. It should be noted that democratic centralism is still considered the basis of the organization and functioning of the PCC:

> This does not deny, but rather presupposes, an increasingly superior democracy in the bosom of the Party, understood as the existence of all the room necessary for the expression of ideas, proposals, opinions, for and against regarding any matter be it controversial or complicated, until the policy is decided or agreed upon, at which point we must support it together, being right or in error and together rectify it.[128]

Escalona, during the 1992 interview, was adamant about the need to reduce the role of the party in relation to the OPP at all levels and instead to emphasize its political role:

> This country has spent thirty years saying that the party cannot administer, and the party has continued to do so. The party professionals must do its real job of political orientation, political work, and ideological orientation and cannot be involved in administration. There is much resistance to keeping the party separate from administration because here we have become accustomed to a style of work. All the transformations that are taking place would be impossible if it had not been for the party's necessary decision to assume its proper role.

Association or activity jeopardizing the status of the PCC is not permitted in Cuba. Four members of the opposition Internal Dissidence Working Group were imprisoned on July 16, 1997, and brought to trial in the beginning of March 1999, following the publication and distribution of a document entitled "The Nation Belongs to Everyone," which advocated a multiparty system. They also publicly called for a boycott of the January 1998 elections for the National Assembly and provincial assemblies, and discouraged foreign companies from investing in Cuba. They were charged with receiving material and financial support from Cuban exile groups in the United States which seek to overthrow the Cuban government, and from the United States government, and with transmitting their messages over Radio Martí which emanates from the United States and is sponsored by the United States government. [129]

Conclusion

The municipal assemblies are important because they are the level of government that takes the most initiative in discovering and resolving the people's problems and satisfying the needs they express. Because of the open neighborhood nomination procedure, the direct, secret, competitive elections, and the close bond and constant contact between delegates and constituents, voters tend to identify closely with their municipal delegates, and delegates are directly responsible to their electors and able to mobilize and express the will of the people. This relationship with constituents is reinforced by the biannual accountability sessions and citizen *planteamientos*. The *consejos populares* have strengthened municipal assemblies and have brought them closer to the people, enhancing the powers of the municipal delegates while broadening and deepening the connection between citizens and their representatives. Close to the majority of provincial assembly delegates and National Assembly deputies are also municipal delegates, so that at all levels of the OPP, those best able to understand and present the needs and preoccupations of the people have an important presence. The municipal delegates serve as the first level of the structure through which national policy is formulated. Without them, representative government in Cuba would lose much of its content.

The principal objectives of the municipal assembly are transmitting voter demands and overseeing the economic activity in its territory. Importance is given to the people's voice by holding the government responsible to address citizens' complaints and suggestions not only on the individual level, but also collectively, by area and category. These citizen mandates help determine policy at all levels.

Excessive centralization and paternalism continue to be of concern. The first priorities referred to by Cuban social scientists for strengthening local representative government is increased economic and political decentralization and local responsibility, especially concerning economic planning and the market. The strong centralism characteristic of the political and economic systems in Cuba has continued to limit the powers of local government and the effectiveness of political participation. Even with the *consejos populares* enhancing decentralization, excessive centralization of power and paternalism have reduced the efficacy of the public's participation and self-management.[130]

For Cuban social scientist Juan Valdés Paz, the impediments to accomplishing decentralization were that political democratization was not always accompanied by economic decentralization. Furthermore, the employment of dual subordination and democratic centralism led to authoritarian tendencies.[131] (As noted above, both were eliminated with regard to the OPP in the 1992 Constitution.) Furthermore, Valdés Paz criticized the lack of boundaries within the system, where the political system subordinates the judiciary, economics, and culture, and the Communist Party supplants the government, state administrations supplant representative bodies, the Council of State supplants the National Assembly, and mass organizations serve more to transmit party and state policies than to represent their members.[132]

Dilla argued for more pluralism, where "civil society should be an area for legitimate expression of socialist policies and not simply an entity subordinate to the circumstantial demands of decision making." However, he did not necessarily identify pluralism with multipartyism; instead, he argued that the Communist Party should be "reconstructed on the basis of consensus between autonomous organizations and supported in a program which includes the ideological and cultural diversity which exists in the society."[133]

Valdés Paz argued that representation of political and mass organizations in local government is insufficient, especially in formulating demands and proposals.[134] For Dilla, the valuable mechanisms for control of authority available to citizens, such as nominations, elections, and accountability sessions, have been weakened because of insufficient information flowing from above.[135]

Valdés Paz recognized that the current local political system is inseparable from being considered a political system in transition to socialism, and that in spite of its weak points, it has brought a level of democratization without precedent in the history of Cuba.[136] Within the Cuban OPP, the municipal assemblies are closest to the prototype set forth by the Paris Commune.

Notes

1. Raúl Castro, speech given on August 22, 1974, *Granma Weekly Review*, September 8, 1974, p. 3.

2. Hugo Ascuy, "La reforma de la Constitución socialista de 1976," in Haroldo Dilla (ed.), *La democracía en Cuba y el diferendo con los Estados Unidos* (Havana: Centro de Estudios sobre América, 1995), pp. 150, 160 (my translation).

3. Carollee Bengelsdorf, "Between Vision and Reality: Democracy in Socialist Theory and Practice: The Cuban Experience," Ph.D. dissertation, Massachusetts Institute of Technology, 1985, pp. 161, 164.

4. Maurice Zeitlin, quoted in ibid., p. 164.

5. Fidel Castro, speech given on July 26, 1974, *Granma Weekly Review*, August 4, 1974, p. 5.

6. Fidel Castro, speech given on September 28, 1967, *Granma Weekly Review*, October 8, 1967, p. 6.

7. Raúl Castro, speech given August 22, 1974, pp. 3–4.

8. Fidel Castro, speech given on November 18, 1971, *Granma Weekly Review*, November 28, 1971, p. 14.

9. William M LeoGrande, "Participation in Cuban Municipal Government: From Local Power to People's Power," in Donald E. Schulz and Jan S. Adams, *Political Participation in Communist Countries* (New York: Pergamen Press, 1981), p. 277.

10. Haroldo Dilla Alfonso, "Democracia y poder revolucionario en Cuba," *Cuadernos de Nuestra America*, Vol. 4, No. 7 (January-June 1987), p. 63 (my translation).

11. Armando Hart, speech given on September 24, 1969, *Granma Weekly Review*, October 5, 1969, p. 4.

12. William M LeoGrande, "Modes of Political Participation in Revolutionary Cuba," paper presented at the annual meeting of the Northeastern Political Science Association, November 10–12, 1977, p. 5. For a more detailed account of "mobilization participation" in Cuba, see Richard Fagen, *The Transformation of Political Culture in Cuba* (Stanford: Stanford University Press, 1969).

13. Fidel Castro, speech given on April 27, 1959, in *El pensamiento de Fidel Castro: Selección temática*, Vol. 1, No. 2 (Havana: Política, 1983), p. 427 (my translation).

14. Haroldo Dilla Alfonso, "Notas sobre la relación centralización-decentralización en la transición socialista cubana," unpublished manuscript, 1989, pp. 7–8 (my translation).

15. Fidel Castro, speech given on November 29, 1971, *Granma Weekly Review*, December 12, 1971, p. 13.

16. Fidel Castro, speech given on May 1, 1971, *Granma Weekly Review*, May 16, 1971, p. 2.

17. Fidel Castro, press conference August 21, 1975, *Granma Weekly Review*, August 31, 1975, p. 9.

18. Gail Lindenberg, "The Labor Union in the Cuban Workplace," *Latin American Perspectives*, Issue 76, Vol. 20, No. 1 (Winter 1993), p. 28.

19. Gail Reed, "Taking the Leap: Cuba's Fourth Party Congress," *Cuba Update*, Vol. 11, No. 4,(Fall 1990), p. 19; see also Esther Mosak, "Democracy: Learning by Doing," *Cuba Update*, Vol. 12, Nos. 1–2 (Winter-Spring 1991), pp. 19–20.

20. Domingo García Cárdenas, *State Organization in Cuba* (Havana: José Martí Publishing House, 1986), pp. 14–15.

21. Haroldo Dilla Alfonso and Gerardo González Núñez, "Participación y desarrollo en los municipios cubanos," unpublished manuscript prepared for the Organizations of Community Power and Grass-Roots Democracy in Central America and the Caribbean, with assistance by the Centro Internacional de Investigaciones para el Desarrollo, Ottawa, Canada, 1991, p. 3 (my translation).

22. Gail Lindenberg, "The Labor Union," pp. 34–35, 37–39; see also Linda Fuller, "The Politics of Workers' Control in Cuba, 1959–1983: The Work Center

and the National Arena," Ph.D. dissertation, University of California, Berkeley, 1985.

23. Fidel Castro, speech given on September 28, 1972, *Granma Weekly Review*, October 8, 1972, p. 3.

24. LeoGrande, "Modes of Political Participation," p. 11.

25. Bengelsdorf, "Between Vision and Reality," p. 250; Dilla, "Notas sobre la relación," p. 14.

26. LeoGrande, "Participation in Cuban Municipal Government," p. 279.

27. García Cárdenas, *State Organization*, p. 15.

28. LeoGrande, "Participation in Cuban Municipal Government," p. 278.

29. Ibid., p. 278.

30. García Cárdenas, *State Organization*, p. 17.

31. Jorge I. Domínguez, *Cuba: Order and Revolution* (Cambridge: Harvard University Press, 1978), p. 243.

32. Ibid.

33. García Cárdenas, *State Organization*, p. 17; see also LeoGrande, "Participation in Cuban Municipal Government," p. 278.

34. Haroldo Dilla, Gerardo González, and Ana Teresa Vincentelli, *Participación popular y desarrollo en los municipios cubanos* (Havana: Centro de Estudios sobre América, 1993), pp. 28–29.

35. Dilla, "Notas sobre la relación," pp. 8–9.

36. Raúl Castro, speech given on August 22, 1974, p. 3.

37. Dilla, "Notas sobre la relación," p. 8 (my translation).

38. Bengelsdorf, "Between Vision and Reality," p. 206.

39. Ibid., p. 209.

40. Ibid., p. 260.

41. Ibid., p. 261.

42. Fidel Castro, speech given on May 20, 1970, *Granma Weekly Review*, May 31, 1970, p. 10.

43. Ibid., p. 9.

44. Ibid., p. 12.

45. Fidel Castro, speech given on July 26, 1970, *Granma Weekly Review*, August 2, 1970, p. 3.

46. Ibid., p. 4.

47. Ibid., p. 5.

48. Ibid., p. 6.

49. Fidel Castro, speech given on August 23, 1970, *Granma Weekly Review*, August 30, 1970, p. 4.

50. Ibid., p. 5.

51. Fidel Castro, speech given on September 3, 1970, *Granma Weekly Review*, September 20, 1970, p. 5.

52. Fidel Castro, speech given on September 28, 1970, *Granma Weekly Review*, October 4, 1970, p. 2.

53. Fidel Castro, speech given on December 7, 1970, *Granma Weekly Review*, December 20, 1970, p. 3.

54. Ibid.

55. Ibid.

56. Georgina Suárez Hernández, "Protagonismo político en Cuba: antecedentes y proyección actual," paper presented at the Cuba Conference, Halifax, Nova Scotia, November 3, 1989, p. 11 (my translation).

57. Carmelo Mesa-Lago, *Cuba in the 1970s* (Albuquerque: University of New Mexico Press, 1974), p. 67.

58. Ibid., pp. 67–68.

59. Suárez, "Protagonismo político," p. 12 (my translation); see also "Cuba Weighs Castro Plan to Decentralize Power," *New York Times*, April 30, 1975, p. 3.

60. "Constitution of the Organs of People's Power," *Center for Cuban Studies Newsletter*, Vol. 2, Nos. 5–6 (October-December, 1975), pp. 4–26.

61. John E. Cooney, "'Popular Power': Cuban Province Takes Initial Steps in Test of Democratic Rule," *Wall Street Journal*, December 4, 1974, p. 1.

62. Ibid., p. 39.

63. Vicente Navarro, "Workers and Community Participation and Democratic Control in Cuba," *International Journal of Health Services*, Vol. 10, No. 2 (1980), p. 206.

64. Fidel Castro, speech given on February 20, 1990, *Granma Resumen Semanal*, March 4, 1990, p. 3 (my translation).

65. "Constitution of the Republic of Cuba," *Granma*, March 7, 1976, pp. 6–7; Also see Michael Waller, *Democratic Centralism: An Historical Commentary* (New York: John Wiley & Sons, 1962), p. 62.

66. "Constitution of the Republic of Cuba," p. 29.

67. Fernando Alvarez Tabio, *Comentarios a la Constitución Socialista* (Havana: Editorial de Ciencias Sociales, 1985), p. 246.

68. Ibid., pp. 301–302.

69. Ibid., p. 302.

70. Fidel Castro, speech given on July 26, 1974, p. 4 (my translation).

71. Dilla, "Notas sobre la relación," p. 11 (my translation).

72. Ibid., pp. 12–13.

73. Maria Julia Mayoral, "Asambleas municipales: Una mirada a las debilidades," *Granma*, January 14, 1999, URL: http://www.granma.cubaweb.cu.

74. "Constitución de la República de Cuba," p. 9.

75. Ascuy, "La reforma," p. 162; Dilla, Gonzalez, and Vincentelli, *Participación popular*, pp. 103–108.

76. "Constitution of the Republic of Cuba," pp. 6–7; "Constitución de la República de Cuba," *Granma*, September 22, 1992, pp. 7, 9.

77. See Chapter 6.

78. See Chapter 4.

79. Fidel Castro, speech given on September 28, 1976, *Granma Weekly Review*, October 10, 1976, p. 2.

80. Bengelsdorf, "Between Vision and Reality," p. 267.

81. Harnecker, *Cuba: Dictatorship or Democracy?* (Westport, Conn.: Lawrence Hill, 1980), p. 117.

82. Peter Roman, "Poder popular en Cuba," *Pensamiento Crítico*, Vol. 11, No. 61, (October-December 1988), p. 5.

83. Bard Jorgensen, "The Interrelationship Between Base and Superstructure in Cuba," *Ibero-Americana, Nordic Journal of Latin American Studies*, Vol. 13, No. 1 (1983), p. 36.

84. Caridad Carrobello, Martha Campos, Pelayo Terry, and Ariel Terrero, "¿Qué piensa el pueblo de su poder?" *Bohemia*, July 6, 1990, p. 7.

85. Dilla, González, and Vincentelli, *Participación popular*, p. 101 (my translation).

86. Mayoral, "Asambleas municipales."

87. Raúl Castro, speech given August 22, 1974, p. 5.

88. Susanna Lee, "Examinan presidentes municipales temas relacionados con la Salud y la Educación," *Granma*, June 12, 1998, p. 3; Susanna Lee, "Asistió Fidel a la sesión final de la IV Reunión de Presidentes Municipales," *Granma*, June 13, 1998, p. 8.

89. Mayoral, "Asambleas Municipales."

90. Ibid.

91. Ibid.

92. See Chapter 4.

93. See Chapter 5.

94. See Chapter 4.

95. Ricardo Alarcón, speech given December 26, 1997, *Trabajadores*, December 29, 1997, p. 8 (my translation).

96. Eloy Concepción, "Para aprobar una ley se necesita," *Trabajadores*, July 20, 1998, p. 16.

97. María Julia Mayoral, "Este es un país de justicia," Granma, February 16, 1999. *URL:http://www.granma.cubaweb.cu*; Roger Ricardo, Sara Más, and María Julia Mayoral, "Indispensable utilizar la fuerza organizada del pueblo," Granma, February 17, 1999, *URL:http://www.granma.cubaweb.cu*; Roger Ricardo, Sara Más, and María Julia Mayoral,"Esta Trinchera tenemos que defenderla," Granma, February 17, 1999, *URL:http://www.granma.cubaweb.cu*.

98. Francisco Rodríguez Cruz, "Prueba de conciencia patriótica, unidad y apoyo al sistema político," *Trabajadores*, December 15, 1997, p. 5 (my translation).

99. María Julia Mayoral, "Diez herramientas claves del Parlamento cubano," *Granma*, July 31, 1998, p. 3.

100. Javier Rodríguez, "Deputados Cubanos analizan producción y autoabastecimiento," *Prensa Latina*, August 24, 1998. URL: http://www.prensa-latina.org

101. Lázaro Barredo Medina, "El consenso, asunto de seguridad nacional," *Trabajadores*, January 27, 1997, p. 4 (my translation).

102. "Asamblea Nacional del Poder Popular: sobre el proceso de elaboración del proyecto de Ley Electoral," *Granma*, October 30, 1992, pp. 4–5 (my translation); "Continuación del debate sobre formación y presentación de candidaturas," *Granma*, October 31, 1992, p. 3 (my translation).

103. Caridad Lafita Navarro, "Salvar la seguridad social," *Trabajadores*, August 8, 1994, p. 3.

104. See Appendix.

105. "Intervención de Fidel en el debate sobre Proyecto de Ley Tributaria," *Granma*, August 6, 1994, p. 3.

106. Mireya Navarron, "Cuba Passes Law to Attract Greater Foreign Investment," *New York Times*, September 7, 1995, p. A–12; "Debate sobre Proyecto de Ley para la Inversión Extranjera," *Granma*, September 5, 1995, p. 3; Vladia Rubio, Isabel Morales, Iraida Calzadilla, Raisa Pagés, María Julia Mayoral, Sara Más, Silvia Martinez, Juan Varela Pérez, Emilio del Barrio, José Antonio de la Osa, José A. Martin, and Roger Ricardo Luis, "Sobre el Régimen Laboral en las Inversiones Extranjeras," *Granma*, September 6, 1995, p. 4.

107. "Al 4 Congreso del Partido!" *Granma Resumen Semanal*, March 25, 1990, p. 3.

108. Carollee Bengelsdorf, "The Matter of Democracy in Cuba: Snapshots of Three Moments," in Sandor Halebsky and John M. Kirk (eds.), *Transformation and Struggle: Cuba Faces the 1990s* (New York: Praeger, 1990), pp. 40–45.

109. Ascuy, "La reforma," p. 163.

110. Ibid., pp. 161, 164–166.

111. Esther Mosak, "Democracy: Learning by Doing," *Cuba Update*, Vol. 12, Nos. 1–2 (Winter-Spring 1991), p. 19; Gail Reed, "Taking the Leap: Cuba's Fourth Party Congress," *Cuba Update*, Vol. 11, No. 4 (Fall 1990), p. 19.

112. Ascuy, "La reforma," pp. 163–164.

113. "Cuban Parliament President Ricardo Alarcón Calls on Deputies and Delegates to Expand Their Work," *Radio Havana Cuba*, April 14, 1998, URL: http://www.radiohc.org.

114. María Julia Mayoral, "Relación deputados-electores: con capacidad para mucho más," *Granma*, May 13, 1998, p. 3 (my translation).

115. Iliana Hautrive, "Modelo de resumen," *Trabajadores*, June 1, 1998, p. 2.

116. Fidel Castro, speech given on July 26, 1974, p. 5.

117. Raúl Castro, speech given August 22, 1974, p. 5.

118. Ibid.

119. Héctor Miranda Pérez, "El Partido controla y dirige no administra ni suplanta funciones," *Granma*, August 7, 1998, URL:http://www.granma.cubaweb.cu.

120. Dilla, González, and Vincentelli, *Participación popular*, pp. 112–114.

121. LeoGrande, "Participation in Cuban Municipal Government," p. 289.

122. Raúl Castro, speech given August 22, 1974, p. 5

123. Dilla, González, and Vincentelli, *Participación popular*, pp. 78–79.

124. Ibid., pp. 78.

125. Ibid., pp. 64–65.

126. Luis Suárez Salazár, "El sistema electoral cubano: Apuntes para una crítica," in Dilla (ed.), *La democracia*, p. 205 (my translation).

127. Ibid.

128. Partido Comunista de Cuba, "El trabajo del Partido en la actual conyuntura (V)," *Granma*, August 21, 1996, p. 3 (my translation).

129. Dalia Acosta, "Rights—Cuba: Opponents Complete Year in Prison Without Charges," *InterPress Service*, July 19, 1998, p. 1. Patricia Grogg, "Rights—Cuba: Group Accused of Sedition Awaiting Verdict," *Interpress Service*, March 5, 1999, pp.1-2.

130. Haroldo Dilla Alfonso, "Los municipios cubanos y los retos del futuro," in Haroldo Dilla (ed.), *La participación, en Cuba y los retos del futuro* (Havana: Centro de Estudios sobre América, 1996) p. 141.

131. Juan Valdés Paz, "Poder local y participación," in Haroldo Dilla (ed.), *La participación*, pp. 121–122.

132. Juan Valdés Paz, "Notas sobre el sistema político cubano," in Dilla (ed.), *La democracía*, pp. 112–113.

133. Haroldo Dilla Alfonso, "Cuba: ¿Cuál es la democracia deseable?" in Dilla (ed.), *La democracía*, pp. 186–187 (my translation).

134. Ibid., p. 127.

135. Haroldo Dilla, "Los municipios cubanos," p. 142.

136. Juan Valdés Paz, "Poder local," p. 131.

4

Nominations and Elections

The election of municipal assembly delegates involves nominations by voters in the electoral district, the compiling and posting within the electoral district of biographies of the candidates, voting by secret ballot, and recall. All citizens who are at least sixteen years old are eligible to nominate candidates and to vote, including members of the armed forces, except those who are mentally incapacitated, who are in prison, or who have been deprived of their political rights. Inclusion on the official list of voters is automatic for those eligible, and there is no sanction for those who do not vote. Municipal delegates must be sixteen years old. The Cuban system mainly differs from the system of the former Soviet Union in that in Cuba, municipal delegates must reside within their electoral district, the municipal assembly elections are competitive by law (there must be at least two candidates per election district, with a maximum of eight), and the Communist Party does not choose the candidates. To win, a candidate must receive more than 50 percent of the votes cast. If no candidate receives a majority, a runoff election between the two candidates with the most votes is held a week later. Municipal assembly delegate elections are held every two and one half years.

Provincial assembly delegates must be sixteen years old, and National Assembly deputies eighteen years old. Neither body has residency requirements. The candidates are nominated by the municipal assemblies from lists compiled by the national, provincial, and municipal candidacy commissions. Elections for these positions are direct but not competitive. Candidates must get a majority of the popular votes cast to be elected. Provincial and national elections are held every five years.

The election process is directed at all levels by electoral commissions, led by the *Comisión Electoral Nacional* (National Electoral Commission, or CEN), which organize, direct and validate each phase of the electoral process. The local electoral commission determines and publicizes the list of eligible voters, organizes the nomination meetings and composes and posts candidates' biographies, encourages people to participate and vote, runs and staffs the polling places, and counts the ballots on election day.[1] Campaigning for and by candidates is not allowed.

The terms for National Assembly deputies, provincial delegates, and municipal delegates were to have ended in Fall 1991, but the elections were postponed for over one year to include the changes contained in the 1992 Constitution and Election Law. The direct elections for the National Assembly deputies and provincial assembly delegates were first held in February 1993 (before this, they were elected by the municipal assembly delegates) and then again in January 1998, and the most recent municipal assembly delegate elections were held in December 1993, July 1995, and October 1997.

Municipal Assembly Delegate Nominations

Nomination assemblies for municipal delegate candidates are held about a month before the elections in subdivisions called *areas* within electoral districts. There are from one to eight areas in a district, depending on the size of its population. An area usually contains several hundred voters in large municipalities like Playa, fewer in smaller municipalities like Bauta. If there is only one area in a municipality, at least two candidates must be nominated from the area. If there is more than one area, each area can nominate at least one. An area can nominate a candidate who has already been chosen in another area, but in the end, there must be at least two candidates; at least one area must nominate someone different. There can be no more than eight candidates.

The local electoral commission organizes the meeting (assembles the loudspeakers and the table and chairs and sets up the lights). To conserve electricity, beginning with the economic crisis in Cuba in the 1990s the nomination meetings have been held together with the regularly scheduled biannual accountability session that delegates hold with their constituents. At the beginning of the meeting, local CDR representatives collect attendance slips in order to establish the percentage of voters attending from that area (these pieces of paper do not contain the names of the voters). Fifty percent of the eligible voters once had to be present for the meeting to take place (in 1992, this requirement was dropped). During regular elections, the national attendance average at nomination meetings has been from 70 to over 90 percent.[2]

Dilla and González highlighted the informal character of the nomination assemblies:

> Those persons most likely to participate actively are the elderly and the women, not only in the debates but also in the preparation of the meeting places, which can be rooms in public buildings (schools, small theaters, etc.,) or simply open areas. Even though there is a rite that determines the order of the assemblies,

they are characterized by a climate of informal debate to which the playing of the neighborhood children, for whom these activities constitute besides an excellent recreational opportunity, contributes decisively.[3]

A member of the local electoral commission opens the meeting and calls for nominations for a president to conduct the meeting and a secretary, who are elected by a show of hands. The person elected president reads the law regarding eligibility for nominations and then calls on the voters present to propose candidates. Only individuals eligible to vote can propose candidates, and those nominated must likewise be eligible to vote, must reside in the electoral district, and must consent to run. (Those proposing candidates and those accepting usually do not have to prove their eligibility because within the area where sessions are held, people for the most part know each other.) People cannot propose themselves as candidates, and no party or organization may propose or publicly support candidates.

The person who proposes a candidate must speak about the person's merits, and others may also do so. In the nomination meetings I attended, the criteria used to recommend those being proposed were similar to those reported in other studies made of the Cuban election process.[4] Membership in the Communist Party is mentioned if applicable but is given no more and no less importance than other factors, such as personal merits, active support of the Cuban Revolution, and job history. A vote by a show of hands is then taken, and the person with the most votes is the candidate from that area.

The nominating meetings I attended in 1988 in Playa and Bauta were part of special elections called to fill municipal assembly seats that were vacant because the voters had previously recalled their delegate, or because the delegate had died or moved out of the electoral district. An officer of the municipal assembly was in attendance at every meeting I attended. In no case was my presence known of beforehand or announced at the meetings. The attendance at these meetings was less than 60 percent of the eligible voters.

At the nomination meeting I attended in Playa (in Area 1 of the Forty-third Electoral District) on December 7, 1987, scheduled because of the recall of the delegate, four people were proposed and three accepted. The person proposing Efrén García called him "a man everyone knows and at the same time is a worker, revolutionary, *internacionalista* [served abroad], and party militant." The statement for a woman being proposed included the following: "I propose a comrade who stands out, who is revolutionary, . . . who has a good attitude, who can truly be a delegate. She is a good worker, a revolutionary. We need comrades who are ready to take steps to help our workers, because there are those who do nothing to solve problems. We must propose comrades who have truly devoted themselves to the neighbors living on the block." She declined the nomination, stating she was not prepared to be a delegate. Two other candidates were proposed. One of these was Jesús Echea Pérez, who, it was stated, "had previously been a delegate and in my opinion can carry out this function well." Another person proposed "has also been a delegate, and everyone knows is dedicated to his work, is very capable and everyone here knows him. His political level is superior, beyond being an official in the armed forces." A vote was then taken by a show of hands to determine which of the three would be the candidate from this area.

In a nomination meeting held on May 10, 1988, in an area in the Eighty-fifth Electoral District in Playa, five persons were proposed, of whom four declined and one was absent. The president of the meeting asked if those present knew the candidate previously accepted in another area, who was said to be enthusiastic and fit for the task. Nobody knew him, but as no other person present would accept the nomination, he was chosen as the candidate from this area also.

On May 11, 12, and 13, 1988, nomination meetings were held in the three areas of the Seventieth Electoral District in the Santa Fe neighborhood of Playa. In the first meeting, in Area 1, a man nicknamed El Chino was proposed. He had run in the previous election and had lost by three votes to the previous delegate. Several people present stated, in his absence, that he wanted to run again, but a woman identified as an aunt of his wife said that as he was studying at night, he did not have time to be a delegate. Because of this confusion, his nomination was not accepted. Four others were proposed as candidates and declined. Finally, one who had declined, an elderly woman who I was told was a respected doctor and president of the nomination meeting, was persuaded to accept. Among the attributes mentioned was her membership in the Communist Party. Another woman was also proposed and accepted. In the subsequent vote, the doctor won and became the candidate from this area.

The next night, Area 2 held its nomination meeting, and El Chino was present. He told the meeting that in fact he did want to be a candidate and that what his wife's aunt had said to the contrary in the Area 1 meeting was wrong. He was then proposed (no other proposals were made) and approved as Area 2's candidate by a show of hands. His Communist Party membership was mentioned among his attributes. The head of the local CDR told me that someone from the local party unit would talk to his wife's aunt to have her explain why she had said that he did not want to run. This was in line with the party's role of intervening in the municipal nomination process only when necessary to ensure its legitimacy.

In the third area's meeting, El Chino and a woman were proposed, and El Chino won by a large majority. On May 29, El Chino won the election as municipal delegate by a seven to five margin of the approximately thirteen hundred votes cast.

In a nomination meeting on May 17, 1988, in Area 2 of the Eighty-fourth Electoral District in Playa, the attendance was 250, a bit over 50 percent of the eligible voters. Three men were proposed and two accepted. The main attributes mentioned were that they were good revolutionaries and very active in the CDR. Party membership was not mentioned. The one who declined had been the delegate for ten years and said he wanted to give others a chance. Furthermore, being a regional CDR officer, he would have had to be absent too often. The winner won the vote 150 to 111.

On May 18, 1988, in the nomination meeting of Area 3 of the Twenty-first Election District in Playa, each of the two persons proposed, Carmen and Mario, had been previously picked as candidates in one of the other two areas of the district. Carmen had been a candidate for delegate in the previous election and had lost by very few votes. At this meeting, each spoke in favor of the other. Again the attributes mentioned included being good revolutionaries and being active in the CDR. Neither belonged to the Communist Party, although a woman stated that Mario was a member and was corrected. The president of the meeting asked if anyone wanted to speak against Mario or Carmen, but no one did.

At the two nomination meetings I attended in Bauta, perhaps because the electoral districts and thus the areas were smaller, those attending seemed more familiar with the candidates proposed. At these meetings, no one declined the nomination. At the meeting held on June 8, 1988, in the Area 1 of the election district, two men were proposed. Manuel Pérez, who won the vote by fifty-three to seven, was described by the person proposing him as young, revolutionary, a party militant, active in the CDR, and a union leader in the large textile factory that dominates Bauta. The second nominee, Ernesto (Pupi) Morales, was at first hesitant to accept since he was a member of the electoral commission in this election district.

In Area 2, a meeting scheduled for June 10, 1988, had to be canceled for lack of sufficient attendance and was rescheduled for June 13, at which time the three proposed nominees all accepted. Raúl, who won with thirty-eight votes, was described as a department head in the textile factory, young, and a member of the UJC. Roberto, who was praised for his experience, got twelve votes. The person speaking in favor of Odalys, who received sixteen votes, described her as a young medical doctor and stressed the importance of having women delegates.

In a survey done by the Cuban magazine *Bohemia*, when asked "Would you accept being delegate from your electoral district?" 31.3 percent answered yes, 40.8 percent answered no, and 27.9 percent answered don't know.[5] The reluctance of some to accept nomination may be due to the great amount of unpaid voluntary work involved and the difficulty of performing the job adequately because of the nature of regular jobs (for example, long hours or the need to be absent for long periods). Many delegates become burned out and decline renomination: There is a turnover of approximately 50 percent in each election. The Cuban journalist Susana Tesoro wrote that a delegate should be

> an exemplary citizen, with proven attributes, because he is agile, has executive skills, is capable of working, is on top of the problems most felt by the population, and feels deeply and rejoices with every step forward taken by the neighborhood. . . . In the case of someone who has no free time—a member of a construction contingent who works fourteen hours daily or a woman who besides being in the *microbrigada* (voluntary work brigade) has children and other responsibilities, it is not enough to be "the best and most capable," for one must also consider a second criterion: "with real possibilities."[6]

In my interviews with delegates, in every case but one they said that, at least the first time they were nominated, they had had no idea that they would be proposed and that the proposal had been made by an individual acting alone rather than being planned beforehand by a group, an organization, or the Communist Party. Typical of the answers I received was that of Norma Estrada, a delegate from Cienfuegos, whom I interviewed in November 1987. She said that she had not attended the nomination meeting in her area with any hope of or even interest in being nominated: "My election as a nominee was a complete surprise." She was elected secretary of the nomination meeting. Subsequently, Elaine Gonzalez, her friend and neighbor from the local CDR, proposed Norma, stating that "she has the qualities to be delegate, participates in all activities, has CDR responsibilities, is a party militant, has a very good attitude in her workplace." When I asked Estrada if she thought people in the local CDR had got together prior to the meeting and agreed that she should be nominated, she replied: "It was an individual act. [Elaine] has known me for a long time, we live in the same neighborhood, we always studied together. No, truly I do not believe that more people were involved in this." In a survey of municipal delegates conducted in Santa Cruz del Norte Municipality during the 1989 electoral process by Dilla, González, and Vincentelli, only 10 percent of the sample said that they had been made aware beforehand that their names were going to be proposed for nomination. Another 19 percent said that in previous terms they had been made aware beforehand of their nomination. Seventy-one percent said they had never received any prior indications.[7]

The main role of the Communist Party in the nomination and election procedure, according to Dilla and Fernández, is played through the local electoral commissions: mobilization of resources, coordination, and guaranteeing the correct application of established norms and respect for the wishes of the voters.[8] However, occasionally in the past, members of a local unit of the Communist Party have decided beforehand to propose and informally promote a candidate for municipal assembly delegate—usually one identified as having leadership capabilities. Efforts to promote certain individuals as candidates have been made for purposes of retaining or placing "persons with leadership capacities with an eye to the future composition of the executive committee. . . . The origin of these manifestations can be traced not only to the local Communist Party committee but also to other organizations and the outgoing municipal government."[9] Dilla and Fernández noted that the party's occasional involvement in the nomination process "could not have had a decisive effect unless the minority of militants were capable of convincing the whole meeting regarding the suitability of their specific proposal, and in this way gaining their approval, taking into account, besides, that such proselytizing could only take place as a personal act and not in the name of the party or any other organization."[10]

Among the 193 people interviewed in 1989 who had participated in nomination sessions, Dilla, González, and Vincentelli found no case or knowledge of attempts to influence the process by the PCC or other organizations. Three said that such intervention had happened in the early election processes. Of the delegates these authors surveyed, 70 percent responded that they had received no indication from any organization that they were to be proposed or should accept being nominated; 11 percent (seventeen delegates) said it had happened either in previous mandates or always. Half of the latter group belonged to the leadership of their municipal assembly.[11]

A concrete example of this kind of local party involvement in the nomination process was related to me in an interview in 1987 by Rafael Fajardo, then vice president of the municipal assembly in Cienfuegos, regarding his nomination in 1986. In an interview on November 24, 1987, he told me that because of his excellent record as director of the local pork industry and favorable reports received by the party in the *estado de opinión*, "There was not the slightest doubt that the party had within its plans that I would go on to a leadership post within the OPP, and I was then elected by the people to be a candidate." A newspaper had done an interview with him before the nomination meeting, and this, he said, had made him "better known to the rest of the electors who did not know me. . . . I would say that [the party] created the possibilities for the people to choose me for this."

Alberto Dan Andrade, head of the Communist Party in Cienfuegos, confirmed in a separate interview on the same day, that the local party unit had, in one or two instances during the 1986 election process, asked party members in an electoral district to propose a certain individual as a candidate. Afterward, the party had used its influence in the candidacy commission of the municipal assembly of Cienfuegos to have the person recommended to be a professional (salaried) member of the municipal assembly's executive committee.

An administrator in the offices of the National Assembly, Felix Moreno, told me in May 1988 that such practice was no longer permitted, and this was confirmed to me by Escalona in February 1992. When, before the 1989 municipal assembly delegate nominations, the municipal party organ became aware through the *estado de opinión* that in two election districts in Playa the party cells were planning to propose candidates, the municipal party advised cells not to become involved in this way.

During the nomination process in 1989, the *New York Times* reported that Roberto Bahamonde, a Cuban dissident and member of the Commission on Human Rights, had challenged "the designated candidate in a neighborhood election. He was defeated, but received thirty votes, compared with sixty for the winner."[12] There are, however, no "designated candidates" in Cuba; Treaster was probably referring to the existing delegate. I found out that this "neighborhood election" was in fact a nomination meeting held in San Miguel del Padron, a municipality in the City of Havana. During the meeting in the area where he resides, Bahamonde had attempted to propose himself as a nominee, which is not allowed. After the meeting he complained to the local electoral commission of unfair treatment, and it responded by convening another nominating meeting in this area. During this second meeting, Bahamonde's wife nominated him. He then attempted to give a talk regarding his platform, an act of self-promotion that is not allowed. In the vote to determine the nominee from this area, Bahamonde lost by a vote of thirty to sixty.

The municipal delegate elections were held on July 9, 1995, during one of the worst years of the economic crisis, with the runoff on July 16 in the cases where no candidate had received a majority. In 97 percent of the election districts, only two candidates were nominated, which meant that very few runoff elections were necessary. Some 6,265,988 people—82.9 percent of those eligible to vote—attended the nomination meetings, about 4 percent more than in 1992; 29,131 candidates were nominated, of which 14,229 were elected. In a poll conducted in all 169 municipalities at the start of the Spring 1995 nomination process by the *Centro de Investigaciones Sociopolíticas y de Opinión del Pueblo* (Center of Sociopolitical Research and of Public Opinion), 93 percent of those interviewed favored the Cuban system for electing municipal delegates;[13] 92 percent stated they planned to attend the nomination assemblies; 72 percent believed they were well represented by their delegates; and 54 percent judged as "good" or "very good" the efforts by delegates on behalf of constituents during the previous term. Carlos Amat, Minister of Justice and president of the National Electoral Commission, stated, "With the situation the country was going through, it is obvious that the delegates have not been able to resolve all the demands of the constituents. Thus we asked ourselves if this would discourage the attendance and the participation of the people. And the result has been just the opposite."[14]

The nomination assemblies were conducted between May 19 and June 18, 1995. Prior to the start of the nominations, the National CDR issued a call to its members to attend and participate in the nomination meetings and to vote in "the most important political process of this year."[15] *Trabajadores* claimed that "the system of our people's state rests on the quality of its delegates and municipal assemblies. This is the cornerstone of a structure that, as distinguished from the past, only has meaning if at the base level, it can count on capable and active men and women."[16] Of the current delegates, 63.2 percent were renominated, constituting 29.9 percent of the 29,131 candidates nominated in 27,789 nominating meetings for the 14,229 contested seats in the 169 municipalities.[17] More than 50 percent of the nominees were between sixteen and forty years old; 60 percent had at least a twelfth-grade education, and 26 percent were university graduates; 35 percent were workers and technicians; and 16 percent were women.[18] Furthermore, in the words of Esteban Lazo, first secretary of the PCC in Havana, "Without the party having to nominate anyone, and without having campaigned for anyone, more than 80 percent of the nominees are militants of the party or of the Union of Young Communists."[19]

Municipal delegate elections were held for the ninth session of the 169 municipal assemblies on October 19, 1997, with the runoff on October 26. There were 14,533 electoral districts, 304 more than in 1995.[20] Nomination assemblies were held from September 3 to 27. To encourage more nominations, the number of inhabitants per nomination area was reduced to below four hundred. According to CEN member Raul Mantilla Ramírez, this reduction was also made to enable the participants to know each other better, to have the assemblies take place closer to where the people live, and to create conditions in which candidates emerge who are supported by and personally acquainted with their neighbors.[21] The number of voters per polling place was reduced to three hundred to make voting easier, to have polling places be closer to where people live, and to speed up the vote count. An average of 86.57 percent of the total of registered voters nationwide attended the assemblies, nominating 31,276 candidates. This percentage was topped only in 1984, when 91.2 percent attended. Of those nominated, 61.87 percent were incumbents, and 73.71 percent were PCC militants. The percentage of women candidates rose 2.39 percent to 18.49 percent, and the percentage of those under thirty years old dropped from 18.20 to 15.66.[22]

During the nomination process, the Cuban press reported on various neighborhood assemblies. Support of a candidacy is supposed to stress personal characteristics and aptitudes such as relations with others and work history and methods, rather than accomplishments and pledges. However, in Matanzas, a woman spoke in favor of renominating the existing delegate, Manuel Reyes Ruiz, claiming that he had performed "miracles" and was also close to the people's sensibilities. She asserted, "Thanks to Reyes we laid asphalt on 500 meters of street, and old problems like those related to water were resolved . . . besides his communist morality," which sounded much like a campaign speech based on accomplishments. The journalist commented on this: "Although it is an error of judgment to associate the authority and efficiency of a delegate to the concrete solutions of problems in these times of material scarcity, it is easy to comprehend that Reyes is held in high esteem in the entire zone."[23] Similarly Yamila Guerrero Donis, a nominee in Guanabcoa, said a delegate should not be judged only by what had been resolved. Yet she spoke of the accomplishments of her father when he was delegate; he had instigated the creation of a secondary school in the neighborhood, the reparation of the primary school, and the operation of a cafeteria. She also listed what was needed to be done: facilitate more cooperation among the various enterprises in the territory, repair the playground and the streets, and do more for recreation. The high school, she stated, was used for selling rum.[24]

The topic of conversation prior to one nomination session was that since the local PCC nucleus had asked its militants to accept nomination if proposed, it was known who would win. A polemic ensued in which one person said, "Then why are we here if so-and-so is going to win," to which another shot back, "That will only happen if the people want it to, since no one can oblige you to raise your hand against your will." Another argued that he agreed with what the party did, as it should ask its militants to act consistently with their position as vanguard, and this would not in any way constrain the selection. Three candidates were proposed—a worker, a retired person, and a vegetable vendor. The only one who was a party militant was proposed by someone who was not a member. The vote was very even. The journalist concluded, "The party's only role is to guarantee that the principles of the electoral process are strictly followed in all its phases."[25]

From Nominations to Elections

The election district electoral commissions have five members who live in the territory and work without pay. About three months prior to the elections, the local CDR give these commissions lists of eligible voters, which are posted in the neighborhoods. Citizens have the right to protest any errors. The commissions also organize the nomination meetings, verify that the candidates nominated possess the necessary requirements, prepare the voting places and inform the public of their locations, and count the votes.

Following the nomination meetings, the commissions write and print biographies of the candidates for each electoral district and, about two weeks before the election, post them with the candidates' photos in store windows and on CDR bulletin boards, and in front of the polling places on election day. The biographies, with some slight variations, stick to the same pattern throughout the country (I obtained copies from Playa, Bauta, and Cienfuegos). They first list the name, age, marital status, education, occupation, and "integration in the revolution" (meaning membership in the party or the UJC, mass organizations, and the military). The rest of the document is an elaboration of these points, and a personal history, including education and work. Of the ones I obtained, only the Cienfuegos biographies had party membership as a separate category (where applicable).

Regarding these biographies, Dilla and González commented that "the method of supplying information is notably sparse."[26] The biographies seem to be more important for supplying information to voters in the larger electoral districts in cities, where voters in one area are less likely than in smaller cities and towns to be familiar with candidates from other areas.

Chilean journalist Marta Harnecker reported that "even though most candidates were known to the majority of voters, at least by sight, not everybody knew all the details of their revolutionary careers, so the revolutionary leadership decided that each candidate should be presented to the people through a political biography sheet accompanied by a photograph." She also mentioned discussions regarding the candidates in gathering places such as the grocery store.[27]

Cuban author and government functionary Domingo García Cárdenas told me in an interview in May 1989 that when he went to read the biographies in his neighborhood, he had to wait for three or four persons to finish reading them before he got his turn. He did not consider voter interest in the biographies atypical. Voters I interviewed at polling places in Havana on election day in 1986 referred to the candidates' biographies among other factors when asked how they decided for whom to vote, even though most were personally acquainted with all the candidates. Two student teachers from Santiago, whom I encountered in a small town in the Sierra Maestra, where they were doing their training, told me that, because they were not personally acquainted with the candidates, they studied the biographies, spoke to local residents, and, in the month between the nominations and elections, tried to verify what they had learned about the candidates in this way.[28]

In their study of Santa Cruz del Norte, a city of twenty-eight thousand inhabitants situated about thirty miles north of Havana, Dilla and Fernández found that the posted biographies were not an important informational source for the voters: "In the interviews done only 32 percent of the electors affirmed having read the biographies and only 9 percent considered them to be the most effective way to obtain information about their candidates."[29] In the survey of voters in *Bohemia*, a university student in Cienfuegos stated, "It is necessary to analyze better those who are elected delegates. We cannot be guided only by a biography that presents many virtues but does not reflect whether they have the capacity to represent the people."[30]

The inadequacy of depending only on posted biographies was conceded by Cuban political commentator Susana Lee, who wrote that the biographies "do not tell all or what they tell is insufficient, and it would be worthwhile to consider for future processes which other things could be done so that . . . each voter could know other aspects of those candidates with whom he is not acquainted."[31] The secretary of the CEN for the 1997 municipal elections, Juan Aizpura Rodríguez, acknowledged the need to include in the posted biographies not only in which important tasks the candidates had participated and the recognition received, but also the candidates' capacity to lead, organize, and mobilize.[32]

Some cubanologists have viewed the use of biographies as a mechanism for excluding those opposed to the government or the socialist system, as such "derogatory" information would be included. Jorge Domínguez has suggested, without citing examples, that because the candidates cannot exclude information in the published biographies, "This has been used in order to discourage candidates who displease the government. In order to avoid humiliations, some candidates have withdrawn from the contest."[33] President Castro has alluded to negative points in candidates' biographies:

> This process also shows that there are citizens who did not have revolutionary merits in the past and, in some cases, they even had shortcomings. . . . Some of the candidates who were nominated have no revolutionary past and some of them even have negative things on their record. . . . The majority of the people in this situation have decided—and we feel the decision is a correct one—that the matter in question be included in the biography and thus be made known to the masses. . . . We feel that any citizen may have made a mistake at a given moment but then he may make great and extraordinary efforts to vindicate himself.[34]

Harnecker related how printing such derogatory information affected the candidates in the 1976 election:

> When the biographical profiles of these candidates were being prepared . . . it was found, that 1,276 (that is, 4.4 percent) had police records. Of these, 78 had been involved in documented counterrevolutionary activities and 60 in other suspicious matters; 80 had belonged to repressive agencies supporting the tyranny, and 251 had applied for passports to leave the country. During ensuing talks with 633 of these candidates 156 decided to drop their candidacy, but 477 opted to remain in the contest, even though this meant that their biographies would note their past offenses. As for the other 643 cases, they involved matters of minor significance, and the charges were omitted from the biographical profiles.[35]

In a discussion with a small group of delegates in the municipality of Cienfuegos on October 10, 1987, I was told that a delegate from Electoral District 21 had once been convicted of falsifying documents, and this fact appeared in his biography. He had been delegate for eight years and had tremendous prestige in his district: "He had made a mistake and paid for it, and the people understood."

Dilla and González also found that whereas the purpose of the campaign biographies is to ensure equality among the candidates, in fact they may operate to the disadvantage of younger candidates and women, who tend to have shorter lists of accomplishments. In the case of women, this can be explained by discriminatory attitudes against women and by lack of time, as women in Cuba usually have to combine work with running the household. Approximately 80 percent of the delegates have been men, the majority being over thirty years old.[36]

As the research of Dilla and Fernández has shown, however, the biographies may be less important in determining voters' preferences than personal acquaintance with or knowledge of the candidates, as well as word of mouth.[37] Although the 1992 Electoral Law allows for candidates to participate in public meetings and visit workplaces, and these activities occurred during the 1993 and 1998 national and provincial elections, this type of formal interchange has not taken place in municipal delegate elections "perhaps for reasons of time, organization or other grounds."[38] The election process is not political. Propaganda in favor of a candidate is not allowed. However, some informal, unorganized campaigning does take place among voters and by candidates. In their public expressions, the candidates cannot issue electoral promises or make gifts with the aim of inducing the voters to vote for them, nor can they carry out campaigns that damage the prestige of any candidate.[39]

According to Gail Reed, "Voters can of course get together informally to argue the pros and cons of the candidates."[40] LeoGrande found that voters do discuss the candidates among themselves: "Informal conversations on the merits of various candidates are frequent and often heated."[41] In all my interviews with delegates and voters, and in all nomination meetings I attended, I heard very few negative references made regarding any of the candidates either by the voters or by other candidates.

One delegate I interviewed in Cienfuegos told me, "There are delegates who do campaign for reelection by visiting the people in the electoral district, showing concern for their problems, but it is not an official campaign." If renominated, delegates can, if they wish, tell voters what they have accomplished in order to get reelected. However, he emphasized, candidates are really not in a position to make campaign promises, such as, for example, promising a family doctor for a neighborhood:

> Look, now there is a demand that is coming from all municipalities and zones and the delegate supports the voters who make the demand. What is the demand? The family doctor. All zones want the family doctor, because it is good

thing to have a doctor close, who looks after the children's health. But this responds to a development plan that gives priority to the zones in the mountains, that are very far from the hospitals. . . . The voters and the delegates want a family doctor, but these are not things within the purview of the delegate.

One theme I heard repeatedly was that in general, voters do not like candidates overtly campaigning. Juan Montelongo, delegate from the Twenty-first Electoral District in Playa, told me in December 1987 that campaigning could hurt rather than help a candidate and gave the example of the opponent he had defeated in the 1986 election: "Carmita visited local CDR offices accompanied by the previous delegate. She then introduced herself and discussed certain problems with the people. This was a way of campaigning in her favor." Harnecker interviewed several voters who complained about a candidate's campaign in Marianao, a municipality within the City of Havana: "He had a few small rallies requesting support in the polling booth. On election day he visited all the polling places so the people could see him. . . . That disgusted us, since for us the delegate must be a humble person, not given to self promotion."[42]

Fajardo told me that voters questioned him after he had been nominated for municipal assembly delegate: "These are the neighbors with whom one is in daily contact. It is not a type of propaganda." His response to voters who asked if he would try to meet local needs was that "one has to be a little conservative because [the delegate] does not control or manage the resources." Furthermore, he made clear to voters that while he might have lacked experience in the OPP, he had had leadership experience and knew that there were things that could and things that could not be resolved: "Thus we must say that we will make the effort to resolve everything that is within our reach."

In an interesting twist, Fajardo told me that there were a few voters in his district who had campaigned against him, with one especially making a great effort to see him defeated, the reason being that word was out that if elected, he would leave his post as administrator of the local pig farm. Workers there did not want him to leave the pig farm, where he had achieved such excellent results, and told people not to vote for him because he was needed in the pork industry and his leaving would hurt the enterprise. Fajardo assured me that nothing negative was said about him in this campaign.

Although their activity does not constitute a campaign, the local media in Cienfuegos have provided preelection publicity for candidates. For example, prior to a municipal election, one of the candidates in one election district was interviewed by the local newspaper, *Cinco de Septiembre*, and the other candidate was interviewed by the local radio station, *Radio Ciudad del Mar*.

Dilla and Fernández found that 82 percent of the voters they interviewed in Santa Cruz had decided whom to vote for prior to election day. Sixty six percent reported that direct personal contact with the candidates and conversations with neighbors and family members were the most important inputs. The high percentage citing these reasons was attributed by the authors to the fact that Santa Cruz is a small city, as opposed to Havana, for example, where such contacts are more sporadic. According to my findings in Havana, most delegates were first nominated in the area where they resided, and where the vote on election day was split, the candidates received the largest majorities in their own areas, indicating the importance voters give to being personally acquainted with the candidates. Next in order of importance after direct personal contact were the arguments made in favor of the candidates at the nomination meetings. In Dilla and Fernández's findings, 33 percent found these presentations useful in determining for whom to vote.[43]

Voters I spoke to at polling places on election day in 1986 justified their support for candidates in terms similar to the statements made in support of proposed candidates in the nomination meetings, referring to age, experience, and revolutionary and personal merits. More concrete reasons were sometimes offered in support of those who were already delegates. For example, in Bauta, a voter pointed out that the delegate had fought to improve the road that passed by the polling place.

Dilla and Fernández found that the most important factors influencing voters' decisions were personal moral considerations, such as honesty. When asked how they had decided for whom to vote, almost invariably voters' answers included that the candidates were "revolutionary," but their explanations of what the adjective *revolutionary* meant tended to emphasize ethical more than political qualities, such as "solidarity with neighbors," "sensitivity toward others," "good human relations," and other qualities less edifying such as "decency" or "good family." Closely linked to these but on a second plane came political considerations, such as "loyalty to the revolution" and "political combativeness." They also referred to the candidates' potential for being effective in their conduct as delegate.[44]

Some voters told me they based their decisions on youth, whereas others preferred maturity and experience. Montelongo told me that when he ran for delegate in 1986, the existing delegate was not renominated because the voters preferred someone younger and perhaps more capable:

> The previous delegate had some problems in his performance. His manner of speaking was confused. Thus while he was conducting accountability sessions with his constituents, at times one could not understand what he was saying, and that bothered the people, even though he might have done good work in carrying through with the *planteamientos*, and in holding discussions with directors of enterprises to find solutions to problems presented by the voters.

Fajardo told me that one possible reason more voters preferred him to the candidate he had defeated was that he had developed a reputation for being very active in meetings and in helping to resolve problems in his electoral district. The delegates I met with in Cienfuegos also stressed prestige in the neighborhood. One told me, "I have lived almost my whole life in this neighborhood. The people know me well; they know my political development; they know my family." Another said that the reasons he had been reelected in Cienfuegos included his becoming directly involved in resolving neighborhood problems, not only soliciting materials to build sidewalks and streets but also contributing his personal labor. When a young, well-regarded professional member of the executive committee in Playa, whose responsibilities included housing, was not reelected in 1989, the explanation offered by other delegates was that his duties on the municipal assembly executive committee, together with his studies, had not left him sufficient time for serving his constituents. One opinion offered was that his constituents felt that because he was in a leadership post, he should have given them preference for better housing. The local FMC and CDR reported that from what they had heard in the neighborhoods before the election, they had not expected him to be reelected.

Prior to the 1995 municipal elections, the Cuban press also stressed the need for nominating and electing qualified candidates, by reviewing the tasks and responsibilities of the municipal delegates: finding solutions for immediate necessities, such as those related to food, health and transportation, explaining why many problems cannot be resolved in the short term, and acting as coordinators for local actions to remedy local difficulties. It was emphasized that delegates should also be the intermediaries between their constituents and the municipal assembly, but that as members of the latter, they must go beyond the interests of their own electoral districts.[45] An editorial in *Trabajadores* stated, "The delegates who will be elected in the next elections should completely abandon the formalistic type of relationship which is only confined to their being accountable to constituents and to receiving complaints and opinions, by converting themselves into sponsors of popular initiatives and into guides for the community."[46] The same points were stressed by Lee: "In judging a good delegate, voters at times do not consider elements which go beyond solving local problems, such as mobilizing the community, displaying and acting on initiatives which benefit the social and political ambiance, because he who always says 'yes' is not always the best."[47]

How is one to explain why over 60 percent of the municipal assembly delegates are members of either the Cuban Communist Party or the UJC, when only about 15 percent of the population belong these organizations? Domínguez attributed this difference in part to what he called the party's right to "distribute propaganda or organize meetings regarding the elections. Thus, government critics cannot exchange points of view nor information; they cannot associate."[48] Ritter, while acknowledging that the individual characteristics of party members are partly responsible, offered the explanation that "collusion, either implicit or explicit, among Party members is probable . . . in view of the organizational monopoly of the Party and its junior affiliate, together with the old-boy networks it nurtures, and the certification of good character and ideological correctness it provides."[49]

Ritter's evidence is that the local electoral commissions have party representatives, which he surmised must "scrutinize and approve or disapprove of nominees." Furthermore, "because of the organizational monopoly of the party, any support for noncompliant nominees is likely to be of a neighborhood favourite-son nature." As opposed to such fragmented support, what Ritter called "the Party/UJC machine" gets its members to support "the certified candidate(s)."[50]

My data lead me to reject this argument, as does Dilla.[51] Dilla and Fernández found that in Santa Cruz, "All the persons interviewed . . . denied that the party or any other organization had exhorted them to propose any candidate, to vote for any candidate or accept being nominated."[52] Similar results were found in other studies.[53]

My findings and those of Dilla indicate that whether or not a perspective nominee or a candidate for municipal delegate is a party member is not a decisive factor in how voters decide for whom to vote. In the nomination meetings I attended, party affiliation was in no case given prominence, and lack of party affiliation was never mentioned as a negative trait. Not one of the voters I interviewed mentioned party affiliation in their evaluation of candidates or delegates.

Responding to my question about what had most influenced her vote in the last municipal election, a constituent of Montelongo's stated that although she had known the three candidates for many years, she had voted for Montelongo because she believed he "had the best possibilities for success in carrying out the tasks, the best understanding and a way with words." She did not mention that he and the other male candidate were party members or, until I brought it up, that the woman candidate was not. She pointed out that Montelongo and his woman opponent had been almost even in the first balloting and that he had only narrowly defeated her in the second round of voting.

In 1988, Carlos Walfrido Rodriguez, a black man and not at that time a party member, had been reelected twice in an electoral district in the Miramar section of Playa, which before the revolution was a white middle- and upper-middle-class neighborhood and now is mixed (poor people having taken over houses abandoned by those who fled). Both times, he had defeated candidates who were party members, and the reason was made clear to me by his constituents: They considered him a marvelous delegate. To be sure, I also found many outstanding delegates who were party members and had been reelected, but party membership did not seem to be a deciding or even a relevant factor in whom voters supported..

Dilla and Fernández reported similar findings. Of the twenty-three people interviewed in Santa Cruz who had proposed candidates in the nomination meetings, only four mentioned the party affiliation in their presentations, and only one considered it important. Among the 150 voters interviewed, only 3 mentioned party affiliation as a desirable factor in their decision about for whom to vote. Yet, in the five electoral districts in which the interviews took place in Santa Cruz, nine of the ten candidates were members of either the party or the UJC. In the nineteen electoral districts in which the contest was between a party member and a nonmember, the latter won in twelve.[54] Finally, a large number of voters were not aware of whether the candidates belonged to the party or the UJC, perhaps because membership is organized by workplace and not by neighborhood.[55]

In line with these data is LeoGrande's explanation of the relatively high percentage of delegates affiliated with the party: "At the municipal level, it is probably because party members are more likely than non-members to be well known and well regarded in their communities."[56]

Given the lack of possibilities of financial gain or privileges for them and the sacrifices involved in the great amount of work required of municipal delegates, those citizens without a desire to serve their constituencies and lacking socialist consciousness are less likely to accept the nomination. But these are the attributes expected of party members, who tend to "have a greater disposition to participate,"[57] and the party expects its members, if possible, to accept such responsibility if nominated.

The party recruits as members some delegates who have shown leadership qualities and are respected and admired by their colleagues. For example, Daniel Morales, the former president of the *consejo popular* in the Santa Fe section of Playa, was not a party member when he was elected municipal delegate and then provincial assembly delegate and chair of the municipal assembly's commerce commission. In May 1989, he had been chosen to be a professional member of the municipal assembly executive committee and at the same time became a candidate for party membership. By 1992, he was a party member, and in 1993, he was elected as a National Assembly deputy from Playa. Similarly, during the late 1980s, Carlos Walfrido Rodriguez was a municipal delegate, a provincial delegate, and a professional member of the Playa municipal assembly executive committee, but he was not a member of the PCC. He became a party member in the early 1990s. Gail Lindenberg, during her study of the labor union of the textile factory in Bauta, found that the person elected as head of the union at the plant was subsequently invited to join the party.[58]

Since the first municipal elections in 1976, the turnout of eligible voters has been above 95 percent in the first round and a bit lower for the runoff elections. On October 19, 1986, 97.7 percent of those eligible voted, electing 12,623 municipal delegates, and where no candidate had received a majority, 93.6 percent voted in the runoff elections a week later, electing the remaining 633 delegates. On April 30, 1989, 98.3 percent of the eligible voters went to the polls to vote for municipal assembly delegates, and 13,815 delegates were elected. However, at a special election in 1987 I observed in Playa, only a little over 50 percent voted. Voters cast secret ballots in enclosed voting booths. Elections are held on Sundays, from seven in the morning until six at night.

When Ernesto Suárez, secretary of the National Assembly and of the National Electoral Commission, was asked, "If someone opted not to vote, would he have problems? Would he be reprimanded?" he responded, "No, no. He would not have any problem; this is precisely one of the liberties that characterizes our democratic process. The vote in Cuba is free and is exercised by that person who is disposed to do so, but there is nothing that obliges him, nor would he be punished."[59] Neither in my interviews and observations in Cuba nor in the research of other scholars (even those very critical of the Cuban system) have I found any evidence or analysis that counters this statement.[60] However, there are informal pressures to vote. Some voters told me that failure to vote could be looked upon unfavorably in a person's work center.

The election districts are small enough, especially in the more rural districts, for voting to be considered a social as well as a political occasion. On October 19, 1986, touring urban and rural polling stations in and near Havana, I found everywhere a concern on the part of those working there to make sure everyone had an opportunity to vote. For example, if a neighbor had not appeared someone might be sent to his or her house to see if there were some problem. Polls open at 7 A.M., and in the polling places I visited, from 75 to over 90 percent had already voted by noon. There was a concerted effort to encourage voting and to make it as convenient as possible for everyone to vote. In rural areas, buses were available to transport to polling sites the elderly and infirm and others unable to provide their own transportation. Those who lived close enough to the voting station could request escorts from Pioneers, the youth group to which most Cuban children, ages six to twelve, belong. For those unable to leave home because of young children, volunteers provided child care while they cast their ballots. I spoke to people in the countryside who had traveled long distances on bicycles and horseback to vote. A local supervisor told me that one man who was unable to leave his job was provided with a ballot delivered by two pioneers to his work place. The municipality in Bauta kept track of the percentage of voters in each election district between 11 A.M. and 3 P.M. in order to be able to respond to problems voters have had in getting to voting stations before they closed at 6 P.M.

On July 9, 1995, 7,568,548 citizens, constituting 97.1 percent of those eligible, voted, electing 97.7 percent of the 14,229 delegates. Of the ballots,

Open air polling station in a rural area on the outskirts of Havana for municipal assembly elections in October 1986. By noon most people in this small election district had already voted.

11.3 percent were not valid: 4.3 percent were blank ballots, and 7 percent were nullified. Violations of the electoral law, such as early closing of the voting places and having candidates' family members in charge at voting places, were found in six electoral districts. In one electoral district, citizens informed authorities that names of people who did not live in the district were found on the list of eligible voters. In these cases, the election was repeated during the second round. Of those registered, 89.2 percent voted in the second round held on July 16 in 332 electoral districts; 330 delegates were elected. Two elections ended in tie votes, necessitating a third round of voting,[61] in which 97.1 percent of those eligible voted. Miguel Centeno's contention, "The local elections of 1995 also revealed significant discontent, especially in La Habana,"[62] is not supported by sources or statistics.

Of the incumbent candidates, 50.8 percent were not reelected by the voters (only in 1979 and 1984 was a lower percentage not reelected), and 40.2 percent of the incumbent municipal assembly presidents and 61.5 percent of the vice presidents were not reelected by the municipal assembly delegates. According to National Assembly Secretary Ernesto Suárez, "Although these results reflect the complete capacity of the system to constantly change and renovate the people's representatives, they could also reflect ... the dissatisfaction of sectors of the population with the performance of a large number of delegates and of the municipal governments."[63] However, Suárez contended that using the electoral system to express voter dissatisfaction reinforces the legitimacy of the political institutions.[64] Miguel Ferrer León, a municipal delegate since the inception of the OPP in 1976, responded to a question on strengthening the government in the series in *Granma* on the twentieth anniversary of the OPP: "Also we must end the instability of the delegates. Where they are changed constantly things cannot go well."[65]

The number of women elected rose from 13.55 percent of the delegates in 1992 to 15.53 percent, even though women make up more than 50 percent of the voting population. Only 6.8 percent of those elected as municipal assembly presidents and vice presidents were women. This outcome led Luis Suárez to conclude that in combating machismo, "More efficient ways must be found to present voters with a better image of women's qualifications and capacity for leadership."[66] After voting in his electoral district in Santiago on July 9, President Castro said that he had carefully read the biographies of the two candidates and had had difficulty choosing among the two: "There was no woman," he explained. "When there is a woman I do not look much at the biographies and I vote for the woman, almost on principle. I have made it a matter of conscience to participate in this manner in the search for equality."[67]

Of the delegates elected in 1995, 71 percent belonged to the Communist Party, 8 percent more than the historical average. Combined with the UJC, Communist Party members made up 80 percent of the delegates, 4 percent more than the average of previous years. PCC and UJC members make up 20 percent of the population. While Suárez attributed these results to the "positive identification of voters with the virtues, qualifications and political vocation possessed by many members of the PCC and UJC," he also favored attempts to increase the number of those who are not members. "This is essential to permanently broadening the base that sustains the social program proclaimed by Cuba's Communist Party."[68]

On election day, October 19, 1997, 97.59 percent of those eligible elected 13,435 of the 14,533 municipal delegates, up from 97.1 percent in 1995. Of the ballots cast, 7.21 percent were left blank or annulled, down from 11.3 percent in 1995. In the second round, held on October 26 in the 1,098 districts where no candidate received a majority, 94.77 percent voted compared with 89.2 percent in the 1995 runoff. Of those who won, 49.5 percent were incumbents, 17 percent were women, 12.5 percent were under thirty years old, 76.18 percent were PCC members, 31.47 held university degrees, and 7.21 percent belonged to the UJC. Representing the different sectors within Cuban society, among the delegates elected were 2,265 workers, 2,649 technicians *(técnicos),* 1,426 administrative workers, 441 employees in the service sector, 5,388 managers *(dirigentes),* 10 students, 380 soldiers, 453 employees of the Interior Ministry, 624 retirees, 170 housewives, 64 self-employed workers, 575 farmers, and 88 in other occupations.[69]

Following the 1995 elections, an editorial in *Trabajadores* complained of the wall of silence in the foreign press, maintaining that when speculations about the vote's indicating strong disagreements or rejection by the population are not confirmed, then the Cuban elections disappear from the news. The message of the seven and a half million Cubans who voted is obscured by the demand that Cuba become a liberal democracy, by the refusal to accept the validity of the Cuban model: "One cannot make a comparison because they are distinct electoral systems which respond to distinct ideals and realities."[70]

In the *New York Times,* the only mention of the 1995 elections came as an afterthought at the end of an article on the lessening of tensions: "When the Government held local elections last month with its usual one party slate, it reported a turnout of 97.1 percent and only a small percentage of blank and nullified ballots."[71] I responded in a Letter to the Editor to correct Golden's error in referring to a one-party slate: "In local elections for municipal delegates, the Communist Party has no say in nominating candidates, nor do candidates have to be members."[72]

Prior to the 1992 Constitution and Electoral Law, the municipal assembly president had been selected by the municipal candidacy commission and ratified by the executive committee, but under the new rules, two candidates (both have to be municipal delegates) are presented to the delegates by the commission. By majority vote, the delegates can accept both or reject one or both of the candidates presented. In a vote by secret ballot, the delegates elect one as the assembly president and the other as vice president, by placing two X's for their choice for president and one X for vice president. For each post, the candidate must have a majority of the votes cast to be elected.[73] The provincial assembly leadership is chosen by the same procedure as in the municipal assembly. From the two candidates proposed by the provincial candidacy commission, both of whom must be delegates, the delegates decide by secret ballot which one will be president and which one vice president.

In the debate on the electoral law at the October 1992 National Assembly session, one deputy stated there should be one election for municipal assembly president and a separate election for vice president. Arguing for keeping one election, Juan Escalona, National Assembly president at the time, stated that the municipal candidacy commissions would have done extensive work to find candidates, and the municipal assembly delegates would have the right to reject either candidate prior to the election. President Castro argued that both candidates needed to have the qualities necessary to be president, and thus one should be president and the other vice president. This clause was not changed.[74]

On June 20, 1995, three weeks prior to the election, the municipal candidacy commissions, presided over by a CTC representative and consisting of representatives from the CDR, the FMC, the ANAP, the FEU, and the FEEM, commenced the search from among the candidates for municipal delegates, for nominees for president and vice president to be presented to the municipal assemblies at the constituent session on July 30. Because some candidates chosen by the candidacy commissions subsequently might not be elected as municipal delegates, and because the municipal assembly delegates could reject any of the proposed candidate prior to the vote, the candidacy commissions had a reserve list of other possible candidates to propose.[75] As with candidacy commissions in prior mandates before the 1992 electoral law, the search process began with far-ranging consultation with municipal delegates, in local work centers and organizations, and with neighbors, involving hundreds of people.

The newly elected municipal assemblies were constituted on July 30, the main order of business being the election of the assembly president and vice president. Responding to international criticisms of the single-candidacy system (presenting only two candidates for the two positions), Lee gave examples where the assemblies had rejected the candidates presented by the commissions:

> There were various municipalities in the country that by a show of hands did not approve of one of the candidates, and I even have information that at least in one, they did not approve of any of the proposals presented by the commission for one position and the candidate then submitted by the assembly was elected, and in another, even after the list of candidates was approved, one did not obtain the majority of the secret votes cast, and a new round of proposals and voting was necessary.[76]

Following the 1997 elections, the newly elected municipal assemblies were constituted on November 2, at which time the municipal candidacy commissions submitted the candidates for assembly presidents and vice presidents. According to reports in the Cuban press, the commissions members began the process of deciding on candidates by attending the neighborhood nominating meetings for municipal delegates to hear the public's opinions. They then analyzed the candidates' biographies posted in the neighborhoods. After the elections, they canvassed their neighborhoods and workplaces or schools regarding the three criteria: capabilities, leadership possibilities, and acceptance by the public. For example, the commission in La Lisa, a municipality in the City of Havana, covered the seven *consejos populares* and consulted with all 108 delegates.[77]

The *consejos populares* are also reorganized following the municipal elections. This reorganization includes new elections for president and vice president, choosing the representatives from the mass organizations and the

UJC, and deciding which local economic entities should belong to the *consejo popular*. In some *consejos,* important economic entities may have been excluded, and new ones may have grown to the point where they should be included.[78]

In Cuba, voters' right to recall their representatives has been historically an integral part of the *mandat impératif.* The rules for the municipal assembly provide for the recall of a delegate who "has systematically failed to fulfill his duties, or has lost the confidence of those who elected him, or has been convicted of a crime proving him unworthy of public trust, or has behaved in a way that is incompatible with the honor of being the people's representative to an organ of People's Power."[79]

Recall may be proposed either by at least 20 percent of the delegates of the municipal assembly to which the delegate belongs or by at least 20 percent of the voters in the electoral district. An assembly officer then calls a meeting of the delegate's constituents, a majority of whom must be present. The petition for recall is presented, along with arguments for and against. The delegate in question is invited to present his side. This meeting then votes on whether there should be a formal, secret recall election. If the delegate is subsequently voted out of office, nomination meetings are convened in the electoral district and followed by the election of a new delegate.[80]

Ritter argued that the threat of recall gives the PCC potential control over the delegates, although he presented no evidence to support this argument and admitted that the voters have the ultimate say on this matter: "While the recall may help to ensure that delegates are responsive and responsible to their electors, it is possible that this mechanism could be used to induce conformity and, in the extreme, to weed out troublemakers and upstarts. . . . Whether a recall of this sort has been carried out is not yet known."[81] In a recall procedure that I observed in Playa in late 1987, the delegate was charged with and admitted having made lewd advances to a young girl. In this case, the municipal assembly initiated the procedures, and the voters agreed and voted to recall him, although he had performed well as delegate.

The voters do not necessarily go along with what the local government and party leaders deem proper. I was told of a case in a municipality in the western Province of Pinar del Río in which the delegate was found to be having an extramarital affair and the local party and municipal assembly leaders initiated a recall, but the voters elected to keep him. It seemed that he was an excellent delegate who served his constituents well.

Again, when voters in a municipality in the center of the country petitioned for the recall of their delegate, their anger had to do with the fact that their houses were not yet connected to electricity—something that was not within the power of their delegate to accomplish. In this case, the delegate decided to resign before the recall could come to a formal vote. Harnecker reported that in a municipality in Sancti Spiritus Province, the voters recalled their delegate "because he didn't do the job. We'd brought a number of problems to his attention, but he did nothing. The *compañeros* would stop by his office, and he wouldn't be in. We also learned that he didn't attend the meetings at the municipality."[82] In the municipality of Marianao, a delegate was found to be in collusion with the local butcher in shortchanging people on their purchases. When he learned that 65 percent of the voters in his district had signed the eight-page document accusing him of wrongdoing and requesting a recall election, he resigned.[83]

The survey of Cuban voters in *Bohemia* indicated that there was a reluctance on the part of voters to use the recall mechanism and widespread ignorance of the procedure. After interviewing a voter in Havana who complained that his delegate responded to constituents' complaints only around election time, the authors concluded that recall was not proposed because "it seems this procedure . . . is little known or unknown; or does it perhaps become difficult in each case to face the advisability and necessity of applying it?"[84]

Candidacy Commissions

Prior to the 1992 Constitution and Election Law, every two and one half years, following the completion of the second round of municipal delegate elections, the municipal assembly met to elect delegates to the provincial assembly and ratify the selection of its executive committee. Every five years, the municipal delegates also elected deputies to the National Assembly. The nominations for these positions were made by the municipal candidacy commission, composed of representatives of the municipal branches of the CDR, the CTC, the FMC, and the UJC and presided over by the municipal party representative. Although the composition of the candidacy commissions and the election procedures have since changed—the PCC and the UJC are no longer represented, the provincial assembly delegates and the National Assembly deputies are elected directly by the people, and the municipal assembly elects its president and vice president—it is relevant to this study to reveal how the commission selected candidates because essentially the same guidelines are still used by the candidacy commissions in choosing potential nominees for these positions.

In May 1989, during the week prior to convening the newly elected municipal assembly in Playa, I participated in some of the activities related to the election of the assembly's executive committee and interviewed the members of the candidacy commission and some of the newly elected members of the executive committee. Near the end of the term, the municipal party bureau had evaluated the performance of all the members of the municipal assembly executive committee and issued written recommendations regarding whether they should continue serving on the executive committee if reelected as delegates. These recommendations became an important part of the material the candidacy commission used to evaluate candidates.

The commission used various other sources in producing their evaluations: the *estado de opinión* compiled by the local PCC, the views of the electoral commission in the delegates' districts, the opinions of other delegates, the neighborhood party nuclei and fellow workers in the delegates' workplaces, and the written report of the secretary of the municipal assembly. The main points taken into account were (1) age; (2) percentage of votes received in the election to be delegate; (3) gender, to achieve a balance between men and women; (4) race, to also include black and mulatto members; (5) place of employment, to avoid having only professionals and excluding manual laborers; (6) track record as delegate; (7) having sufficient time to serve; and (8) the likelihood of being elected as member of the executive committee. Party affiliation was not mentioned as a criterion. Of the 104 delegates, 50 were initially selected as potential candidates, and this number was narrowed to 29 and then to 19 (12 of them party members). Of the nineteen, 13 had not previously been members of the executive committee.

The commission also determined which of these, if elected to the executive committee, would be recommended to the newly elected executive committee to fill the professional slots on the committee (those in charge of specific sectors like health and education). Because this recommendation was contingent on their being elected delegate and to the executive committee, the commission had a reserve candidate for each professional position. The qualities mentioned with regard to professional members were charisma, intelligence, leadership potential, and the party's opinion. The president of Playa's municipal assembly told me that, especially for the post of assembly president, it was important that the individual have won the election for delegate by a wide margin. Finally, priority was given to those who had served as professional members and had received good evaluations. Three candidates who were not party members were elected to the executive committee and were chosen and ratified for the professional positions overseeing construction and housing, education, and commerce and gastronomy.

The new executive committee met immediately, and the candidate for assembly president was proposed by the first secretary of the municipal party and elected by the committee. Next, the candidates for the other professional slots were presented to the executive committee by the president of the candidacy commission and voted on and approved. The results were then ratified by the municipal assembly delegates by a show of hands. In fact, these selections had been more-or-less determined beforehand. Members of the commission had canvassed all 19 candidates prior to the convening session of the municipal assembly to determine if they were willing to serve. The candidates to be recommended for the professional positions were informed that they were being considered and were asked whether they would be willing to take leave from their regular jobs. In the case of a high school teacher, the commission had also consulted the municipal director of education regarding the delegate's taking leave from his teaching post.

Special elections for executive committee positions occurred in Bauta and Playa in 1988. Mario García of Bauta and Roberto Diaz Vence of Playa, who had served as municipal assembly presidents for many years and were respected in their municipal assemblies and well-known in their municipalities, resigned to assume administrative positions in their respective provinces.[85] In Bauta, a special session of the assembly was convened, during which the president announced that the executive committee recommended that the vice president become president. This recommendation was approved by the delegates and, because it did not concern electing a new member to the executive committee, was approved by a show of hands. Subsequently the candidacy commission proposed two candidates for the election of a new vice president by secret ballot.

At a special assembly held in Playa, it was announced by the president that the executive committee had recommended that the vice president, Luis Olivera, become president, and that the woman in charge of education become vice president. An election was then held to fill the education position on the executive committee. The election was conducted by the president of the candidacy commission, with candidates recommended by this commission. Carlos Walfrido Rodríguez was elected by a vote of sixty to nine. Olivera remained in office after the 1989 election but shortly thereafter began having difficulties, mainly of style and communication, that brought complaints from the delegates. In fact, prior to his becoming president, I had heard him express his reluctance to assume this office. He discussed his problems with the executive committee, and then he and the committee met with the candidacy commission and an agreement was reached that he would resign. It was he who presented to the assembly the candidate to succeed him as president, and he stayed on as a delegate. His resignation had nothing to do with ideology or policy, and in any case, it did not appear to have been initiated by the party.

Prior to 1992, every two and one half years the municipal assembly elected the provincial assembly delegates. The municipal candidacy commission presented the municipal assembly with a list of candidates. Then as now, provincial delegates could be municipal delegates (*de base*) or other citizens (*directos*). The president of the municipal assembly served as delegate to the provincial assembly ex officio. In May 1988, I attended a meeting of the municipal candidacy commission in Playa called to choose candidates to fill three mid-term vacancies for provincial delegates. The vacancies to be filled had come about for different reasons: one because the delegate had left for an international mission, a second because the delegate had moved out of the municipality, and a third because the delegate had been recalled by the voters in his district. Present at the meeting were the secretary general of the municipal branch of the FMC, the municipal coordinator of the CDR, the first secretary of the Playa CTC, the first secretary of the Playa UJC, and, as chair, Nérida Quintero, a member of the party's municipal bureau.

The fact that Quintero chaired the meeting did not necessarily mean that she dominated. The most influential person seemed to be Manuel Avila, the CDR coordinator, because he had the most information regarding the delegates: He was best acquainted with the delegates; had attended many neighborhood meetings, including accountability sessions; and was best informed as to how the people regarded their delegates. Party membership was not one of the criteria discussed and did not seem to be an important consideration. None of the four candidates proposed by the commission was a party member at that time. All were municipal delegates, as all the positions had been previously filled by *de base* delegates.

During the ten days prior to the meeting, the members of the candidacy commission studied the biographies of the ninety-five municipal delegates. The commission took into account the opinion of the neighborhood party nucleus and the electoral commission. Among the first criteria discussed was support for the delegates among their constituents, including the number of votes received when nominated, the number of votes received when elected, and whether or not it had been necessary to go to a second round in the voting.

At the commission's request, the secretary of the municipal assembly of Playa, Mercedes Rodriguez, provided information regarding each delegate and reported that the executive committee had recommended fifteen delegates as possible candidates. The commission members commenced their deliberations by eliminating from consideration delegates who were National Assembly deputies or members of the Playa executive committee, those whose work would not allow them sufficient time, those who were too old, and those who lacked experience. Ideological factors were not mentioned, but strong support for the Cuban Revolution was obviously presupposed.

Seventeen potential candidates were eliminated for a variety of reasons— insufficient involvement with constituents and problems in the workplace, too many time-consuming responsibilities, immaturity, negative reports from local CDR leaders or other sources regarding effectiveness as delegates, or insufficient social and intellectual development and sophistication. There was also an attempt to avoid having all candidates be intellectuals or professionals, for example, as opposed to manual laborers. The main sources of information were the municipal assembly secretary's report (especially concerning performance as municipal delegate) and the resources and contacts of the CDR coordinator. After this screening process, ten names remained, and four of those were selected as candidates. These four had support from the party nuclei and the CDR of their electoral districts. One was Daniel

Morales, a high school teacher in his early thirties. His electoral district was in the community of Santa Fe. Avila said that the people there had for some time been demanding representation in higher-level representative bodies: "You know that in Santa Fe the people feel strongly about such things." Thus it was agreed that it would be good to have a representative of Santa Fe in the provincial assembly. There was also general agreement that Daniel had been an excellent delegate and was young and full of energy.[86]

Another candidate, Carlos Walfrido Rodríguez, was a university professor, forty-eight years old at the time, who had been elected municipal delegate three times and had maintained strong support among the voters. In the 1986 election, he had won 1,200 out of 1,833 votes. This strong support, it was felt, was related to the attention he gave his constituents. Avila remarked, "You've got to see his accountability sessions." It was pointed out that he had administrative experience from his work as president of the Playa assembly's education commission.

A third candidate was Guillermo Pérez, thirty-eight years old, a worker in an electric plant with an excellent work record. On the plus side was his work with his CDR and the fact that he was a manual laborer, a class of workers the commission members were desirous of having represented on the provincial level. He had been elected municipal delegate in the last three elections, but a question was raised about whether he had had sufficiently strong backing in his electoral district in the last election.

The fourth candidate was Gerardo Salgado, forty-three years old, who worked in a medical clinic. The four candidates selected coincided with the recommendations made by the municipal assembly executive committee.

Quintero closed the meeting stating that it would be necessary to contact the four delegates selected to see if they would agree to be candidates. If there were no problems, she would ask the municipal assembly secretary to prepare the biographies and the ballots for the assembly session to be held on June 11. The longest biography by far was that of Rodríguez. Of those elected provincial delegate, he had won the most votes (sixty-eight), followed by Pérez (fifty-five) and Morales (fifty-one). Salgado, with forty-five votes, was not elected.

National and Provincial Assembly Nominations

The 1992 constitutional and electoral reform included the election of provincial assembly delegates and National Assembly deputies by the direct vote of the citizens, whereas formerly they had been elected by the municipal assemblies. These elections are not competitive, as the number of candidates is equal to the number of positions to be filled. Deputies and provincial delegates are nominated by municipal assemblies and are elected by voters within a municipality, or within up to four districts in municipalities where the population exceeds 100,000 inhabitants. To be elected, a candidate must receive a majority of the votes cast. Voters can vote for the whole slate (*voto unido*) in their municipality or district, or for as many individual candidates as they choose. In the 1998 election, 601 deputies and 1,193 provincial delegates were nominated and elected. The provincial delegates' term was changed from two and one half to five years to coincide with the election of the National Assembly deputies. Provincial assembly delegates may also be deputies.

The requirement that at least one half of the deputies and provincial delegates must also be municipal (*de base*) delegates was changed to a stipulation that no more than one half can be municipal delegates. This change means that a significant proportion of the deputies in the highest organ of Cuban representative government and of the provincial delegates are still also municipal delegates, with very close ties to the people who nominated and elected them. It also turns out that the *de base* representatives are usually the most outspoken in assembly debates and most active within assembly commissions.

The rest (*directos*) are selected to represent various sectors of Cuban society and include those with important government and/or party posts and those representing various sectors of society—sports, the arts, science, trade unions, students, teachers, factory workers, farmers, and retired people. Defending this type of sectorial representation, Cuban journalist Fabio Raimundo Torrado quoted from an article in *The Modernization of Latin American Legislatures* published by the Center for Electoral Advising, which is affiliated with the Inter-American Institute of Human Rights in Costa Rica: "In Latin America, the legislatures' weakness is expressed in the insufficiency of legitimate representation: broad sectors do not feel duly represented in their legislatures and see them as a bit distant from their problems."[87]

The *directos* have no residency requirement. Especially in the case of deputy candidates, it is not always possible for the candidates to be elected from the municipality in which they live or work, because those with important positions usually live and work in Havana. The candidacy commission attempts, where possible, to link candidates to municipalities from which they are nominated and elected through birthplace or hometown or through job-related or historical ties (Fidel Castro was a candidate from Santiago). "To go by only the municipality where they live, would result in a disproportionate number of *directo* deputies from the capital city as compared to the rest of the country."[88] It would also leave few openings for less-well-known candidates from Havana. The argument made to support this view was that the National Assembly should not necessarily be a gathering of representatives of municipalities, but that the deputies should be the most capable and represent all sectors of Cuban society so as to compose a national forum. Castro explained that "the deputy should do whatever possible for the district or municipality, without entering into contradiction, but if there is contradiction, the duty of the deputy is to defend the national interests above all."[89] When possible the *directos* attend sessions of the municipal assemblies from which they were nominated, and toward the end of the five-year term, deputies and provincial delegates report to this municipal assembly on how they have carried out their duties.

Because candidates do not necessarily reside in the municipalities that they are to represent, the commissions have to decide, in consultation with the municipal delegates, from which municipalities nationally well-known figures should be candidates. In 1993, I heard resentment of the fact that one candidate for Bauta was from San Antonio de los Baños, the neighboring municipality. The president of the City of Havana Provincial Assembly in 1993, Pedro Chávez, was a provincial assembly candidate from one municipality and National Assembly deputy candidate from another. In six cases, one candidate represented two municipalities in the different bodies to prevent one municipality's voting for the same person twice, and thus having fewer candidates to vote for.

According to the 1992 Electoral Law, suggestions for precandidates for National Assembly deputies and provincial assembly delegates are proposed to the candidacy commissions at all levels mainly by mass organizations, trade unions, and student federations. The provincial and municipal candidacy commissions submit their proposals for deputy candidates to the National Candidacy Commission, which formulates the final list of precandidates, and the municipal candidacy commissions submit their proposals for provincial delegates to the provincial candidacy commissions, which make up the final lists of precandidates. The municipal candidacy commissions are mainly responsible for proposing precandidates who are also municipal delegates. The municipal candidacy commissions subsequently present to the municipal assemblies a list of precandidates equal to the number to be elected from the municipality (together with alternatives if any should be rejected) for nomination as candidates for National Assembly deputies and provincial assembly delegates. Each name submitted is voted on separately by a show of hands, and the precandidate must get a majority of the votes to be nominated. If a precandidate does not receive a majority vote, the candidacy commission must substitute another name.

Proposals for substituting names in place of those submitted by the candidacy commission can be made from the floor and need a majority vote to be accepted. Except for this loophole, only officially sanctioned precandidates are presented for nomination. The opinion of some Cuban social scientists I consulted was that the precandidates for National Assembly deputies were selected at the highest level of the party and government and then filtered through the mass organizations, trade unions, and the municipal assemblies to weed out those unacceptable, unpalatable, or lacking sufficient support within these constituencies.

Dissident groups have complained that this nomination procedure not only denies the possibility that those not accepted by the mass organizations will become candidates on the provincial and national levels, but also the right of choosing to run, of proposing oneself as a candidate or arranging to be proposed. Alarcón, on the other hand, has lauded the Cuban nomination procedures, citing the fact that candidacies are initiated in neighborhood meetings (for municipal delegates) and in mass organizations (for provincial delegates and national deputies) as another of the characteristics that "distinguish us from what is in fashion in the rest of the world" and has said, "The very essence of our system [is that the] candidate is not the person who says: 'I want to aspire to such office, and I launch my candidacy with my funds, with my tools, to steal votes from old people, to threaten others, to bribe, etc., because I want to occupy such office.'"[90]

For the 1993 election, 1.5 million people were consulted, and 70,000 nominees were initially recommended by the main organizations and groups in Cuban society.[91] Given that the candidacy commissions have no party representatives, *El Diario* and *The Economist* were incorrect in reporting that the PCC had a formal role in selecting candidates.[92] All precandidates were interviewed by the commissions. The president of the City of Havana candidacy commission spoke of visiting precandidates in their homes, to know the family situation and the opinion of the neighbors.[93] For example, workers at the factory of a precandidate suggested by the CTC were consulted. The president of the National Candidacy Commission was asked about consultation with the people: "Definitely the masses approve all proposals, be it by neighbors in electoral districts or by workers at work sites, or by plenary meetings of organizations, or a combination of the three. There have been proposals which after consultation were rejected. . . . I know of the case of a vanguard [exemplary] worker who was not accepted because he was no longer a vanguard worker."[94]

For the national and provincial elections held in January 1998, the mass organizations, trade unions, farmers' associations, and student federations recommended precandidates to the candidacy commissions at their national and provincial meetings during September 1997, and at their municipal meetings in September and October. The *de base* precandidates were recommended after the October 19 municipal assembly elections. The National Candidacy Commission split into three working groups covering the eastern, central, and western parts of Cuba. According to commission member Silvano Merced Sen, the consulting process included the workplace, subordinates and superiors, organizations, and neighbors, in order to evaluate the prospective candidates' acceptance within their radius of action. According to the Cuban press, more than 60,000 names were proposed and 1.6 million open consultative meetings were held by the candidacy commissions.[95]

The municipal candidacy commissions submitted the precandidates selected for nomination to the municipal assemblies on January 24, 1993, and on November 28, 1997. The number presented was equal to the number to be nominated, and each candidate was voted on separately. Candidates could be rejected by majority vote of the delegates. In 1993 in Playa, several municipal delegates complained during the municipal assembly session that there had been insufficient consultation with municipal delegates. During the 1997 nominations, *Trabajadores* reported that disagreements were expressed regarding candidates in some municipal assemblies, which made it necessary for the municipal candidacy commission to submit other names. In the municipality Diez de Octubre, some candidates were approved by unanimous votes, and others were approved by a majority in a divided vote, some so close that recounts had to be made. Concerns were raised about the need for more youths and greater diversity among the candidates.[96]

In an interview for an article in *Granma* regarding the nomination process just before the names were submitted in 1997 to the Playa municipal assembly for approval, municipal delegate Daniel Morales reaffirmed the thoroughness of the selection process: "The municipal candidacy commission has conversed with each of us individually four times. First they asked for our opinions about the precandidates who are municipal assembly delegates and then about other colleagues at the provincial or national levels."[97] However, it is curious that with all the consultations and searches to find the best candidates, someone like Morales, who had been president of the Santa Fe *Consejo Popular* and a National Assembly deputy elected in 1993, to his surprise was not presented as a precandidate for *de base* deputy and thus not renominated. To my knowledge, no municipal delegate from Santa Fe was in closer contact or was better known or more admired in the territory than Daniel, desirable characteristics laid out in the press as criteria for being deputy, so one wonders on what basis he was passed over and why there was no protest from the municipal delegates in Playa during the nomination procedure.

Among the National Assembly deputy candidates nominated in 1993, diverse sectors of the society were represented, including two religious leaders, sports figures, journalists, culture and show business personalities, youth representatives (forty-seven were less than thirty years old), family doctors, and important political and economic figures. Only about 20 percent were incumbents. There were fewer historical figures (mainly participants in the revolutionary war) because they were dying off. Workers directly involved in production numbered 123. A little less than half were municipal delegates (*de base*). Eighty-nine presidents of *consejos populares* were candidates; 20 percent were nationally known personalities; and 23 percent were women.[98] Seventy percent of deputies were members of the party, in contrast to the percentage in the previous election, held in 1986, when all but four of the deputies were members either of the Communist Party or the UJC. Of the 601 National Assembly candidates for the 1998 elections, 145 (24.1 percent) were production or service sector workers; 278 (46.25 percent) were municipal delegates, including 90 presidents and vice presidents of *consejos populares*; 166 (27.62 percent) were female, which was an increase of 32, and 209 (34.8 percent) were incumbents.[99]

National and Provincial Assembly Elections

The issue of having closed, noncompetitive candidate lists was brought up in the 1992 National Assembly debate on the proposed election law. One deputy proposed expanding the list of candidates for provincial delegates and National Assembly deputies to include the election of reserves to fill future vacancies. National Assembly President Juan Escalona responded that the electoral law left it to the Council of State to decide how to fill future vacancies. Jorge Lescano, the first secretary of the party in the City of Havana at that time, stated, "One cannot suppose that having a greater number of candidates than positions to elect would convert the process into a more democratic one. The democratic essence is found within the candidacy commissions. We should not take into account the attacks that our enemies make to make concessions." Another deputy, Patricia Varona, argued for having more candidates than slots to fill. Escalona responded that voters would be able to vote for the number of candidates they wanted to, and not necessarily everyone on the ballot. He stressed the multiple criteria used to make up the candidacy. Minister of Culture Armando Hart stressed the need for unity and maximum participation and the importance of an adequate process of candidacy selection. A woman deputy said having more candidates would "disperse" the voting. Various deputies said that the essence of democracy was the revolution itself. President Castro joined the debate, stating that the new law would be more democratic than the laws in other countries because elsewhere political parties do the nominating. He referred several times directly to Patricia Varona, saying that her uneasiness was shared by others. He emphasized that the mechanisms in the new law were there to prevent politicking, political fighting, and individualism. If people wanted to have more candidates, it would be sufficient to raise the number of deputies by 50 percent. Just having competition among candidates would mean that those with the most influence or those who could get space in the press would be favored. Division among candidates should not exist in our elections. The need to get more than 50 percent of the vote to win is democratic. The closed list means giving more importance to a good selection of candidates and would make possible the election of candidates with tremendous experience and of great value, who are not well known, but whose presence is very necessary in the National Assembly. A way would be found for them to have contact with the public. He asked whether competitive elections would be giving counterrevolutionaries the opportunity not to vote for the most revolutionary candidates. They could destroy the revolution by trying to block the best candidates. The majority has the sacred obligation to maintain the revolution. He mentioned the challenge of having the elections during the special period (the economic crisis of the 1990s brought on by the disappearance of the Soviet Union), because when direct elections were first discussed, Cuba was not yet in the special period, and no other country would dare to have elections in such abnormal and difficult times.[100] The system of noncompetitive elections was left in place and approved by the National Assembly as part of the 1992 Electoral Law. Varona was not renominated for the 1993 elections.

Castro has emphasized the close ties of the legislators with the people they represent as a unique feature of the Cuban system: "One of the things which most moves me regarding our electoral system is that a humble citizen can be deputy of the National Assembly."[101] The main rationale used by Cuban authorities to justify noncompetitive elections is that it makes it possible for such relatively unknown candidates (especially the *de base* candidates) to be elected:

> Tell the electors that here you have five or six candidates; to choose two or three would have placed at a disadvantage a large part of those proposed as candidates: women and men of great merit, but with recognition earned in small fields of action such as a municipal assembly election district, the territory of a people's council, a work or research center, a school, a military unit. . . . The latent danger would be that, in the name of choosing only the best known, this minority of the candidates would win, and a great act of injustice would be committed regarding the rest.[102]

In making the argument against competitive elections, National Assembly President Ricardo Alarcón has linked the concern for electing lesser-known candidates with advocating for voting for the entire slate (*voto unido*):

> There are candidates whose names, when mentioned once, are recognized and known by the people because of the responsibility we have, because we appear more in the mass media, for whatever reason; and there are others who may be very well known, in a work center, in a neighborhood, but with difficulty are known to the same degree in the whole zone, in the whole electoral district. . . . Neither confrontation between candidates, nor competition among candidates, such as capitalism displays, which makes them equivalent to merchandise, and to objects of consumption, nor exclusivity, which gives space only to those

who are well known, to the national figures, who are more well known for one reason or another.[103]

In an interview with me on February 25, 1994, Alarcón personalized the argument:

I will give you an example. I was nominated and elected deputy as a candidate of the municipality of Plaza in the City of Havana. It is divided into three electoral districts, and I was a candidate in District 2. There were two women who were also candidates in District 2. One is María Llorens, who is a municipal delegate in Plaza. The other is Tania Pérez Enríquez, who is president of the medical students of Havana. I was foreign minister at the time. Of the three, the only one who the people in Plaza knew was me, my face, my name, etc. In the electoral campaign, everyone knew who I was. But not the other two, who were known only in their base of operations, María in the jurisdiction from which she was elected municipal delegate. A competitive election would lead to a fight among the candidates that would be totally unequal, because I would have to tell absolutely no one who I am, nor would I have to show anyone my biography.

The example of the deputy candidate from District 1 of Bayamo, Teovaldo de la Paz, a garbage collector and union leader, was highlighted in the Cuban press during the 1998 campaign. He was on "a list of candidates in which there is also a well-known government minister. But I do not harbor fears. The *voto unido* [vote for the entire slate of candidates] will make no distinctions between this humble revolutionary and exemplary worker in his job in municipal services, and the minister, also exemplary in his accomplishments and work."[104]

The competitive elections on the municipal assembly level do not create a similar barrier for candidates who are without national recognition or stature, as they must live in the district and are nominated and usually well known by their neighbors. In the final analysis, the lack of competition may not be very significant in the elections for Cuba's national legislative organ because the airing of policy alternatives by candidates is not permitted during the campaigns. As voters do not nominate candidates, there remains little significant basis on which voters can make a well-grounded choice among those who are not well known.

In an interview in the CTC newspaper *Trabajadores* in April 1995, Alarcón compared the 1995 municipal delegate elections to the 1993 national and provincial elections:

In the past [provincial and national] general elections there was, as was logical, a national mobilization; there was the presence of Fidel in that whole process. More than for one or another concrete candidate, the people felt that it was voting for the fatherland, for the Revolution. The process which will now take place does not have those attributes. . . . There can be no *voto unido*. One must go to the neighborhood, in the midst of all the tensions which we experiencing, to elect a grassroots combatant who is confronting problems which in many cases do not have solutions.[105]

Voting for the entire slate was the dominant theme in both the 1993 and 1998 elections, which were considered more as plebiscites on the Cuban Revolution than as elections.[106] Prior to the 1993 provincial and national elections, there was an intense campaign in the press, on television, and with banners in the streets urging the *voto unido* and "Vote for Cuba" *(Si por Cuba)*. It was insinuated strongly that not to vote for all would be counter-revolutionary. This was in part a response to the massive campaign on Radio Martí and other sources from Miami, including Florida governor, Lawton Chiles, for Cubans to annul ballots in order to discredit the election process. Carlos Lage, secretary of the Council of Ministers and Council of State, stated that the *voto unido* would be a demonstration of the force of the revolution and a reaffirmation of the people's unity. In an interview on TV on March 1, 1993, Castro said that although it was not called a plebiscite, the election had become a plebiscite because it was a battle, and a confrontation of concepts, of ideas, of policies: "It was a battle between the Cuban people and imperialism, between the present, future and past, between socialism and capitalism. . . . I believe the most exceptional thing about this plebiscite is the fact that it was done during the special period."[107]

President Castro's speeches during the 1993 campaign, as reported in *Granma* and *Trabajadores* during January and February, repeated the main themes and arguments he had made in the 1992 National Assembly debate on the new electoral law, during which he had defended the lack of competitive elections and urged all to vote for the entire slate.[108] He implied that those who did not vote for all would be selling out their country—likening it to selling one's mother, brother, children. The revolutionary, patriotic vote should not be divided. It is good for the country, which needs the spirit of unity for the special period. He also reiterated that the right of those who don't want to vote for all the candidates must be respected.

Castro argued that rather than choosing among well-known personalities, the essence of the electoral outcome was geared to result in all sectors being represented. Candidates were selected by virtue of their principles and not because of any influence exerted. Elections should be based not on popularity but on merits and capacities. The reason that the elections would not be competitive was that there should be no competition among revolutionaries. Furthermore, if the elections were competitive, it would be hard for less well-known people to be elected, such as young people without much revolutionary history and municipal delegates who were unknown outside their electoral district, because to win, a candidate had to get more than twenty thousand votes. Revolutionary elections are held to elect not only well-known candidates, but all candidates with merit, quality, and capacity who are patriotic and revolutionary. Voters should have confidence in the selection process of the candidacy commissions. Dispersing votes among competing candidates helps counterrevolutionaries.

The call for the *voto unido* was repeated prior to the 1998 elections and similarly linked to patriotism and viewed as a plebiscite on Cuban socialism: "A plebiscite for the Revolution, for democracy, for socialism; for social justice, for the human right for work and life; for the dignity of men, will be what will come about in Cuba. . . ."[109] The election results were referred to as "a plebiscite in favor of the world we dream of and of the political project we defend."[110]

Castro noted that voters had a right to vote as they wish: "If there is someone who does not want to vote for any, he is within his rights to not vote for anyone. He has the right to vote for all, for some for one or for none, and the citizen should feel truly free."[111] At the National Assembly session in December 1997, he affirmed that the *voto unido* was an arm of the Cuban Revolution and an expression of unity, but people should be won over by persuasion and reasoning rather than by sloganeering. He told the deputies that he disagreed with an editorial in *Trabajadores* that directly linked the *voto unido* to the struggle against the U.S. economic blockade.[112] During the same session, Alarcón said that the *voto unido* would be a proof of conscience and patriotism.[113] The national coordinator of the CDR, Juan Contino Asián, declared that all patriots should know that unity has always ensured victory and that the *voto unido* was a vote for Cuba's independence and socialism. This was reiterated by the president of ANAP, Orlando Lugo Fonte. Pedro Ross Leal, general secretary of the CTC, said that the call for the *voto unido* should be adhered to, because the increasing aggressivity of imperialism required greater unity.[114] Otto Rivero, first secretary of the UJC, emphasized that a united vote would "demonstrate how the new generations support the system in force on the island."[115]

Along with the biographies and photos posted in neighborhoods, as in the municipal elections, the 1992 Electoral Law allows the candidates at the three levels of the OPP "to participate together in presentations, meetings and visits to work centers and exchange opinions with workers, which at the same time will allow the people get to know the candidates personally without this being considered a campaign with electoral propaganda."[116] However, as is the case in the municipal elections, candidates offer voters neither policy alternatives nor campaign promises to solve problems faced by the people. The reason is that, in the words of Alarcón:

> Possibly there are tons and tons too many promises in the world that no one has thought to keep not even at the time when they were made. In our case, as our

A large, well-attended rally held in the center of Havana on election eve for the 1993 elections for National Assembly deputies and provincial assembly delegates. The rally was televised nationally, candidates spoke and popular singers performed. The main theme was the *voto unido*.

system must exclude demagogy and politicking, we are frank, and in these candidate meetings, no one has promised anything to anybody, nor would it be correct to do so, in terms of things that materially benefit the people. . . . The search for the solutions to our problems is not found in anyone's demagogic propositions, but rather will be the result of the effort and sacrifice of all.[117]

In 1993 and 1998, candidates appeared at public meetings in their municipalities or districts. In 1993, some voters told me that they had not been invited to or notified of these encounters with the candidates. That year, I attended meetings of candidates with voters in Bauta, Diez de Octubre, and Cerro, all in the City of Havana. No one asked questions, but several voters did speak on the need to vote for all candidates. The candidates also spoke, exhorting the voters to vote for all, identifying the vote as a plebiscite for the revolution and for Fidel. However, I did find out that at another meeting voters asked questions about (1) tourism—complaints about the separation of tourists from the public; (2) joint ventures with foreign capital; (3) the economic crisis, especially regarding the availability of food and the plan for food distribution; (4) problems with energy; and (5) social security—some complained that medical permission for leaving work was given too freely, and others thought one year off work for child care at 60 percent salary was too much. At a meeting in Habana Vieja, the voters complained bitterly to the then provincial assembly president, Pedro Chávez, about the abysmal state of housing, said they did not want to hear excuses about lack of resources due to the economic crisis, and wanted to know what he was going to do about it because this was a critical problem that had to be resolved.

In 1997 in Centro Habana municipality, I was told of people waiting in line for food, complaining about being told how to vote, and declaring publicly that they wouldn't vote. In the suburbs of Havana, I heard some people complain about the lack of competitive elections, the fact that the old leadership resisted giving up power, and the lack of possibility for self-nomination. One person told me that if dissidents wanted to, they should run, and even if they got 30 percent of the vote, it would be a tremendous victory for the Revolution.

Just prior to the 1998 elections, I attended election rallies in four municipalities within the City of Havana—Plaza, Marianao, Diez de Octubre, and Playa—with the provincial and national candidates from the district present. The larger and better-organized ones included nationally prominent guests and speakers and, in one case, questions from the audience. However, not even in the small neighborhood gatherings did I witness any meaningful exchange between the candidates and the public. There were no discussions of Cuba's problems, no questions about or mention of policies and possible alternatives, and no presentation of any of the candidates' ideas and capabilities as potential members of the national legislature. Rather, at each gathering, the main thrust of those who spoke as well as of those who participated from the audience was the need and the pledge to vote for all the candidates and a rejection of the type of elections held in Cuba prior to 1959 and in the United States.

On January 6, I went to a rally in Marianao with over four thousand people in attendance. The main speaker was the Reverend Raúl Suarez, a candidate for National Assembly deputy, and the director of the Martin Luther King, Jr., Memorial Center. The pastor equated Cuban socialism and democracy with Christianity in terms of social justice, equality, and attending to the weakest, and quoting Ernesto "Che" Guevara, he stated that the religion of the Cuban Revolution is national unity. Comments and questions were solicited from members of the audience. There were those, including children, who repeated slogans exhorting all to heed the call for the *voto unido*. The president of the national electoral commission answered questions from the audience on the difference in voting procedure for national deputies and provincial delegates, whether voting booths would be set up for those who were working in the countryside and those interned in hospitals, voting if one was out of town, and voting if one was in prison.

Alarcón was present in Marianao and was the main speaker at three other rallies I attended. His main theme revolved around a comparison of the Cuban elections to the corruption found in Miami's mayoral election, citing reports from the *Miami Herald* that even the dead voted. He also stressed that Cuba had been defeated in the past because of lack of unity, that unity was one of Fidel Castro's main achievements, and that the *voto unido* was the best way to demonstrate and support unity.

On January 10, the day before the elections, I accompanied the national and provincial candidates from District 1 in Playa (the westernmost sections), together with the president of the municipal candidacy commission, traveling in a van to six small neighborhood meetings. At each stop, either the president or one of the candidates began a short speech by briefly introducing all the candidates and then urged all to vote for the entire slate. At only one stop did one deputy candidate, Raúl Garcia, who is also the president of the Playa Municipal Assembly, explain to the voters what the *Poder Popular* had done for the community, what was left to do, and why the National Assembly was important. The only audience participation came from neighborhood CDR and election commission leaders, promising that everyone in their district would vote early and for the entire slate. The atmosphere stressed conformity and support and was not conducive to questioning and dialogue focused on substantive issues such as Cuba's severe economic crisis. In these meetings, as in the posted biographies and in articles in the press, the emphasis was on the candidates' patriotism, integrity, and role in society, and on the general process by which they had been chosen, with no mention of their ideas, knowledge, expertise, or legislative skills and no attempt to differentiate the candidates from each other or to familiarize the audience with the lesser-known candidates.

Beginning in mid-December of 1997, *Granma* ran a series of articles on the encounters between candidates and voters that stressed what the people told the candidates about their work and communities, rather than what voters learned about the candidates. In Aguada de Pasajeros in Cienfuegos Province, candidates visited the workers who process sugarcane: "Dulce María Albellán, a municipal delegate and candidate for deputy, explained that carrying out the program of these visits permitted the candidates to know better the economic reality of the municipality in all aspects and converse with a large number of voters, and as a result, as candidates, they now feel much more committed to represent their constituents effectively in the organs of government."[118] Reporting on a meeting in Guisa in the Sierra Maestra, the journalist wrote, "The only 'promises' of the candidates are to continue being faithful to the Revolution, the people, the fatherland and to work together for economic recuperation in all fields, and to contribute to improving of the organs of government and the electoral system."[119]

During the election campaigns, media commentators repeatedly explained the process and the differences from the municipal assembly elections. The pictures of all National Assembly candidates for deputy appeared in the newspapers and on television.

There can be severe consequences for those who openly defy the system. For example, the *New York Times* reported that during the 1992–1993 local and national elections, Ismael Sambra, a Cuban writer and television producer, and his son Guillermo had distributed unauthorized election material, and had been found guilty of "rebellion" and sentenced to ten- and eight-year prison terms, respectively. They had slipped pamphlets under doorways that called for "liberty, dignity, independence" and had challenged Castro's chant, "Socialism or death," with "No socialism. No death. No Castro." Both subsequently went to live in exile in Canada.[120]

In February 1993, 99.6 percent of those eligible voted. All the national and provincial candidates were elected. In the elections for National Assembly deputies, only four candidates got less than 90 percent, including City of Havana party chief Lescano; 94.99 percent of those who cast valid ballots voted for the entire slate. The Cuban government reported that 7.27 percent of the voters cast blank or annulled ballots (14.66 percent in the City of Havana), figures confirmed by Agence France Presse, "in spite of the fact that the 'exile' Cuban organizations in the United States as well as the minuscule . . . internal 'dissidence' had called on people to abstain, cast blank ballots or annul their vote as an expression of rejection of the single party system."[121] The Mexican media reported an annulment rate of 15 to 20 percent, and Miguel Angel Centeno claimed that "31 percent of the ballots were invalidated or left blank," citing as sources Beloyra and Jorge Domínguez, two well-known critics of the Cuban Revolution.[122] In 1998, 98.35 percent of those eligible voted (acknowledged by the Spanish EFE News Service[123]), 94.37 percent who cast valid ballots voted for the entire slate, and 5 percent cast blank or annulled ballots.[124] The election process, if viewed as a plebiscite, had been a success. Elizardo Sánchez, president of the opposition Cuban Commission for Human Rights and National Reconciliation, recognized that the January 1998 elections "signified the renovation of the mandates and the legitimacy of the government" of Castro.[125]

In the constituent session of the National Assembly, the deputies elect the officers of the National Assembly and the officers and other members of Council of State, from a closed list of candidates, offering no choice, selected by the National Candidacy Commission after consultation with each deputy. Prior to voting, the deputies must approve the list of candidates. However, as Escalona made clear in his interview with me, the PCC continues to have the final decision as to who will fill these positions. As mandated by the Cuban Constitution, the president of the Council of State is also the president of the Council of Ministers, and thus the same person is head of state and head of government. Fidel Castro has held this combined position since the inception of the OPP. InterPress Service's speculation that following the 1998 elections, a constitutional reform would eliminate this combined position, leading to a separation of powers in Cuba, proved to be unfounded.[126]

Conclusion

The electoral process for municipal delegates that I observed was characterized by active, uncoerced citizen participation, commitment, and involvement. At the municipal level, voters nominated and for the most part knew the candidates, sometimes personally, and the Communist Party had no role in determining who was nominated and elected—and continues to have no role because the 1992 Electoral Law did not change this part of the election process.

Prior to 1992, the party played a more active and intrusive role in nominations for the municipal assembly leadership positions, provincial assembly delegates, and National Assembly deputies, and in fact, its formal participation progressively increased, the higher the office. It was in these areas that major changes were instituted in 1992. The PCC and the UJC no longer have seats on the candidacy commissions at any level, so that formal party involvement in the selection of candidates has been eliminated for all of these offices. The municipal assembly president and vice president are elected by the assembly delegates. The process of nominating candidates for provincial assembly delegates and National Assembly deputies involves the candidacy commissions and the municipal assembly delegates, and they are elected in direct, secret, though not competitive, elections. The party continues to be directly involved in selecting the National Assembly leadership, as well as the composition of the Council of Ministers and the Council of State.

As discussed in previous chapters, Marx supported elections devoid of politics, and partisan politics were absent in the elections to the local soviets in 1917 and in the Leninist concept of the one-party state. In line with this tradition, the Cuban election campaigns at all levels are devoid of campaign promises and the presentation of policy options. Juan Valdés considers the election of the municipal delegate, which must be competitive by law, to be where the Cuban political system reaches the greatest degree of democratization, but with its legitimacy nonetheless limited by its being a contest between persons and not between those favoring different policy alternatives and diverse interests.[127] On the provincial and national levels, the nomination process potentially excludes those who disagree with all or some aspects of government policies and those who may be too outspoken. Thus Castro's January 1989 contention in reference to municipal elections, and repeated regarding National Assembly elections in December 1997, that "if the counterrevolution had a majority, it could win the elections and take power peacefully"[128] could be valid for municipal elections, but virtually impossible at the provincial and national levels. The arguments for noncompetitive elections and the *voto unido* center around ensuring, on the one hand, the election of lesser-known candidates, especially the *de base* candidates, following the Marxian principle of a government in which the representatives are socially indistinguishable from those they serve, and, on the other, ensuring representation from all sectors of Cuban society. It thus becomes more of a selection than an election process, with the outcome measured as a plebiscite rather than an indication of public support for specific policies or candidates.

A 1994 Gallup poll, the only independent study done in Cuba, found that the majority of the population believed that the revolution had had more achievements (58 percent) than failures (31 percent); that 48 percent identified themselves as revolutionary, 11 percent as communist, and 10 percent as socialist; and that 23 percent said they were not integrated into the revolution.[129] Thus, although support for the Cuban government is considered high even though some are critical of the government,[130] according to the 1994 poll it was not as high as the 94 percent who voted for the entire slate in 1998. But this lower percentage does not invalidate the 1998 elections as a plebiscite showing general support for the revolution and the OPP. While the percentage of those eligible who voted may seem unrealistically high, compared to participation in U.S. elections, voters in Cuba are not legally or in other ways forced to vote, although indirect pressures may come into play. The high percentage of those who voted for the entire slate in 1993 and 1998 may have resulted from the lack of choice and the lack of policy distinctions in and definitions of what the candidates represented.

Notes

1. Haroldo Dilla Alfonso and Armando Fernández Soriano, "Las elecciones municipales en Cuba: un estudio de caso," *El Caribe Contemporaneo*, No. 23 (July-December 1991), p. 88.

2. Haroldo Dilla Alfonso, Gerardo González, and Ana Teresa Vincentelli, "Los municipios en Cuba: una experiencia más allá de los paradigmas," paper presented at the annual meeting of the Latin American Studies Association, Washington, D.C., 1991, p. 10.

3. Haroldo Dilla Alfonso and Gerardo González Nuñez, "Participación y desarrollo en los municipios cubanos," unpublished manuscript prepared for the Organizations of Community Power and Grassroots Democracy in Central America and the Caribbean, 1991, p. 19 (my translation).

4. Marta Harnecker, *Cuba: Dictatorship or Democracy?* (Westport, Conn.: Lawrence Hill, 1980), pp. 78–82; see also Dilla and Fernández, "Las elecciones municipales," p. 83; José Prado, "De nuestras elecciones: Un caso singular en una asamblea normal," *Trabajadores*, April 4, 1989, p. 4.

5. Caridad Carrobello, Martha Campos, Pelayo Terry, and Ariel Terrero, "¿Qué piensa el pueblo de su poder?" *Bohemia*, July 6, 1990, p. 7.

6. Susana Tesoro, "Punto de vista: vale más precaver," *Bohemia*, February 17, 1989, p. 29 (my translation).

7. Dilla, González, and Vincentelli, "Los municipios," p. 13.

8. Dilla and Fernández, "Las elecciones municipales," p. 82.

9. Dilla, González, and Vincentelli, "Los municipios," p. 13 (my translation).

10. Dilla and Fernández, "Las elecciones municipales," p. 82 (my translation).

11. Haroldo Dilla, Gerardo González, and Ana Teresa Vincentelli, *Participación popular y desarrollo en los municipios cubanos* (Havana: Centro de Estudios sobre América, 1993), p. 62.

12. Joseph B Treaster, "Cubans Arrested During Soviet Visit," *New York Times*, April 5, 1989, p. A8.

13. María Julia Mayoral, "Democracía electoral, no sólo en las urnas," *Granma*, June 15, 1995, p. 5.

14. Julio García Luis, "Yo participo: el pueblo dirá lo final de este proceso," *Trabajadores*, June 19, 1995, p. 16 (my translation).

15. Coordinación Nacional de los CDR, "LLamamiento a todos los cederistas," *Granma*, May 13, 1995, p. 8.

16. Julio García Luis, "Tener mejores elecciones que nunca," *Trabajadores*, May 15, 1995, p. 16.

17. Susana Lee, "A las próximas elecciones del 9 de junio," *Granma*, June 27, 1995, p. 1; "El reciente proceso de nominación de candidatos," *Granma*, June 24, 1995, p. 8.

18. "El pueblo sabe," *Trabajadores*, July 3, 1995, p. 2; Julio García Luis, "Yo participo," p. 16.

19. Esteban Lazo, "El voto por la dignidad, por la soberanía, por la independencia de la Patria," *Trabajadores*, July 3, 1995, p. 4 (my translation).

20. Susana Lee, "Determinadas 14,533 circunscripciones electorales para los próximos comicios," *Granma*, July 8, 1997, p. 8.

21. Julio García Luis, "Se trabaja con mucha seriedad para las elecciones," *Trabajadores*, August 18, 1997, p. 3.

22. Alberto Núñez Betancourt, "Resultan participación popular en el proceso de nominación de candidatos," *Granma*, October 1, 1997, p. 3.

23. Ventura de Jesús, "La propuesta de Rosa," *Granma*, September 10, 1997, p. 3 (my translation).

24. María Julia Mayoral, "Yamil, entre la alegría y el qué vendrá," *Granma*, September 12, 1997, p. 3.

25. María Julia Mayoral, "Por el mejor y con cabeza propia," *Granma*, September 19, 1997, p. 4 (my translation).

26. Dilla and González, "Participación y desarrollo," p. 20.

27. Harnecker, *Cuba: Dictatorship?* p. 74.

28. Peter Roman, "A Preliminary Report on the October 1986 Municipal Elections in Cuba," *Socialism and Democracy*, No. 5 (Fall-Winter 1987), p. 97.

29. Dilla and Fernández, "Las elecciones municipales," p. 86.

30. Carrobello et al., "Qué piensa?" p. 6 (my translation).

31. Susana Lee, "Pensando en mi candidato," *Granma*, July 4, 1995, p. 3.

32. María Julia Mayoral, "Destaca secretario de la Comisión Electoral Nacional importancia de las asambleas de nominación," *Granma*, August 29, 1997, p. 8.

33. Jorge I. Domínguez, "Derechos políticos y el sistema político Cubano," *Revista Occidental*, No. 2 (January-April 1984), p. 257 (my translation). For a similar point of view, also without citing any examples, see Archibald R. M. Ritter, "The Authenticity of Participatory Democracy in Cuba," in Archibald R. M. Ritter and David Pollock (eds.), *Latin American Prospects for the 1980s: Equity, Democratization and Development* (New York: Praeger, 1983), p. 196.

34. Fidel Castro, speech given on September 28, 1976, *Granma Weekly Review*, October 10, 1976, p. 2.

35. Harnecker, *Cuba: Dictatorship?* pp. 82–83.

36. Dilla and González, "Participación y desarrollo," pp. 27–28.

37. Dilla and Fernández, "Las elecciones municipales," p. 86.

38. María Julia Mayoral, "Ganar en calor humano," *Granma*, May 26, 1995, p. 2 (my translation).

39. María Julia Mayoral, "Nuestras elecciones: limpias y justas," *Granma*, May 17, 1995, p. 1 (my translation).

40. Gail Reed, "April 8: Election Day in Cuba," *Granma Weekly Review*, April 15, 1979, p. 4.

41. William M. LeoGrande, "Participation in Cuban Municipal Government: From Local Power to People's Power," in Donald E. Schulz and Jan S. Adams (eds.), *Political Participation in Communist Countries* (New York: Pergamon Press, 1991), p. 284.

42. Harnecker, *Cuba: Dictatorship?* p. 98.

43. Dilla and Fernández, "Las elecciones municipales," pp. 86–87.

44. Ibid., p. 83.

45. María Julia Mayoral, "Delegados: con ser buenos no basta," *Granma*, May 23, 1995, p. 8.

46. "El pueblo sabe," p. 2 (my translation).

47. Susana Lee, "¿Quién es el mejor y el más capaz?" *Granma*, July 5, 1995, p. 3 (my translation).

48. Domínguez does not give examples or explain to which propaganda and meetings he is referring The only propaganda I observed during the municipal election period were banners made by the electoral commissions exhorting the people to "vote for the best." The only public meetings were the nomination meetings. Domínguez, "Derechos políticos," p. 257.

49. Archibald R. M. Ritter, "People's Power and the Communist Party," in Sandor Halebsky and John M. Kirk (eds.), *Cuba: Twenty-five Years of Revolution, 1959—1984* (New York: Praeger, 1985), p. 278.

50. Ibid., pp. 278–280.

51. Haroldo Dilla Alfonso, "Notas sobre la relación centralización-decentralización en la transición socialista cubana," unpublished manuscript, 1989, p. 36.

52. Dilla and Fernández, "Las elecciones municipales," p. 82 (my translation).

53. Dilla, González, and Vincentelli, "Los municipios," p. 13.

54. Dilla and Fernández, "Las elecciones municipales," p. 83.

55. Dilla, González, and Vincentelli, "Los municipios," p. 13.

56. William M LeoGrande, "The Communist Party of Cuba Since the First Congress," in Stephen White and Daniel Nelson (eds.), *Communist Politics: A Reader* (New York: New York University Press, 1986), p. 190.

57. Dilla, "Notas sobre la relación," p. 36 (my translation).

58. Gail Lindenberg, "The Labor Union in the Cuban Workplace," *Latin American Perspectives*, Issue 76, Vol. 20, No. 1 (Winter 1993), pp. 28–39.

59. Grisell Rodriguez, "Elecciones en Cuba: un derecho ciudadano" (Interview with Ernesto Suárez), *Poder Popular*, Vol. 8, No. 3 (1989), p. 3 (my translation).

60. Roman, "Preliminary Report," p. 96.

61. María Julia Mayoral, "Extraordinaria victoria revolucionaria en pleno período especial," *Granma*, July 11, 1995, p. 1; María Julia Mayoral, "El número de vueltas no determina la elección de los delegados," *Granma*, July 18, 1995, p. 1.

62. Miguel Angel Centeno, "Cuba's Search for Alternatives," in Miguel Angel Centeno and Mauricio Font (eds.), *Towards a New Cuba? Legacies of a Revolution* (Boulder: Lynne Rienner, 1997), p. 11.

63. Luis Suárez Salazar, "The 1995 Municipal Elections: A Different Angle," *Cuban Review*, October 1995, p. 7.

64. Ibid.

65. Pastor Batista Valdés, "Ni mentiras, ni falsas promesas," *Granma*, September 25, 1996, p. 4 (my translation).

66. Luis Suárez Salazar, "The 1995 municipal elections," p. 7.

67. Susana Lee, "Las sociedades de consumo no son la fórmula, ni la democracía capitalista; nosotros podemos adoptar en lo económico algunas medidas pero en lo demás no vamos a apartarnos de lo hecho," *Granma*, July 10, 1995, p. 4 (my translation).

68. Luis Suárez Salazar, "The 1995 municipal elections," pp. 7–8.

69. María Julia Mayoral, "Tomarán mañana posesión de sus cargos los 14,533 delegados elegidos recientemente," *Granma*, November 1, 1997, p. 1.

70. "La muralla del silencio," *Trabajadores*, July 17, 1995, p. 2 (my translation).

71. Tim Golden, "A Year After Boat Exodus, Threat to Castro Dissipates," *New York Times*, August 15, 1995, p. A–6.

72. Peter Roman, "When Cubans Vote," *New York Times*, August 24, 1995, p. A–22.

73. "Ley Electoral," *Gaceta Oficial de la República de Cuba*, November 2, 1992, pp. 62–63.

74. "Asamblea Nacional del Poder Popular: sobre el proceso de elaboración del proyecto de Ley Electoral," *Granma*, October 30, 1992, pp. 4–5 (my translation).

75. María Julia Mayoral, "Entrarán en funciones las comisiones de candidaturas," *Granma*, June 10, 1995, p. 1.

76. Susana Lee, "Excepciones que confirman la regla," *Granma*, August 3, 1995, p. 2 (my translation).

77. María Julia Mayoral, "Presentarán candidaturas a presidentes y vicepresidents de Asambleas Municipales," *Granma*, p. 1; Julio García Luis, "La Lisa: una entre 169," *Trabajadores*, November 3, 1997, p. 16.

78. María Julia Mayoral, "Después de las elecciones: reordenan consejos populares," *Granma*, August 11, 1996, p. 1.

79. Domingo Garcia Cárdenas, *State Organization in Cuba*, (Havana: José Martí, 1986), p. 45.

80. *Ley Electoral-Poder Popular* (Havana: Ciencias Sociales, 1984), pp. 68–72.

81. Ritter, "The Authenticity," p. 198.

82. Harnecker, *Cuba: Dictatorship?* p. 102.

83. Ibid., pp. 95–110.

84. Carrobello et al., "¿Qué piensa?" p. 6 (my translation).

85. The "promotion" of municipal assembly leaders to positions in the provincial government may create discontent among constituents. A young man from a small municipality in Cienfuegos Province told me that the municipal assembly had had an excellent president, one who was well known throughout the municipality, who had been a good advocate for the people, and who thus had given a lot of prestige to the local government. His capabilities had soon been noticed by the provincial government, and within a year, he had been given a position in the province. His departure left the people in his municipality angry and disappointed.

86. Morales later became the president of the *consejo popular* in Santa Fe. See Chapter 6.

87. Cited in Fabio Raimundo torrado, "Differences and Similarities," *Granma Internacional,* January 3, 1998, *URL: http://www.granma.cu.*

88. Susana Tesoro, "Elecciones 'Todo acto o voz genial viene del pueblo,'" *Bohemia,* December 5, 1997, p. B39 (my translation).

89. Fidel Castro, Intervention in the National Assembly debate December 13, 1997, Granma, December 19, 1997, p. 6 (my translation).

90. Ricardo Alarcón, speech given December 26, 1997, *Trabajadores*, December 29, 1997, pp. 7–8 (my translation).

91. María Julia Mayoral, "Consultarán a los electores para conformar precandidaturas," *Granma*, June 27, 1997, p. 3.

92. "Fidel sugiere que podría dejar el poder," *El Diario/La Prensa*, February 26, 1993, p. 11; Ann Wroe, "Heroic Illusions: A Survey of Cuba," *The Economist*, April 6, 1996, p. survey 5.

93. María Julia Mayoral, "Indagación para bién de todos: vivencias de la Presidenta de una Comisión de Candidaturas," *Granma*, January 22, 1993, p. 3.

94. Isabel Morales, "¿Puede haber consulta más exhaustiva y popular? Entrevista a Manuel Mendez Castellanos, presidente de la Comisión de Candidaturas Nacional, acerca de la marcha del proceso electoral," *Granma*, December 9, 1992, p. 3.

95. Rodolfo Casals, "Cuba Ratifies Its Socialist Option," *Granma Internacional*, March 1, 1998. URL:*http://www.granma.cu/.*

96. Francisco Rodríguez Cruz, "Nominación de candidatos: No fué ejercicio carítico," *Trabajadores,* December 1, 1997, p. 5.

97. María Julia Mayoral, "Buscando lo que la gente piensa," *Granma*, November 26, 1997, p. 3 (my translation).

98. Antonio Raluy, "Una campaña electoral 'a la cubana,'" *El Diario/La Prensa*, February 7, 1993, p. 17.

99. Maria Alonso, "Who Are the Candidates?," *Granma Internacional*, December 19, 1997, URL: http://www.granma.cu; Maria Julia Mayoral, "Proyecto de candi-

datura para preidencia de la Asamblea Nacional genera amplio análisis," *Granma*, February 20, 1998, p. 3.

100. "Continuación del debate sobre formación y presentación de candidaturas," *Granma*, October 31, 1992, p. 3 (my translation).

101. Fidel Castro, speech given December 29, 1997, *Granma*, January 2, 1998, p. 6 (my translation).

102. María Julia Mayoral, "Ni competencia ni figuras de relleno," *Granma*, January 8, 1998, p. 5 (my translation).

103. Ricardo Alarcón, speech given on December 26, 1997, pp. 8–9 (my translation).

104. Caridad Nafite Navarro, "¿Quién es Teovaldo?" *Trabajadores*, January 9, 1998, p. 3 (my translation).

105. Frank Agero Gómez and Julio Gracía Luis, "Tenemos que demostrar que aquí el destino nuestro lo decidimos nosotros," *Trabajadores*, April 10, 1995, p. 3 (my translation).

106. Luis Suárez Salazar, "Crisis, reestructuración y democracía en Cuba: apuntes para un debate," *Cuadernos de Nuestra America*, Vol. 10, No. 20 (July-December 1993), p. 76.

107. Fidel Castro, television interview, March 1, 1993, *Granma*, March 3, 1993, p. 3 (my translation).

108. Fidel Castro, speech given February 6, 1993, *Granma*, February 10, 1993, pp. 5–8.

109. Marcos Alfonso, "Plebiscito por la Patria," *Granma*, January 10, 1998, p. 5 (my translation).

110. Marcos Alfonso, "La penúltima diatriba," *Granma*, January 15, 1998, p. 3 (my translation).

111. Fidel Castro, speech on December 29, 1997, p. 7 (my translation).

112. Fidel Castro, speech on December 13, 1997, *Granma*, December 18, 1998, p. 8; "El voto unido: suprema unidad," *Trabajadores*, December 8, 1997, p. 2.

113. "Synthesis Cuba," *Prensa Latina*, December 15, 1997, URL: http://www.prensa-latina.org.

114. Juan Antonio Borrego, "La unidad es garantía de la victoria, afirma el movimiento sindical," *Granma*, December 5, 1997.

115. "Synthesis Cuba," *Prensa Latina*, December 5, 1997, URL: http://www.prensa-latina.org.

116. "Ley Electoral", *Gaceta Oficial de la Republica de Cuba*, Article 171, November 2, 1992 (my translation).

117. Alarcón, speech given on December 26, 1997, p. 9 (my translation).

118. Alexis Rojas Aguilera. "Continúan encuentros de candidatos con los electores," *Granma*, December 16, 1997, p. 8.

119. Jorge Luis Batista, "Encuentro de candidatos de Güisa con su pueblo," *Granma*, January 3, 1998, p. 8.

120. Anthony DePalma, "It's Everything Castro Promised, on Lake Ontario," *New York Times*, June 11, 1998, p. A–4.

121. Luis Suárez Salazar, "Crisis, reestructuración," p. 75 (my translation); María Julia Mayoral, "585 diputados obtienen más de 90% de los votos," *Granma*, February 27, 1993, p. 8.

122. Centeno, "Cuba's Search," p. 11.

123. "Declaraciones y aclaraciones," *Trabajadores,* June 29, 1998, p. 2.

124. Fidel Castro, Interview on January 16, 1998, *Trabajadores* (supplement), January 19, 1998, p. 4; Dalia Acosta, "Cuba: Alta participación electoral, otra victoria de Fidel Castro," *InterPress Service,* January 16, 1998, p. 1.

125. Dalia Acosta, "Cuba: nuevo parlamento revelara el rumbo de Fidel Castro," *InterPress Service,* February 23, 1998, p. 2 (my translation).

126. Ibid., p. 1.

127. Juan Valdés Paz, "Poder local y participación," in Haroldo Dilla (ed.), *La participación en Cuba y los retos del futuro* (Havana: Centro de Estudios sobre América, 1996), p. 125.

128. Fidel Castro, speech given on December 13, 1997, *Granma,* December 18, 1997, p. 6 (my translation); Fidel Castro, speech on January 4, 1989, in Fidel Castro, *In Defense of Socialism: Four Speeches on the 30th Anniversary of the Cuban Revolution* (New York: Pathfinder, 1989).

129. Sandra Levinson, "Gallup Poll in Cuba," *Cuba Update,* Vol. 16, No. 1 (February 1995), p. 9; Acosta, "Cuba: Alta participación," p. 2.

130. Centeno, "Cuba's Search," p. 11.

5

Accountability

The purpose of this chapter is to analyze the main activities of the municipal assembly delegates as they relate to accountability and responsiveness to the electorate and participation and input by the electorate. Following the tradition of the *mandat impératif*, these activities involve meeting with constituents in accountability sessions, which delegates hold twice a year with groups of their constituents in areas within their electoral district (the same areas demarcated for the nominating meetings*), and with individuals at weekly office hours, in both cases to gather and respond to previous citizens' mandates (*planteamientos*), usually relating to local issues or problems. The *planteamientos* conveyed during the delegates' office hours are usually more private or individual, and those transmitted at the accountability sessions are about local problems with social repercussions, such as public transportation, distribution and sale of food and other goods, and water and sewage. For Dilla, González, and Vincentelli, the accountability sessions have become "one of the most original and fruitful processes within the framework of the People's Power at the local level, and without a doubt, a valid experience beyond the national boundaries."[1]

Responding to a statement by President Bill Clinton in May 1994, transmitted to Cuba over Radio Martí, criticizing the Cubans for lack of democracy and accountability, Felix Pita Astudillo wrote in *Granma:*

> He says this about the only government in the hemisphere, including the United States, that not only is subject to direct accountability sessions by the people, but also ... subjects to popular debate entire policies such as the island's finances [referring to the workers' parliaments†]. Where can the average

---

*See Chapter 3.

†See Appendix.

North American formally register opinions on the financial or tax policies of Washington, to ratify or oppose the decisions of the cabinet, the legislature and a select group of corporation plutocrats? To which voters and to what people is the government accountable when it decides to undertake the arms race or star wars?[2]

The Mandate System in Cuba

The *mandat impératif* aspect of the OPP is manifested most clearly in the biannual neighborhood accountability sessions, during which municipal assembly delegates receive *planteamientos* from their constituents and provide responses to previous ones.

The right to petition in bourgeois constitutions can be traced to England's Bill of Rights of 1689,[3] and it has been part of Cuban constitutions since the founding of the republic. According to the 1901 Constitution, "Everyone has the right to direct petitions at the authorities: that the petitions be resolved and that the resolution be communicated to the complainant." The 1934 and 1940 Constitutions contained almost identical articles.[4] Benigno Pablo Castellanos pointed out that "this bourgeois regulation did not go further than a formal proclamation since its effective enforcement was far from a reality . . . lacking concrete mechanisms for carrying it out."[5]

Article 36 of the Fundamental Law of Cuba, enacted with the triumph of the revolution in 1959, was taken from the 1940 Constitution: "Every person has the right to address petitions to the authorities and to have them attended to and decided within a period of not more than forty-five days, with notice of the decision made."[6] This provision remained in effect until the new Cuban Constitution of 1976 and, according to Castellanos, prepared the way for the present system: "In effect in this period the right to redress grievances, even though adequate institutions were often lacking, was implemented in practice because of the profound identification of the people with the revolutionary state. It can be said that in this period which lasted about seventeen years, the bases were created for an effective exercise of the right to redress of grievances."[7]

The Constitution of the Organs of People's Power, written in 1974, associates the meetings of delegates with their electorate with "fulfilling their mission as the true vehicle of communication between their electorate and the Organs of People's Power of which they form a part,"[8] and with the "obligation which all the institutions and elected have to be accountable for all their activities to the electorate."[9] During the 1974 pilot project of the OPP in Matanzas Province, Raúl Castro likewise associated the accountability sessions with the Marxist concepts of the delegate as the intermediary between the electorate and the government, and of the *mandat impératif*:

> In every collective contact with his electors the delegate should report on the activities and different responsibilities of municipal people's power, on his personal activity as a delegate, the way in which the problems which the electors asked him to put before the organs of people's power have been handled. . . . A complaint, suggestion or opinion . . . must be submitted by the delegate to the organs of people's power, even if he himself is not in agreement. The delegate does not represent himself but the mass of electors who have elected him and his duty is to act in the interests of the opinions expressed and the problems of the masses and not his personal opinions and problems.[10]

Article 62 of the 1976 Cuban Constitution is also taken from earlier constitutions: "Every citizen has the right to file complaints with and send petitions to the authorities and to be given the pertinent response or attention within a reasonable length of time in keeping with the law." Article 113 provides the mechanism to deal with the complaints and petitions: municipal delegates must

> (A) make the opinions, needs and problems expressed by their electors known to the Assembly; (B) report to their electors on the policy of the Assembly and the measures adopted for solving the problems raised by the people or outline the reasons why they have not been solved; and (C) render accounts of their work on a regular basis to their electors and to the Assembly to which they belong.[11]

The 1992 Constitution retains this language with a few minor changes.[12] For Fernando Alvarez Tabio, these articles provide the underpinnings for the establishment of close relations and ongoing contact between the representatives and the represented, participation by the public in governmental affairs, the gathering of the population's opinions and suggestions, and the assessment of public opinion.[13]

At the neighborhood accountability sessions, the delegates report on the municipal assembly's and their own activities during the previous six months, present a crime report for the district, and report on the resolution of *planteamientos* raised in the previous meeting. Those attending then can raise new *planteamientos*. Delegates are usually able to resolve the majority of these (especially those not requiring material resources) or at least to provide explanations. There is competition between municipalities within a province to achieve the highest percentage of *planteamientos* resolved. Official statistics indicate that about 70 percent of the *planteamientos* are solved. However, according to Dilla, González, and Vincentelli, these statistics do not compare them in terms of quality and impact with *planteamientos* that have not been resolved and do not affirm that the answers satisfied the complainants. Furthermore, in their survey of delegates, only 37 percent believed that the municipal government had demonstrated efficiency in responding to *planteamientos.*[14]

The municipal assembly officers, aided by the provincial government, spend a great deal of effort on preparing and evaluating the accountability sessions. Before the process begins, there are seminars to brief the delegates regarding social and economic problems about which they will be asked by the public and meetings with representatives of state enterprises to try to resolve the remaining *planteamientos* from the previous session. The municipal and provincial governments and the municipal PCC send representatives to the accountability sessions to evaluate them and to suggest improvements to the delegate, and representatives of the state agencies, especially those cited in previous *planteamientos,* are expected to attend to make themselves available to respond to citizens' questions.

Delegates prepare for, organize, and preside over the accountability sessions. They transmit citizen *planteamientos* voiced at these neighborhood meetings or during weekly office hours or simply on the street to the proper state organ at the appropriate level of government. Both the delegate and the person making the complaint must receive an answer from the agency to which the *planteamiento* was transmitted. Delegates must submit monthly reports to the municipal assembly secretary concerning the status of citizen *planteamientos.* Delegates meet with representatives of government enterprises and entities to receive and discuss the written answers to these concerns. They visit citizens at home to discuss the acceptability of the responses received. If a response is deemed unacceptable, the question can be raised again at the municipal assembly administrative council. Delegates and/or citizens can and do appeal such issues all the way to the National Assembly if necessary, but local solutions are encouraged whenever possible.

Citizen mandates receive ample consideration. All *planteamientos* are recorded by *consejo popular* officers immediately after the accountability sessions, and these officers, together with the delegate, make the initial attempts to resolve them. The municipal assembly commissions review the *planteamientos* that fall within their areas, and commission members visit the targets of the complaints and the citizens who make them. The municipal assembly president and secretary read all the *planteamientos* received and send copies of those that correspond to their areas of responsibility to the members of the administrative council, to the assembly commissions, to the state enterprises or entities affected, and to the provincial assembly and National Assembly. The administrative council members monitor and often help the delegates with difficult problems that fall within their areas of responsibilities, and with those corresponding to agencies on the provincial or national levels. The commissions also issue a written statement of the process.

The municipal assembly secretary writes a monthly report to the executive committee regarding the resolution of *planteamientos*, listed according to category, that have emanated from the prior accountability sessions. Just prior to the start of the new sessions, the secretary composes a biannual report evaluating the previous accountability process. The citizen who submits a complaint or receives visits at home from a representative of the enterprise or entity involved, (in some instances) a member of the corresponding assembly commission, and the local delegate to verify that a satisfactory answer has been received.

Citizen complaints, suggestions, and denunciations of a more individual nature, called *quejas*, may be taken in person to *consejo popular* officers, to the administrative council members of the municipal assembly, or sent by mail to the municipal, provincial, or National Assembly; to the Cuban president; to the PCC; or to the press. The municipal administrative council members monitor and also act to resolve *quejas* that fall within their areas of responsibility. Most of these concern housing problems and difficulties in finding employment and are similar to the *planteamientos* heard by delegates during office hours. The municipal assembly president reads all of the letters and reports of the personal interviews. The municipal government is required by law to respond to them within sixty days. Compliance with this requirement is checked by the provincial assembly and also by the National Assembly. A quarterly report on *quejas* goes to the administrative council and an annual report to the municipal and provincial assemblies.

The provincial assemblies work with the municipalities in resolving *planteamientos* and *quejas;* for example, they help obtain the needed resources. The provincial assemblies help to prepare municipal delegates for their biannual accountability sessions. The members of the provincial assembly administrative council read all the *planteamientos* received from the municipalities and the *quejas* that correspond to their areas of responsibility. In the City of Havana Province, given the large number of *planteamientos* (over thirty thousand every half year), the administrative council analyzes them according to the numbers compiled in each category and concentrates on resolving those that have to do with the greatest collective needs. The commissions of the provincial assemblies work with provincial enterprises and entities and receive the *planteamientos* from the municipalities that can be resolved only at the level of the province. These commissions monitor their resolution and visit the citizens who made them.

The municipal assemblies also receive information regarding citizens' concerns through public opinion polls conducted by the Cuban Institute for Consumer Research and Demand Guidance and by the PCC and through the monthly *estado de opinión* reports from the municipal party organization regarding opinions on local issues overheard in the neighborhoods and work centers. These reports are combined at the provincial and national levels of government. Among those who receive these monthly reports are the presidents of the provincial and municipal assemblies, as a tool for orienting the work of the assemblies. I reviewed the *estado de opinión* reports received in Bauta, Playa, and Pinar del Rio and found that, regarding local issues, the findings were very similar to *planteamientos* received by delegates from their constituents. In Pinar del Rio, for example, complaints included irregularities in distribution of goods to the stores and missing items, poor quality of the offerings, rude treatment of customers by store and restaurant attendants, long lines, butting in line, poor quality of the coffee, and administrators lying about going to meetings to explain their excessive absences.

Delegate Accountability and Citizen Input

The regular, systematic process of delegate accountability to citizens has been identified as the main difference between socialist democracy and bourgeois democracy.[15] It is the manner in which citizen input influences and affects policy decisions: "The will of the masses, expressed in the meetings of these government cells, forms an integral and inseparable part of governmental decisions."[16] The biannual neighborhood accountability sessions and the delegates' weekly office hours to meet with individual constituents serve as the main point of contact between delegate and constituents, for citizen participation and input, and for delegate accountability and government responsiveness to the voters. Eldon Kenworthy of Cornell University compared the accountability sessions to a New England town meeting: "The delegate and his constituents addressed one another as equals and discussed community issues in an open, critical way devoid of ideological abstraction and ritual praise. . . . Here was a local authority taking citizen questions seriously and citizens receiving apparently straight talk in return."[17]

Also contributing to close delegate-constituent ties is the delegates' obligation to give primary attention to issues raised specifically by their constituents. For example, at an accountability session I attended in Camerones in the municipality of Palmira in April 1988, the delegate refused to recognize a man who attempted to raise a *planteamiento* but who did not live in the delegate's electoral district.

According to Humberto Pérez, the former director of the Central Planning Board (*Junta Central de Planificación,* or JUCEPLAN), the decentralized structure of the OPP was "designed to increase participation by the masses and lower levels of administration in the solution of problems."[18] When asked in the 1990 *Bohemia* survey, "Do you feel that you participate in the government of the country?" 60.7 percent of respondents said yes, 26 percent said somewhat, and 13 percent answered no.[19] The accountability sessions clearly constitute a major vehicle for citizen participation. Dilla considered these sessions "probably . . . the most consistent and effective participatory act of the Cuban political system, both for the opportunity they provide for public discussion and as a direct channel for conveying information from and to the population."[20] Elsewhere Dilla reiterated his contention that of all the forms of popular participation, "the most significant are the accountability sessions, because of their originality and the massive character of the participation."[21]

Attendance at the accountability sessions is relatively high, ranging between 70 and 80 percent of the eligible voters.[22] Attendance is not mandatory. During several accountability sessions at which I was present, some of those not attending were at home right on the same block with their televisions blaring, obviously making no attempt to hide their absence. Rafael Hernández and Dilla explained this high rate of participation by first alluding to the historical "precedent of Cuban municipal life and, after the revolution, of the CDR and the brief experiment with Poder Local [Local Power],"[23] and then the characteristics of the OPP:

> In the first place, the very simplicity of the governmental structures and participatory mechanisms and the sense of nativeness about them have facilitated learning and internalization of them on the part of citizens. In the second place, and closely related, in this combination of practices of direct democracy with practices of technical representative ones, it is the first that are preeminent by virtue of a certain attachment to the principles of the imperative mandate, which at the same time assumes dynamic flows of information (ascending and descending) and considerable demystification of the techno-bureaucracy. Lastly, the town council was endowed with the powers necessary to transform demands into public policies and to generate sufficient output to reproduce its own legitimacy. . . . It is no exaggeration to say that its effectiveness has lain in its having fostered active participation by the population.[24]

Accountability sessions have also become a vehicle for promoting voluntary citizen participation in work projects, generally organized by the delegate, for solving local problems where possible. In 1987 and 1988, delegates in Cienfuegos and Bauta showed me sidewalks that had been constructed by volunteers from the community, usually on Sundays, in response to *planteamientos*. One Sunday, I witnessed volunteers from the Santa Fe district of Playa and their delegate fixing the roof of the local hardware store. Also in Santa Fe, neighbors participated in the construction of the new produce market, which was initiated because of citizen *planteamientos*. In one electoral district in Bauta, the delegate organized the neighborhood party nucleus, made up largely of retired people, to do minor repairs, such as replacing fallen street signs, that had been requested during the accountability sessions. At an accountability session in Playa, the delegate solicited volunteers for brigades *(microbrigadas)* to do major home repairs.

Citizen participation has not always been automatic or forthcoming. In their survey of delegates, Dilla, González, and Vincentelli found that 57 percent of the delegates surveyed responded that the population did not actively participate in resolving local problems, a response that they attributed to dissatisfaction with the municipal government's efforts, or to lack of mechanisms to facilitate participation, or to the weak role played by the mass organizations in organizing participation. The people surveyed stated that many delegates neither summoned the people nor asked for help even in cases where it was necessary.[25]

With the severe economic crisis beginning in the early 1990s, the call went out for increased citizen involvement in resolving *planteamientos.* Anticipating the Fall 1990 accountability sessions, Ernesto Suárez, secretary of the National Assembly, announced that "each delegate should encourage in the sessions an active participation of the masses in solving the problems of the electoral district . . . and, furthermore, mobilize the resources that exist in his area with the aid of the administrators and mass organizations at this level."[26] Similarly an editorial in *Trabajadores* at the time of the Spring 1992 accountability sessions called for them to organize those who were out of work but receiving salaries to aid in distribution of goods, to encourage cultivating neighborhood vegetable gardens, and to participate in local crime watches.[27] The emphasis on participation by constituents in resolving neighborhood problems has continued throughout the decade. Dario Machado, of the PCC Political Bureau, reported that in the Fall 1997 accountability sessions, the people agreed to participate in solving 40.5 percent of the 119,972 *planteamientos* in Cuba.[28]

Representation and Accountability

Meaningful participation by citizens, according to Dilla, depends on faithful representation and truthful and relevant information passed on to the citizens. Cuban laws and regulations imply a strict interpretation of the role of delegates as representing the needs and interests of the citizens.[29] However, Domingo García Cárdenas pointed out, "This does not mean that they should be passive beings, merely transmitting to the assembly what their electors tell them."[30]

Furthermore, the municipal assemblies were designed to be the main bulwark against tendencies toward bureaucratic centralization. According to Dilla, the municipal assemblies "establish the preeminence of the representative institutions over the administrative ones starting from the accountability sessions;"[31] the accountability sessions are based "on the principle of the supervision of the state conduct by the masses."[32]

Municipal delegates have no administrative powers. They do not direct production and service units. According to Escalona, delegates only govern as part of the municipal assembly when it is in session.[33] García Cárdenas elaborated on this point:

> When delegates act individually in their electoral districts, they do not head the production and service units in those territories. They only act in an administrative function in regard to production and service units and other activities when they are in session in the municipal assemblies. As individuals they do not have authority over local administration, while when they are in session in the assembly they have the highest authority over local administration.[34]

"Performance of delegates and assemblies is measured by the handling of *planteamientos*," according to Sheryl Lutjens.[35] For Max Azicri, the accountability session is "a way in which elected representatives remain responsible to those who elected them."[36] William LeoGrande recognized that the rendering of accounts to voters by municipal delegates provides citizens with easy access to delegates "with a consequent increase in government responsiveness to mass political demands" and that "the mechanism for maintaining close contact between delegates and constituents gives the populace an unprecedented opportunity to communicate their interests and demands to local decision makers and to learn how those demands are processed." He concluded, however,

> The major limitation on popular input to decision making seems to be the limitations of the local Organs of People's Power in the overall policy making process. The municipal OPP deals exclusively with local issues. The criticism and suggestions generated at the accountability sessions tend to be "concrete," aimed at local problems. The sessions, for the most part, have not been forums for criticizing or even discussing major national policy, since such issues fall outside the jurisdiction of the local OPP.[37]

Some cubanologists argue that accountability is limited in that it really pertains only to the mundane problems on the municipal level and is lacking in decision-making power. While admitting that it is responsive, Rhoda Rabkin finds the merits of the Cuban accountability system limited because it is restricted to local problems: "Although the regime is adamantly opposed to open debate on fundamentals, it has been willing and even anxious to encourage the expression of popular dissatisfaction on such subjects as bad service, product shortages, and poor quality of goods."[38] Jorge Domínguez pointed out that citizens can complain only about such issues as potholes, garbage collection, and bus service, though he recognized the ultimate value of such a "mechanism by which the citizens make some local public officials responsible for the performance of the governmental institutions."[39]

Alfredo Prieto and Dilla take issue with Domínguez's position that the significance of delegates' rendering accounts is of only minimal, local importance:

> These supposedly unimportant themes are strategically linked to very important questions. The same examples that Domínguez cites, to which we could add others frequently brought up in popular discussions—such as the distribution of consumer goods, the efficiency of medical services or the water supply—are none other than parts of a broader discussion of the efficacy of the new type of state in meeting the growing needs of the population.[40]

They offered as an example the public debate on women's rights, incorporating profound transformations in human and family relations, as a demonstration of the wider ramifications of criticizing the state on specific local issues. Citizens' *planteamientos* situated this debate in the context of seemingly mundane issues such as the incorporation of women into the labor force or into technical training programs.[41]

Bard Jorgensen found in Nuevitas Municipality that to a degree, citizens limited their demands to issues that had a reasonable chance of being resolved with the available resources. The understanding, for example, that severe economic limitations caused by external factors such as the U.S. blockade might limit the local government bodies' influence tended to produce

> self-restraint when confronted with problems and needs that may arise. This is expressed by the fact that the operation and services of local grocery stores is criticized more often than the system of distribution of consumer goods as a whole. The population accepts (and adapts to) this reality, and only problems that are considered likely to be solved are taken to governing bodies or representatives.[42]

Dilla, González, and Vincentelli stressed the influence of the locale on the *planteamientos*, arguing that "the accountability sessions seem a legitimate channel for the transmission of demands and the encouragement of input, and in this sense citizens make extensive use of them. Above all, it is observable that the themes of the demands produced in each municipality correspond with the types of conflictive situations that are present."[43]

My observations support Jorgensen's position. People tended not to bring up issues of national or foreign politics because the municipal delegate is perceived as having little or no direct influence; rather, they stuck to the issues where it was perceived that the delegate could provide help. Pedro Chávez, then president of the City of Havana provincial assembly, told me in February 1988 that "the population does not bring up issues when it is known there are no solutions." Following the Spring 1992 accountability sessions, which were held during the serious economic crisis of the special period, Mirtha Cardona, then secretary of the City of Havana provincial assembly, "emphasized that the population's *planteamientos* showed a high level of political consciousness, since they did not have to do with material requests that the country is not in conditions to offer at this time."[44]

The best examples of how local *planteamientos* affect national policies involve their influence on economic planning and the budget. Some *planteamientos* I witnessed required solutions beyond the immediate capacity of the delegates, such as those dealing with problems and shortages in national production and investment. For example, one complaint had to do with the inability to buy a replacement part for a toilet without having to buy the whole mechanism. Others had to do with the lack of nipples for baby bottles, the shoddiness of shoes offered for sale, money spent for tourists and not the Cuban population, and the need for a hospital (in Playa) and for rural electrification (in Palmira).

I was told of a human rights issue's being brought up at an accountability session. Carlos Walfrido Rodríguez, the black delegate from the Miramar section in Playa, told me in February 1992 that although known "dissidents" such as Elizardo Sánchez lived in his electoral district, they did not usually attend the accountability sessions. However, a *planteamiento* was instigated by Sánchez at one of Rodríguez's accountability sessions at the time of the visit to Cuba by the United Nations Commission of Human Rights in 1991. Rodríguez told me the following account of the session:

> Sánchez used a person from his block. They got him drunk so as to get him to say at the session that in Cuba there were no human rights to bring up certain things. I explained to him what human rights were. I explained to him what a society with humanity is, what rights gained by humanity we have to defend, what human rights were being defended in Cuba and not being defended in other places. He had the right to make this *planteamiento*, and we recorded it right away. The man said, "I want you to respond. What are human rights and why is it stated that in Cuba there are no human rights?" In other words, he asked me a question not in order that it be brought to the government nor to Fidel but rather to me in the session. That was a provocation, and I responded to him there. He is a black man about fifty years old. "Do you realize," I said to him, "that this neighborhood where you and I are living now, we would not have been allowed to live here before the revolution?"

Whatever the wider ramifications may be, people have been accustomed to discussing topics in accountability sessions and other local forums that could be categorized, using C. Wright Mills's terminology, as "personal troubles of milieu" instead of "public issues of social structure."[45] In other words, although the solutions may involve public issues, the context in which problems are presented is usually more personal. This became evident when in 1990, the Communist Party published the "call" to the Fourth Party Congress held the following year. The document, distributed nationally for the purpose of organizing discussions at all levels of society (workplaces, block committees, party cells, mass organizations) opened for debate such topics as the economy and social development, the electoral process, the operation of institutions of the state, government, administration, foreign policy, and the Communist Party.[46]

The public meetings to debate these items were abandoned after a few months, because the people were not, for the most part, debating national issues. "The problem was that nobody was *debating* anything—at least not the vital issues facing the country. The meetings had either turned into cheerleading sessions for the Revolution, or had waned to a fine drizzle of opinions on mundane items."[47] To be sure, these were not accountability sessions, but as Carlos Aldana, the former ideology secretary of the Central Committee, admitted, they demonstrated that, concerning national issues, "we're just not used to debating."[48]

The debates were resumed only after people had been convinced that there was no "correct" line and that their comments would be taken seriously. Esther Mosak reported on a meeting in September 1990 in a workplace in the communications field where the topics included the need to overhaul the National Assembly and to have the deputies directly elected by the people and more accountable to them. Also brought up for debate were policies of the Ministry of Education on high schools, corruption in the rationing system, the effects of "socialist emulation" on worker productivity, service cooperatives for restaurants (similar to the existing agricultural cooperatives), small-scale free enterprise, the need for more information from the press, opening up the party's ranks, and avoiding some of the mistakes of the former socialist countries.[49]

Problems in Accountability

Resolving *planteamientos* by citizens does not necessarily mean solving them. It may mean explaining to the constituents' satisfaction why they cannot be solved. Kenworthy defined accountability under the Cuban system as "the idea that citizens are entitled to an explanation for why things are the way they are. OPP's motto might be: solutions when possible but explanations right away."[50] *Planteamientos* are about equally divided between those that require a material solution (such as housing) and those based on problems that can be solved without material expense (such as bad service at a pharmacy). Obviously, the latter are, for the most part, easier to solve.

The overall percentage of *planteamientos* resolved has been between 60 and 70 percent, but the success is rate lower for those requiring investments.[51] Mirroring this high rate of success has been a generally high level of public satisfaction with and confidence in the ability of delegates to deal effectively with constituents' needs. But problems with the system have surfaced, some revolving around delegates' insufficient authority over the administrative agencies involved in resolving *planteamientos,* and others due to lack of initiative by delegates.

In June 1978, this problem was debated in the National Assembly in the context of complaints concerning housing construction, repair, and maintenance, which had constituted over 75 percent of the *planteamientos* that year.[52] Faustino Pérez, reporting to the assembly as the head of the Office of Attention to the Local Organs of Popular Power (created to aid local assemblies and to coordinate their activities with the higher bodies), criticized the municipal delegates for failing to deal adequately with the housing problem, pointing to a "lack of initiative on the part of delegates at the base level" and "a loss of confidence in the initiative of the delegate."[53] A heated four-hour debate ensued in which forty-seven deputies participated, all of them *de base* (municipal assembly delegates). They claimed that the problem was not so much the delegates as the lack of resources, lack of transportation for the resources, lack of efficient workers, and untimely and or unacceptable responses by administrators.[54]

Problems related to accountability sessions and *planteamientos* were discussed by Fidel Castro in his main address to the Second Party Congress in 1980:

> We should struggle to eliminate the causes that have led many rendering-of-accounts sessions to become mere formalities. We should . . . keep up a permanent struggle against the tendency toward bureaucratic mismanagement, stickiness in problem-solving, red tape, negligence and indifference to the problems and needs of the population. The local bodies of People's Power should be more demanding with regard to the administrative dependencies, enterprises, and units, so as to make them work more efficiently in providing adequate solutions to the problems raised by the people and to give them satisfactory explanations when immediate solutions are not possible.[55]

By 1982, new regulations were promulgated for all levels of the OPP. On the municipal level, the intent was to give the municipal assembly more authority to get adequate and timely responses to constituents' problems. However, by the late 1980s, a lack of sufficient local authority was still being reported. Municipal delegates from Boyeros in the City of Havana were interviewed in the publication *Poder Popular.* José Ferrer Sánchez said, "The delegates at times want to do a lot, but we can't. The voters understand provided that they get good explanations." Elena González stated, "We believe that on occasion the answers that the administrations give us to *planteamientos* made by the voters are not the best. Many are formal answers that are given sitting in an office, without analyzing the objective conditions at the site, and at times the answers are given by the secretaries or office workers, easy answers just to get by."[56] The minutes of the executive committee meeting in Playa of August 27, 1987, regarding the Spring 1987 accountability sessions report, included the following: "An effort has been made to raise the level of resolution of the *planteamientos* above 60 percent. . . . Concern was communicated to the provincial assembly executive committee regarding the provincial and national entities that have not yet provided answers."[57] The summary of the results of the Fall 1987 accountability sessions in Cienfuegos included an item critical of some of the delegates: "It was determined that low turnout at the accountability session had been due to the delegates' not resolving anything."[58]

In January 1988, representatives from the Havana provincial assembly conducted an inspection of the Bauta Municipal Assembly, a process called *control y ayuda* (supervision and assistance). I attended a meeting in which municipal delegates complained to the provincial representatives that they had not received answers for over one year to most of the *planteamientos* transmitted to the province, even though their resolution required neither resources nor investments and the municipal executive committee had intervened to help them. They pointed out that this kind of delay did not often occur on the municipal level.

Dilla linked problems related to the lack of sufficient authority at the municipal level to economic difficulties at the national level and the priority given to long-range development projects.[59] For example, the availability of construction materials including cement for home construction and repair depends partly on their production in Cuba, partly on imports, and partly on national distribution—matters that are beyond the control of the municipal delegate. A report in *Pueblo* (the publication of the provincial assembly in Sancti Spiritus) in 1987 provides an example of the problem of limited resources. After noting the many successes in resolving citizen *planteamientos* of Guillermo Díaz Pita, a delegate from Las Tozas who "knows everything that happens in his neighborhood like the palm of his hand," the article mentions his inability to get a major leak repaired in the tank that supplies water to Las Tozas. According to Díaz Pita, what was needed was a new tank: "Municipal Services repaired it, but everything remained the same. According to them the solution depends on an investment, that is to say, constructing a new tank, and that is not possible this year."[60]

Bureaucratic runaround is another issue frequently mentioned. A provincial delegate from Santiago de Cuba said in an assembly session in 1988:

> Four years ago in my election district, a pharmacy was closed with the promise that a new one would replace it, and nevertheless the problem still exists and is brought up in each accountability session. You go to see the compañeros from the Medicinal Enterprise and they tell you to go to Construction Maintenance, where I was told it was not Construction Maintenance, and in conclusion no one constructed the pharmacy and this problem affects an area with fifty-two thousand inhabitants.[61]

Friends of mine in the municipality Plaza de la Revolución in the City of Havana lived in a stately old apartment house whose leaky water tanks on the roof were destroying it. My friends had been bringing up this problem at accountability sessions since the late 1970s and kept being told that new tanks were not available. In 1988 I mentioned the case to the person in charge of citizen complaints at the National Assembly, who spoke to the secretary of the municipal assembly in question and was told that my friends were first on the list for a new tank. However, nothing happened. When my friends inquired, they were told that they were sixtieth on the list. Months later, the new tanks appeared on the front lawn, where they remained for more than six months because no one seemed to be able to arrange to have them lifted to the roof.

In the 1990 survey of voters in *Bohemia*, 48.6 percent of the voters interviewed said that their delegates lacked sufficient authority to resolve the problems brought up in the electoral district: "The repetition of problems without solution has reduced people's interest in accountability sessions. . . . The lack of resources to find solutions to many of the problems tends to lessen the faith of the electors in their representative."[62]

One of those interviewed, Teresa Reyes, an engineer from El Cangre, a small municipality in Havana Province near a sugar refinery, reported:

> In many assemblies of People's Power in El Cangre we have requested that the bus pass through the town before seven in the morning in order to avoid late arrivals for children and workers. The delegate goes to the Madruga bus terminal and states the problem, but everything remains as if nothing had been done. And here the solution is not related to lack of resources because we are not asking for more buses. What authority does the delegate have?[63]

Eduardo Ren Abad of Granma Province said that people had been waiting for five years for a solution to water problems and he had stopped attending the accountability sessions. Juan Valdés Peña, a director in the Ministry of Sugar in the City of Havana, complained that the delegates' great vulnerability was a detriment to their ability to solve problems. In the opinion of José Rodríguez, a construction worker in Matanzas Province, the delegate possessed less authority than in the early years of the OPP.[64] Among the criticisms related to the OPP raised in public forums preparatory to the Fourth Party Congress in 1991 were that municipal delegates had insufficient authority and had lost credibility.[65]

When asked their opinion of the OPP as a form of government, 40.6 percent of those surveyed in *Bohemia* said that they performed adequately, 3.6 percent said that they were inadequate, and 55.8 percent said that they needed improvement. When asked for suggestions, 70.5 percent answered that more agile and efficient methods should be found for dealing with citizens' concerns, however, without changing the present structures.[66]

Municipal delegates often feel frustrated, as is evident in the following statement by a former delegate:

> What's missing from the People's Power is the power. People would come to us and lodge scores of complaints, which I would run around trying to solve. But I didn't have the authority to solve the problems, not even a problem like getting a stop sign put in at a busy street corner, or ensuring better service at the local pizzeria. So people started blaming me, when the solutions were out of my hands. Often times, the solution was impossible because we didn't have the resources. . . . But when it's simple things that should be taken care of quickly but aren't because of some bureaucratic red tape, that's when people get disillusioned.[67]

In a follow-up article in *Bohemia*, Caridad Carrobello and colleagues interviewed eleven delegates from five provinces. Luis Colás, from Holguín Province, said that he felt that the difficulties involved in getting administrators to respond meant that the administrators had more power to govern than the OPP. Others said that this was especially the case in dealing with government agencies at the provincial and national levels: "In this area it is only possible to advance by relying on the personal relations that the members of the executive committee have with the administrations of these enterprises."[68]

Lack of adequate and timely response by administrators and delegates not taking full advantage of their status to compel adequate responses were cited by Dilla, who offered the following quote from the October 10, 1986, issue of *Bohemia*:

> The administrative agencies prolong the time in which to supply answers and respond a week before the accountability sessions when the delegate has no time to complain and has to go before the neighbors with no real acceptable answer, and at best can only tell you: "I know that this answer that they have just given me is without much meaning, or I know that it does not correspond to reality, I am not in agreement with it, but in any case I will tell you what it is," and then he reads what is at times nonsense with which no one is in agreement.[69]

Some of the delegates interviewed in *Bohemia* said that success in resolving *planteamientos* also depended on the level of preparation and effort put forth by individual delegates. At times, delegates deemed it necessary to attempt to resolve problems themselves, for example, by finding needed materials or even making administrative decisions. Melba Aldama Baró, from Matanzas, said that the regulations governing the municipal assemblies did not give the delegates sufficient authority, and that at times, it was necessary to assume more authority to carry out the assignments given them by the electorate. She also stressed that the delegate had to be firm: "The director of an enterprise must receive me and show me in practice that a matter cannot be resolved and make it clear to me why."[70]

A similar attitude was expressed by Raquel Mediavilla, from the municipality Diez de Octubre in the City of Havana, in an interview with Marta Harnecker:

> I'd like to say that we are instructed by our executive committee that we are under no obligation to accept unconvincing answers. For example, yesterday I rejected four answers given to me by various departments. . . because I couldn't understand them, and if I can't understand them, then I can't possibly make them clear to my constituents. . . . The delegate must know the problem inside out so she can discuss the matter properly with the pertinent department. For instance, if this can't be done, why not? What are the measures you're going to take? So I can explain everything to my people. The delegate must show the people that their problems were handled properly in the appropriate bureaus. She must be able to face up to an administrator and ask: "Well, what's this? How many times do I have to hear the same thing?"[71]

In 1997, a random sample survey of 3,371 voters evaluating the municipal assemblies and the delegates found that 10 percent thought that the local government was making less of an effort than prior to 1990 and the onset of the special period. 6 percent evaluated the work of their delegates as excellent, 11 percent as very good, 40 percent as good, 31 percent as average, 6 percent as bad, 1 percent as very bad, and 1 percent as awful, and 4 percent did not know or did not answer.[72]

Information and Input

Besides being designed for collective discussion and resolution of local problems, the accountability sessions were created as a mechanism for exchanging information between the government and the community. In fact, participation by citizens and accountability of representatives to the voters can be meaningful only if based on the circulation of relevant information from top to bottom and bottom to top, as well as horizontally through discussion and interaction among neighbors.[73]

In the accountability sessions, the first order of business is the report read by the delegates on the activities of the municipal assembly and its leadership during the previous six months (the same report is read by all delegates in a municipality). Next on the agenda is a report on the delegates' own activities (commission work, activities as provincial delegate or National Assembly deputy if applicable). My observation is that these reports constituted the least effective segment of the meeting because few of those in the audience seemed to be paying much attention. The delegate was limited to reading the reports without much interchange with the audience, although those attending could ask questions and voted to approve the report. This segment is followed by a report on crime in the district over the same period.

Dilla and colleagues characterized as scanty the results of the flow of information from the government to the community during the accountability sessions "because of the excessively stilted presentation, unattractive for the common citizen, of the information offered. This has definitely placed limits on the capacity of the citizens to exercise their right of oversight over public activity."[74] The problem has also been recognized at all levels of the OPP. For example, the analysis made by the National Assembly of the deficiencies found during the spring 1988 process of accountability sessions mentioned "reports offered by some delegates regarding the measures taken by the executive committee, extensive and loaded with numbers, as were the reports on their own efforts, which also lacked the required quality."[75]

Improving the flow of information to the population was made urgent in 1990 by the severe economic crisis. The accountability sessions were used to convey the causes of the shortages, to explain the measures taken by the government, and to mobilize people to solve their own problems where possible. Just prior to the Fall 1990 accountability sessions, Ernesto Suárez recommended that the sessions become more "a lively interchange of ideas and dialogue between delegate and constituents."[76] The leadership of the National Assembly issued a proclamation prior to the Spring 1992 accountability sessions, calling for a true interchange of opinions with the population regarding the situation that confronted and the efforts of the leadership of the country first to obtain necessary food, the minimum of fuel, medicine, and the things essential for life and also to increase the nation's income and as far as possible avoid closing factories. It also recommended "adequate individual preparation and prior search for the necessary information to be able to explain correctly in each accountability session the problems and situations that exist."[77]

An editorial in *Trabajadores* during the same period called it "essential that these [accountability] sessions be developed without formalism and constituted as tribunals for collective analysis of the way in which the concrete situation confronting the country is manifested on the local level."[78] Throughout the 1990s, reports in the Cuban press have criticized these reports by the delegates as formalistic and lacking content, but the recurrence of the criticism indicates that the problems continue.

After concluding this initial phase of the accountability session, the delegate informs those present of the status of the *planteamientos* made in the previous session. This segment is much livelier than the preceding ones, involving frequent participation by the public as well as administrators invited to explain their answers.

Information that flows from the population to the government with regard to problems that affect everyday life serves as input for governmental decisions at all levels.[79] According to Dilla, "It would be difficult for a local government that aspired to any legitimacy to seek to ignore the results of the accountability sessions . . . , and that is perfectly understood by the citizens and their representatives."[80] However, *planteamientos* made at accountability sessions do not necessarily promote concerted or collective action, since "these are regularly formulated and presented individually. Of more than six thousand demands studied . . . only 6 percent had some level of collective planning,"[81] that is to say, little evidence of people getting together prior to the sessions to determine collectively what *planteamientos* should be made. At the same time, it is clear that *planteamientos* do affect government decisions and policies when considered collectively. At the discretion of the delegate, some *planteamientos* may be submitted to a vote by the citizens attending the session and then presented collectively. Carlos Walfrido Rodríguez told me that he asked for the opinions of those present at the accountability sessions regarding *planteamientos* for which collective approval seems appropriate. *Planteamientos* are also considered collectively in reports issued by the municipal and provincial assemblies and the National Assembly, where they are categorized and enumerated by subject (transportation, commerce, etc.).

Domínguez conceded that "balancing everything, these procedures seem to have bettered in a practical way the life of common Cubans."[82] There is general agreement among scholars that one of the best illustrations of the influence of *planteamientos* is that of housing construction and repair, especially in the late 1970s and early 1980s. Jill Hamberg wrote, "The budget for maintenance and repair of housing and community facilities increased dramatically as a result of complaints expressed in meetings held periodically between local People's Power delegates and their constituents. . . . Between 1977 and 1983, local agencies increased their maintenance and repair budgets fivefold."[83] Similarly, Bengelsdorf correlated citizen demands with the rapid development of housing policy in the late 1970s: "It became quickly apparent that the repair and maintenance of all housing, as well as the construction of new housing, were problems of national proportions, problems which dominated [accountability] assemblies throughout the island."[84] Rabkin concurred, concluding that housing complaints made to delegates were

> forcefully and insistently brought to the attention of the political elite. The responsiveness of the system can be seen in the surge of the construction sector of the Cuban economy in the first half of the 1980s. . . . After years of stagnation in the housing sector, an average 67,000 housing units were constructed annually in 1981–1985. In 1984, after substantial increases in previous years, there was a 45 percent increase in home repairs under the jurisdiction of local government.[85]

In November 1986, a special television program narrated by the then minister of education José Fernández explained the education reform enacted in response to concerns expressed by the population regarding the quality of teaching, student promotion practices, testing, and boarding schools, among other problems. Fernández told me in January 1989 that the complaints had come to the attention of his ministry via citizen *planteamientos* as well as through municipal and provincial assembly education commission reports and the Communist Party's *estado de opinión*.

Faustino Pérez of the Office of Attention to the Local Organs of People's Power, in an interview in January 1989, gave me some later examples of the influence of *planteamientos* on a provincial and national scale. Bottlenecks in bus construction in Las Tunas Province were eliminated and production was increased in large part because of widespread citizen complaints. In the National Assembly debate on transportation in December 1988, the arguments of deputies who were also municipal delegates regarding the need to change the places where trains stopped were based on citizen complaints. A hospital constructed in Playa had been proposed by the municipality in response to citizens' requests. Gilberto Valdez and Julio Arias of JUCEPLAN told me in January 1989 that the Province of Sancti Spiritus had communicated the need for a baseball stadium, a hospital, and an old-age home, using citizen *planteamientos* as supporting evidence. (The appeal had gone to and been approved by JUCEPLAN because the province's resources were insufficient for these projects.) Pedro Chávez offered further evidence of the importance of *planteamientos* in shaping policy for the City of Havana Province. In the Alamar district of the municipality Habana del Este, needs for a new supermarket, street lighting, and the widening of a major avenue were all problems brought up by numerous citizens in accountability sessions. Similarly, in the Flores section of Playa, citizens consistently complained of flooding due to problems in the water and sewer system. Because these problems were beyond the financial capability of the municipalities and could not be resolved immediately because of the large investments required, these projects were included in three-year provincial construction plans.

José Machado Ventura of the Communist Party's political bureau and Felix Pérez Milián, head of the Department of Judicial and State Agencies of the party's Central Committee, explained to me in May 1989 how the PCC gets involved in helping to resolve *planteamientos*. The example they used came from a rural area in Holguin Province that lacked electricity and had been asking for it for a long time without success. After being told by the delegate at an accountability session that the problem could not be solved, the constituents responded that they would no longer attend these sessions. Because the installation of rural electricity involved the grouping of dispersed peasants into new communities that, in turn, required other services, providing electricity was beyond the capability of the province. The party, informed of the growing discontent, saw to it that this request for electrification was considered in the national plan and subsequently implemented.

The municipal assembly of Palmira was confronted with resistance by peasants to moving to more densely settled communities, which was required if their homes were to be given electricity. I attended the Palmira Municipal Assembly session in Palmira on November 7, 1987, where delegates reported discontent expressed to them by those who had lived in their isolated homes for many years and did not want to move from zones that have not been declared settlements *(asentamientos)* sufficiently populated for electricity or for further home construction and urged the executive committee to send urban specialists to continue trying to persuade the peasants to support the policy regarding *asentamientos.* Tomás Cabrera, then president of the assembly, stated that "this problem has been explained to the population so that the people understand the need to group houses together in order to use the resources offered in these communities, and that they cannot necessarily construct where they want to, but rather where it has been planned." It was decided to send representatives from the provincial office of physical planning and the assembly's executive committee "to visit the areas in question and provide full answers."[86] However, the policy of requiring *asentamientos* was kept.

President Roberto Díaz Vence of the municipal assembly in Playa told me in March 1988 that he had been alerted of serious delays in the distribution of food through *planteamientos* at accountability sessions:

> We realized that something was wrong. We called the ministers, we called the enterprises, and we had meetings in the ministries presided over by vice ministers. The problem was examined and solved. This is not easy to detect, because you must understand how our distribution system works. There is a certain quantity for each person, and any error or difficulty can affect some people, and if one or two persons are affected here and two others over there and two more somewhere else, it adds up. Perhaps these people don't complain at the moment it happens, but they do complain in the accountability sessions, and then we see the problem.

Another example of how citizen input affected policy in Playa comes from a municipal assembly session I attended on June 11, 1988. Orestes Mont, an administrator from the provincial agency that bought fruits and vegetables from private farmers and farmer cooperatives for sale to the population, took the podium to summarize the written report submitted by this agency to the assembly and to respond to delegates' inquiries.

The delegates complained about the pricing policies. One delegate stated, "The personal experience of the population does not correspond with what is expressed in the report. . . . The vegetable products are kept at the same price even when they are in bad shape, and the population suggests that preference is given to having them spoil rather than being bought by the people." Another said that in his district, the practice of not lowering the prices when the products began to spoil was "the cause of constant complaints on the part of consumers." Other delegates cited specific examples and used statements such as "It creates a general situation that produces unrest among the population" and "Those in charge of applying pricing policy are making the people angry. . . . The products that arrive at the small food stores *(bodegas)* are sometimes not fit to be thrown to the pigs." Some delegates also complained that prices were different in *bodegas* and in supermarkets and varied among municipalities within the same province for no apparent reason. One delegate said that his constituents had complained that the quality of goods in the *bodegas* differed from that in the produce markets even though the prices were the same. Two delegates argued that consumer demand must be considered: "The agricultural sector should not plant just to plant but rather take into account the tastes of the people and the demand for different products, since some that are in great demand are lacking and many others that are abundant are little consumed." Mont responded by citing the regulation that governed pricing policy and explaining that in every commercial zone, it is the manager alone who is authorized to lower prices. Díaz Vence responded "that what compañero Orestes Mont has explained reflects the mechanism that should be used, but this is not being carried out, for if this were so, the people would not be complaining. It has become evident in the course of the session that something is going wrong. . . . The answer of compañero Mont does not satisfy the issues that have been raised."[87]

A proposal was approved by the assembly to set up a commission to analyze the complaints about the distribution and sale of fruits and vegetables. The commission members were to receive reports from delegates regarding problems with the enterprise in their districts, and the commission was to report to the provincial assembly (because it was a provincial enterprise). The delegates then voted not to accept the enterprise's report. The following week, representatives from the enterprise and the provincial assembly met with the leadership of Playa, and it was decided to dismiss Orestes Mont from his position as administrator and to initiate necessary reforms in the enterprise's operations.

Bread production and distribution have also been modified by *planteamientos.* Mirtha Cardona explained that it had been decided in the 1970s that bread would be baked in central bakeries, but when many people complained to their delegates that they wanted their bread to be fresh and warm when they bought it, bread began to be baked locally. The steep decline in wheat imports beginning in 1991 caused by the changing relations between Cuba and the former Soviet Union led to a sharp drop in bread production and the need for the reimposition of rationing in areas where it had been eliminated. A declaration issued by the Ministries of Internal Commerce and Food Industry at the time regarding bread distribution mentions *planteamientos* raised by citizens in the previous accountability sessions as contributing to the decision to set the per capita share of bread at eighty grams daily per consumer "as the most equitable and dependable way for the acquisition of this food."[88]

Topics of debate during a special session of the City of Havana Provincial Assembly, held on November 4, 1993, were the quality of services provided by neighborhood family doctors and nurses and the difficulties incurred in the distribution of medicine, responding "to the problems pointed out by the population during the recently completed process of accountability sessions."[89]

Many categories of complaints have never been satisfactorily resolved and recur in every series of accountability sessions. However, as *planteamientos* do indeed contribute to resolving societal problems, the population gains confidence in the system, and according to Chávez, this confidence encourages more and different types of requests. Efraín Ferradáz, then executive committee member overseeing economic affairs in Havana Province (subsequently he became Cuba's Minister of Foreign Investments), told me in an interview in May 1988 that the massive construction of nursery schools in 1988–1989 was an example how *planteamientos* evolve: "The national government is being influenced by *planteamientos*, and thus has created a national program in response to them, and the whole country is being supplied with nursery schools. What is happening is that because the *planteamientos* have resolved the problem of child care, now nobody complains of nursery schools but rather of other things." Georgina Suárez also contended that *planteamientos* change in the process of social development: "Thus, the satisfaction of a group of needs constantly gives rise to new expectations. . . . For example, whereas once a number of requests in the public health sector were directed toward the establishment of particular medical or related services or specialized installations, once these demands are satisfied the requests are directed fundamentally toward the quality of the services."[90] There is also a tendency for the number of *planteamientos* to increase at the beginning of a delegate's term and then gradually diminish over time. Dilla attributed the initial increase to "the expectations awakened in the electorate to the potential initiatives which a new delegate may display."[91]

Economic Planning

In a context of economic scarcity, it is in decisions regarding the distribution of resources, according to Harry Magdoff, that "the issue of democracy in a socialist society should be located."[92] Resolving *planteamientos* that require resources and investments means, in a socialist society, that they must become part of the economic plan. In the journal of the PCC, Lorenzo Hernández wrote that for *planteamientos* that require resources, linking them with local economic and social development plans is the best way to respond.[93] Ferradáz said that the core of popular input and participation in the economic planning process was the accountability of the municipal delegates to their constituents rather than the debates on the economic plans in assembly sessions, which, at all levels of the OPP, have tended to be limited and lacking in substance.

For investments under state control,* economic planning in Cuba takes place at all levels of the economy, with the involvement of the municipal, provincial, and national governments. Citizens' *planteamientos* constitute important input in adjusting the choices made for investments that directly affect the needs of the population. These needs, to be sure, are weighed in relation to the possibilities under conditions of scarce resources and the investment requirements for long-run economic development.† An article in the provincial party newspaper in Cienfuegos explained during the October 1987 accountability sessions, "Many of the *planteamientos* formulated need to be included in future economic-social plans and budgets because they require resources that have not been within the reach of the local government or entities . . . or because they are about important centralized national investments."[94] The guide for training seminars for deputies, delegates, and administrators of the OPP, published by the Cuban National Assembly, di-

---

*Foreign investments in Cuba increased dramatically during the 1990s, especially after the National Assembly passed legislation on foreign investments in 1995, and by 1998, they had reached a value of $2.2 billion. These investments have been concentrated mainly in tourism, nickel, telecommunications, and industrial production for the internal market. Lazara Rodríguez Alemán, "Crecen las relaciones económicas de Cuba, a pesar de Helms Burton," *Prensa Latina*, December 12, 1998, URL: http:\\www.prensa-latina.org.

†It is my intention not to explain the entire economic planning process in Cuba, but to focus on how citizen *planteamientos* are part of this process Besides the literature on this topic, my information comes mainly from interviews conducted in 1988 and 1989 with the following persons: (1) Gilberto Valdez and Julio Arias of JUCEPLAN; (2) Efraín Ferradáz, the member of the executive committee of the Havana provincial assembly in charge of economic affairs; (3) Alberto Durruthy, the subdirector of planning for City of Havana Province; (4) Omar Torres, budget director for Cienfuegos Province (and also a Cienfuegos municipal delegate); (5) Pedro Chávez, president of the City of Havana provincial assembly; (6) Roberto Díaz Vence, president of the Playa municipal assembly; (7) Luis Olivera, vice president of the Playa Municipal Assembly (in charge of economic affairs); (8) Sylvia María León Rodríguez, municipal director of planning for Bauta; (9) René Lozada, municipal director of planning for Cienfuegos; (10) Juana Fonseca, municipal director of planning for Palmira; and (11) Faustino Pérez and (12) Domingo García Cárdenas, both of the Office of Attention to the Local Organs of Popular Power of the Council of Ministers. Although there are variations among municipalities and provinces (especially in the City of Havana Province), the basic procedures are similar.

rectly relates voters' *planteamientos* to economic planning. In 1982, a system of information and oversight was developed that permitted each level of government to receive the data necessary for analyzing this input. Among the objectives to which this system responds is

> the incorporation of the demands of the population into the economic plans and budgets of the territories. . . . [Under the heading] "*Planteamientos* to Be Included in the Next Economic Plans" is the *planteamiento* whose solution is not possible within the year. It is formulated because of the quantity of resources it requires but because of its importance should be analyzed during the planning process in order to determine the possibility of including it in the following economic plan or the plans for subsequent years.[95]

The municipality is required to send the province periodic reports of the *planteamientos*, classified by type, and to inform the province about *planteamientos* to be included in the economic plans, and the province, in turn, reports to the nation: "The objective is that the higher levels know, in forecasting economic plans, to what extent the *planteamientos* formulated by the voters should be taken into account, whose solution requires inclusion in these plans."[96]

One reason for establishing a uniform system for reporting these data is that prior to 1982, each province used different methods, often without any systematic analysis. In an interview published in 1985, Elia García Patiño, then head of the Office of Attention to the OLPPs, said that the system had been put into practice that year with the aim of identifying on a national scale the concerns of the citizens and determining which of them should be included in the national economic plans. García expected this system to "assist the agencies of the central state administration in planning, in investing resources, and in taking measures to resolve the issues that most preoccupy the population."[97]

Among the modifications to the central planning system approved by the political bureau of the Communist Party in February 1988 were a number related to strengthening the participation of local governments in economic planning, thereby making possible greater input on the part of the population. As reported in *Trabajadores*, "The elaboration of the Plan for Economic and Social Development, according to the approved document, should be conceived of as an uninterrupted and ongoing process at all levels. . . . Each link should not wait for the other to begin its tasks, starting from the numbers approved by the central levels, that is to say, the work should be carried out in parallel."[98]

In the Cuban economic planning process, there is a constant flow of information from top to bottom and from bottom to top. The preliminary figures issued by JUCEPLAN for the nation's yearly economic plan, which form the bases for provincial and municipal plans, are sent to the provinces and municipalities. These estimates are based on (1) the requirements of the long-range plan in progress, (2) information from national ministries and agencies, and (3) information received beforehand from the OLPP. This third category contains the needs of the population as expressed in *planteamientos* as well as in other ways. According to Valdez and Arias of JUCEPLAN, a significant part of the national economic plan comes from the combination of provincial plans, which, in turn, are to a great extent made up of municipal plans. The concept of starting the planning process with municipalities and using the municipal planning apparatus as an active rather than a passive force began in the late 1970s in Camagüey Province.

Allocation of resources by the central government through JUCEPLAN is divided into two categories: (1) investments designated and defined by the national government *(nominales)* for projects under national, provincial, and municipal jurisdiction and (2) undesignated *(no-nominales)* to be determined by national enterprises and by the provincial and municipal assemblies. Municipal and provincial economic plans include all expenditures and investments, *nominales* and *no-nominales*. Citizen input influences both categories, but most directly the latter.

On the local level, the undesignated investments consist mainly of construction, repair, and maintenance of projects directly controlled by provincial and municipal governments, such as warehouses, bakeries, gas stations, markets, primary schools, and quarters for family doctors. The sizes of the local budgets are not inconsiderable; according to the Cuban economist Nelson Mata Monfort, in 1984, these budgets included 23 percent of Cuba's investments financing 89 percent of housing and local services, 82 percent of education, 92 percent of public health costs, and 71 percent of the social and cultural activities such as libraries, social clubs, old-age homes, and sports. Mata summarized these figures: "Thus the local budgets of socialist society can be defined as the aggregate of the economic relations that foster the redistribution of the national state income . . . and finance the major part of the socio-domestic infrastructure of the national economy."[99] For example, in Havana Province, the provincial assembly invests part of the undesignated investment funds for projects under direct provincial control and distributes the rest to be invested by the municipalities according to their needs as communicated to, verified by, and approved by the province. Approximately 30 percent is invested by the province and 70 percent by the municipalities. *Planteamientos* influence the process of identifying and substantiating investment priorities on both levels.

The *planteamientos* assembled by municipal delegates by means of the *consejos populares* are sent to the presidents of the municipal and provincial assemblies and planning offices, which keep a register of them. After being categorized by area of concern and proper level of economic jurisdiction, they are sent to local enterprises and entities (bakeries, schools, transportation, clinics, etc.) and to members of the municipal and provincial administrative councils and assembly commissions according to their domains (public health, commerce, education, construction, etc.). The municipal planning office sends the figures for the amount of money available, received from JUCEPLAN for economic planning purposes, to local enterprises and agencies for input in determining undesignated investments. These agencies use *planteamientos* to help identify problems (repair and maintenance) and to establish new investment priorities and are consulted by the director of planning in evaluating a local enterprise's request for investment. Undesignated investments in Bauta's plan for 1989 included constructing bakeries, warehouses, and offices and living space for family doctors; enlarging a school; and opening a parallel market (which sold only unrationed goods).

In practice, not all the undesignated investments have been left to the discretion or under the control of the municipalities and provinces, and citizen demands have, in some instances, been ignored. During the 1980s, the Ministry of Culture decided that part of these funds should be used for the construction of theaters, although many municipalities would have preferred other investments. In the late 1980s, in one neighborhood in the municipality Chambas in Ciego de Avila Province, the *planteamientos* from an accountability session demonstrated an urgent need for a nursery school. The municipal government claimed there were insufficient resources but pledged to continue searching for funds. When a state agency vacated a building that could have been converted to a nursery school without great expense, the citizens repeated the *planteamientos.* The municipal government wanted to use undesignated investments for the conversion but were overruled by the central government's decision to use the building as a computing center for young people.[100] Dilla told me that a delegate who attempted to call attention to this discrepancy at a municipal assembly session was prevented from doing so by the assembly president.

Before a municipal plan is submitted to the assembly's leadership, the planning director solicits the input of the professional members of the assembly's administrative council, based, in part, on the *planteamientos* and *quejas* of the areas over which they are in charge. The provincial planning director meets with the municipal planning directors to make sure that the problems brought up by the public will be dealt with in municipal plans. Once approved by the assembly, the municipal plan is sent to the province for inclusion in the provincial plan, which is essentially the summation and coordination of the municipal plans in the province plus investments and expenditures under the jurisdiction of the province. The provincial planning director and the provincial assembly leadership analyze the proposals of the municipalities and other interests of the province, including those arising from citizen complaints and suggestions that correspond to this level of government. However, as Ferradáz told me, the province must attempt to meet needs expressed by the public that are beyond the reach of municipalities: "The citizen will complain that rice and beans do not arrive on time to the stores, but will not propose building a warehouse to store the rice and the beans. But the government of the province does have this responsibility because if this warehouse is not constructed in time the distribution of the provisions to the population will not be guaranteed."

The investments and expenditures in the designated category, although specified by JUCEPLAN, become part of the municipal plan insofar as the particular venture is under municipal control. Here *planteamientos* similarly play a role in substantiating a municipality's needs when requesting (via the province) these investments. In 1988, three large nursery schools, a health clinic, and an old-age home were among the designated investments approved for Playa. For centrally designated investments deemed necessary by municipalities but under national control, the municipality makes its requests to the province, which forwards them, once approved, to the relevant national ministries. Playa's request for a new hospital, sent to the province because obviously it would also serve other municipalities, was based on health needs substantiated by the provincial government but beyond the capacity to respond to. It eventually reached the Public Health Ministry and was approved.

Municipalities submit their requests in the order of priority given each. Obviously not all municipal and provincial requests can be approved and included in economic plans, especially under crisis conditions. Not all *planteamientos*, even taken collectively, can or should be included, but there is no question that needs expressed by the population are part of the economic planning process.

Commenting on the absence of debate that I had observed at the three levels of the OPP on the yearly economic plans and budgets, due in great part to time constraints and lack of timely information, Escalona told me that major changes were envisioned in the planning process, such as putting more emphasis on the needs of various sectors of the economy without the time constraints of yearly economic plans, giving more initiative to municipalities and enterprises, and eliminating much of the overlapping bureaucracy:

> If you refer to the [Fourth] Party Congress resolution which deals with the economy, you will see that it suggests planning by sector and not necessarily by time periods. The economic planning system has been our ruin. It was brought to us on a silver platter from the socialist countries and it is a huge piece of rubbish, because it has not in any way produced results in this country. First it divided the government, and when there were objections to the plan, it was said: "Well, there is no time because the National Assembly meets in fifteen days." And then the plan arrived at the National Assembly the same day as the vote on it. . . . The problem is much more serious than the formal act of approving the plan: it is that we have to go to the bottom to see how we are going to manage

our economy, and we are now performing various types of experiments, that is to say opening the possibilities for organisms, enterprise units, factories, etc. to make direct contracts. A series of national experiments are being conducted, unhurried, because this country cannot withstand being mistaken again. . . . It cannot continue being the system that demonstrated its inefficiency in the socialist countries and almost drowned us. There is a Central Planning Board that has changed and now it is much more serious. For example, regarding modifications in the local governments, we will create an apparatus sufficiently flexible to deal with whatever decision is made. . . . All this became a bureaucracy, with all the ministries interfering to express their opinions.

Despite the many economic changes introduced during the special period, *planteamientos* continued to play a major role in economic planning. At the second annual meeting of the 169 presidents of municipal assemblies, held on September 13 and 14, 1996, part of the discussion centered on citizens' *planteamientos* as an important aspect of the relation of the assemblies with their constituents, and on the experience of the past two processes of accountability sessions. Carlos Lage, secretary of the Council of Ministers, stated that the interchange of information between local governments and the central government helps the former in the efforts to find effective solutions to the needs of the people.[101]

The economic and social plan submitted for approval to the National Assembly has become more decentralized and serves as an instrument of control and oversight and to forecast macroeconomic objectives. Up until 1990, plans were based on a system of centralized assignment of tasks and distribution of material resources for production. In 1995, short-term planning was reintroduced employing financial instruments and decentralized control and regulation, especially taking into account income and expenditures in hard currency. However, money is still centrally allocated, based on needs, for social expenditures, including public consumption and food and fuel imports, because of their economic and social importance.[102]

Accountability Sessions

I attended accountability sessions held by municipal delegates with their constituents in 1987, 1988, and 1996. I was present at various activities held in relation to the accountability sessions of Fall 1987 and Spring 1988. I attended seminars held prior to the sessions to prepare the delegates for the sessions and to attempt to resolve the unresolved *planteamientos* from previous sessions, as well as meetings to coordinate the preparations of the sessions. I accompanied delegates on visits to the homes of citizens to discuss the possible resolution of *planteamientos* they had made in the previous accountability sessions. I participated in biweekly meetings between delegates and administrators held to resolve pending *planteamientos*.

In October 1987, I attended seven accountability sessions. In April 1988, I attended fourteen accountability sessions, five of them with the same delegates as in October, so that it was possible in some cases to follow the process of making and then resolving the same *planteamientos*. In May 1996, I attended four sessions. All but two of the sessions I attended were in one of the four municipalities included in my study. For some of the October 1987 sessions, I was accompanied by a representative of the municipal government because I had not yet had a chance to make my own contacts, and it is possible that the delegates were informed that I would be present. Except for these sessions, I went unaccompanied and usually unannounced to all other meetings, seminars, visits to constituents, and accountability sessions.

Although I did not give the delegates prior notice, when possible I greeted them prior to the start of the session. With the exception of two sessions, my presence was not announced to the citizens attending, and I attempted to remain in the background to attract as little attention as possible. For the most part, I believe I remained relatively unnoticed, and my presence did not seem to affect the audience participation.

The discussions and interchanges at the accountability sessions were lively but, for the most part, respectful, with many of those attending willing to complain, criticize, voice opinions, and disagree with the delegate or administrators present. I found very little difference in tone and substance from cosmopolitan Miramar and Cienfuegos to suburban Santa Fe and Bauta, and to rural Camerones. The sessions in what could be called shantytowns *(barrios insalubres)* differed little from the others except for the nature of some of the problems raised. The delegates whose sessions I attended included ones with years of experience and new ones, men and women, black and white. Some were in leadership positions in their municipal assembly. One was a *consejo popular* president. I chose four who were also National Assembly deputies to see if issues relating to national policy were more likely to be raised. I did not observe any significant differences that could be attributed to any of these categories. Furthermore, those held in the late 1980s were similar in all respects to those held in 1996, including the nature of the *planteamientos;* that is, the same types of problems recurred and could not be satisfactorily or totally resolved.

The excerpts from these sessions presented here should not necessarily be considered typical or representative; rather, they have been selected to show the interaction between constituents, delegates, and administrators; the range of topics under discussion, the willingness of the public to criticize governmental authorities; and the efforts of the delegates to resolve *planteamientos*.

From my observations, a great deal of time and effort are spent preparing the delegates for the accountability sessions. According to Domingo García Cárdenas:

> The CDR, the FMC and the ANAP . . . in coordination with the municipal executive committee and the delegates are responsible for setting up the meeting and publicizing it, stressing its importance in order to encourage the electors' participation. . . . the delegates prepare information, with the help of the administrative departments and enterprises, on the status of matters brought up in previous meetings and individual contacts.[103]

In preparation for the April 1988 accountability sessions, the municipal delegates in Playa held a meeting led by assembly President Roberto Díaz Vence on March 19. On March 25, they met with the head of the municipal party unit, and on March 26, all the municipal delegates from the City of Havana Province attended a preparatory session led by provincial assembly President Chávez.

At the March 19 meeting, after some procedural guidelines had been discussed, delegates complained that responses to *planteamientos* raised by constituents during delegates' office hours were not given the same importance by administrators as those raised in the accountability sessions, as only the former were counted in determining which municipality within the province had resolved the largest number of *planteamientos*. Díaz Vence responded that coming in first is not as important as satisfying the people. He also told the delegates that if they observed problems in their districts beyond those brought up by constituents, it was their responsibility to try to solve them. Specifically with regard to the upcoming accountability sessions, delegates complained of the difficulties of getting administrators to attend. Díaz Vence suggested that delegates should seek help from party members in their districts in resolving *planteamientos*. The meeting closed with a talk by an administrator of public transportation regarding problems that might be brought up at the accountability sessions. At the March 25 meeting with the municipal party leader in Playa, the delegates discussed problems in resolving *planteamientos* due to inefficiencies of city and state agencies.

On March 26, all the municipal delegates from the City of Havana Province met to hear reports from the provincial director of transportation and the provincial director of *microbrigadas* on their accomplishments and continuing problems. The latter asked delegates to encourage the population to participate in construction projects. One delegate demanded that more resources be provided for volunteer brigades doing home repairs. Mirtha Cardona, the provincial assembly secretary, reported that 65 percent of the *planteamientos* from the previous October accountability sessions had been resolved, in contrast to only 17 percent of those submitted through delegates' offices. The municipality Plaza de la Revolución had come in first with 93 percent. It was announced that the two types of *planteamientos* would thereafter be given equal weight in these tallies. The meeting ended with a speech by the provincial party leader.

On March 17, 1988, Bauta delegates met with municipal administrators to attempt to find solutions to the 161 unresolved *planteamientos* (out of 761 made the previous October); 59 of these were considered to have a chance of being resolved before the April accountability sessions, which would result in a 73 percent solution rate. Each of the 59 was discussed. In some cases, administrators and delegates disagreed, and here the delegates had the final say. Delegates were told to encourage the participation of the population in projects such as constructing sidewalks. Bauta delegates met again on March 24 to hear from local administrators from the departments of transportation, commerce, and public health regarding difficulties and perspectives, information to be shared with the public at the April accountability sessions. A final meeting was held on March 31 to resolve the last remaining *planteamientos.* Delegates were told to explain to the public that openings in nursery schools would remain limited until the construction of a new one that was in the following year's economic plan.

The February 1989 bulletin of the Cienfuegos executive committee informed the delegates on six topics proposed for discussion in the spring accountability sessions. Under the heading "Do you know that for these sessions you should have answers ready to these questions?" it was explained why it would not be immediately possible to (1) replace the cafeteria in the provincial hospital, (2) electrify all new housing, (3) repair all small grocery stores, (4) expand telephone lines, (5) increase urban bus routes, and (6) conduct repairs in the city's rooming houses.[104]

Delegates, together with representatives of the mass organizations and the party in their electoral district, hold coordination meetings, to prepare for the accountability sessions. I attended the March 29, 1988, meeting with Carlos Walfrido Rodríguez in Playa. The local CDR president chaired the meeting because this organization has the major responsibility for setting up the lights, tables and benches, and microphone and loudspeakers; bringing the record player and the recording of the national anthem; hanging the Cuban flag; and mobilizing the citizens to attend. The local CDR president announced that members of the Pioneers youth organization would lend assistance at the session so that young people could identify with the political process. The neighborhood party nucleus, composed mainly of retired people and housewives, also helped with the preparation. Rodríguez told me that the party nuclei in workplaces located in his electoral district also contribute, lending a hand if there are problems, for example, getting an audio system.[105] At the meeting, Rodríguez announced some changes from past sessions: (1) There would no longer be any voting on *planteamientos,* (2) *planteamientos* were to concern more social rather than personal issues, (3) *planteamientos* submitted through the delegates' office were to be given equal weight with those given at the sessions, (4) possible solutions to *planteamientos* were to be discussed, and (5) an attempt was to be made to get volunteers to join the volunteer brigades for housing repairs *(microbrigadas sociales)*.

The various sessions are coordinated by the municipal assembly secretary, who determines at what sessions administrators should be present to answer questions and which delegates will attend to evaluate the participation of the constituents present and the overall performance of the delegate conducting the session. Observers from the local CDR, the municipal PCC, and the provincial assembly also attend and report back to their respective bodies. Chávez told me that provincial assembly leaders, members, and administrators helped with the preparations and then attended as many accountability sessions as possible, their main interest being the mood of the population.

At the accountability session of Enrique Bravo in Playa that I attended on April 5, 1988, there was a delegate sent by the municipal assembly executive committee to evaluate the session, along with a party observer and representatives from the local commerce and education offices. Afterward they all met with Bravo and talked about the session. The written evaluation covered the organization of the meeting, the attendance, the delegate's report and explanations, the participation of the constituents, and the issues that most animated those present. One criticism was that Bravo should have announced the presence of the administrators to encourage *planteamientos* on commerce and education.

In Cienfuegos, the evaluation of a member of the executive committee of an accountability session in October 1987 contained the following criticisms:

> (a) The delegate, not the secretary of the session, should read the answers to the constituents. (b) Mobilization of the constituents to attend the session was poor in relation to the number in the electoral district, and we found out later that there are problems with the local CDR leadership. (c) The delegate should look to more support from the local leadership and militants of the party and the UJC.

Beforehand each voter in the area is given a slip to hand to a representative of the CDR at the beginning of the session, in order to determine the approximate percentage of voters attending. (These slips do not bear the voters' names and thus are not used to find out who was absent.) At the start of the accountability session, those present elect a secretary to take minutes, which include the number attending and the percentage in relation to the number of voters in the last election, the opinions expressed by the constituents on the delegate's reports, and the new *planteamientos*. Immediately after the sessions, the *planteamientos* are recorded by the *consejo popular* officers and subsequently passed along to the relevant state enterprises, to the municipal and provincial leadership, and to the appropriate municipal and provincial assembly commissions, which investigate and report on the conditions that led to complaints.

Racquel García, the municipal assembly secretary in Cienfuegos, told me that she met after the accountability sessions with municipal party representatives to discuss the written evaluations of the sessions. Monthly statistics on the resolution of *planteamientos* were used to determine which delegates were having problems. According to García, women delegates often had more difficulty getting answers from administrators. Toward the end of every month, she met with each delegate to review the monthly report on the status of the *planteamientos*. Delegates also submitted written opinions of the administrators and their responses. Each member of the Cienfuegos municipal executive committee was assigned to supervise and help a certain number of delegates. García oversaw eighteen.

García gave me examples of how responses were dealt with on the municipal level. One *planteamiento* had to do with the lack of organization and hygiene at the local bakery. The response by the bakery administrator was that measures were being taken to eliminate the causes of the disorganization and that hygiene had improved substantially. The delegate rejected this response, stating that although the administrator was new, no real improvements had been made, and that what was needed was a general effort to clean up and embellish the bakery. In support of the delegate, García wrote that the entrance to the bakery was causing a bad impression and needed some brightening up, that the interior needed painting, and that the counter and shelves needed repair. A *planteamiento* in Cienfuegos for which the response was deemed acceptable concerned the need for the construction of a home and office for a family doctor in the neighborhood. The municipal director of public health responded that the problem had been recognized, construction of three family doctor homes/offices had commenced, and a new one was planned.

Reviewing suggestions for improvement and reports in the Cuban press of accountability sessions from 1994 to 1996, and having attended four sessions in Santa Fe in May 1996, I found little evidence of any major changes in content or procedures since 1986. Bread, water, and streetlights continued to be among the *planteamientos* brought up. There was concern expressed in the press that the severe economic crisis might discourage attendance and participation, as, because of the lack of material resources, finding solutions for *planteamientos* was becoming more difficult. However, attendance did not diminish.[106]

A recurring theme was that the sessions should go beyond local concerns. In a letter to delegates just prior to the Spring 1994 accountability process, National Assembly President Ricardo Alarcón called for a continuation of the economic policy themes of the recently concluded workers' parliaments and National Assembly sessions, to convert the traditional session into "a massive movement of exchange of opinions, of explanations, and of argumentation, regarding the recent agreements and pronouncements of the National Assembly."[107] This topic was repeated during the municipal election and accountability process in 1995. Cuban journalist and political commentator Susana Lee reiterated that the sessions should involve discussions of local, provincial, and national problems. However, in the reports in the press and during the sessions I attended in 1996, I found only a few instances where *planteamientos* and discussions referred to issues beyond the locality. In Santa Fe, a man complained about hard currency being used mainly for tourism, and the press noted denunciations in some accountability sessions of the U.S. Helms-Burton law strengthening the U.S. economic blockade of Cuba.

The exhortation that constituents, in the context of the accountability sessions, should participate actively in finding solutions and resolving problems seems to have met with more success. According to Lee, this 180-degree change from the previously predominant "ask for" and "receive" mentality was necessary because of the increase in difficult conditions, as reflected in citizens' *planteamientos*, and the decrease in the materials to solve them.[108]

For example, in the Fall 1994 accountability process, there were press reports of a session in Cotorro in the City of Havana. The lack of water was no longer a problem because previously the residents had dug the ditches and brought in the pipes by hand because of the lack of machinery. They had also started the construction of the clinic for the family doctor. Those attending agreed in this session to build and maintain the neighborhood vegetable gardens.[109]

In a 1995 interview published in *Trabajadores*, Alarcón said that the essence of Cuban democracy is collective action, not an isolated delegate, such as organizing repair brigades to resolve problems: "I was present in an assembly where an administrative director was absence, and there the people decided: 'lets organize a commission of neighbors to visit this administrator.'"[110] Raúl Ramírez commented in *Trabajadores* about what he termed the three "magical" words: "analysis, participation and solutions. . . . I ask myself why these three very often recurring terms are so difficult to link together in the affairs of delegates and constituents."[111] Lee took up the same theme:

> Only if we go—delegates and constituents—further than the merely recounting of resolved and pending *planteamientos*, and formulating new ones . . . and dedicate a part to expressing our opinions, to giving ideas, to finding formulas together in order to face up to problems that trouble us and whose solution do not only depend on resources, which are presently very scarce, will we be on the road in which this process impels, reinforces, and consolidates popular participation in the principal decisions which concern the communities.[112]

Reducing the number of participants to no more than 120 per session by scheduling more sessions per electoral district was one measure taken to increase constituent participation, according to Jaime Crombet, vice president of the National Assembly.[113] This has meant more sessions for each delegate. For example, in Camagüey, Lee reported that whereas before each delegate had had up to three sessions, as of Fall 1995 the number was from four to ten or even more.[114] Therefore the period set aside for accountability sessions has been stretched from about one month to more than two months. In Spring 1996, it went from mid-April to mid-June. Having accountability sessions with smaller groups met with approval, according to an August 1997 survey, which found that 73 percent considered this an improvement, 61 percent said that it resulted in more people speaking up, and 45 percent acknowledged that new problems were brought up.[115]

Lee reiterated the need for the delegate to have community respect, involvement, and support for solving problems, as well as timely cooperation from administrative entities. She cited an example from a "difficult" electoral district in the municipality Cerro in the City of Havana, where the delegate complained that the municipal administrators had waited until just before the accountability session to inform him that nothing had been done to solve housing problems, which had been often brought up in the past. This lack of action results in the constituents' losing confidence in the delegate, discourages dialogue, and affects the quality of the session.[116] National Assembly VicePresident Jaime Crombet stated that administrators who do not support the delegates "should be immediately replaced."[117]

The lack of attendance by administrators at the accountability sessions continued to be a problem mentioned in the press and by Alarcón. The municipal governments were considered responsible for their being present, and the delegates and popular council presidents should specify the specific sessions each administrator should attend.[118] Municipal and provincial administrators should attend to respond to constituents' concerns, but above all, the family doctor, the director of the public health clinic and of the nursery school, and the local administrators of the bakery, the *bodega*, the vegetable market, and the fish and meat store.[119]

Tomás Cárdenas, president of the National Assembly Commission on Local Organs of the Poder Popular, evaluated the Spring 1996 accountability process. Having the provincial assemblies be in overall charge permitted better scheduling and preparation of the delegates. He criticized the insufficient dissemination of information in the media, excepting some radio stations, and the insufficient use of graphic publicity. The goal of reducing the number of participants in each session had been met in most places. The number of *planteamientos* raised by citizens as well as the number of solutions presented by the delegates had increased. However, if a problem had no solution, the delegate must present his or her constituents with the necessary arguments and not accept the demand as a *planteamiento*. Cárdenas repeated the need for the sessions to go beyond delegates' responding to constituents, to "become an instrument to channel popular participation, which we hope in the future will arrive at a higher plane: control by the people over matters and actions on which they agree."[120]

I attended the accountability session on October 26, 1987. for Area 3 of the Second Electoral District in Bauta. The delegate, Felix Gómez, a retiree, spoke of the status of two *planteamientos* from the previous session of April 1987. One, which Gómez reported as being 50 percent resolved, concerned letting high school students enter the school grounds before school started because the students' waiting in the street was bothering the neighbors. The school officials replied that this would not be a problem at 7 A.M. because there were no students in class at that time, but it would be impossible for students entering at 1 P.M. because the students allowed to enter early would bother those in class. However, after checking on the day of this session, Gómez found that in fact, the students were not being let in at 7 A.M., and he told those assembled:

> Today I spent the day trying to find the school's director and the municipal director of education. I found the school's director, who told me the problem is that the workers would have to start work at 7 instead of 7:20. I told him, "Chico, I told the voter who made the *planteamiento* to go check it out, and now I go to check it and you have not opened the door or called anybody. In other words, you did not comply with the solution that you promised to the electoral district." I asked when he would open that door at 7 A.M. He told me, "Tomorrow." Besides, he told me, "I want to know who the voter is in order to speak with him and explain the situation to him." Carlos [the complainant] should come tomorrow to check to see if it is true that the doors open at 7 A.M. This is a hard struggle, because it means changing customs and to be sure would mean more work to have the children inside the school instead of on the street.

The other *planteamiento* was that an attendant be placed in the bathroom at a bus stop, with those using the facility paying five centavos to the attendant to keep it clean. The municipal unit in charge agreed and was granted permission from a higher level, and a person was being sought to fill the position.

It is customary when presenting new *planteamientos* for constituents to give their names and addresses. The first two new *planteamientos* at this session, presented by one man, concerned street repair and the availability of construction materials for housing. The next person, Pedro Luis López, also presented two *planteamientos*:

> The first is with relation to the sewage water from the Nuevo Vedado district, which flows into the river, which carries it to the Maurín Dam. This sewage wa-

ter thus does not pass through a sewage treatment facility and flows contaminated right to this dam. This water is then utilized for irrigating the pastures where the cows eat, and this can cause a whole series of transmissions of diseases. My *planteamiento* is that a study be made of the possibilities of establishing a sewage treatment plant for this water so it should not arrive contaminated.

For his second *planteamiento,* López spoke of his opposition to having Bauta's summer street parties held within the populated areas because of sanitation problems:

Our revolution spends millions of pesos taking care of the health of the people, and the medical services in Cuba we can say are our pride on a world scale, but we have breaches, and one of these breaches is precisely what I pointed out with relation to the sewage water, and the other is due to these parties. Latrines have to be set up in the city, because the people drink a lot of beer and have to go to the bathroom to empty the bladder during the three days of the party, and this brings as a consequence stench and flies, which are intolerable. One latrine that was placed—and I criticized this a lot to many friends—right in front of the *bodega* where we make our purchases, where they are selling food products—I don't know who had the idea of putting a latrine there. These kinds of parties should take place outside of populated areas.

Gómez responded that the first *planteamiento* had been brought up frequently about five years earlier, as a result of which an oxidation pond had been constructed (an example of *planteamientos* influencing investments), and now López was suggesting that this was not sufficient: "We will take up this *planteamiento* and get a response as soon as possible." Other *planteamientos* presented at the session concerned housing construction, delivery of construction materials, and high electricity rates.

On March 31, 1988, just prior to the April accountability sessions, I accompanied Gómez on a visit to López's house to speak about sewage treatment and summer parties. On the sewage problem, Gómez had informed the leadership of the municipal assembly and arranged a meeting with López attended by the executive committee member overseeing public services, an administrator from the municipal public services department, and a technician from public health. They explained the situation to López and tried to convince him that the methods now being used were sufficient. He was not convinced and told Gómez that he planned to write to the National Assembly:

The sewage waters that go into the pond carry a series of microscopic organisms, and I do not consider that they explained to me that these would be destroyed by the biological action of the plants, fish, and sun. . . . This water is used to irrigate pastures and sugarcane fields, and I consider that there exists a degree of danger in the transmission of viruses. . . . I consider this to be a serious problem that should be analyzed at a higher level with a greater degree of responsibility with the goal of finding an adequate solution or giving me a satisfactory and scientific response that convinces me that this oxidation pond leaves no contamination in the water. . . . If the National Assembly gives me an answer that does not satisfy me, well, at least I will have fulfilled my duty as citizen to point out the problem, to make it known.

On the problem of summer parties, Gómez told López that he had been informed that there was no suitable alternative place to hold them. The municipal assembly had commissioned a person to study the situation, and it had been determined that the parties should be spaced out more and not concentrated in just a few areas and that latrines should not be put in front of food stores. After reiterating emphatically what a scandal this had been, López said he was satisfied that with the measures recommended, things would improve. I asked him if Gómez was well known among his constituents. "Of course," he responded. "He is known even to the cats. Everyone knows him in all parts."

During the accountability session of April 7, 1988, Gómez referred to the response on the sewage problem: "The answer said that there is an oxidation pond, which sufficiently purifies the sewage water that goes to the dam, and thus it is not necessary to build a treatment facility, which certainly would improve the purity of the water but which costs too much and is not considered necessary for irrigating the pastures and for animals' drinking water." He referred to the steps taken and López's intention to take the matter to the National Assembly.* López answered affirmatively when asked whether he continued to reject the response. Gómez then discussed the solution proposed for the latrines during the summer parties and asked López if this was all right, and López answered yes.

At an accountability session held in Playa, Area 5 of the Seventy-seventh Electoral District, on October 15, 1987, the delegate, José Enrique Cardoso, was corrected by members of the audience when he said that he had been informed that the *planteamiento* from the previous session held in

---

*As appears in the official National Assembly minutes, the matter was brought up in debate, probably not coincidentally, during the July 1988 National Assembly session. During the discussion of the response by the commission on public health to the report from the Academy of Sciences, a deputy referred to problems with using sewage water from oxidation ponds for irrigation in terms similar to López's *planteamiento*, and complaining of lack of technical supervision and qualified personnel. Rosa Elena Simión, a deputy from the commission, responded, "Undeniably the oxidation ponds are a problem, most seriously in some cases due to lack of maintenance, and in others because the pond as such does not have sufficient capacity to destroy all the organic material, which is the case the deputy refers to, and because of this, there has been a search for other alternatives [by the Academy of Sciences]." She said the issue would be discussed in the December 1988 National Assembly session.

Felix Gómez, left, municipal delegate in Bauta, meeting with a constituent during his visits to constituents' homes to discuss *planteamientos* made at accountability sessions.

April 1987, regarding poor performance by an inspector at a bus stop, had been resolved. One citizen complained:

> With respect to the bus inspector, he maintains the same attitude that was brought up here in April. When the bus drivers arrive here, we form a line. However, when the three bus doors are opened, people scatter and there is disorder, and those not in line get in, and the people waiting in line get angry. The inspector is insensitive to the problems of the line. He just stays in the doorway of the cafeteria conversing. He pays no attention to any problems related to the buses. This is not just my personal opinion; you can do a survey of those waiting in line. Nothing has changed. . . . We want to know what the role of a bus inspector is. He sees kids hanging from the bus windows and is incapable of telling the driver to stop. The problems are seen here every day. The inspector has the same attitude. He has not changed.

Another man added, "The inspector is lazy. He should show the same respect that I have seen other inspectors have, who help people get on buses. This compañero is just a decorative figure. He doesn't help those of us who take the bus there every day."

After another person had reiterated the complaints against the inspector, Cardoso said, "I believe what is being brought up here is very fair. Those in favor of rejecting the answer to this *planteamiento* raise your hands." (Cardoso called for a vote on all *planteamientos.*) As a result of a favorable vote the complaint was registered again. This item was brought up again in the same area during the spring accountability session, after which, on April 1, Cardoso wrote the following letter to the head of the inspection department of the Urban Bus Enterprise:

> The object of this letter is to make you aware of some deficiencies detected by voters in Electoral District 77 of Playa in relation to the performance of the inspector who works at the bus stop of Avenue 19 and 70. . . . The answer to the *planteamiento* of April 1987 was that discussions had been held with the compañero and that he had promised to improve his work. Now, the response to the *planteamiento* of October 1987 was that this inspector's work had been checked and "no irregularity whatever was detected." . . . We thought that at last the situation was resolved, but the constituent has told us that the situation continues. Concerned by the proximity of the new accountability session . . . I decided personally to observe this situation, as others had brought it up, too, and in any case, the answer could be rejected. . . . In reality, I was able to prove one of the points made at the sessions: HE IS INDIFFERENT TO THE PUBLIC THAT RIDES THE BUSES. . . . You are the ones who know what the duties of the inspectors are . . . but an abysmal difference exists between the work of this compañero and that of other inspectors whom the public considers true friends and men of the people, concerned with alleviating the difficulties with transportation that all of us are aware of. . . . We have left this case pending in the accountability session that took place last night until we receive from you the results of the analysis that you will surely make regarding this communication.

Among other *planteamientos* made at Cardoso's October session was the need for extensive repair of a sidewalk. Cardoso responded that he was aware of the problem but mentioned the labor shortage and suggested that the neighbors perform the task with voluntary labor as people in the Santa Fe district had done, identifying this as "the style of work that our commander in chief has counseled." Later on, a man commented that it must be determined who could work and what needed to be done before this brigade was organized: "This is not just a case of arriving and throwing the concrete there, because then we would be leaving the sidewalk worse than it is now." Other *planteamientos* concerned the poor quality of replacement parts for television repair and the failure to turn on city water as scheduled for apartment buildings. Regarding the second, a man said, "We know there are problems with the water, because we live in Cuba—it doesn't rain and water cannot be manufactured. But what we want is that they not deceive us. . . . We want them to give us an answer." The final *planteamiento* was that work crews had repeatedly torn up the street to repair underground pipes but had never returned to fix the street.

At an accountability session held on October 20, 1987, by delegate Fidel Martínez in Camerones, a relatively isolated settlement in Palmira, the *planteamientos* concerned insufficient milk supply (to have been resolved by the completion of the new milk-processing plant), repair of the only road leading into the town, the need for construction materials for building and repairing houses, and problems with the telephones and the water supply.

On October 21, at the session of the delegate Norma Estrada in the Ninety-fifth Electoral District in Cienfuegos, the *planteamientos* were about clogged street-sewer drains, the need for paving streets and sidewalks and for streetlights, faulty electric meters, leaky roofs and other housing repair, garbage thrown in the streets, and moving graves in the cemetery.

At the accountability session on October 21 of Enma Torres in Anafe, a small settlement just outside of Bauta, the *planteamientos* dealt with inconsistent and late meat deliveries to the local store; the poor quality of the bread ("At times, not even the chickens will eat it"), which the constituent recognized was a national problem that persisted despite the bread bakers' salaries having been raised; the constant breakdown of the turbines pumping water to the houses due to the failure to finish the shelter that was to protect them from inclement weather (the constituent recognized the efforts made by the delegate to guarantee the flow of water and suggested that the local population, including himself, volunteer to finish the construction of the shelter); a dangerous ditch by the local highway that was causing many accidents; and the fact that the fourth-graders in the local school had gone two weeks without a teacher.

Just prior to the April 1988 accountability sessions, I accompanied José Enrique Cardoso on his constituent visits in Playa. On the first of these, the issue was the irregular delivery of milk to the stores. Cardoso admitted that the answer supplied did not say anything and expressed concern that the administrator had not visited the woman at home. This constituent had also made *planteamientos* concerning bus transportation that could not be resolved, and about a rash of stealing gas meters (because of a shortage, thieves were able to sell them), the solution for which was to attach the meters to the house walls and to develop a new protective device to be attached around the meters. Asked her opinion of the accountability system, this constituent responded, "One can freely say what one feels, and if then one finds the solution, it seems to me the best way. No one is afraid to speak, and one can determine where deficiencies are." She told me Cardoso was well known in his district. In the next home, a young couple had complained about a space unused for years on the first floor of their apartment building, which was deteriorating because of lack of ventilation, causing damage to the

José Enrique Cardoso, municipal delegate in Playa, meeting with a constituent during his weekly office hours.

building and attracting rats. Cardoso informed them that a confectionary store would be put there, and the couple offered to help with the labor.

On March 22, I accompanied Carlos Walfrido Rodríguez from Playa on his constituent visits. At the home of a middle-aged professional couple, the issue was the bad quality of the flushing mechanism for toilets and the fact that if a part broke, one had to buy the whole set, which meant unnecessary expenditure for the consumer. A representative of the Ministry of Light Industry had told them that the ministry was working on improving the quality. Rodríguez had learned from the ministry, however, that what was being proposed was a modification in the flotation arm mechanism—an interim step rather than a solution to the quality problem, which required materials not immediately available. Besides, separate parts still were not being sold, although that was promised for the near future. The constituent said that he was not satisfied with the response, although he did expect the issue to be resolved satisfactorily. At the accountability session held on April 14, Rodríguez reported that the problem was being worked on, with the ministry agreeing to inform the delegate specifically how the toilet tank parts would be improved. Asked their opinion of the *planteamiento* system, these constituents told me that the delegate was their entree to government agencies; without him, "One wouldn't get past the front door, but with the delegate we can because it becomes something that affects not just one person." Before the revolution, it had been very difficult to see one's government representative, whereas "now the representatives are well known. Everyone knows Carlos. If I want to see him, I go to his house. We can see him any time we want. If he needs something from us, he also can knock on our door."

On April 2, 1988, I made the rounds with a delegate from the rural outskirts of Bauta. The first person visited was the head of the local CDR, who had complained about the long lines at the pharmacy, due mainly to the employees' poor work habits. It had been determined that the pharmacy's administrator was to blame. He was replaced, and the problem was resolved. The delegate informed other constituents that their request for lights on the road to the milk factory for those who work the night shift had been denied for that year because of the need to use the lamps in areas that had been given a higher priority. Similarly, a request for new electrical cable was delayed because the existing cable was destined for use at the local slaughterhouse and a new clinic for dentures. A paved road damaged by tractors from the cane fields had been repaired, and a new sidewalk by the rural bus stop had been built by local voluntary labor, both items in response to *planteamientos.*

At an accountability session in Playa on April 6, 1988, where the attendance was 65.8 percent, the lively discussion focused on the failure of the police to control youths, and on the performance of the delegate, María Correa, who was also a National Assembly deputy. Although she mentioned this during the report on her activities, none of the *planteamientos* were directed to her in that capacity. She was interrupted while giving the crime report for her electoral district, with many complaints about police ineptitude. One man said, "With the quantity of robberies there are in the streets and buses, it seems that we have the doors open in Cuba. I don't see the police taking any measures, neither the police in the district, nor those patrolling in cars. I don't see any, not any! I have not yet seen a patrol car stop a bus and arrest anyone." Another said, "What has bothered me for some time are the so-called dancers *[bailarines],* that is, those who hang onto the outside of buses, and because of them, the bus doors are not closed, and there have been injuries." Another said, "This should be resolved by us who are party militants, who are Communists. We ourselves must cooperate. We cannot wait for the police to resolve everything. Certainly if there are police on a corner, they should be called." Correa responded, "The compañero's concern is a *planteamiento* to which we can respond. I completely agree with him that the police, if present, can corroborate and contribute, independent of the fact that all the people can help to keep the youth from doing these things and to keep them from breaking the bus." Another man said:

> This is not an easy problem for a party militant alone, confronting twenty or twenty-five youths who even go riding on the bus's roof. It seems incredible when we consider other countries in the world and see that possibly this is the most peaceful, that such behavior exists in our system. It was announced that buses are being bought, that 250 more buses will be incorporated. How much does it cost to bring these buses here? Do you believe it is correct to make this expenditure? If we solve nothing else we must stop them from traveling as they wish, hanging from the windows. . . . This is a problem for all of us, not just the police.

This was followed by applause.

Correa said that just as the blacksmith worked on his anvil and the cane cutter cut sugarcane, the police had to do their job; that was what the state paid them for. But everyone, party militant or not, had to cooperate—the local FMC and CDR, social workers, parents by educating their children. She emphasized that most young people in Cuba were not delinquents, and the people applauded. She said that this complaint would be the first *planteamiento.**

A man complained about an unresolved *planteamiento* concerning a water tank in an apartment building that had been leaking for five years and was destroying the building. The authorities had not even come to see the problem: "If you don't see it, you can't feel it." When Correa tried to get in a word, he said, "Pardon me, but it seems that this doesn't interest you and you don't want to let me finish." Correa responded that the person he was denouncing had been unable to resolve the issue because of the lack of new tanks. She then defended herself:

> When I received this *planteamiento,* unfortunately there were no tanks. Some of the neighbors remember that some days ago I climbed onto the roof at 7 A.M. with the building's manager and the person in charge of housing repair, trying to resolve the problem. . . . I am fully aware of this situation—don't believe that I haven't tried to make the effort—and when I said here that it couldn't be resolved, it's because I really couldn't resolve it. The compañeros here know that I investigate each and every complaint, and when they give me an answer that one can't be resolved, I go back and examine the problem and try to draw out a

---

*I heard of other accountability sessions where people complained about the police. In one, held in the late 1980s in the municipality of Plaza in the City of Havana, complaints about prostitution and other illegal activities around the tourist hotels with the police standing by and doing nothing were followed by applause.

solution where there is none. I know that you elected me to resolve your problems, but it must also be said that at times it is out of my hands and at times out
of the hands of the enterprise directors, because you know the situation of our
country, that we are a poor country, independent of the fact that at times there
has been negligence.

On April 1, 1988, I attended the accountability session of Orlando
Medioceja in Romerillo, a slum neighborhood in Playa with many ram-
shackle homes, unpaved streets, and septic tanks instead of a sewage system.
The attendance was 60 percent. The *planteamientos* included the poor quality of the shoes being sold; lack of cotton in the stores; problems with the local butcher shop; the city water being turned on only between 2 A.M. and 4
A.M., when most people were not awake to be able to fill their tanks; open,
overflowing garbage cans in front of the local family doctor's office; the selling of baby bottles with no nipples; faulty electric meters; and problems with
water bills. The main discussion centered on antisocial youths who climbed
on buses and cars and disturbed the neighbors. A woman announced that a
neighborhood commission, whose membership would include the delegate,
the local CDR president, and retired party members, was being formed to
work with troubled youths and deal with other social problems. She argued
that every CDR unit should have a person in charge of preventing juvenile
delinquency. Another person pointed out the need for recreation areas and
sports facilities for young people. The delegate responded that the municipality could not build new ones at the moment but that he could arrange for
them to use other facilities nearby. Also related to antisocial behavior was another woman's *planteamiento* about burned-out streetlights. She said that
she had to go to work in complete darkness ("like the inside of a wolf's
mouth") at 3 A.M. and was plagued by peeping toms *(mirahuecos)* and had
been robbed four times in one week. The delegate suggested that she call
the company to install new bulbs. One final *planteamiento* was about the
need to empty septic tanks before they overflowed onto the street (which
was occurring). The delegate said that when the septic tank filled up, the
owner must report it and pay a few pesos to have it cleaned: "As delegate I
am not here to report your septic tank to anyone. I am here for when a job is
poorly done or not done in time and someone wants to complain."

In another poor neighborhood on the outskirts of Playa in Santa Fe,
called Bajos de Santana, the *planteamientos* at the accountability session of
April 8, where the attendance was 54 percent of registered voters, were (1)
unexplained variations in food prices; (2) lack of variety of items in the produce market, especially in comparison with those nearby in the municipality
of Marianao; (3) the irregularity of buses, with long waits, followed by three
or four buses arriving together; (4) the rationing of kerosene, which was not
rationed in neighboring municipalities; (5) the schedule for the local family

doctor being inconvenient for the patients; (6) the delay in the construction of new housing and in repair of existing housing; and (7) the poor quality of bread at the local bakery.

At a raucous accountability session of José Enrique Cardoso on April 5 in Playa, with 57 percent attendance, the first *planteamiento* was the price and quality of cream cheese. The second, about which numerous people spoke in angry tones, was an intolerable mosquito problem from stagnant water in the street caused by clogged sewer drains. When Cardoso said that the public health department should be informed, a woman answered that they had already informed the local clinic but nothing had been done. Next, a woman complained about the lack of batteries for her new portable radio: "Did I spend money not to be able to hear the radio I have?" A man added, "We want an explanation of the problems in producing these batteries." Another constituent reported that for last two years, cooking gas had never been delivered to his apartment building on time and the people living there had regularly had to go five to ten days without gas. At the time of this session, the gas was already three days late. The tenants had gone to the gas company several times and had gotten the runaround, either being assured that there would be no problem in resolving the problem, being told that the problem was solved, or having the blame placed on someone not present. The complainant said, "From what I could perceive, the major problem they have is organizational; that is, it didn't take me long to realize that there was confusion at the time of gas distribution. . . . I propose that if they can't meet their delivery obligation of every twenty days, they should give us a larger gas tank." When Cardoso asked him what concretely was his *planteamiento*, he interrupted, declaring, "It's practically an accusation!"

After a *planteamiento* on the availability and quality of bread, a concern was expressed about the many gallons of city water that were leaking onto the street and stagnating there because of clogged sewer drains. The man said that he and many others had contacted the responsible city agency, the CDR, and the party, but no one had come to solve the problem: "Nevertheless, the population is asked to make an effort to save water, and then they waste it. It is similar to the case of streetlights. Avenues around here are lit from morning till night, and then they ask the population to save electricity." Cardoso responded that the province was making a huge investment in fixing the underground pipes in order to solve the water problem, but that at the same time, the people had to continue to save water wherever possible.

Finally, it was suggested that the local bakery also sell pizza. Cardoso responded that this was impossible at the moment because the money was unavailable and therefore there was "nothing to be gained by processing this *planteamiento*." Another woman suggested that if this were not possible, those assembled would demand that the bakery also be a confectionary store. The woman who had made the *planteamiento* became angry and said,

"I'm leaving, because I want to tell all of you one thing. I am sixty-seven years old, I am arriving at my life's end, and I'm not going to have a pizzeria or a confectionary store, none of these!" Cardoso responded, "Well, we will not see many things, but we have worked for many years for our children to have a better life, although we may not enjoy it."

At the accountability session in Playa on April 4, 1988, Carlos Walfrido Rodríguez told those assembled that during the last round, Playa had had the most *planteamientos* for the number of inhabitants in the City of Havana Province. He also disclosed that

> the day is not far off when the electoral district may assume some control over the budget, and we must learn starting now where to use the resources that they give us each year, what to do, what to expand, what to repair, what needs to satisfy. . . . Thus, as voters, not only must we assume the role of demanding and solving problems, but also we have to begin to think about administering adequately the resources at our disposal.

He asked for full-time volunteers to sign up for two brigades for house repairs, to be formed at the electoral district level. Any delay, he announced, would leave the district behind in solving repair problems, as other electoral districts would get the resources, materials, and technical assistance first. He suggested that along with the volunteer workers, these brigades would also provide work, salaries, and training for unemployed youths. A woman made a *planteamiento* that workers who had supposedly come to fix her roof had instead taken roofing tiles and boards from her house to be used for the house being converted into a new funeral parlor in Playa, which was all the more serious since she had a sick person at home. Furthermore, the house being converted had belonged to provincial assembly president Pedro Chávez, but they weren't taking building materials from his new dwelling.* She asked, "What has greater priority, the funeral home or the sick person?" Rodríguez responded that it was necessary to reconcile the needs of the living and the dead. The municipal government determined that the funeral home was a priority because Playa did not have one. Because the workers had pledged to finish the funeral home on time, they had wrongly taken the materials from the complainant's house. The provincial director of apartment buildings later promised Rodríguez that the her home would be repaired within the month.

---

*Denouncing abuse by those in power was not unheard of. For example, in one accountability session, there was a report of a fight in a building because the high government official who lived in the penthouse was using all the water in the building and would not give people access to the roof to place television antennas. The demand was that these problems be brought up in the appropriate municipal assembly commission.

At the accountability session of Omar Torres in Cienfuegos on April 16, milk delivery was a major topic of conversation, as it was in most sessions held in Cienfuegos Province. The solution lay in the completion of the new milk-processing plant. One man bitterly complained that in the long lines for buying milk, some people were selling up to five places in line. He called on everyone to denounce these people to the police instead of patronizing them, and he argued that measures should be taken to stop this abuse. Another man said that whereas admission was free for everyone for sports events at the municipal stadium, and local people had participated in its construction, he was incensed that choice box seats were being "reserved" by stadium employees for "friends." He added, "I could get [these favors], but I don't want this. Since admission is free, no one has the right to reserve a box seat for whomever he wants."

The sessions for Spring 1995 began on May 19 and lasted until June 18. Each accountability session was immediately followed by ameeting to nominate candidates for municipal delegates. Reports on various sessions plus interviews with Alarcón, members of the National Electoral Commissions, National Assembly deputies, provincial and municipal delegates, and constituents were transmitted on Radio Progreso on weekdays at noon. At these sessions, 30,228 *planteamientos* were made, with water supply problems the most reiterated, followed by requests for road repairs and complaints about the quality of the bread, lack of public transport, sewers, housing and school repairs, family doctors, public lighting, the distribution of food and medicine, and surly service in restaurants.[121]

In a session in the Los Olivos section of Sancti Spiritus, the delegate reported on building repairs, the patching of potholes, new food services, a public telephone, parking for bicycles, improvements in garbage collection, and cleaning the water tank. New *planteamientos* included rodent control, availability of medicines, and community hygiene. The delegate also mentioned efforts to resolve problems concerning the train station, the waterproofing of roofs, and the repair of a turbine. It was decided that cleaning the water tank would be done with help by the community.[122]

November 1 marked the beginning of the Fall 1995 accountability sessions, and the debut sessions for over seven hundred municipal assembly delegates elected for the first time in July 1995. In Camagüey, the number of *planteamientos* rose from 370 and 872 in the previous sessions to 1,172, and the problems most frequently brought up had to do with public lighting and sewers. Lee reported that the sessions, averaging less than two hundred neighbors, were "almost like family gatherings since practically all those present know each other and have common problems, the dialogue takes place in a natural way and when it deals with a *planteamiento* or complaint, opinions and proposals for solutions surge from the audience."[123]

Granma reported on the accountability sessions held in November 1995 in the town of Nueva Gerona on the Isla de la Juventud. The *planteamientos* in one session dealt with community participation in repairing roofs and constructing houses for those affected by storms, repairing an alternative well for emergencies, and making better use of the family doctor and nurse. In another session, the neighbors expressed their satisfaction with the improvements in the water supply and street lighting. They organized brigades to fix the roads and waterproof the roofing on buildings. In a third session, the constituents agreed to cooperate in repairing roofs, fixing up the family doctor's dispensary, improving the cultivation of medicinal plants, and aiding the local school. The article concludes that "what predominates . . . is the open and sincere interchange among neighbors, the dialogue of the people exercising their authentic government, with language and initiative from the neighborhood and the demand and action of masses committed to a common task and where they do not accept monologues, administrative evasions, or unjustifiable answers."[124]

The weekly *Tribuna de la Habana* reported on a session in Plaza in the City of Havana that took place in May 1996. The soap opera was not on the television that night and thus was not an obstacle to attendance.* There were complaints that although the garbage was collected daily between 8 and 9 A.M., shortly afterward garbage began to accumulate and stink. Those present understood that a second pickup would not be possible and that the neighbors should respect the community's hygiene. The bad quality of the bread was mentioned, although just before the accountability session it had begun to improve. Other problems included streetlights, sewer drains, water pumps, housing repair (the article mentioned the importance of a *consejo popular* capable of pulling strings to find solutions to common problems). It was noted that here, as at many other times, there were inexplicable incidents: During the previous month, holes had been made in the street to install new gas pipes; the new pipes had arrived, as had the work brigade, but the pipes were not installed; the ditches were not closed and were filled with water and mosquitoes. Unfortunately, the administrators needed to give explanations to the public did not attend.[125]

In May 1996, I attended four accountability sessions in the *consejo popular* in Santa Fe, which is a suburb in Playa in the City of Havana. Each night after the sessions, the delegates came to the *consejo popular* office to record the attendance and *planteamientos*.

---

*Televised soap operas are extremely popular in Cuba and come on at 9 P.M. Thus the accountability sessions I attended in May 1996 were scheduled to end before that hour so people could watch the programs.

Daniel Morales, then president of the Santa Fe *Consejo Popular*, led the session on May 10 at 8 P.M. At 7:30, he had gone to the agricultural market where the meeting was to be held, to check with the CDR people about preparations—the Cuban flag, a table, a record player with a recording of the national anthem—reminding constituents to attend. About fifty people attended. Daniel announced the presence of the family doctor, the local police chief, and the administrators of the hardware store and the agricultural market (where private farmers sold their food). He spoke of the problems and accomplishments in Santa Fe during the previous six months, including the *planteamientos* made at the last session.

One *planteamiento* concerned automobiles driving at high speeds through the main streets of Santa Fe. The police officer present explained the measures taken to deal with this problem. The solution to the complaint made regarding the water supply problems depended on new pipes, which were not available because of the country's economic crisis. Furthermore, the main water pump depended on batteries that had been stolen twice. The truck that cleaned septic tanks had been repaired, and Daniel told the people to inform him if there were service delays of over one week. With the participation of the agricultural market administrator, Daniel discussed the availability and prices of certain food items. He congratulated the sanitation workers for making Santa Fe one of the cleanest neighborhoods in Playa, and he exhorted the neighbors to help keep the streets clean.

Daniel announced that the province of Granada in Spain, the province of their sister city Santa Fe, had purchased an ambulance for the local health clinic. Although the license plates had not arrived, it was nevertheless being used. Always of great concern to Cubans is the quality of the bread, which was rationed. He explained that the bread was not up to par because of problems with using Cuban instead of imported flour. In one *planteamiento*, a man complained that the police did not sufficiently regulate traffic flow in Santa Fe. Another objected to the bus schedules.

On May 13, I attended an accountability session of Omar Fuentes, a delegate from Santa Fe. About sixty constituents out of 107 attended, as did the bakery administrator. Omar informed those present about the new ambulance, the arrival of medicine to be distributed by the family doctor, the opening of a new discotheque for young people, and the first hard currency shop in Santa Fe.

During the previous six months, there had been five *planteamientos* about the lack of bread at the scheduled times. The bakery administrator responded that the bread usually arrived at the scheduled time, but at times, the quality was so bad that the bread was not sold. No consumer had complained directly to him. Omar said that consumers should first complain to the administrator and, in the case of an unsatisfactory response, resort to the delegate. The police officer attending was asked to comment on recently committed crimes in the area. He complained that vigilance on the part of the neighborhood CDR had been practically nonexistent, leaving the police with "little strength in the territory."

Omar announced his weekly office hours for receiving constituents. He then called for new *planteamientos.* A man compared bus lines 40 and 9, which serve Santa Fe: "When you change from one to the other, it is like leaving one country and entering another—from Europe to Haiti. On the Number 40, the service is friendly, calm, tranquil. On the 9, it is gross and offends people, lack of respect. To get on a 40 is happiness. To board the 9 is hell." [I found out later that many black people took the 9, which may explain the reference to Haiti.]. In a second *planteamiento,* the same man complained that there was no place in Santa Fe to pay the fines for driving tickets. The person in the police station who was supposed to take the money was never there. Fines then multiplied because they were paid late, as the alternative was to pay in the center of town, which was far from Santa Fe and meant having to use scarce, expensive gasoline, and having to take off from work.

In another *planteamiento,* a lady complained that when one went to a shop to buy a replacement part for a bicycle or appliance, the attendant said there were no parts, but after hours, this same person offered to sell a part to you for four or five times the price. A young man complained of the high prices for the discotheque—two pesos to park and five pesos to enter. A man protested that the police were not doing enough to control nighttime disturbances in the streets after the discotheque closed. The kids shouted and caused disruption. Another man and a woman added that they threw bottles and other items: "It seems like it's carnival." The police officer responded that a car would be dispatched to control the situation.

A woman made a *planteamiento* about the lack of streetlights. Omar responded that there were no bulbs or posts and the people would have to wait, but his constituents did not accept this explanation. One man said that they should be bought with dollars as was the case for lights in tourist areas. Priority should be given to streets that needed light. (In fact, Daniel Morales had just used money donated by Granada Province in Spain to buy lightbulbs and posts.).

On May 14, Daniel led an accountability session in the area where he lived. Just before the meeting, Daniel visited many of his neighbors to remind them to attend, as it seemed the CDR person had failed to do so. One *planteamiento* made by Daniel's father concerned the high speed at which cars drove down one of the main streets of Santa Fe, especially by the primary school. Another concerned abuses of Plan Jaba, whereby people with jobs with long hours got to go to the front in the lines to buy food. Daniel replied that those who worked in the stores should check those who claimed this privilege, and the public should also report abuses. Daniel then spoke of shops that were being painted and repaired, including the conversion of the fish store into a new *bodega* that was closer to this neighborhood. The people applauded this announcement.

On May 17, I attended an accountability session led by a delegate named Monet. Daniel was also present and spoke at various times. The first *planteamiento* dealt with the garbage accumulating in cans in the streets, bringing flies and mosquitoes, as well as diseases that were difficult to cure because of the difficulty of purchasing medicine with Cuban pesos, although, the complainant added, one could purchase all the medicine one needed with dollars. Many of those present spoke of problems with electricity and the lack of response by the electrical company of Playa. They had reported burned-out equipment, low voltage, fluctuating electric bills when the use of electricity had not varied, and lack of streetlights (the inspector had not shown up in two months). Monet repeatedly promised to contact the electric company to get action as soon as possibly and said he had brought up the issue at the session of the municipal assembly of Playa the day before. Another woman complained about the lack of cigarettes in the market. One woman criticized the quality of the bread and the lack of respect one got at the bakery. One *planteamiento* was that five pesos was too much for a ticket to enter the discotheque. There were complaints about robberies and lack of police response. Monet responded that all present here were revolutionaries and must help the police, whose numbers had diminished, by doing (CDR) guard duty at night—one group until 2 A.M., another from 2 A.M. to 7 A.M. One man complained that Santa Fe was the only sector of the City of Havana that did not have a bus line that went directly to the center of Havana. To get there, one had to take one bus to the end of the line and then take another.

During the Spring 1997 accountability sessions, 6,450,533, representing 83.4 percent of the electorate, participated; 118,147 *planteamientos* were formulated, the majority of which revolved around difficulties with the water supply, the need to repair the streets, and lack of streetlights.[126] Complaints at the accountability sessions also revolved around problems associated with tourism. The delegate from the electoral district where the exclusive Copacaban Hotel is located explained that whereas Cubans had been used to social equality, tourism was creating social differences. Tourist hotel workers had access to dollars. Households situated near such priority facilities always had electricity, whereas most others were affected by the blackouts. The delegate explained, "We had a lot of discussions about these problems in the community meetings. At first, many people were opposed to the building of tourist hotels in their area. Eventually that changed. We even invited the hotel's manager to the meetings to answer questions and to explain how the hotel's hard currency revenues help fund the country's health care, schools, and other necessities." Other related *planteamientos* concerned excess noise from the hotel's disco, which was reduced, and prostitution. The delegate told how he had worked with the four prostitutes from the neighborhood; as a result, three had got jobs, and one had left the country.[127]

Conclusion

The Cuban version of the *mandat impératif* is applied mainly through the accountability sessions, which help identify and resolve the problems of everyday life, encourage citizen participation in solving these problems, define the workload of the delegate, make possible citizen input into government policy, and constitute the foundation of local parliamentary government in Cuba.

That the issues raised are mainly commonplace ones flows from the fact that these are the issues that have a chance of being resolved with the help of the delegate, and the people know it. These are the issues over which people believe they have some control. They are not necessarily trivial, and they indicate what people regard as important to the quality of their lives. Most citizens seem to know what to expect, and they are not afraid to speak their minds.

Because in Cuba the market has not play a dominant role in determining the quality and allocation of goods and services, *planteamientos* combined with socialist consciousness supposedly fill the void. In capitalist societies, some of the types of problems raised by the Cuban populace through *planteamientos* are dealt with through the market, in some cases more successfully but with less equality and access for common citizens. With problems such as the supply of necessary services to the lower end of the income spectrum, the market solution is less successful. Furthermore, where the marketplace is not a factor in capitalist societies, such as in government-run enterprises, there is no system like *planteamientos* to correct abuses or failures. When buses in New York City do not run on schedule and then four come at once, to whom can one complain and be treated with respect and guaranteed at least an attempt to resolve the problem?

The way in which *planteamientos* are presented often reflects socialist values, as well as an awareness of Cuba's accomplishments and the problems, both bureaucratic and economic, that it faces. Citizens expressed outrage over favoritism in the reservation of box seats at the stadium; they volunteered their labor; they pointed to the country's achievements in the health field while complaining about stagnant water in the streets, sewage treatment, and mosquitoes; they deplored the damage caused by youths to the imported buses that the Cuban people had had to work hard to pay for; they complained of abuse by the more powerful. Most citizens were aware of the great amount of work involved, were appreciative of the almost constant accessibility of the delegate, and were appreciative, especially taking into consideration that the delegate is not paid for doing this work. To be sure, a few people at one accountability session in Playa, for example, did not hesitate to express their dissatisfaction with their delegate's efforts with regard to the leaking water tanks, and the delegate did not hesitate to defend herself.

Most Cubans know who their delegates are and often are personally acquainted with them, and the familiarity inherent in delegate-constituent relations is constantly being manifested, whether at accountability sessions or just walking through the neighborhood streets with the delegate, where one notes that most people use the greeting "*delegado*." Compare this to the New York City Council, for example, where, according to the *New York Times*, "Few voters know their Council members."[128]

Dilla defined participation under socialism as socialization of power going beyond voting, which has functioned in Cuba in formulating and implementing the public's demands, but less so in direct input for national policy selection.[129] According to Cuban sociologist Juan Valdés, public participation continues to be far more important in the execution of policy than in decision making and control. He linked direct community participation in the processes of decision making with the identification, elaboration, approval, and implementation of demands. However, "This participation continues being very high in the implementation of decisions . . . and very low in their approval."[130] Dilla recognized that the municipal assemblies have intensified the public's participation in determining local policy and choosing capable and responsive leadership, but he advocated for greater autonomy for the participation process and for nongovernmental organizations.[131]

With all the difficulties of the accountability process, there is little question of the importance of *planteamientos* for the solution of individual or neighborhood problems and, taken collectively, for providing citizen input into local and national economic and social planning. Citizens readily participate in the process and seem to value its importance. Accountability sessions fall within the tradition of the *mandat impératif* because the main (but not the only) task of municipal delegates is to transmit and facilitate the resolution of citizen *planteamientos*, and the parameters for this task are set by the constituents of the delegate.

Notes

1. Haroldo Dilla Alfonso, Gerardo González, and Ana Teresa Vincentelli, *Participación popular y desarrollo en los municipios cubanos* (Havana: Centro de Estudios sobre América, 1993), p. 87 (my translation).

2. Felix Pita Astudillo, "Un mensaje insultante para los cubanos: Fariseísmo," *Granma*, May 26, 1996, p. 3 (my translation).

3. Fernando Alvarez Tabio, *Comentarios a la Constitución Socialista* (Havana: Editorial de Ciencias Sociales, 1985), p. 228.

4. Benigno Pablo Castellanos, *Quejas contra burocratismo: problemas actuales del perfeccionamiento de la democracia socialista en Cuba* (Havana: Política, 1988), pp. 38–41 (my translation).

5. Ibid., p. 41.

6. *Fundamental Law of Cuba 1959* (Washington, D.C.: Pan American Union, 1959), p. 12.

7. Castellanos, *Quejas contra burocratismo*, p. 42 (my translation).

8. "Constitution of the Organs of People's Power," *Center for Cuban Studies Newsletter*, Vol. 2, No. 5–6 (October-December 1975), p. 22.

9. Ibid., p. 9.

10. Raúl Castro, speech given August 22, 1974, *Granma Weekly Review*, September 8, 1974, p. 4.

11. "Constitution of the Republic of Cuba," *Granma Weekly Review*, March 7, 1976, pp. 6, 10.

12. "Constitución de la República de Cuba," *Granma*, September 22, 1992, pp. 7, 9.

13. Alvarez Tabio, *Comentarios a la constitución socialista*, pp. 229, 350–351; see also Castellanos, *Quejas contra burocratismo*, pp. 44–45.

14. Dilla, González, and Vincentelli, *Participación popular*, p. 89.

15. Lorenzo Hernández Martínez, "La rendición de cuenta: expresión práctica de la democrácia socialista," *El Militante Comunista*, April 1984, p. 47.

16. Ibid., p. 49.

17. Eldon Kenworthy, "Institutionalizing Community Politics in Cuba: Cultural Proclivities and Revolutionary Dilemmas," paper presented at the annual meeting of the Latin American Studies Association, March 6, 1982, pp. 13–14.

18. Quoted in ibid., p. 15.

19. Caridad Carrobello, Martha Campos, Pelayo Terry, and Ariel Terrero, "¿Qué piensa el pueblo de su poder?" *Bohemia*, July 6 , 1990, p. 7 (my translation).

20. Harold Dilla Alfonso, "Notas sobre la relación centralización-decentralización en la transición socialista Cubana," unpublished manuscript, 1989, pp. 38–39 (my translation).

21. Harold Dilla Alfonso, Gerardo González, and Ana Theresa Vincentelli, "Los municipios en Cuba: Una experiencia más allá de los paradigmas," paper presented at the annual meeting of the Latin American Studies Association, Washington, D.C., 1991, p. 10 (my translations).

22. Sheryl Lutjens, "Democracy and Socialist Cuba," in Sandor Halebsky and John M Kirk (eds.), *Cuba in Transition: Crisis and Transformation* (Boulder: Westview Press, 1992), p. 65; Rafael Hernández and Haroldo Dilla, "Political Culture and Popular Participation in Cuba," *Latin American Perspectives*, Issue 69, Vol. 18, No. 2 (Spring 1991), p. 51.

23. Hernández and Dilla, "Political Culture," p. 50.

24. Ibid., p. 51.

25. Dilla, González, and Vincentelli, *Participación popular*, p. 94

26. José Gabriel Gumá, "Desde el lunes rendición de cuenta," *Granma*, September 28, 1990, p. 1 (my translation).

27. "Un intercambio de opiniones," *Trabajadores*, March 16, 1991, p. 2.

28. Dario L. Machado Rodriguez, "La lección del pueblo," *Granma*, October 25, 1997, p. 8.

29. Haroldo Dilla Alfonso, "Participación popular y gobiernos locales en Cuba," paper presented at the Second Workshop of the Organizations of Community Power and Grassroots Democracy in Central America and the Caribbean, Havana, Cuba, November 28-December 2, 1988, pp. 7–8.

30. Domingo García Cárdenas, *State Organization in Cuba* (Havana: José Martí, 1986), p. 116.

31. Dilla, "Notas sobre la relación," pp. 37–38 (my translation).

32. Dilla, "Democracia y poder," p. 69 (my translation).

33. Susana Tesoro, "A pecho descubierto: Una conversación con el recin estrenado presidente de la Asamblea Nacional, Juan Escalona Reguera," *Bohemia*, July 20, 1990, p. 52.

34. García Cárdenas, *State Organization,* pp. 114–115.

35. Lutjens, "Democracy and Socialist Cuba," p. 65.

36. Max Azicri, "Twenty-six Years of Cuban Revolutionary Politics: An Appraisal," *Contemporary Marxism*, No 14 (Fall 1986), p. 89.

37. William M. LeoGrande, "Participation in Cuban Municipal Government: From Local Power to People's Power," in Donald E. Schulz and Jan S. Adams (eds.),*Political Participation in Communist Countries* (New York: Pergamon Press, 1981), pp. 288, 290.

38. Rhoda Rabkin, "Cuba: The Aging of a Revolution," in Sergio Roca (ed.), *Socialist Cuba: Past Interpretations and Future Challenges* (Boulder: Westview Press, 1988), p. 46.

39. Jorge Domínguez, "Derechos Políticos y el Sistema Político Cubano," *Revista Occidental*, No. 2 (January-April 1984), p. 258 (my translation).

40. Alfredo Prieto González and Haroldo Dilla Alfonso, "Para una reflexion sobre la democracia en Cuba (A propósito de un artículo de Jorge Domínguez)," *El Caribe Contemporáneo*, Nos. 1, 2 (1988), p. 45 (my translation).

41. Ibid.

42. Bard Jorgensen, "The Interrelationship Between Base and Superstructure in Cuba," *Ibero-Americana: Nordic Journal of Latin American Studies*, Vol. 13, No. 1 (1983), p. 37.

43. Dilla, González, and Vincentelli, "Los municipios," p. 17 (my translation).

44. María Julia Mayoral, "Concluyó rendición de cuenta en la capital," *Granma*, May 8, 1992, p. 1 (my translation).

45. Kenworthy, "Institutionalizing Community Politics," p. 14.

46. Esther Mosak, "Democracy: Learning by Doing," *Cuba Update*, Vol. 12, Nos. 1–2 (Winter-Spring 1991), p. 19; Gail Reed, "Taking the Leap: Cuba's Fourth Party Congress," *Granma Weekly Review*, Vol. 11, No. 4 (Fall 1990), p. 19.

47. Reed, "Taking the Leap," p. 19.

48. Quoted in ibid.

49. Mosak, "Democracy: Learning by Doing," pp. 19–20, 22.

50. Kenworthy, "Institutionalizing Community Politics," p. 15.

51. Lutjens, "Democracy and Socialist Cuba," p. 65; Hernández and Dilla, "Political Culture," pp. 45, 51.

52. Carollee Bengelsdorf, "The Matter of Democracy in Cuba: Snapshots of Three Moments," in Sandor Halebsky and John M Kirk (eds.), *Transformation and Struggle: Cuba Faces the 1990s* (New York: Praeger, 1990), p. 42.

53. Quoted in ibid.

54. Ibid., pp. 42–43.

55. Fidel Castro, "Main Report to the Second Congress," *Cuba Update*, Vol. 2, No. 1 (March 1981), p. 12.

56. "Opiniones de Delegados," *Poder Popular*, Vol 5 (1986), p. 13 (my translation).

57. "Chequeo de acuerdos, Acuerdo #483," *Acta #20, Comité Ejecutivo Playa*, August 27, 1987 (my translation).

58. "Informe valorativo sobre el resultado del II proceso asambleario de rendición de cuenta del delegado," Municipio de Cienfuegos, October 1987 (my translation).

59. Dilla, "Notas sobre la relación," p. 43. Regarding constraints due to the "special period" of the 1990s, see Lázaro Barredo Medina, "Autoridad mayor para los delegados al Poder Popular," *Trabajadores*, January 18, 1993, p. 2.

60. Reinaldo García Blanco, "Queremos tanto a Guillermo!" *Pueblo*, Vol. 1, No. 4 (October 1987), pp. 15–16 (my translation).

61. "Intervención de los delegados en la Asamblea Provincial," *Correo Del Delegado*, No. 11 (January 1988), p. 3.

62. Carrobello et al., "¿Que piensa?" pp. 6–7.

63. Ibid., p. 6.

64. Ibid., pp. 6–7.

65. Reed, "Taking the Leap," p. 19.

66. Carrobello, "¿Que piensa?" pp. 7–8.

67. Medea Benjamin, "Soul Searching," *NACLA Report on the Americas*, Vol. 24, No. 2 (August 1990), p. 29.

68. Caridad Carrobello, Susana Tesoro, Martha Campos, Pelayo Terry, and Ariel Terrero, "Debate público: Los caminos del poder," *Bohemia*, July 13, 1990, p. 5 (my translation).

69. Quoted in Dilla, "Notas sobre la relación," p. 59.

70. Carrobello et al., "Debate público," pp. 6–7.

71. Marta Harnecker, *Cuba: Dictatorship or Democracy?* (Wesport, Conn.: Lawrence Hill & Co. 1980), pp. 122–123.

72. Machado Rodriguez, "La lección del pueblo," p. 8.

73. Dilla, "Participación popular," pp. 9–10.

74. Dilla, González, and Vincentelli, "Los municipios," p. 18.

75. Asamblea Nacional del Poder Popular, *Analisis tercer proceso de rendición de cuenta -V- Mandato*, June 1988, p. 4 (my translation).

76. Gumá, "Desde el lunes rendición," p. 1 (my translation).

77. José Gabriel Gumá, "Rendición de cuenta: un verdadero intercambio de opiniones con la población," *Granma*, February 26, 1992, p. 1 (my translation).

78. "Un intercambio de opiniones," p. 2 (my translation).

79. Dilla, González, and Vincentelli, "Los municipios," pp. 16, 18.

80. Ibid., p. 18.

81. Ibid., p. 19.

82. Domínguez, "Derechos politicos," p. 258.

83. Jill Hamberg, "The Dynamics of Cuban Housing Policy," in Rachel Bratt, Chester Hartman, and Ann Meyerson (eds.), *Critical Perspectives on Housing* (Philadelphia: Temple University Press, 1986), p. 604.

84. Bengelsdorf, "The Matter of Democracy," p. 42.

85. Rabkin, "The Aging of a Revolution," pp. 46–47.

86. *Acta: Asamblea Municipal del Poder Popular Palmira: II Sesión Ordinaria del V Mandato*, pp. 4–5 (my translation).

87. *Acta: Asamblea Municipal Poder Popular Playa: Tercera Sesión Ordinaria Quinto Período de Mandato*, pp. 23–27 (my translation).

88. "Información a la población," *Granma*, May 28, 1991, p. 2 (my translation).

89. "Analizan funcionamiento del médico y enfermera de la familia," *Granma*, November 6, 1993, p. 2 (my translation).

90. Georgina Suárez Hernandez,, "Protagonismo político en Cuba: Antecedentes y proyección actual," paper presented at the Cuba Conference, Halifax, Nova Scotia, November 3, 1989, p. 21 (my translation).

91. Dilla, "Notas sobre la relación," p. 44.

92. Harry Magdoff, "Socialism, Democracy and Planning: Remarks at a Conference," *Monthly Review*, Vol. 33, No. 2 (June 1981), p. 26.

93. Hernández Martínez, "La rendición," pp. 49–50.

94. Mireya Ojeda, "Comentario a propósito de las asambleas de rendición de cuenta del delegado," *Cinco de Septiembre*, October 27, 1987, p. 2 (my translation).

95. Asamblea Nacional del Poder Popular, *Temas para seminarios a diputados, delegados y cuadros del Poder Popular* (Matanzas: Girón, 1982), pp. 7.2–7.3 (my translation).

96. Ibid., p. 7.5.

97. Carmen R. Alfonso, "Puede haber un planteamiento sin respuesta? Entrevista a la diputada Elia García Patiño," *La Nación Cubana*, No. 3 (1985), p. 45 (my translation).

98. "Cambios organizativos en la planificación," *Trabajadores*, May 26, 1988, p. 10 (my translation).

99. Nelson Mata Monfort, "Los gastos del presupuesto de los OLPP," *Finanzas y Crédito*, No. 5 (January-May 1986), pp. 47–48 (my translation).

100. Dilla, González, and Vincentelli, *Participación popular*, pp. 90–91.

101. Susana Lee, "Fructúferas jornadas de información, orientación e intercambio," *Granma*, September 17, 1996, pp. 4–5; Julio Garcia Luis, "Coordinación, comprensión y unidad como nunca antes," *Trabajadores*, September 16, 1996, p. 16.

102. Francisco Rodríguez Cruz, "¿Cómo se planifica hoy en Cuba?" *Trabajadores*, December 8, 1997, p. 3.

103. García Cárdenas, *State Organization*, pp. 117.

104. *Poder Popular: Boletín del Comité Ejecutivo Municipal de Cienfuegos*, No. 2 (February 1989), pp. 9–12.

105. Raul Mantilla Ramirez, "El partido y la rendición de cuenta de los delegados a sus electores," *El Militante Comunista*, April 1988, pp. 28–30.

106. María Julia Mayoral, "Mucho más que un derecho democrático," *Granma*, June 9, 1995, p. 2.

107. Susana Lee, "Encaminar este proceso en función de las medidas que hay que adoptar," *Granma*, May 19, 1994, p. 8 (my translation).

108. Susana Lee, "Analizar lo bueno y lo malo," *Granma*, May 18, 1995, p. 1 (my translation).

109. María Julia Mayoral, "Rendición de cuenta en la capital: Margarita con buenos jardineros," *Granma*, November 8, 1994, p. 2.

110. Frank Agero Gómez and Julio García Luis, "Tenemos que demostrar que aquí el destino nuestro le decidimos nosotros," *Trabajadores*, April 10, 1995, p. 3 (my translation).

111. Raul Ramírez Manzano, "Por un diálogo directo," *Trabajadores*, November 13, 1995, p. 4 (my translation).

112. Susana Lee, "Comenzó la rendición de cuenta del delegado a sus electores," *Granma*, November 2, 1995, p. 1 (my translation).

113. Susana Lee, "Convocan proceso de rendición de cuenta del delegado," *Granma*, October 17, 1995, p. 3; Manolo Rodríguez Salas, "Desde el Ministro hasta el bodeguero tienen que apoyar al delegado," *Granma*, November 10, 1995, p. 4.

114. Susana Lee, "Rendición de cuenta en Camaguey: Se hace diálogo al andar," *Granma*, December 15, 1995, p. 3.

115. Machado, "La lección del pueblo," p. 8.

116. Susana Lee, "Para que las reuniones sean un diálogo abierto," *Granma*, November 9, 1995, p. 3 (my translation).

117. Rodríguez Salas, "Desde el ministro," p. 4 (my translation).

118. María Julia Mayoral, "Comenzará en octubre rendición de cuenta de los delegados," *Granma*, September 23, 1994, p. 1 (my translation).

119. Ramírez, "Por un diálogo," p. 4.

120. Maria Julia Mayoral, "Rendición de cuenta: estamos hablando de cambios," *Granma*, August 22, 1996, p. 5 (my translation).

121. "Demostración fehaciente de la confianza del pueblo en la Revolución y en sus instituciones," *Granma*, June 24, 1995, p. 8.

122. Juan Antonio Borrego, "Conversación en Los Olivos," *Granma*, June 8, 1995, p. 2.

123. Lee, "Rendición de cuenta," p. 3 (my translation).

124. Diego Rodríguez Molina, "Rendición de cuenta de delegados: Un diálogo de pueblo," *Granma*, November 18, 1995, p. 3 (my translation).

125. R.S., "Asuntos del barrio," *Tribuna de la Habana*, May 19, 1996, p. 2.

126. Maria Julia Mayoral, "Alta participación del electorado en asambleas de rendición de cuenta," *Granma*, July 19, 1997, p. 2.

127. Martin Koppel, "Cuban Vote Registers Support for Revolution," *Militant*, November 10, 1997, p. 1.

128. James C. McKinley, Jr., "New York City Council Sees Little Upheaval in Elections," *New York Times*, August 19, 1993, p. A–1.

129. Haroldo Dilla Alfonso, "Comunidad, participación y socialism: reinterpretando el dilema cubano," in Haroldo Dilla Alfonso (ed.), *La participación en Cuba y los retos del futuro* (Havana: Centro de Estudios sobre América, 1996), pp. 22–23.

130. Juan Valdés Paz, "Poder local y participación," in Dilla (ed.), *La participación en Cuba*, pp. 129–130 (my translation); Haroldo Dilla Alfonso, "Los municipios cubanos y los retos del futuro," in Dilla (ed.), *La participación*, p. 141.

131. Dilla, "Comunidad, participación," pp. 22–23.

6

The People's Councils

The newest and most decentralized level of government in what constitute the Local Organs of People's Power in Cuba, the *consejos populares* (people's councils), were conceived at the Third Party Congress of the Communist Party in 1986.[1] The historical precedents were the deputies groups in the former Soviet Union.[2] The initial concept was to place full-time governmental representatives and offices in settlements that had been seats of municipal government prior to the political-administrative division of 1976 but were no longer, to enable their residents to solve problems locally and have a strong collective voice vis-à-vis the municipal government. This chapter traces their development since they were instituted in 1989 and describes their current structure, function, and practice. The field study concentrates mainly on the *consejo popular* in Santa Fe, located on the western outskirts of Havana.

In 1989 several pilot projects were introduced in the municipality of Habana del Este in the City of Havana. Expanding the concept and purpose, ninety-three *consejos populares* were created in 1990 including all the electoral districts within the fifteen municipalities in the City of Havana, each *consejo* having up to forty thousand inhabitants.[3] By 1992 the plan was to spread them across the island, which can be linked to the economic crisis and shortages of the 1990s (the "special period"), brought on by the fall of socialism in the Soviet Union and Eastern Europe. They were incorporated into the 1992 Constitution, converting them into a permanent part of the state structure. Article 104 states that the *consejos populares* "work actively for efficiency in the development of the activities of production and services and for the satisfaction of the medical, economic, educational, cultural, and social necessities of the population, promoting the greatest participation by the population and local initiatives for the solution of its problems."[4]

The *consejos populares* group together the municipal assembly delegates of an average of fifteen contiguous electoral districts, although some in the City of Havana contain up to thirty districts. They also include representatives of mass organizations and state enterprises located in the territories. The presidents and vice presidents must be delegates and are elected by the delegates. The presidents, and sometimes the vice presidents, work full-time for the *consejos.*

The *consejos populares* are linked to the higher branches of the Cuban government. The municipal assemblies check the work of the *consejos* annually. Each *consejo* president meets weekly with the municipal assembly president. The National Assembly Commission on the OLPP evaluates proposals for creating new *consejos* and analyzes the economic and social oversight functions of the *consejos,* their links with the municipal assemblies, and how the local administrators work with the *consejos.*[5] Just prior to the December 1996 session of the National Assembly, this commission met to debate on how to improve the *consejos,* focusing on organization, functioning, integration, the authority of the presidents, and the control they should exercise.[6] The *consejo* presidents in the City of Havana meet regularly with President Fidel Castro, other members of the Council of Ministers, and the leadership of the provincial assembly.

The 1990 Council of State resolution presented the *consejo popular* in the City of Havana as

> an entity which constitutes an authority in direct and immediate contact with the social, economic and service activities in the neighborhoods, communities and settlements with real capacity to pursue solutions to problems with agility and that at the same time assists in maintaining and improving the level of service the population receives, controls the units of production and services attached to the territory, works for the development of an adequate social, administrative and work discipline, and contributes to confronting unlawful activities and other antisocial manifestations which may take place.[7]

The resolution also stated that the *consejos* were to have only consultative functions and that the attributions of the council president were not to be delegated to any other member of the *consejo.*

According to Cuban sociologist Jesús P. García Brigo, the philosophy behind the *consejos* is to

- strengthen the authority of the municipal Delegate;
- improve the control and oversight of the administrative entities, regardless of the level of subordination;
- find formulas that incorporate all the elements of the community in solving its problems; and
- have a strong government figure at the neighborhood level who would be able to organize the forces of the community to solve local problems.[8]

With emphasis on the decentralization of power, the primary purpose of the *consejos* is to respond quickly at the local level to issues such as corruption, inefficiency, and citizen complaints, with the minimum of bureaucracy, and with immediate access to the local and higher levels of government. The *consejos populares* have been granted considerable power and authority, including the right to act on local economic crimes such as food hoarding and bribery of store managers, to intercede in municipal, provincial, and national state enterprises, to inspect, control, and coordinate all national, provincial, and municipal economic activity and support the development of local industry within the territory, propose new services, and manage culture and recreation. They were also charged with overseeing the special period measures involving service industries, the food programs, hygiene, local work centers, mass transport, public health, crime control and prevention, and education.

Juan Escalona, president of the National Assembly when I interviewed him in 1992, commented on the need for and the decentralized authority of the *consejos populares*:

> I am convinced that the social problems do not have solutions at the level of central governments. If we do not connect the community to the solution of its own problems then there will be no solution ever, as there will not be in any country in the world. No government can respond to the level of a pipe that broke in the entrance to your house and is spilling water into the street. . . . The president of the *consejo* has resources at hand, although he does not administer anything. That is to say the president calls the local director of commerce and tells him for example, "This administrator cannot continue here because he is not performing up to par, and this butcher is stealing so investigate and get rid of him." Why? Because he is in his zone all day, that is to say, not like the [municipal] delegate who has to go to work and can only be there at night, who thus can hear people's complaints regarding a store or a butcher shop only after they are closed. . . . The *consejos populares* that we created have more power than the municipal [assembly] executive committees, because a resolution of the Council of State gave them power to intervene in everything located within their territory.

A constant theme is that although the *consejos* have considerable authority, they are not to be part of the administrative apparatus. President Fidel Castro, speaking at the meeting of the presidents of the newly created *consejos populares* in Havana in October 1990, told them that they needed strong authority to comply with their obligations.[9] The municipal delegates will have more authority because

> they will have somebody representing them full-time and calling the municipal offices and the provincial offices or wherever is necessary. I will meet every so often with the 93 presidents of the people's councils and they can tell us what is

going on in the grocery stores, butcher shops, the restaurants, the cafeterias or any other services. . . . They will not be administrators, there won't be paperwork or bureaucracy.[10]

Escalona clarified this concept:

When the officers of the *consejo popular* call an administrative director, and say that a worker must be replaced, he is replaced. But it is not the president of the *consejo* who replaces him. This is done by the administrative apparatus in the municipality. And when the presidents need resources in order to, for example, fix a street, they find the entities or enterprises which then resolve the complaints.

To mark the fifth anniversary of the founding of the *consejos populares* in the City of Havana, the *consejo* presidents met with provincial and national government and party leaders, including Fidel Castro and National Assembly President Ricardo Alarcón. Conrado Martínez, president of the City of Havana Provincial Assembly, spoke of their strengths and weaknesses. The authority of the municipal delegate was strengthened, the quality of the accountability sessions improved, there was more unity among the delegates and more consultation in making decisions, control over administrative entities increased, and there was more awareness of local problems by municipal and provincial entities. Among the difficulties he mentioned were too many meetings, bureaucratic problems, and lack of attention and participation by directors and administrators at higher levels. Among the suggestions made by the *consejo* presidents were to increase the level of preparation and information for the *consejo* officers, increase decentralization, and better define the role of the mass organizations represented in the *consejo popular*. "The most common deficiencies revolve around the necessity to continue strengthening the concept and the practice that the *Consejos Populares* do not administer."[11]

Cuban journalist María Julia Mayoral attempted to clarify further the confusion between control and administration: The *consejo popular* should not carry out administrative tasks, nor should it substitute for the economic, administrative, and social entities in its territory. *Consejo* presidents should not make administrative decisions such as those concerning food distribution, store schedules, and prices. At times, *consejo* presidents, reacting to the lethargy of administrators in resolving problems and anxious to find solutions, incorrectly make administrative decisions. The *consejos* should coordinate and exercise control and oversight over economic and service activities and help them perform adequately instead of assuming their responsibilities.[12]

During the first two years the ninety-three *consejo* presidents in the City of Havana met on numerous occasions with the executive committees of the provincial assembly and of the Council of Ministers, and crime detection and prevention emerged as an important topic. The *consejos* were given an increased role in inspecting commercial and service entities, especially for black market and other criminal activities. To cut down on corruption the *consejo* presidents were to supervise the distribution of agricultural products to the public.[13] A *consejo* in Havana that includes a section of the Malecón (the city's oceanfront), where much black market activity was taking place, intervened by informing authorities of citizens' complaints and by participating in reconnaissance to finger the delinquents.[14] The *consejo* presidents also complained about the slow criminal court procedures.[15] Consequently in February 1992 municipal court subdivisions were created in each of the ninety-three *consejos*. The *consejos populares* provided these local courts with the sites and the items needed to function.[16]

By mid–1992 there were a thousand *consejos populares* spread throughout the country. In April and May of that year Raúl Castro, Minister of Defense and Second Secretary of the Cuban Communist Party, met with *consejo* presidents in the provinces. In rural areas self-sufficiency in food production and other necessities was a constant topic, as was bringing basic services and government offices to the community to diminish the need for citizens to travel (especially difficult during the special period). Those living in rural areas in Cienfuegos Province were making on average almost three trips per weekday to the location of the municipality or to the provincial capital. By placing government and bank offices, as well as repair and other services, in rural *consejos populares*, the number of trips was cut by more than thirty-two thousand per month.[17] Similarly, seventeen municipal government offices were situated in a rural *consejo popular* in Holguin Province, including a notary public, a civil register, lawyers, and a municipal court, as well as services such as equipment and shoe repair centers, barbers, and beauty parlors, further reducing the need to travel to the municipal seat of government. The *consejo* also arranged for pensions for elderly people to be given to them directly in their homes.[18] To cut the need to travel long distances to work in Havana, the State Committee on Work and Social Security (CETSS) placed a representative in each *consejo popular* to facilitate workers changing jobs or finding new work.[19] The *consejos* in the countryside also assisted in agricultural production. In Guantánamo Province at the eastern end of the island they participated in all phases of the coffee harvest.[20]

Representatives from the municipal departments, including gastronomy, commerce, public works, and water and sewers, joined the *consejos* in 1992, creating greater decentralization of authority. The president of a *consejo* in Havana with twenty-eight electoral districts and almost forty thousand inhabitants stated that their presence meant, "We do not have to call on the municipality to discuss many incidents; the delegates receive with dispatch an answer concerning the constituents' inquiries and complaints and we can make demands directly to those responsible."[21]

By 1993 the number of *consejos* in Havana rose to 102. Schools were made part of their agenda, including repairing classrooms and desks and collecting pencils, notebooks, books, and other teaching materials: "Help from municipal delegates, parents, teachers, neighbors and even students from higher grades is traditional in preparing the schools; but since the emergence of the *consejos* and of education representatives in these zones, this work has gained in cohesion and participants."[22] By the end of 1993 the *consejos* had become more involved in public health, especially regarding the availability and distribution of medicine.[23] During the debate on the budget in the December 1996 session of the National Assembly, it was recommended that the *consejos* be the vehicle to promote a culture of hygiene among the population.[24]

In 1994 community architects were being assigned to the *consejos populares* on request of the population, to plan home repairs and improvements and new housing and give advice regarding the advisability of trading homes.[25] In 1996 *Granma* reported on the activities of the *consejo* in Los Pocitos–El Palmar, with eighteen electoral districts and twenty-seven thousand inhabitants, in the municipality of Marianao in the City of Havana. The delegates organized a group of neighbors to grow vegetables on vacant land. The president and a delegate spoke to the workers of a construction brigade, which belonged to the *consejo*, that donated leftover cement to repair housing. The eighteen delegates agreed that when they attended to problems that affected the constituents of various electoral districts, they would demand solutions for all from administrative entities rather than just for their own district.[26] In April 1997 the campaign launched by the Committee for the Defense of the Revolution (CDR) against unauthorized internal migration to Havana and related illegal construction of houses, and against private workers who failed to pay taxes, was carried out in part through the *consejos populares*.[27]

Fieldwork

Between 1992 and 1996 I did fieldwork with the presidents of three *consejos populares*, Miramar, Almendares Sierra, and Santa Fe, in the municipality of Playa in the City of Havana Province, located by the seacoast in the western part of the city. I interviewed the *consejo* officers, accompanied the officers on their rounds, and participated in their meetings with constituents. Playa has a variety of neighborhoods, including elegant sections populated by diplomats, other foreigners, and wealthy Cubans, tourist hotels, and some of the worst slums in the city.*

---

*I make no claim that the Consejo Popular Santa Fe, which I studied in greatest detail, or the other two *consejos*, are representative of the *consejos* nationally. Certainly there are differences between rural and urban *consejos*, as well as between those in the City of Havana as compared with the provinces and among those in the capital city. Within Playa, I was told of problems in some *consejos* due in part to lack of neighborhood cohesion. In fact, as noted in the text, the Almendares Consejo was separated from the one in Miramar because it was unmanageable due to its size. However, in terms of methodology, a *consejo popular* in a well-defined neighborhood like Santa Fe, with a very capable, well-known leader like Daniel Morales, demonstrates the possibilities and limits of the *consejos* in perhaps the best of circumstances.

On February 23, 1994, I followed Mirium Pabón, president of the *Consejo Popular* Miramar, on her monthly rounds through the neighborhood. The president of retired members of the PCC residing within the *consejo*, a family doctor, the supermarket administrator, the coordinator of the local CDR, and municipal delegates from the *consejo* also formed part of the entourage.

Along the way the supermarket administrator spoke to Pabón regarding her needs and problems related to robberies, staff, water, and *mensajeros* (self-employed people who wait in food lines and carry the groceries to the homes of those who work all day). The supermarket had no food in it, but outside the market grapefruits were being sold without being rationed. Pabón ordered that they be rationed so that some would remain for those who got off work after 5 P.M. Similarly, after discussing supplies with those working in the pharmacy, she ordered limits on the sale of some medicines so that the pharmacy would not run out of supplies. This kind of administrative decision was supposedly beyond the purview of *consejo* presidents, but I found it to be commonplace in the other *consejos* I studied as well.

The municipal delegates discussed with Pabón the status of various *planteamientos* made by constituents at the accountability sessions. She stopped to see a woman who had made a *planteamiento* concerning leaks in her roof. Pabón asked her if those who were supposed to check the problem and schedule the repair had come. The woman responded that they had not, and Pabón promised action.

The following day I visited Mario Cubota, the president of the *Consejo Popular* Almendares Sierra, located adjacent to Miramar, with thirty-four thousand people and fifteen electoral districts. It was separated from the Miramar *Consejo* in 1993, which was deemed to have been too large and unwieldy.

Cubota was at the biweekly session where constituents came to speak to administrators or to Cubota looking for solutions to problems. These were held during both daytime and evenings to give maximum opportunity for constituents to attend. Besides Cubota there were representatives from the divisions of city water and sewers (*acueducto*) and housing construction and repair (*arquitectura*). One person came to report on a leaky roof. Another needed roofing paper for repairs, which is imported and is scarce. Cubota told me that the *consejo* in consultation with the neighbors and the delegate of the district involved must reach a consensus as to where the paper is most needed. A delegate came in looking for gasoline to run the compressor she had obtained for the septic system in her building. A woman wanted Cubota to sign a paper to enable her to obtain the wood she needed to finish the roof for the two new rooms she was building. She said her delegate was aware of the problem but that she had come to see Cubota in order to alleviate the work of her delegate, who had helped with this problem but "who has so many things to do and so many problems to resolve, besides so many meetings to attend." Cubota told me that her house is in bad condition and her roof was damaged in a storm. After her delegate had helped solve the problem she had tried to take advantage of the situation by adding rooms to the house for which she was now requesting more wood.

Oversight and inspection of the activities within the territory, according to Cubota, constitute the major portion of the *consejo's* mandate. Both local and national state entities that belong to the *consejo* must report periodically to the *consejo*. The state telephone company, which is a national enterprise, was scheduled to report the following month. *Aqueducto* had just reported because of problems with septic tanks and street drains. Among other problems cited (common in Cuba) were the lack of equipment to break up the streets and to replace the pipes. The previous month the local bread-flour industry had had to account for supply problems hindering making bread. The municipal budget was also discussed in relation to the *consejo* and the government agencies it contains, with emphasis on imposing controls where deficits exist. For example, it was decided that the public should pay to enter some of the planned cultural activities that in the past had been free.

Cubota was aware that the *consejo* presidents should not be administrators but should indicate their criteria and priorities to the local directors. But he told me that they had to comply with the *consejo's* demands: "If not, we take measures with the directors of the enterprise." In the three *consejos* I studied the presidents did make what would be called on-the-spot administrative decisions such as rationing sales. Cubota told me that he has had to step into chaotic situations that could have caused political problems. "We arrived at the bakery and there was no bread, the population was complaining and the administrator could not be found. We could not wait seven hours, we had to make a decision in that moment to solve the problem."

The *consejo* was watching the bread bakeries closely because the public had reported illicit distribution of bread. When steps were not taken to correct the situation, Cubota got the director of the enterprise to replace the bakery's administrator, and things improved. The *consejo* also demanded that the enterprise take a series of administrative steps to improve efficiency. The public also reported that food products such as rice and sugar were missing from a local *bodega*. Cubota went to the *bodega*, and when the administrator did not give him satisfactory answers he had the director of the enterprise replace the administrator, who was found guilty of stealing the food. While making the rounds Cubota found some *acueducto* workers privately selling their labor power during their worktime and using state resources. The incident was immediately reported to the local director of *acueducto*, who took measures against the workers.

Consejo officers inform and assist municipal assembly delegates, most of whom work during the week, regarding problems and issues in their electoral districts and the *consejo*. The *consejo* helped delegates resolve constituents' grievances and problems, especially in dealing with government agencies in the territory where the *consejo* has more influence than the individual delegate. Cubota compiled copies of all constituents' *planteamientos* that he had received from the delegates and insisted on rapid responses from administrative entities.

Santa Fe has an area of 5.2 square kilometers with approximately twenty-two thousand inhabitants, located in the extreme western sector of the Havana city limits. It is a self-contained and well-defined neighborhood, suited for a *consejo popular*. Most houses are one- or two-family residences, although there are some apartment houses. To the south and west are mainly rural parts of the municipality Bauta in Havana Province, and it faces the sea to the north. Originally it was a small fishing village. With the construction of the highway linking Santa Fe with Havana in the 1930s, middle-class families from the city built summer homes there. Many of these families emigrated during the 1960s, and their homes were taken by farming families from other provinces, who came to work at the nearby naval base. In the 1980s poor immigrants from the eastern provinces settled and built the slum neighborhood near the western edge called Bajos de Santana.[28]

The *consejo popular* in Santa Fe consists of one municipal delegate from each of the eleven election districts in the territory and representatives from the Federation of Cuban Women (FMC), the CDR, and from seven administrative entities–the PCC school Nico López, the Marina Hemingway Tourist Center, the Sanchez Villar workers' social organization (restaurants, cabaret, sports), the VeraCuba tourist bus terminal, the Base for Repairing Agricultural Airplanes, the Cuban Service Enterprise (ECUSE), and the Arturo Díaz quarry. The president, Daniel Morales, and the vice president, William Milanés, were longtime delegates and well-known in Santa Fe, especially Daniel (everyone in Santa Fe called him by his first name), who was also a National Assembly deputy. Both worked full-time in the *consejo*. Even before the *consejo popular* was incorporated, Santa Fe informally functioned in a similar coherent manner, with Daniel as its recognized leader. He was known as the "mayor of Santa Fe."

I interviewed Daniel in 1992 together with then-delegate and member of the Playa executive committee Carlos Walfrido Rodríguez, and again in 1994, together with Milanés. In 1996 I spent ten days with him, participating in his activities, observing what he did. Almost everyone was on a first-name basis with him. Recognizing his authority, those with problems tended to seek him out instead of their own delegate. Seven days a week he usually left his house at 7 A.M. and did not return until 9 P.M. He was constantly checking up on things in the neighborhood. People came to his house at all hours of the night. He was continually being called to meetings at the municipal and provincial government. He had not had a vacation for years. He got paid 310 pesos per month (less than $14), which corresponded to the

Daniel Morales, president of the *Consejo Popular* Santa Fe, attending to constituents while making his rounds.

salary of a schoolteacher (his prior employment). The great amount of work and time required, intensified by the problems and shortages of the special period, eventually wore Daniel out and in general probably has been a major reason for the high turnover among *consejo* presidents.

I was told by Rodríguez that Daniel had considerable influence since it was known that he was popular and was likely to be elected continuously as both delegate and *consejo* president, and government officials at higher levels were reluctant to oppose him. Government ministers responded when he called. The Minister of Transportation visited Santa Fe twice in 1991 and assigned more bus lines to serve the neighborhood; they are important given the distance to the center of Havana.

Consejo presidents do things on their own, often contrary to stated regulations. For example, there was supposed to be only one private agricultural market (*mercado agropecuario*) per municipality, but many *consejos*, including Santa Fe, set them up in their neighborhoods. Contrary to regulations Daniel put up stands to sell *guarapo* (sugar-cane juice). He allowed private food stands to sell cigarettes, which was not legally permitted. However, he insisted they also sell food and threatened to close one that failed to do so. To ensure the availability of flowers in Santa Fe, Daniel allowed private flower vendors, even though the legislation allowing private vendors excluded flowers. Daniel explained the reasons for taking such actions:

I took on this authority knowing full well that I could count on the support of the people of Santa Fe, that all the citizens applaud that I have brought back the *guarapo* vendor. If you want to drink *guarapo* you can drink it there. In other *consejos* this may not exist, because they have accepted the regulation. But we did it because it is a solution for our people. They ordered us to remove the vendors and I said no. Santa Fe is in the extreme western part of the capital city, not close to the center of town. If you wanted to buy some flowers you would have had to at least go to Marianao. But we have the flower vendors here. Not because I want it but because the people of Santa Fe asked me for it.

Similarly to what I had observed in Miramar, Daniel made administrative decisions when necessary, such as controlling the sale of scarce goods, even though he was not suppose to administer. For example, in 1994 a medical ointment had been scheduled to be sold without limit. However, the demand was great and the supply limited, so people lined up many times to buy large quantities, most likely to resell them at a higher price. The *consejo* in Santa Fe decided to ration the sale of the ointment to two containers per family. Daniel stated in the interview in 1994, "This is to administer. This goes against what had been stipulated. And what happened? A large part of the population got the ointment. Do you understand? We involved ourselves in making a decision that was outside our area. This is not authorized, but well, we kept the people happy because they could purchase the ointment." During the 1992 interview Daniel related another example of having to make an administrative decision. When one bakery needed sugar to continue producing bread and the other bakery in Santa Fe did not have any, Daniel authorized moving ten sacks of sugar stored in another entity to the bakery. During my 1996 visit a truckload of green bananas arrived. Daniel had arranged for a farm cooperative in another province to sell them on the street.

As occurred in Almendares Sierra, *consejo* presidents can have local administrators dismissed. Rodríguez said that Daniel probably had greater leverage in removing administrators than the leadership of the municipal assembly. Daniel had administrators removed numerous times. In 1992 he told me the *consejo* officers discovered that an administrator was taking beef from one store to another without legal documents, and they reported this to the economic commission. The administrator was fired and tried for this crime. According to Daniel, "The people complain to us and we evaluate the complaints. We see to it that the measures we apply correspond to the deed. We do not apply sanctions but propose them to the enterprise." In the 1994 interview he was more emphatic: "We can order that people be dismissed. For example I tell the enterprise director that a local administrator cannot continue for such and such reasons. And the director faced with a signal from the *consejo* must act. We tell him the bread is sold late. It arrives late, burned, or dirty. Or the administrator is never there."

In May 1996 Daniel met with the administrator of a local agricultural market, together with the municipal assembly president and the municipal delegate in whose district the market was located. The administrator had been cited by many people as being arrogant and unfriendly, so Daniel decided that he must be replaced, and he was.

The *consejo* meets at least once a month. Local directors (*jefes de la zona*) from municipal government entities located within the *consejo*, including commerce, public health, services, aqueduct, education, street cleaning and garbage collection, restaurants, and electricity, meet regularly with and report periodically to the *consejo*. During my stay in 1996 I was invited to attend a meeting of the Santa Fe Consejo, which was canceled because of lack of a quorum (attributed to the heavy rains that day). The agenda items were to have been an analysis of sports and culture, including the plan for the summer.

I was given the official minutes from a *consejo* meeting in Santa Fe held on November 6, 1993. The first item on the agenda was an analysis of the work of the housing repair brigade (*microbrigada social*), based on its report. Questions were raised about the crew, such as why seven of the nineteen workers were supervisors. The local director said that the government agency said that lack of funds was the reason more workers were not sent, and also that some of the workers assigned to Santa Fe were working elsewhere. He also mentioned the excessive and unexcused absences of one technician. Other problems cited were poor working conditions (no snack or lunch, lack of tools), low salaries (one reason why workers left), and lack of construction materials. Delegates were told to meet with their constituents to explain the difficulties and delays. The agency, which had undergone many leadership changes, was subjected to heavy criticism by those at the meeting, and it was decided that the problems should be analyzed by the municipal assembly administrative council, which should conduct a fiscal audit. The agency was asked to submit a report to the *consejo* within thirty days offering solutions (the report was issued on December 6). A commission was formed with three delegates to oversee the resolution of the problems in Santa Fe and to report back to the *consejo* at the next meeting.

The *consejo* presidents from the City of Havana Province meet as a group every two months with the leadership of the provincial assembly, and also periodically with the country's leadership. Each *consejo* president in Playa meets once a month with the municipal assembly president. The assembly president also makes monthly tours of each *consejo* in the municipality. Every two weeks the *consejo* president and/or vice president meets with the municipal assembly's administrative council and municipal directors, in order to, in Daniel's words, "bring up the problems we have with gastronomy, with services, with aqueduct, with telephones, with electricity, with public health, with education. The municipal directors offer solutions or responses on how and when they plan to solve these problems. The *consejo* may then inform those affected among the public."

Twice a year the *consejo* sends a written report to the municipal assembly, recounting what has occurred and projecting the problems it will tackle during the period to follow. The report issued by the Santa Fe *Consejo* in June 1991, covering the first seven months of its existence, listed the thirteen meetings held (eight regular and five special), their purpose, and the attendance (noting the continued unexcused absences of the Confederation of Cuban Workers representative). It noted which agencies had reported to the *consejo* and divulged that housing needed to focus more on detecting illegal construction and occupations. Among the achievements recorded were the creation of a watch shop, a small-appliance repair shop, an ironworks shop, a housing repair brigade, and two agricultural markets; preparations for opening a nursing home; and garbage collection and food distribution to restaurants, using animal transport to save fuel. Also reported were improvements in conditions at the public schools, in city water distribution, and in the city sewers and a reduction in the crime rate due to greater police presence. Among the items planned were an ice-cream store, a large-appliance repair shop, a children's park, a video theater, and improved conditions on the public beach. Finally the report called for more municipal agency control over offices located in the *consejo*.

During my stay in 1996 Daniel had a meeting at the Playa municipal assembly headquarters concerning *planteamientos* in Santa Fe (the biannual accountability sessions of delegates with constituents were taking place at the time, and Daniel held several). He was summoned to the provincial assembly, as were the other *consejo* presidents in Havana, to be interviewed regarding the housing situation in the *consejo* and to meet with the provinces commission on the OLPP regarding the transmission and status of *planteamientos* from the accountability sessions in progress. He attended a meeting of all the *consejo* presidents from the City of Havana with the president of the provincial assembly, the first secretary of the provincial PCC, and Alarcón, held at the provincial assembly. The agenda was (1) the completion of the plan for the principal concerns in the trimester, including economic factors, farmers markets, infant mortality rates and other public health issues, housing, street cleaning and repairs, and tourism, and (2) a review of the spring 1996 process of accountability sessions. Daniel also attended a session of the Playa Municipal Assembly held that week.

The *consejos* have substituted for the municipal government in the immediate supervision of the municipal delegates' accountability sessions. Daniel and Milanés attended at least one of the sessions of every delegate and, when necessary, responded to constituents' questions. Each evening after the sessions the delegates gathered at the *consejo* office to discuss and record the *planteamientos* made by constituents.

Daniel and Milanés worked with delegates to improve their effectiveness:

> For example we saw a delegate who did not project well to the audience, who
> was not prepared, who was not visiting constituents who were making angry
> *planteamientos.* We sat down with the delegate and discussed the situation with
> him, "You are doing things incorrectly; people left your sessions; you are not
> visiting constituents; you did not do a follow-up check on the store, people are
> making complaints and you do not have the answer." The municipal govern-
> ment cannot do this with every delegate who needs it, but our *consejo* can do it
> with its ten delegates.

Prior to the *consejos* the delegate would attempt to resolve *planteamientos*
at the municipal level, but now they are evaluated at the *consejo* level because
almost all government agencies have their representative at this level. Within
the *consejo* there are contacts and resources to help resolve most
planteamientos, because, according to Daniel,

> When all is said and done, the essentials for resolving problems are here. Not
> all! Because we have administrative entities here where you really almost have to
> punch them and knock them down, because they do not comply with the rules
> and are slow in solving problems. With them you really have to insist. If the lo-
> cal director cannot resolve it then the municipal director is called.

Once a week each delegate holds office hours to meet constituents individually and register their *planteamientos.* In an example of people preferring
to consult Daniel rather than their own delegate, during his office hours I attended on May 16, 1996, only seven of the seventeen people waiting to see
Daniel were from his district (the rest were from districts of other delegates
within the *consejo*), and he attended to them first. Daniel suggested that
those from other parts of Santa Fe see their own delegate, but most remained. There were complaints of theft and domestic violence. Most problems concerned lack of housing and employment–in some cases a fallout of
Cuba's economic crisis resulting in unauthorized internal migration together
with illegal housing construction on state-owned land, resulting from a great
influx into Santa Fe from other parts of Havana (given the greater availability of vacant land) and from other provinces.

Prior to the *consejos populares*, people also could register their complaints
of a more individual nature (*quejas*) directly with the member of the municipal assembly leadership in charge of the issue involved. This practice continues, but the *consejos* now handle most of the *quejas* when local directors participate in regular meetings with the public, as described above in the
Almendares Sierra Consejo. Alarcón received a *queja* in the mail from Santa
Fe and asked Daniel, who was a National Assembly deputy, to follow up.
The complaint involved the excessive planting of trees that do not bear edi-
ble fruit. The complainant protested that the people could not eat wood but

like to eat mangos or oranges and said that a vice minister of agriculture should be put in charge of planting fruit trees. Daniel spoke to the person who told him, "Look, you see that this nursery school in front of my house has seven trees. If guava, coconut or orange trees had been planted, the children there could eat the fruit and drink the juice instead of having a tree that only provides shade." Daniel communicated this to Alarcón, who replied that the corresponding vice minister would be in contact with Daniel and the constituent to respond to the issue.

The main tasks of the *consejo popular*, under the purview of Daniel in Santa Fe, involved oversight, supervision, inspection, and control of all government and private economic and service activity in the territory, including enterprises under national, provincial, and municipal control. The purpose was to attain efficiency and guarantee the quality of goods and services and to root out corruption. The *consejo* does not replace but rather supplements the inspections done by the municipal assembly commissions.

Daniel explained:

> We check up on what is produced, what is repaired or that the services rendered are done correctly as is authorized. Besides the *consejo* is able to see up close how these entities employ their resources, because we control them fundamentally from the point of view of financing, planning and economic control, so that they do not use unnecessary labor, so that the budget is used adequately, and to check how the budget is drawn up. We control all the resources within the *consejo* and their distribution to stores and restaurants. I have the power to requisition the inventory on a store's invoices.

There is a schedule for inspections by the *consejo* of all state and private entities in the territory, including restaurants, food stands, stores and service centers, health clinics, schools, and other state enterprises. The inspectors at the *consejo* level also respond to citizen complaints, such as that a store has run out of chickens, or that the rice being sold is spoiled. Daniel asserted that it is easier for the *consejo* to check the few local restaurants for service and quality and weight of products sold than for the municipal government to supervise effectively the numerous restaurants in the municipality: "We inspect state food stores for example, comparing what has entered with what has been sold. For example, if a hundred cartons of eggs were brought, we review the receipts to see how many eggs were sold, and we arrive at the difference." Daniel finds out why products fail to arrive at the stores as scheduled: "If they do not arrive I go to each office and ask to see the distribution plan. We show the plan to the director and to the municipal government. The power that the *consejo* has is great."

The *consejo* meets frequently to discuss local problems with those in charge of food distribution (availability and equitable distribution), repair services (for televisions, refrigerators, radios, irons, fans, blenders, bicycles), water, electricity, restaurants, education, commerce, and agriculture and other local industry. A municipal delegate with a problem related to water consults the local representative in the *consejo* instead of having to go to the municipal office.

By 1995 private restaurants (*paladares*), private food stands selling sandwiches and beverages (*cafeterias*), private agricultural markets, and self-employed workers (*por cuenta propia*) were allowed, regulated by the *consejos populares*, which check on prices, sanitary conditions, quality, and so on. The *consejo* president approves the licenses to operate and can take them away.

Petty theft and corruption increased during times of growing scarcity. Information about corruption, theft, and diversion of resources comes mainly from constituents and inspections by *consejo* officers. However, a clever bread baker knows that even with all the controls and vigilance he can beat the system. Because he is allowed a margin of error, he can make each loaf of bread weigh 380 grams instead of the required 400 grams, a difference that is not easily detected. He then makes more bread, which he sells under the counter, and pockets the money with the collusion of those who buy it. It is difficult to catch him because those who can buy more bread (which is rationed) benefit and do not denounce him. Daniel concluded, "Our controls are not always effective; that is a reality. We might detect a bakery administrator stealing bread, but two blocks down the street a shopkeeper is selling rice illegally."

Among the successes attributed to the *consejo* in Santa Fe has been adding, in response to requests by the population, services and other amenities to the neighborhood, which previously were located far away. In 1994 the management of the city water flow was shifted from the province to local control by the *consejo*. The *consejo* demanded and got public telephones for Santa Fe, determined where they would be placed, and insisted that a telephone exchange be built in Santa Fe to improve service and to enable the population to make international calls from their home phones. By 1996 the *consejo* had gotten a hard currency store for Santa Fe (the government agency in charge had also agreed to paint some houses and stores in the neighborhood), a construction materials store, a discotheque, a video theater, a repair facility for small appliances, and an agricultural market. Pending were a notary public and a marriage chapel.

Daniel had visited Santa Fe in the province of Granada in Spain, which donated money for an ambulance for the public health clinic. Even before license plates were obtained, he had it running. Granada also donated money for supplies that Daniel used to purchase switches and bulbs for streetlights, cleaning materials for the local schools, and a pump for city water. He spent one morning going from office to office trying to untangle a bureaucratic mess to get approval to spend the money.

During my 1996 visit a dispute arose regarding the placement of a funeral parlor, which people had requested. For the site the municipal government decided to renovate a house infrequently used by the local CDR located on a street bordering a public park. I accompanied Daniel to meet there with the municipal assembly president, the municipal assembly delegate for that area, the head of the local CDR, the local Communist Party chief, and the local administrator whose responsibilities included funeral parlors. The delegate, supported by the local CDR leader, vehemently opposed using the house, arguing that it was used for meetings and that it was inappropriate to situate a funeral parlor next to a park that was being refurbished and was used for neighborhood festivities and recreation. His constituents had told him they did not want to see dead people arriving while they were enjoying the park. The municipal assembly president got angry and told the delegate that as he could not provide an alternative he should accept the site. The delegate proposed constructing a new building elsewhere, to which the president responded that there was a severe shortage of building materials. The delegate said he was responding to his constituents, to which the president countered by saying he should consider the needs not just of his constituents but also of the municipality and that he was being individualistic and not sufficiently revolutionary. The president then said he would arrange for a meeting with all CDR heads and all municipal delegates from the Santa Fe Consejo to resolve the issue. It was subsequently decided to locate the funeral parlor elsewhere.

Daniel was constantly on the move all day and well into the night during my eleven-day visit in 1996. Besides approaching him on the street, many people came to his house at all hours. A lady came to his house to ask for a cleaning job in the new store. The director of the primary school came to his house because the school's refrigerator was broken (she told me that almost everyone in Santa Fe comes to see Daniel, based on trust). A man came to tell him he was afraid the state was going to destroy his illegal dwelling, which he had built on state-owned land, and that he would have no place to live. At 2:15 A.M. on a Sunday a couple woke up Daniel to tell him their electricity was not working. He gave them a number to call. One man came to his house to complain about treatment on his job, and another told Daniel his truck, which he needed for his job, had been stolen and so he had been fired. Still another told him that people were spreading rumors on the street that only Daniel's friends were getting jobs in the new hard currency store.

Daniel often mobilized neighbors for tasks such as repairing stores, state-owned cafeterias, schools, and bakeries and cleaning and cutting weeds in the streets. Several times during my visit he checked on the remodeling of the building that was being converted to become the hard currency store. One night, after his accountability session with constituents, he visited one of the local bakeries to see if the flour had arrived for the next day. On another night he found the reason the streetlights in one section were out (he twisted wires together at a pole to turn them on again). On a Saturday evening he went to the public health clinic to check on the ambulance, because there had been problems with juveniles fooling around with it on weekends. From 6 P.M. to 10 P.M. one evening he helped neighborhood volunteers paint a store.

One night he was called to a local *paladar* by the owner (like many in Santa Fe, a longtime friend of Daniel), who complained of the high taxes he and his workers had to pay, equal to those exacted from more prosperous private restaurants in areas with more tourist traffic, which charge in dollars. He also told Daniel that some *paladar* owners were concerned about the rumor that Daniel was going to move out of Santa Fe and thus no longer be president of the *consejo*. Daniel told him he would meet with other owners and then appeal to the administrative council of the Playa Municipal Assembly for lower taxes in Santa Fe. He also said he would insist that municipal inspectors not be so rough on *paladares*, especially for first violations, which should first be discussed with the owners before sanctions were levied. However, the taxes were not lowered, which forced this and seven other *paladares* to close, leaving only three in Santa Fe.

Indicative of local initiative and popular participation supported by the *consejo* are the horticulture clubs, founded in 1993 as a result of food shortages and the government drive to use vacant city lots (*huertas*) for growing food. The founder and leader was Luis Sanchez, whose apartment door sign in Santa Fe read, "Agricultural and Veterinary Consultant" and who wrote in a pamphlet about the clubs:

> The characteristics of growth and development of the urban community of Santa Fe has left open spaces which were not occupied. . . . In other cases, these open spaces have surrounded multi-family apartment buildings. In many cases, these areas were invaded by weeds, or became deposits for garbage and contamination. As an alternative that could contribute to the food self-sufficiency of agricultural products in the community, a strong campaign within the population developed to utilize these open spaces in order to produce food stuffs for direct consumption. . . . There exist 915 cultivable spaces which are worked by some 1,130 horticulturists. Within this area of 75 hectares, they produce vegetables, tubers, root crops, grains, fruits, as well as raise small animals such as birds, bees, rabbits, goats, sheep and cows among others.[29]

There are fourteen horticulture clubs in Santa Fe, each with eight to ten families, divided according to electoral districts in Santa Fe (a few districts have more than one club), along with a club for raising rabbits, a club for viniculture and preserves, and a youth club called *Amigos del Bosque* (Friends of the Forest). On average, those cultivating the land put in eighteen hours per week. About 40 percent are retired people. What is not consumed by club members is sold to neighbors, at prices usually below those of the

private agricultural markets, and is donated to nursing homes, hospitals, and
nursery schools. Sanchez, who was employed by the Agricultural Ministry,
provided organizational and technical assistance, seeds, and fertilizers; he
also distributed bulletins and gave classes in schools. All farming is organic.
The horticultural movement has spread throughout the City of Havana,
which has 870 clubs and seventy-seven agricultural technicians.

Sanchez told me in 1996 that plans included the cultivation and processing of medicinal plants in Santa Fe and the adjoining Cangrejeras *Consejo
Popular* in Bauta. After determining the most frequent illnesses from the
family doctors in the area, those participating would cultivate plants, and an
institute in the region affiliated with the Agricultural Ministry would produce the appropriate medicines, to be sold to the community in a special
pharmacy. The Cangrejeras *Consejo Popular* organized this whole project, including the participation of the Agricultural Ministry. Plans existed to build
a small factory to produce preserves and one to produce improved animal
feed.

The Santa Fe clubs collaborate with and are in part funded by money from
Germany funneled through the Cuban Council of Churches; the United
Nations Children's Fund and the Food and Agricultural Organization; non-
governmental organizations from Italy, Holland, and Austria; and the Center of Information and Study on Interamerican Relations and the Institute of
Fundamental Investigations on Tropical Agriculture. Support also comes
from the Cuban government, the local Cuban Communist Party, and agencies belonging to the Santa Fe Consejo.

However, from the outset, most of the impetus, organization, and support has come from the Santa Fe *Consejo Popular.* Initially the state land was
converted to *huertas*, to be cultivated by those selected and approved of by
the *consejo*. The technical advice and help are a service of the *consejo*, of
which Sanchez was a member. Cuban sociologists Armando Fernández and
Rubén Otazo found a close and fruitful relationship between the Santa Fe
horticulturist movement and the *consejo popular.* In a survey, 97 percent of
those interviewed in Santa Fe defined the relationship between the *consejo
popular*, its president, and the horticulturist movement as very positive. The
consejo has obtained seeds from the Agricultural Ministry. The failure to drill
sufficient wells for irrigation was attributed by those interviewed not to the
inefficiency of the *consejo* but to municipal and provincial government agencies outside the jurisdiction of the *consejo*.[30] Daniel told me that he and
Sanchez worked together to deal with government agencies and to resolve
political and practical problems. For example, if Sanchez needed more land,
the *consejo* tried to get it for him.

After the October 1997 municipal delegate elections, Mirium Pabón,
Mario Cubota, and Daniel Morales were no longer presidents of their *consejos populares*, and William Milanés was no longer a vice president. All but

Vegetable gardens in Santa Fe cultivated by the horticulture clubs.

Daniel chose not to run again for municipal delegate. Thus, only Daniel remained as a municipal delegate, and he decided not to be a candidate for
president of the *consejo popular* and had secured another job. To his surprise,
however, he was not renominated as a National Assembly deputy candidate
for the January 1998 elections. Luis Sanchez left the post of agricultural
consultant in Santa Fe, accepting a higher-paying job within the Agricultural
Ministry.

Conclusion

The *consejos populares* mesh with the characteristics and province of the
Cuban municipal assembly and help carry out its functions. The convergence of civil and political societies-constituents resemble and maintain
close, frequent personal contact with their elected representatives, and hold
them in high estimation-and the *mandat impératif*- the responses to and responsibilities of municipal delegates regarding citizens' *planteamientos*-are
enhanced through the *consejos populares*. Furthermore, the consejos have become the mechanism and conduit for people's participation in monitoring
and controling local economic activity.

A workshop entitled "Los consejos populares: La gestión del desarrollo y
la participación popular en Cuba" (The People's Council: Efforts Toward

Development and Popular Participation in Cuba) was held at the *Centro de Estudios sobre América* (CEA) on October 31, 1995. Among the participants were *consejo* presidents, functionaries of institutions connected to the *consejos'* activities, and social scientists. A report on the workshop issued on November 13, 1995, states:

> The creation of the *consejos populares* and their subsequent spread over the whole country represent one of the most effective and efficient means in the process of political decentralization, of institutionalizing a people's government at the base and of developing new forms of popular participation.[31]

My fieldwork, especially in Santa Fe, makes a stronger case for the possibility of decentralizing power than for introducing new forms of political participation. Rather than being just another layer of government, in many ways the *consejo* has demonstrated greater potentiality than the municipality for cutting through the bureaucracy and getting results. Clearly Daniel, as a neighborhood leader and advocate constantly on the scene, had both the residents' support and political clout, which those in higher government positions and those working in the *consejo* territory had to take into account. Although the municipal assembly monitored, supported, and sometimes was in conflict with the *consejos*, in the examples studied the *consejo* supplemented and at times replaced the municipal government as the focal point for dealing with local problems in general, for recording, resolving, transmitting, and following up on citizens' *planteamientos* and *quejas* and monitoring the delegates' accountability sessions, and for inspecting state and private stores, restaurants, service centers, bakeries, and public health facilities.

People were mobilized in the Santa Fe Consejo to paint and repair stores, facilities, and homes and to accomplish other tasks, but this kind of participation existed on a smaller scale at the level of the individual electoral district prior to the *consejos populares*. Clearly, however, having these endeavors encompass the whole *consejo* represents an important change, since the projects serve the whole community and not just the electoral district in which they are located, and the undertakings become more effective with the *consejo* organizing the efforts and acquiring the construction materials and tools.

Yet the horticulturist clubs presented a different way of incorporating members of the community in solving local problems, and thus they can be classified as a new form of participation, instigated, organized, and supported by the *consejo*. Another workshop at the CEA entitled "Municipios, economía local y economía popular" (Municipalities, Local Economy, and Popular Economy), held March 7–8, 1996, made recommendations regarding popular participation emanating from community efforts, which allow people to identify their problems and propose solutions and involve leaders and institutions to spur such projects. The workshop's report cited the horticulturist movement of Santa Fe as an example: "It was created with the idea of making use of existing unused lots by means of urban agriculture and thus help resolve the food supply problems of the population . . . with the help of the *consejo popular*, Santa Fe has been the setting for other communitarian projects related to the environment, aid for the elderly, etc."[32]

The *consejo* officers in this study used *planteamientos* and other requests made by citizens as an important method in defining community needs and soliciting remedies and in rooting out crime and corruption. It was also demonstrated that the *consejo* in Santa Fe was responsible for requesting and obtaining improvements in services for the territory, such as telephones, the hard currency store, and repair centers, to name a few.* The 1995 workshop report called for the *consejos* to have a greater role in economic planning and to work with the Institute for Physical Planning in regulating land use. Cuban economist Carlos García Pleyán wrote that community participation in local economic and physical planning has taken place through the *consejos*, especially in providing information, evaluating local problems, and creating and implementing solutions. Projects have included rehabilitation of slums, construction of new housing, and water and sewage projects. Planning should take into account input from local administrators and technical workers with the criteria of the economic sector they represent, as well as from "the community, perhaps without the same rigor (or rhetoric) as the technicians, but with the realism of those whose needs are based on their own experience . . . which expresses by means of delegates and *Consejos Populares*, problems, preoccupations, opinions, proposals and initiatives which the local government should evaluate and take into consideration in its decision making."[33] The importance of the *consejo* president, as well as the delegate, having a say in physical planning, bolstered by citizen input, was clear in the dispute over the placement of the funeral home in Santa Fe.

The examples cited above of *consejo* presidents assuming administrative tasks and their relationship to the local administrators and administrative agencies give substantiation to the criticism made in the 1995 workshop report regarding the lack of a concise legal definition of the *consejo*'s structure, character, functions, and relations.[34] Regarding oversight and control, the report states that the *consejos* should act as constructive critics (*contrapartida*) in relation to the administration and local government rather than becoming an executive-administrative organ. The country's leaders and the press have continuously stressed the point that the *consejos populares* should not administer. Yet in practice, as was seen to varying degrees in the *consejos* studied, the attempt to keep *consejo* presidents from performing administrative functions and making administrative decisions has proved to be unwork-

---

*See Chapter 5 regarding the use of citizens' *planteamientos* for local input in the economic planning process.

able. In their daily operations in the field they devise and execute guidelines and assume other functions paralleling government agencies. Pabón ordered that the sale of grapefruits be rationed, and both she and Daniel saw to it that medicine was rationed. Cubota took charge in a crisis in a bakery when the administrator was missing and directed that bread sales be rationed. Daniel arranged for the truckload of bananas to be sold on the street, made the agreement with the government agency controlling the hard currency shop to supply the materials for painting stores and houses, ordered the sacks of sugar to be moved to another bakery, and set guidelines for the private sale of flowers and of cigarettes at street refreshment stands.

The workshop on the *consejos populares* pointed out that government agencies situated in the territory, especially those directly subordinate to the central government, are not necessarily bound to comply with the resolutions of the *consejos*. Furthermore, the 1995 workshop's report alludes to a contradiction between the role of representing community interests and promoting popular participation, on the one hand, and representing, coordinating, and controlling entities connected to the local government on the other.[35] This lack of a precise legal definition of the *consejos'* relations with these agencies leads to dependence on the prestige of the *consejo* presidents and their willingness to act, potentially leading instead to overdependence on a strong personality (*personalismo*). In Santa Fe, Daniel's following, recognition, and strength were such that he could not be ignored by officials at all levels of government. Daniel and Cubota fully expected that at their requests administrators would be replaced.

A deficiency in the *consejo* structure pointed out in the 1995 workshop was the lack of decentralized financial independence and resources to develop the local economy according to community needs.[36] It was recommended that funds for the *consejos* come from local taxes on production and services. The advantage of fiscal access and control was demonstrated by the funds obtained from Spain that the Santa Fe *Consejo* used to purchase an ambulance and other important supplies not available from higher government sources.

Among the rationales for creating the *consejos populares* was the need to strengthen the municipal assembly delegates. However, my research has shown that this goal is in contradiction with another of the stated rationales—that of having a strong government figure at the neighborhood level.[37] The importance, authority, and availability of the *consejo* president have decentralized governmental authority and enabled people and their delegates to find solutions for local problems. Daniel was, for example, an advocate for the municipal delegate in the dispute regarding placing the funeral home by the park. However, at the same time the position of the *consejo* president has weakened or diminished the role of the other municipal delegates. During the weekly meeting with constituents, people sought

Cubota's assistance rather than relying on their delegate, as did most of those who came to see Daniel during his office hours. In Santa Fe, faced with crises or problems, especially the more immediate ones, people logically usually went to see Daniel.

The workshop on the *consejos populares* report concluded, "It is necessary to focus on the *consejo popular* as an embryo of popular self government in a model socialist project. . . . "[38] However, the fieldwork shows that rather than provide for new forms of local self-government—or be regarded as the inception of a model socialist project—the *consejos populares* do represent a potentially positive development in decentralized, effective, and responsive representative government. In the examples studied they brought what existed at the municipal level to the neighborhoods—oversight and control over and more access to government agencies and services, scrutiny over private economic activities in the territory, and vigilance regarding economic crimes. They have provided new clout as people's advocates in pursuing solutions for the needs of the population. To be sure, Santa Fe is not necessarily a representative case. Neighborhoods, especially in the cities, do not necessarily have the cohesion of Santa Fe. *Consejo* presidents do not always have Daniel's energy and support and are not necessarily as well known. Most would probably not be willing to sacrifice their family life to the same extent by expending equal amounts of energy and time, which in the end wore Daniel out. Yet Santa Fe, as led by Daniel, illustrates the potential for the *consejos populares* in Cuba.

Notes

1. *Resoluciones Aprobadas por el III Congreso del Partido Comunista de Cuba* (Havana: Editora Política, 1986), pp. 14–19.

2. Jeffrey W. Hahn, *Soviet Grassroots: Citizen Participation in Local Soviet Government* (Princeton: Princeton University Press, 1988), pp. 163–164.

3. José Gabriel Gumá and Alberto Nuñez, "Consejos Populares en la capital: una bienvenida optimista," *Granma*, October 6, 1990, p. 3.

4. "Constitución de la República de Cuba," *Granma*, September 22, 1992, p. 9 (my translation).

5. María Julia Mayoral, "Acción de los diputados en las rendiciones de cuenta," *Granma*, August 12, 1993, p. 1.

6. "Pasan revista a importantes asuntos en comisiones del Parlamento," *Granma*, December 24, 1996, p. 8.

7. Cited in Jesús P. García Brigos, "Cinco tesis sobre los Consejos Populares," *Revista Cubana de Ciencias Sociales*, No. 31, 1996 (my translation).

8. José Gabriel Gumá and Alberto Nuñez, "Consejos Populares," p. 3.

9. José Gabriel Gumá, "El Consejo Popular comenzará a actuar de inmediato y a adoptar las medidas oportunas," *Granma*, October 12, 1990, p. 3.

10. Fidel Castro, in a speech given on September 28, 1990, *Granma Weekly Review*, October 10, 1990, p. 5 (my translation).

11. Susana Lee, "Algún día la historia tendrá que consignar que hemos resistido en parte importante gracias a los Consejos Populares," *Granma*, November 14, 1995, p. 3 (my translation, Lee's emphasis).

12. María Julia Mayoral, "Confusiones sobre los Consejos Populares," *Granma*, July 10, 1998, p. 4.

13. Pedro Prada, "Analizan distribución de productos agrícolas," *Granma*, April 11, 1992, p. 3.

14. Vladia Rubio, "Sábado ejemplaizante en el Malecón," *Granma*, November 19, 1991, p. 2.

15. María Julia Mayoral, "Tratan Consejos Populares sobre lucha contra el delito," *Granma*, October 29, 1991, p. 2.

16. Teresa Valdés, "Crean secciones penales de los Tribunales Municipales a nivel de Consejo Popular," *Granma*, February 1, 1992, p. 2.

17. Susana Lee, "Acercar trámites, simplificar gestiones = menos viajes," *Granma*, September 2, 1992, p. 3.

18. Alexis Rojas Aguilera, "El Consejo Popular de la Gallega," *Granma*, July 2, 1992, p. 3.

19. Reynoldo Rass, "Permutas laborales a partir del próximo Lunes," *Granma*, January 31, 1992, p, 4.

20. Agustín Pérez Hechavarría, "Afanza influencia de Consejos Populares," *Granma*, September 11, 1993, p. 2.

21. María Julia Mayoral, "Armas de un Consejo," *Granma*, June 18, 1992, p. 2 (my translation).

22. María Julia Mayoral, "Consejos Populares apoyan curso escolar," *Granma*, August 28, 1993, p. 3 (my translation).

23. José A. Martín, "Salud Pública en la agenda de los Consejos Populares," *Granma*, November 27, 1993, p. 2; José A. de la Osa, "Analizan presidentes de los Consejos Populares apoyo al programa de medicamentos," *Granma*, May 17, 1994, p. 1.

24. Raisa Pagés and Isabel Morales, "Diputados abogan por mayor control de los recursos materiales y financieros," *Granma*, December 25, 1996, p. 3.

25. "La experiencia del arquitecto de la comunidad," *Granma*, October 22, 1994, p. 2.

26. Maria Julia Mayoral, "Este Consejo echa raíces," *Granma*, September 5, 1996, p. 5.

27. Vladia Rubio, "Unidad: arma principal en la lucha contra la indisciplina social," *Granma*, May 6, 1997, p. 2; Susana Lee, "La batalla contra las ilegalidades y las indiciplinas sociales no se ganará sin los CDR," *Granma*, April 25, 1997, p. 3; Eloy Concepción, "Crear conciencia de rechazo a las ilegalidades, las indiciplinas sociales y el delito: Entrevista con Juan Contino, Coordinador Nacional de los CDR," *Trabajadores*, May 19, 1997, p. 8; Fidel Castro, in a speech given on April 4, 1997, *Granma*, April 8, 1997, pp. 5–6.

28. Armando Fernández Soriano and Rubén Otazo Conde, "Comunidad, autogestión, participación y medio ambiente," Haroldo Dilla Alfonso (ed.), *La partici-*

pación en Cuba y los retos del futuro (Havana: Centro de Estudios sobre América, 1996), pp. 229–230.

29. Luis Sanchez, "From Consumers to Producers: Work Experiences with Small Agricultural Groups to Improve the Food Self-Sufficiency among the Members of a Community," unpublished manuscript.

30. Fernández and Otazo, "Comunidad, autogestión," pp. 232, 234.

31. Centro de Estudios sobre América, *Informe sobre el taller: Los consejos populares: La gestión del desarrollo y la participación popular en Cuba* (Havana: Centro de Estudios sobre América, 1995), p. 2 (my translation).

32. Centro de Estudios sobre América, *Relatoria del taller: Municipios, economía local y economía popular* (Havana: Centro de Estudios sobre América, 1996), p. 3 (my translation).

33. Carols García Peyán, "Participación y decentralización en el planeamiento territorial," in Dilla (ed.), *La participación*, pp. 189–190 (my translation).

34. Centro de Estudios sobre América, *Informe sobre el taller*, p. 2.

35. Ibid., p. 6.

36. Ibid., p. 8.

37. García Brigos, "Cinco tesis."

38. Centro de Estudios sobre América, *Informe sobre el taller*, p. 2.

Conclusion

To understand what Cuban municipal assembly delegates do in relation to their constituents and why, I found it helpful to trace the tradition to the political thought of Rousseau, Marx, and Lenin and to the historical events of the Paris Commune of 1871, the 1905 and 1917 soviets, the Russian Revolution and its immediate aftermath, and the development of the Soviet Union. Most relevant to Cuba in Rousseau's writings are his emphasis on (1) inequality and the convergence of the social and civil realms, expressed in Cuba in the stress on economic and political equality—municipal assembly delegates being nonprofessionals who do not form a separate political caste; (2) partial or parochial interests subservient to the what might be likened to the general will, which in Cuba finds its expression in the lack of antagonistic class divisions and the emphasis on political harmony and unity; (3) the strong, close identity between delegates and constituents in the setting of a small body politic and political participation by the electorate; (4) active involvement of and participation by the electorate, in Cuba manifested in the nomination assemblies and accountability sessions and in voluntary efforts to solve local problems; and (5) the combination of the mandate system of representative government with the presentation of grievances in periodic public meetings, evident in Cuba in the accountability sessions and *planteamientos* and the role of Cuban municipal delegates as transmitters of constituents' concerns.

Marx and Lenin added to these themes a class analysis of the state and the concept of the dictatorship of the proletariat, and these form the theoretical underpinnings of the Cuban Organs of People's Power. Furthermore, for both these writers, the theory of the withering away of the state included the concept of its depoliticization, which in Cuba is most notable in the elections devoid of election campaigning for or against particular candidates, and in the nonpolitical parliamentary debates.

Marx and Lenin relied for their political theory on historical and unfolding political events, among them the Paris Commune of 1871 and (for Lenin) the 1905 and 1917 soviets and the Russian Revolution and its aftermath. From these events emerged a pattern that became the historical foundation for working-class government and, in particular, both the Soviet parliamentary system and the Cuban OPP. Neither Marx nor Lenin can be considered the initial or even main organizer of these workers' parliaments. Although the Communards in Paris did not invent all the forms (the *mandat impératif* can be traced to the French Estates General in the Middle Ages), there was an element of spontaneity in the manner in which the Paris Commune was constituted and structured. The first soviets created by and for the Russian proletariat included characteristics of the Paris Commune, but again, there was an element of the unrehearsed in their organization. The 1905 soviets set the pattern for the 1917 soviets, which in turn provided the basic model for parliamentary government immediately after the Russian Revolution (Lenin, it will be recalled, had little to do with drafting the first constitution), for the subsequent constitutions of the Soviet Union, and, following the historical thread, for Cuba.

Cuba borrowed deeply from the experience of the Soviet Union, most importantly the mandate system and delegate recall, representatives who are not professional politicians, the structure of the assemblies, and the Communist Party in both instances having the primary role in policymaking. Cuba also made significant changes that brought it closer to model of its earlier predecessors, among them nominations by constituents and competitive municipal elections, a process not controlled by the Cuban Communist Party; a more definite separation between local parliaments and the party; and the requirement that municipal delegates reside in their electoral districts, all of which have served to increase the esteem in which local government is held by the people and to strengthen the bonds between Cuban delegates and constituents. Whereas in the Soviet Union candidates for soviet deputies at all levels were selected by the party and there was only one candidate for each position, in Cuba the voters themselves, with no outside interference even by the Communist Party, nominate their candidates for municipal assembly delegates, and by law, the elections must be competitive.

However, the voters do not participate directly in the nominations for National Assembly deputies and provincial assembly delegates, and the elections for these offices are not competitive. This model is closer to what existed in the Soviet Union, except that in Cuba the Communist Party has no formal role. With the 1992 Cuban Constitution and Electoral Law, the party no longer has any representative on candidacy commissions and no longer approves candidates for these positions, at least not officially.

In the Soviet Union, even after the reforms initiated by Gorbachev in the late 1980s, there was no requirement that the local deputies reside in the electoral districts. In Cuba, the municipal delegates reside within the electoral districts throughout their tenure. This requirement, combined with the nomination procedures and competitive elections, has resulted in a very close identity between delegates and constituents because delegates are, in effect, neighbors and are therefore familiar, available, accessible, and accountable to their constituents. There is, however, no residency requirement for National Assembly deputies and provincial assembly delegates, and even after the direct elections brought on by 1992 reforms, most people do not seem to be aware of what the provincial assemblies and National Assembly do and who their representatives are, and even fewer are personally acquainted with them. While only the National Assembly has legislative powers, and its importance has grown, it is still mainly a responsive body rather than one that takes independent initiatives.

The *consejos populares* can be traced to the deputies' groups in the Soviet Union. They are similar in combining municipal delegates from a neighborhood to give them more presence in the community and more strength in representing the needs of the population.

Accountability to constituents is also enhanced by Cuba's adoption of the mandate system of representative government. This system is very similar in form to the one that existed in the Soviet Union, consisting of periodic meetings between constituents and delegates, called accountability sessions, whose main purpose is the presentation of mandates (i.e., *planteamientos*) by the constituents to the delegates and a report on the status of those made at previous sessions. Helping to resolve *planteamientos* raised by constituents may well be the municipal delegates' major task and the most important factor in the legitimization of the OPP in the eyes of the Cuban populace. As the delegates are bound, where possible and within reason, to attempt to facilitate the resolution of the *planteamientos*, the mandates can be categorized as imperative.

Among the differences between the mandate system as practiced in Cuba and the historical concept of the *mandat impératif* is that the latter has been associated with parliaments as legislative bodies. In Cuba, citizen *planteamientos* are almost never directed toward legislation or national policy because neither is within the purview of the municipal assembly. The limitation in practice on the scope of public debate was demonstrated in 1991 when the national debate preparatory to the Fourth Party Congress had to be temporarily suspended because citizens at first regarded it as an extension of their accountability sessions rather than as a discussion of proposed changes in national political and governmental structure. However, during the second round, suggestions for national reforms became prevalent, as was also the case in the workers' parliaments held in 1994.

Although most *planteamientos* are made by individuals and revolve around local problems, collectively they constitute an important input that has affected policy at all levels, as is clearly demonstrated in housing and public health. Citizen *planteamientos* taken collectively have been an important element in the formulation of municipal economic plans and have provided input into the provincial and national economic planning processes.

However, viewed from this collective perspective, citizen mandates lose much of their imperative quality, for neither policymakers nor legislators are directly obliged to consider or act upon them, either because of more pressing national priorities or because of bureaucratic inflexibility. To be sure, there is little awareness on the part of the Cuban public that their *planteamientos* have an impact beyond their neighborhoods and can affect and have affected national policy.

Cuban municipal assembly delegates are legitimate elected representatives of the population. They are, for the most part, humble working people selected by their neighbors from their midst, and they tend to remain an integral and active part of the milieu from which they emanate. They are the point of immediate contact between the people and the government, giving citizens a known entity, someone tangible and accessible, to turn to in time of need for help in solving problems. Municipal delegates have become the embodiment of the integration of civil and political societies in Cuba. Although their involvement in the governing of Cuba may at first glance seem limited in range, their tasks are considered of vital importance to the population to which they are immediately and directly accountable and ultimately have important implications for national policy. Cuba's municipal assemblies and delegates can therefore be considered a vital, effective, and representative component of the Cuban government.

Appendix

Workers' Parliaments in Cuba

During the special period in time of peace beginning in 1990 following the collapse of socialism in Eastern Europe and the Soviet Union, Cuba's economy suffered severe contraction.

"Workers' parliaments" sponsored by the Central de Trabajadores de Cuba (Cuban Workers' Federation—CTC) were held between January and March, 1994, in 80,000 work places, and 3 million workers (85 percent of the work force) were invited to propose solutions to problems in their work places, and in the national economy. Summaries of the workers' suggestions were then discussed in municipal and provincial meetings of the CTC, with municipal and provincial assembly delegates and National Assembly deputies from the region also present, and provided input for the special session of the National Assembly held on May 1 and 2, 1994, and the regular session on August 3 and 4, 1994. According to Cuban reporter Susana Lee, this represents "the undeniable fact of a people participating in the formation of a massive national consensus without precedent in the world, consolidating the process initiated in the last session of the National Assembly [December 1993] and forming the basis for the continuation of these deliberations in its next extraordinary session [May 1994]."[1]

The CTC newspaper *Trabajadores* contrasted this consultation with the Cuban workers with the issuance of decrees:

> Again we salute the wisdom of the National Assembly for postponing decision making and rejecting categorically the intention of formulating a supposed "package of measures." In reality, the concept of a "package of measures" smells too much of Third World capitalism, of neo-liberal policies whereby one day workers wake up with the news of prices shooting up, of the privatization of enterprises that leaves half of them unemployed, of reduced salaries and abruptly eliminated social services.[2]

For Lee the workers' parliaments demonstrated

This article was originally published in *Latin American Perspectives*, Issue 87, Vol. 22 (Fall 1995), and is reprinted hre with the approval of the publisher.

In the first place the validity of bringing the debate on such vital themes as economic efficiency and the improvement of our internal finances to the heart of
the workers' collectives. Secondly, the comprehension by the majority of participants in these encounters of the principal problems which we face today.
. . . And thirdly, the raising of economic and political consciousness.[3]

Problems at the workplace have historically been discussed in production assemblies,[4] but the Cuban people have had few avenues or opportunities to participate directly in debates on national policy. National consultations had been held prior to the
vote on the 1976 Constitution, for specific legislation such as the labor code, and
prior to the Fourth Congress of the Partido Comunista de Cuba (Cuban Communist
Party—PCC). The biannual accountability sessions between municipal delegates and
their constituents, while having potential national ramifications, predominantly involve local community issues.[5]

According to a survey of Cuban workers regarding the workers' parliaments done
by the Centro de Estudios Sociopoliticos y de Opinión, the skepticism expressed at
the start of the process in mid-January 1994, was somewhat reduced by mid-Febru-
ary. When asked whether the workers' parliaments had aroused enthusiasm among
the workers, 62 percent answered yes in January, and 80 percent in February. To the
question whether useful proposals would be received, 75 percent answered yes in
January and 84 percent in February.[6] A survey of workers done by the same center in
October 1993, found that 68 percent favored using pricing policy to help resolve the
financial crisis, as compared with 74 percent in February 1994, "although this topic
cannot count on a majority consensus when specific products and services are discussed." In February, 50 percent favored price increases for alcoholic beverages, and
45 percent for cigarettes, and 60 percent for electricity use over basic consumption.
71 percent favored eliminating subsidies and giveaways for other than basic items.
There was no consensus on the possible introduction of taxes. "To the question what
was the greatest concern with regard to the economic measures, the new study produced a definite group of responses: the fate of surplus workers, the affects on low income workers and their families, the enrichment of people making illegal sales and
other crooks, and the effectiveness of the economic measures finally adopted."[7]

Every workers' parliament session that I attended began with a report from the director, and the reading aloud of excerpts from an editorial in the CTC newspaper
Trabajadores:

What actions should be taken to stimulate work discipline and morale? How can
more be produced, of better quality and at lower costs? Where do we need to
rationalize the use of personnel? What policy should be adopted with regard to
surplus workers? What can be done to reduce or eliminate state subsidies? . . .
How should we confront the excess of money in circulation? How should we
resolve the budget deficit? Should money of dubious origin and accumulated in
large quantities by small sectors of the population be confiscated? What free
items and services should be maintained? By what means and up to what point
should unprofitable enterprises be subsidized? What role should prices play? Is a
system of income tax appropriate?[8]

At the workers' parliament in the Partagás Cigar Factory in Havana, led by Pedro
Ross, Secretary General of the CTC, a worker said,

You say our biggest problem is absenteeism and you may be right. But I want to know why, given all the hard currency we earn for the country, we're driven to work on a flat bed truck while others ride on buses! . . . We say there's not enough tobacco leaves and the quality is poor. What we do get is not always properly dried. You say our factory made a lot of hard currency? We didn't make any hard currency; we made pesos and only pesos! Padrón [in charge of the tobacco export business] got the hard currency; the sales people who sell to the tourists got the hard currency; the thieves who steal the tobacco to sell on the black market got the hard currency; but this factory and this workforce, where the cigars are produced, didn't see any hard currency! . . . Where does all the money go? We don't see any of it![9]

Another worker complained about the lack of food in the lunchroom. "If we earn so much hard currency, why doesn't the state pay more attention to this factory?" Ross responded that their cafeteria received more food than other places which do not produce for export (such as the cafeteria for Cuban journalists) and suggested they follow the example of his office and grow their own food.[10] The causes of the deficits in the tobacco industry were attributed by workers not just to stealing, but also to technical and organizational problems leading to losses in quality of raw materials, excessive expenditures, and poor management.[11]

At the workers' parliament at the Ariguanabo textile factory in Bauta, which experienced a loss of 12.4 million pesos in 1993, the workers referred to management inefficiencies, salaries paid during work stoppages due to lack of electricity and raw materials, fixed costs with reduced production, labor instability, absenteeism, and insufficient demands placed on the workers. They demanded action against thieves, speculators and *macetas* (those who amass small fortunes through illicit activities), all of whom feed off state resources, and called for price controls for the self-employed.[12]

Workers at the Planta Mecánica de Santa Clara, demanded decentralization, said they were underworked due to lack of demand for their products, and suggested alternative production.[13] Regarding absenteeism, one worker, complaining about the sudden hike in train fares, asked, "Do you think that a worker will get up in the morning and come here and just barely cover the cost of his transportation?" There were complaints of low salaries, the monthly salary being equal to the cost of ten pounds of rice on the black market. At a cigarette factory in Santa Clara the workers wanted to take the initiative more, such as in rejecting defective raw materials.[14]

At a workers' parliament in a match factory in Havana, at first no one wanted to talk: "Almost two decades of bringing up the same items without getting concrete answers filled the atmosphere with some skepticism." When asked to speak some responded, "For me this is just another meeting," "where will our complaints be taken?," and "we here are all very tired." Others expressed severe criticisms regarding the lack of attention paid to workers and working conditions, and the lack of machinery and tools. They demanded more autonomy for the factory, which had had too many changes in the administration (eight in one year), and poor food preparation in the cafeteria. One protested the need to get up at 3 A.M. because of lack of transportation and to arrive without even the inducement of a refreshment, and another that low salaries were causing skilled workers to leave.[15]

The problem of phony medical leaves, causing high rates of absenteeism emerged in many workers' parliaments. A lack of oversight and faked illnesses resulted in medical leaves being used as a legal pretext to get out of work and engage in illicit activities. It was suggested that the time a medical leave permits a worker to be away from work while still receiving a salary should be limited.[16]

Another theme emphasized in the Cuban press was *igualitarismo*—equal pay for workers regardless of their productivity. *Trabajadores* editorialized that the union movement, understanding the pernicious effect of paternalistic practices and *igualitarismo*, favored measures that raised the real income of workers on the basis of higher levels of production. Tobacco workers proposed individual and collective material incentives rigorously linked to efficiency and raising production.[17] Dario Machado Rodríguez, director of the Centro de Estudios Sociopolíticos y de Opinión, spoke of the contradiction between *igualitarismo* as having been a goal of the Cuban revolutionary process and Cuba's economic recovery based on rejecting this concept. He attributed changes in attitudes by workers in part to the workers' parliaments, which contributed to a more realistic grasp of the economic situation. "In a study made in October-November 1993 we asked a representative sample of the Cuban adult population if everyone should receive the same, and 61 per cent said yes. Last February [1994] we repeated the question, expressing it better: 'As you know, one of the problems most debated now is the so-called *igualitarismo*. We want to know your criteria with respect to whether we all should receive the same,' and 50 per cent of those questioned responded affirmatively."[18]

The first workers' parliament I attended was for the news service workers (including reporters) in the Instituto Cubano de Radio y Televisión (Cuban Institute for Radio and Television—ICRT) on February 23, 1994. Ricardo Alarcón, President of the National Assembly, attended and Ross presided. The first to speak stated that television news lacked credibility among the populace, and that it is not enough just to report, for example, that some factory has produced more than the plan. Another reporter reiterated the problem of content, which was causing a decline in the audience for news. She cited the fear of dealing with the negative aspects of Cuban economic crisis and suggested that television news should also discuss themes and problems such as adolescents and divorce. She felt that journalists had become accustomed to limiting themselves with regards to what they covered and that they themselves should choose what appeared on television news programs.

Another participant claimed that Cuban television news had lost some credibility, because of a lack of variety of news sources:

> I absolutely don't believe that we should always use the same source. I don't believe it is feasible, nor credible, or helpful in any way. To the contrary, even when we are not in agreement with the source we are citing, we should present these opinions. This country has changed a lot in the past five years and we have to be entrusted to report what we are experiencing. I consider that television, not to mention the press, is as it was in 1990, blind! . . . We must advance opinions. I can say this categorically because I have offered my opinions. I have offered my opinions regarding these parliaments, which have not been very well received in some places, but it is my opinion and I have the right, as do all reporters who transmit information, and I defend it and claim it, and my right to be mistaken. What I cannot claim is the right to keep quiet because of fear of being mistaken. . . . We must deal with alternate sources. We must mention

them because the people know them. They find out in the *bodega*, on the corner, playing dominoes. . . . Let's make space available on television for the opposition.

A man rose to say while there was no censorship, nobody said anything to censure. When Ross said that journalists could say whatever they want, people began to murmur. One man asked, "Doesn't one have to be in agreement with the party?" Ross cited the workers' parliaments as examples of people complaining, of saying everything, and that *Trabajadores* was publishing everything. Again murmurs arose from the audience. Someone shouted that Ross was taking the floor from a woman who proceeded to claim that the television news was not credible but also boring, and that was also true of *Granma* and furthermore that neither central government organisms nor the party's central committee give reporters clear information. When she said that there were articles that could not be published, shouts were heard from the audience: "The ones about cigarettes!" Regarding the lack of cigarettes available for purchase by the public, she had been told by the director of the cigarette institute that the problem would be solved by November 1993. But in November he was sick, and when she visited the cigarette factories in Havana she discovered that she had not been told the truth. "I come to give this information to the people because besides being part of a press office I am a member of the party. . . . We went to the minister and vice-minister of agriculture, and no one wanted to give us information about the case." This was greeted with applause and shouts of "Bravo!" A man shouted, "I would like to see *Trabajadores* publish this information," and this was met with shouts of approval. Ross responded that permission from above was not necessary and that it would be stupid not to publish it. The woman told Ross to be quiet, that she had the floor, and continued, "The only thing that interests those in authority here is a silenced press."

A man brought up the problem of the scarcity of gasoline and complained that he had been given incorrect statistics by the ministry that were not believed by the public. When Ross asked how to gain the people's trust, the man responded, "Tell the truth!" Another man stated that what was lacking was an information policy, and that "there are many instances when in reality no one says no, but no one dares to publish it." He also noted that while an economic program was needed, "we do not speak of economic alternatives," even though people were discussing such alternatives. He proposed programs about how the foreign press treats Cuba. "Let's take the *Miami Herald*, let's take other newspapers . . . . We have our arguments. We have weighty arguments to convince people." He also brought up the subject of who decides on news programming.

"Who gives orders in the press in Cuba? Are the ministers the ones who decide whether some piece of information can or cannot be published? . . . Does the director of an enterprise decide? Does the minister of internal commerce decide? Who decides?"

Another woman complained about self-censorship: "We report good news about tobacco when there isn't any about tobacco. . . . We say it is raining tomatoes when there are no tomatoes. We say how well the parliaments are going and there are parliaments where no one attends." It is not, she claimed, that reporters were not allowed, but rather had to find a correct way to say things. Ross asked why she could not report this, and she replied that nobody, including *Trabajadores*, would publish it. Ross interrupted again to accuse her of not reading *Trabajadores*.

He pointed out that the February 21, 1994 issue had published an article criticizing some workers' parliaments. (The article to which he referred said that the discussions of the country's economic problems in some of the workers' parliaments tended toward simplicity and sketchiness.[19]) He went on to say that at the workers' parliaments they were attempting to introduce unpopular themes into the discussions, such as taxes:

> What do we gain by doing something without content? What do we gain with going through this process without debate and ending up with nothing? Is this a simple exercise in rhetoric? No! . . . This is why I say that it is necessary for the news media to give opinions about what is happening—whether the assembly is good or bad, whether they debate the issues or not. Come on! You are authorized by me, since I am the head of this process and no one can stop you.

The woman reporter replied,

> It is not whether or not we are authorized; it is our problem within ourselves, understand? We must become accustomed to expressing not what we are authorized but rather what we authorize ourselves to. . . . We have been misled by the same persons who have directed the news and who have directed us for many years have created a pattern of behavior that we have not yet been able to break. . . . At times I believe that those who direct the news think that the people are in the '40s, the '50s, or the '60s. They don't realize that the people have achieved an eighth or ninth grade education and that the leadership of this country has taught them to think.

She went on to say that when several Cubans sought asylum in the Mexican embassy it was not reported on Cuban television or radio and thus people turned to Radio Martí and other Miami stations to find out what was happening. She asked Ross to tell the country's leaders that they needed equipment. When a co-worker went out to film a story on the street, not one of her three batteries was working. There were not enough microphones for recording, since they had been stolen because of lack of sufficient controls. They had almost run out of tape cassettes while recording the December 1993 session of the National Assembly.

Another woman complained that scarce medicine was being sold in dollars, and since she had broken with her relatives in Miami she had no access to dollars. Ross responded that he had heard this complaint in other workers' parliaments and he would see to it that medicines for Cubans were sold only for pesos.

A workers' parliament was held on February 24, 1994, at the Instituto de Medicina Tropical Pedro Kouri (Pedro Kouri Institute for Tropical Medicine—IPK), whose work earns hard currency for Cuba and has been given high priority. Ross again presided. The first person to speak said that products that the state was incapable of supplying to the people could be found for sale in enormous quantities on the black market. Soap, for example, cost 50 pesos on the street. More inspections and vigilance were needed. Stores were empty, and while he earned 200 pesos a month, shoes cost up to 1500 pesos on the street. "Do I have to steal them?" he asked, adding that goods were stolen from workplaces, for example blankets, gauze and medicine from the IPK. Ross responded that the problem was where and how to introduce the controls to stop stealing from workplaces, "including [controls] for the police—it would be necessary to police the police. . . . I agree with you that controls by the administration and by the workers' collectives are lacking in workplaces all over the country."

When another man said that those who work in *bodegas* were stealing food and selling it on the black market, Ross responded that this should be checked by the elected municipal delegates and the presidents of the people's councils, since they have the authority to adopt whatever measures they consider appropriate to protect the population and see to it that the laws were in force. "If they don't work, we're finished. And if they don't work, the citizens have the duty and obligation to change them."

A young woman stated that more controls were not enough. "The person who is supposed to stop the stealing of soap has no soap in his home. And the policeman who has to do the work of the police hasn't a decent roof on his house. . . . What we have to resolve is not the control but the shortages. . . . I can't be giving dose after dose of medicine to calm someone who is tense; I have to get to the cause of the stress. And we are in the same situation." While she was treated well at work, and given a good lunch, she said, when she returned home she had no eggs, no cooking oil, no soap to bathe or wash her clothes with. She admitted that she took pieces of cotton from work because it is impossible to buy sanitary napkins. Ross interrupted at this point, and she said, "Wait, let me finish." She continued that it is not so bad for those who received dollars from outside the country, but she has no access to dollars. For many years moral incentives have been used to urge people to work harder, but this was no longer enough. This IPK earned dollars, yet "I am not given even one dollar. . . . If I create a computer program and with this program a certain quantity of dollars enter the country, a small percentage should please go to the one who created it." She felt that with such incentives, projects that earned hard currency would flourish. More material incentives would also help increase food production, she said, going on to suggest reinstating the free farmers' markets which were briefly allowed in the early 1980s, but this time with high taxes to keep this sector of the population from getting too rich. "I live with many moral resources, with pride in working here, with the professional satisfaction of the achievements gained through research, with the great thing one has in doing research and advancing in education. . . . I believe that in this moment the workers of IPK are among the most privileged." Nevertheless, she felt that the workers there should be given a small part of the fruits of their labor. She stressed the disincentive of having workers in the same category earn the same salary even though some work more than others and concluded by citing the socialist maxim: "From each according to his ability, to each according to what he produces."

Another woman complained about the proposed income tax. "I never would accept another tax, because really my salary as a researcher is hardly enough to feed myself poorly." Ross admitted that most workers had been opposing income taxes. She argued that taxes should be placed on "the self-employed workers who earn 100 pesos in five minutes. I have seen it myself." She also proposed taxing the profits on private farm cooperatives that had obtained their land from the state and private sale.

Another complained that more vigilance was needed over private vendors of vegetables in the street, who sold at exorbitant prices and did not pay taxes. "Not even capitalism, where everyone sells what he has however he wants to, has the disorganization that is going on today." No one was doing anything about the thieves who stole from the people and then sold the stolen goods. She had reported these thieves to the local government, but nothing had been done.

A woman added that the population is not given adequate information and explanations regarding the food supply. When she said that people call agricultural products "the artists" because they are only seen on television, everyone, including Ross, burst into sustained laughter. She said that the reason people did business with the self-employed was that if you needed a replacement piece for your television set your best chance was with them rather than in the state shop. She went on to demand that the state find out where the private vendors got the severely rationed milk to make the butter and yogurt they sold.

A man stated that Cubans were losing their dignity, that the poor under capitalism were taught to be honest and now everybody in Cuba had to steal. His salary was practically worthless, while a private street vendor earned in an hour what he earned in a month. He spoke of the need to control those in high positions with access to goods. Another woman claimed that while she resented that those engaged in illicit activities had access to scarce goods, she "wouldn't stop being a revolutionary, not for 20 television sets." The people applauded.

Another workers' parliament I attended held on February 26, 1994, involved the eighth brigade of the Unión Nacional de Empresas Constructores del Caribe (National Union of Construction Enterprises of the Caribbean—UNECA), who build tourist hotels in Havana. Alarcón attended, and the meeting was covered by *Trabajadores*. Workers complained of deficiencies in the attention given to their needs which affected worker efficiency.[20] One worker complained, "We are not animals but human beings." Another said that while the workers arrive at 7 A.M. there were usually no materials at the work site until 10 A.M., which meant they were getting paid for three hours of doing nothing. Often the same job was done two or three times. Quality suffered when workers had to improvise. Cement was often wasted. Participants reported the lack of tools, and a debate ensued as to whether having the workers buy their own tools would lead to their taking better care of them. It was recognized that more vigilance on the part of the construction chiefs was needed, but the workers agreed that those who broke or lost their tools or did shoddy work should have 20 percent deducted from their salaries. (This was also to apply to those in charge, including government ministers. Five chiefs and technicians forfeited the 20 percent in February.[21]) Workers declared that those who made money by illicit means are counterrevolutionaries and said the state should get rid of these parasites. It was mainly corrupt inspectors and police who allowed these activities to flourish. Taxes should be levied not on salaries but on savings and on cigarettes and rum, and the state should charge for potable water.

In a closing speech, Alarcón pointed out that 60 percent of the state enterprises were unprofitable. Economic problems had to be resolved by increasing efficiency in each workplace using socialist methods, without lowering salaries or shutting down factories. The excessive amount of money circulating was a disincentive to work. Whereas in other countries economic measures were announced in the middle of the night, without worker involvement or input, this could not be done under socialism. Workers could help solve the deficit problem by finding ways to make factories profitable. Those present should remember that workers in capitalist countries, especially the poorer countries, "live in a permanent special period."

The National Assembly met in special session on May 1 and 2 to formulate economic measures in consideration of the suggestions made in the workers' parliaments. Constant references were made to the workers' parliaments in the debate. Ross's speech summarized their results, citing the calls for more efficiency and better use of resources through increased worker involvement in decision making, more attention to the welfare of the workers, and an end to the theft of state resources that fueled the black market. It also noted workers' reports of unnecessary paternalism, insufficient demands made by administrators, and the misuse of medical leaves and their belief that any solution to the problem of overinflated payrolls should provide economically justifiable employment for those displaced from their jobs. Ross reported fundamental agreement on retaining free education and medical care except for elective surgery and dentistry and on requiring those responsible for accidents and assaults to pay the victims' medical costs. Workers suggested that people should pay for previously free peripheral items such as school meals for boarding students, school uniforms, some aspects of higher education, and sports and cultural events; that bus fares should not be raised, but cigarettes and rum should be removed from the ration book and sold at higher prices; that bank interest should be increased to stimulate savings; that prices in the workers' cafeterias should more closely reflect costs but the quality should be improved; that a charge be imposed for municipal water service and the rates for electricity and telephones should be raised providing that the service improves, but that that lower-income families should be protected from the effects of higher prices. The great majority of workers opposed an income tax but favored a tax on self-employed workers and private farmers. There was almost total agreement on confiscating illegally obtained goods and money and more severely sanctioning those who committed economic crimes. Ross concluded by declaring that the workers' parliaments had taught the CTC the need to be more communicative with the workers in resolving economic problems.[22]

One deputy noted, "For the first time we must face, as a Parliament, a collection of actions and measures that have a certain degree of unpopularity but which are necessary and vital for our process."[23] A reporter for *Trabajadores* criticized the debate: "It served to emphasize principles, clarify concepts and tackle some particular situations, but was unable to go beyond the road previously traveled over. . . . Some of the statements make one think that the revolutionary purity and passion still needs to be reinforced with greater concrete knowledge."[24]

As is usual in the National Assembly, the ensuing resolution passed unanimously. It pointed to the areas where action was needed and directed other bodies to take action. It began by acknowledging the process of consultation in the workers' parliaments. It calls on (1) municipal and provincial assemblies to monitor strictly the budget process and exact savings where possible; (2) National Assembly deputies, municipal and provincial assembly delegates, and people's councils to help the workers comply with proposals made in the workers' parliaments regarding rationalization of the workplace; and (3) the Council of State and government to adopt all necessary measures to halt illegal economic activities. It mandated the government to reduce subsidies in order to halt the fiscal deficit; increase bank savings; control the circulation of hard currency; increase production for internal consumption; increase prices for items not considered basic necessities; gradually introduce a system of taxation; examine the possibility of introducing new currency; and take other measures considered necessary for improving the economy.[25]

On May 4, 1994, the Council of State passed Decree 149, "regarding confiscation of goods and earnings obtained by unjustified enrichment," including theft, speculation, diversion of state resources, and black market activities.[26] Lee compared the support in Cuba for this decree with the condemnations in the international press:

> As was to be expected—due to the broad consensus that this demand had in the parliaments in the work centers and in the deliberations of the deputies—the new legislation can count on majority popular support. . . . As was to be expected, the international repercussion to this initial measure after the parliamentary session has provoked a variety of interpretations from [foreign] "observers" who have come to talk even of "witch hunts," and confronted with these cabled dispatches, one asks oneself, what do they want? First they write that there is robbery, black market, new millionaires and that the population is dissatisfied, protests, etc., and now, when the State announces that it will act energetically against these manifestations they indicate certain alarm in their appraisals. You can't win.[27]

On May 20, 1994, the Executive Committee of the Council of Ministers passed a resolution which raised prices of cigarettes and cigars, beer, rum, brandy, gasoline, electricity, inter-city public transportation, water and sewage services, postage and telegrams, and lunch in workers' cafeterias.[28] In July Decree 150 of the Council of State increased penalties for crimes related to the national economy, and empowered the state to seize goods stolen from the state.[29]

On July 7, 1994, the Executive Committee of the Council of Ministers issued a resolution eliminating many of the items which had been free, including lunch for boarding students, language school, vitamins, sports and cultural events, and higher education. The resolution provided for assistance for low income families. Lee then compared Cuba to other Third World countries:

> But even today, in the depths of the crisis of the special period, when in the Third World budgets destined for basic social areas are cut and cut, when we face so many material fluctuations, the Cuban state preserves, without modification, its social policy, maintaining unaltered the principles of universality and without charge of the basic services such as education and health, as was the overwhelming view of the workers' parliaments and the consensus of the National Assembly. . . . Moreover, these measures are less harsh than might have been expected if one takes into account what was suggested in this very broad popular consultation regarding measures for the stabilization of our internal finances.[30]

The Secretariat of the CTC reported at the end of July 1994, that hard currency certificates had been introduced for workers in sectors that earned hard currency and had strategic economic importance.[31]

The workers had rejected an income tax for themselves while favoring taxes on salaries of self-employed workers and private farmers and on farm cooperatives. Yet clearly Cuban economists saw the need for income taxes to help reduce the excess of pesos in circulation.[32] The issue was brought to a head in the August, 1994, session of the National Assembly with the debate and passage of the new tax law. The bill allowed taxes on personal income other than salaries, but included self-employed workers and those with hard currency incomes, on farm cooperatives, homes, surface transport and idle land, and reinstatement of the contributions of workers towards their social security that had been eliminated in 1967. The law was modified during the session on August 4 to allow for the possibility of an income tax on workers' salaries. During the debate, "various deputies, mainly union leaders, put forward arguments related to why such an element should not appear in the law."[33] Castro said, "Notwithstanding the will to follow the spirit of the discussions, as can be noted in many of the measures adopted prior to this session of this parliament, it would not be possible to abide by all the desires and concerns expressed by the workers in these meetings in their workplaces." He stressed the need to create a consciousness among the population of the need for such taxes.[34] He argued that as a principle it should not be excluded from the new legislation, even though the hope was never to have to resort to it, and proposed the following amendment, which was accepted: "All income, including salary, in proportions according to the amounts, are susceptible to taxation."[35] Ross proposed a new round of workers' assemblies to explain the possible implementation of an income tax.[36]

Castro also identified the need to distinguish between an income tax and workers' contributions to social security. He stated that for each 3 pesos 17 centavos paid out, the social security fund received 1 peso, and there is no other source available. The options were either workers' contributions on a progressive scale or a reduction of social security payments, and the law was amended to included the former and passed unanimously.[37]

In mid-September 1994 the Council of State issued a decree reinstating the free farmers markets, which had been closed in the mid–1980s, a demand emanating from the workers' parliaments. All surplus farm products, including those from cooperatives and small vegetable plots could now be sold, subject to license requirement and taxation of profits.[38]

Conclusion

It seems obvious that if Cuba were really a totalitarian state in which everyone was afraid to criticize the leaders and their policies, the kind of meetings I witnessed would not have occurred. What was said accentuates the existence and awareness of deep problems beyond the economic crisis, including censorship, moral decay, and lack of local decision-making power. It is undeniable that workers were consulted, and it is notable that this consultation occurred in the depths of Cuba's severe economic crisis. Much of what workers requested and suggested was later adopted. Furthermore, it is certain that in most so-called democratic countries, economic measures are announced by the government rather than being subject to a structured national consultation. Castro made reference to this in his explanation that under

Cuba's concept of democracy, "We take months—it doesn't matter that months go by—in assemblies of one type or another, gathering the opinions of the workers, explaining, explaining again, persuading, illustrating things that are not well understood, in order to achieve a consensus on what we must do, and in this way we continue to succeed."[39] While consultations with workers regarding problems had long been a regular part of union activity in the workplace, the suggestions made in the workers' parliaments were given much more importance and publicity, and national policy issues were included, with follow-up in the National Assembly.

Constant reference was made to the workers' parliaments during the National Assembly debates, as well as in the resolutions and legislation passed by the National Assembly and the decrees passed by the Council of State. The most frequent demands made by the workers were met; one exception was that there be no income tax on workers' salaries. During the National Assembly debate in August, 1994, some deputies from the CTC opposed the income tax.

Also noteworthy is the realization by many workers that some of the accepted norms of the Cuban Revolution, such as *igualitarismo*, paternalism, and a plethora of free goods and services from the state, are no longer possible or desirable. At the same time, there was a strong sense of the need to maintain the basic gains of the revolution, such as free education and health care, and special attention for the poorest segments of the population. Finally noteworthy was the despair that I heard in terms of morale and morality—people do not like to accept stealing as normal or the black market as necessary, and they do not understand why those who steal from the government get rich while workers' salaries lose value.

Notes

1. Susana Lee, "El parlamento en los centros laborales," *Granma*, February 22, 1994, p. 3 (my translation).

2. "Lo político, la situación económica y las finanzas," *Trabajadores*, January 17, 1994, p. 2 (my translation).

3. Lee, "El parlamento," p. 3 (my translation).

4. Gail Lindenberg, "The Labor Union in the Cuban Workplace," *Latin American Perspectives*, No. 20 (Winter 1993), p. 34.

5. Peter Roman, "Representative Government in Socialist Cuba," *Latin American Perspectives*, No. 20 (Winter 1993), pp. 10–11; Peter Roman, "The Cuban Municipal Assembly: Local Representative Government Under Socialism," Ph.D. dissertation, Princeton University, 1994, pp. 276–368.

6. Susana Lee, "Parlamento en los centros laborales: no quede sólo en la reflexión colectiva," *Granma*, February 26, 1994, p. 3; "Encuesta de opinión: sí o no a los parlamentos," *Trabajadores*, March 14, 1994, p. 7.

7. "Encuesta de opinión," p. 7 (my translation).

8. "Quienes son los políticos de nuestra política," *Trabajadores*, January 10, 1994, p. 2 (my translation).

9. Quoted in Mary Murray and Marc Frank, "The Cuban Letter," *Cuban Action*, No. 7 (Spring 1994), p. 7.

10. Ibid.

11. Silvia Martínez, "A debate el palpitar de la sociedad," *Granma*, March 12, 1994, p. 3.

12. Isabel Morales and Silvia Martínez, "Parlamento obrero: un desafío a enfrentar con trabajo," *Granma*, January 22, 1994, p. 3.

13. "Miremos primero hacía dentro," *Trabajadores*, March 14, 1994, p. 2.

14. Julio García Luis, "¿Saldremos? La respuesta la tiene 'Holguín,'" *Trabajadores*, March 7, 1994, p. 6 (my translation).

15. Rebeca Antúñez, "¿Una reunión más?" *Trabajadores,* February 21, 1994, p. 6 (my translation).

16. "Ausentismo: reto a la vergüenza colectiva," *Trabajadores*, February 28, 1994, p. 2.

17. "Medidas de precios, ingresos reales y estimulación," *Trabajadores*, June 13, 1994

18. "Firmeza de pricipios y cambio de mentalidad," *Granma*, March 19, 1994, p. 3 (my translation).

19. Julio García Luís, "No es captar la 'onda,' sino pensar hondo," *Trabajadores*, February 21, 1994, p. 7.

20. Iliana Hautrive, "Discutir abiertament entre todos," *Trabajadores*, February 28, 1998, p. 6.

21. Ibid.

22. Pedro Ross, speech on May 1, 1994, *Trabajadores*, May 2, 1994, pp. 8–9.

23. "Reseña de los debates de la última jornada," *Granma*, May 3, 1994, p. 4 (my translation).

24. García Luís, "¿Saldremos?" p. 6 (my translation).

25. Asamblea Nacional del Poder Popular, "Acuerdo," *Granma*, May 3, 1994, p. 5.

26. "Decreto-Ley No. 149," *Granma*, May 5, 1994, p. 2 (my translation).

27. Susana Lee, "Ya se está actuando," *Granma*, May 12, 1994, p. 3 (my translation).

28. "Sobre precios y tarifas," *Trabajadores*, May 23, 1994, p. 2.

29. "Decreto-Ley 150 de 1994," *Granma*, July 5, 1994, p. 1.

30. Susana Lee, "Acerca de la eliminación de gratuidades," *Granma*, July 9, 1994, p. 3 (my translation).

31. Iliana Hautrive and Julio García Luís, "Discutir abiertamente entre todos," *Trabajadores*, July 25, 1994, p. 3.

32. Roberto Alvarez Quiñones, "Impuestos," *Granma*, March 5, 1994, p. 3.

33. Caridad Lafita Navarro, "Salvar la seguridad social," *Trabajadores*, August 8, 1994, p. 3 (my translation).

34. "Debate sobre el Proyecto de Ley del Sistema Tributario," *Granma*, August 5, 1994, p. 3 (my translation).

35. "Intervención de Fidel en el debate sobre Proyecto de Ley Tributaria," *Granma*, August 6, 1994, p. 3 (my translation).

36. "Debates de la última jornada," *Granma*, August 6, 1994, p. 2.

37. "Intervención de Fidel," p. 2.

38. Tim Golden, "Cubans Get a Taste of Capitalism," *New York Times*, September 25, 1994, p. A–8.

39. Fidel Castro, speech on December 5, 1994, *Granma*, December 7, 1994, p. 3 (my translation).

Bibliography

Acosta, Dalia, "Cuba: Alta participación electoral, otra victoria de Fidel Castro," *InterPress Service*, January 16, 1998.

———, "Cuba: Nuevo parlamento revelara el rumbo de Fidel Castro," *InterPress Service*, February 23, 1998.

———, "Rights—Cuba: Opponents Complete Year in Prison Without Charges," *InterPress Service*, July 19, 1998.

Acta: Asamblea Municipal Poder Popular Playa: Tercera Sesión Ordinaria Quinto Período de Mandato, efectuada el de 11 Junio de 198.

Acta: Asamblea Municipal del Poder Popular Palmira: II Sesión Ordinaria del V Mandato, efectuada el 7 de Noviembre de 1987.

Acta correspondiente a la Primera Sesión Extraordinaria de la Asamblea Municipal Playa en su Quinto Período de Mandato, efectuada el 27 de Noviembre de 1986.

Acta #20, Comité Ejecutivo Playa, "Chequeo de acuerdos, Acuerdo #483," August 27, 1987.

"After Fidel Castro," *New York Times*, February 4, 1998, p. A–22.

Agero Gómez, Frank, and Julio Gracía Luis, "Tenemos que demostrar que aquí el destino nuestro lo decidimos nosotros," *Trabajadores*, April 10, 1995, p. 3.

"Al 4 Congreso del Partido!" *Granma Resumen Semanal*, March 25, 1990, p. 3.

Alarcón, Ricardo, speech given on December 26, 1997, *Trabajadores*, December 29, 1997, pp. 7–8.

Alfonso, Carmen R., "Puede haber un planteamiento sin respuesta? Entrevista a la diputada Elia García Patiño," *La Nación Cubana*, No. 3 (1985), pp. 42–45.

Alfonso, Marcos, "Plebiscito por la Patria," *Granma*, January 10, 1998, p. 5.

———, "La penúltima diatriba," *Granma*, January 15, 1998, p. 3.

Alonso, Maria, "Who Are the Candidates?," *Granma Internacional*, December 19, 1997, URL: http://www.granma.cu/.

Alvarez Quiñones, Roberto, "Impuestos," *Granma*, March 5, 1994, p. 3.

Alvarez Tabio, Fernando, *Comentarios a la Constitución Socialista*, Havana: Ciencias Sociales, 1985.

"Analizan funcionamiento del médico y enfermera de la familia," *Granma*, November 6, 1993, p. 2.

Anderson, Perry, "Acerca de las relaciones entre el socialismo existente y socialismo posible," *Nueva Sociedad*, No. 56–57 (September-December 1981), pp. 185–191.

Antuñez, Rebeca, "¿Una reunión mas?" *Trabajadores*, February 21, 1994, p. 6.

Anweiler, Oskar, *The Soviets: The Russian Workers, Peasants, and Soldiers Councils, 1905–1921*, New York: Random House, 1974.

"Apuntes sobre el tercer proceso de rendición de cuenta," *Poder Popular*, Vol. 7, No. 7 (1988), p. 3.

Asamblea Nacional del Poder Popular, *Temas para Seminarios a diputados, delegados y cuadros del Poder Popular*, Matanzas: Girón, 1982.

_____, *Analisis Tercer Proceso de Rendición de Cuenta -V- Mandato*, June 1988.

_____, "Asamblea Nacional del Poder Popular: sobre el proceso de elaboración del proyecto de Ley Electoral," *Granma*, October 30, 1992, pp. 4–5.

_____, "Acuerdo," *Granma*, May 3, 1994, p. 5.

Ascuy, Hugo, "La reforma de la Constitución socialista de 1976," in Haroldo Dilla alfonso (ed.), *La democracia en Cuba y el diferendo con los Estados Unidos*, Havana: Centro de Estudios sobre América, 1995.

"Ausentismo: reto a la vergüenza colectiva," *Trabajadores*, February 28, 1994, p. 2.

Azicri, Max, "Twenty-six Years of Cuban Revolutionary Politics: An Appraisal," *Contemporary Marxism*, No. 14 (Fall 1986), pp. 65–96.

Bahro, Rudolf, *The Alternative in Eastern Europe*, London: Verso, 1981.

Bambirra, Vania, and Theotonio dos Santos, *La estrategia y la táctica socialista de Marx y Engels a Lenin*, Vol. 2, Mexico: Era, 1981.

Barredo Medina, Lázaro, "Autoridad mayor para los delegados al Poder Popular," *Trabajadores*, January 18, 1993, p. 2.

_____, "El consenso, asunto de seguridad nacional," *Trabajadores*, January 27, 1997, p. 4

Batista, Jorge Luis, "Encuentro de candidatos de Güisa con su pueblo," *Granma*, January 3, 1998, p. 8.

Batista Valdés, Pastor, "Ni mentiras, ni falsas promesas," *Granma*, September 25, 1996, p. 4.

Bellis, Paul, *Marxism and the USSR: The Theory of the Proletarian Dictatorship and the Marxist Analysis of Soviet Society*, Atlantic Highlands, N.J.: Humanities Press, 1979.

Bengelsdorf, Carollee, "Between Vision and Reality: Democracy in Socialist Theory and Practice: the Cuban Experience," Ph.D. dissertation, Massachusetts Institute of Technology, 1985.

_____, "The Matter of Democracy in Cuba: Snapshots of Three Moments," in Sandor Halebsky and John M. Kirk (eds.), *Transformation and Struggle: Cuba Faces the 1990s*, New York: Praeger, 1990.

Benjamin, Medea, "Soul Searching," *North American Congress on Latin America Report on the Americas*, Vol. 24, No. 2 (August 1990), p. 23–31.

Bezúglov, Anatoli, *El diputado sovietico: Estatuto jurídico*, Moscow: Editorial Progreso, 1976.

Bobbio, Noberto, *Which Socialism? Marxism, Socialism and Democracy* (Richard Bellamy, ed.). Worcester, England: Polity Press, 1987.

Borrego, Juan Antonio, "Conversación en Los Olivos," *Granma*, June 8, 1995, p. 2.

_____, "La unidad es garantía de la victoria, afirma el movimiento sindical," *Granma*, December 5, 1997.

Brown, Archie, "Political Power and the Soviet State: Western and Soviet Perspectives." in Neil Harding (ed.), *The State in Socialist Society*, Albany: State University of New York Press, 1984.

Brundenius, Claes, "Cuba: Redistribution and Growth with Equity," in Sandor Halebsky and John M. Kirk (eds.), *Cuba: Twenty-five Years of Revolution, 1959–1984*, New York: Praeger Publishers, 1985.

"Cambios organizativos en la planificación," *Trabajadores*, May, 26, 1988, p. 10.

Caputo, Philip, "The Wei That Wasn't," *New York Times Magazine*, June 21, 1998, pp. 26–31.

Carr, E. H., *The Bolshevik Revolution, 1917–1923*, Vol. 1, Baltimore: Penguin Books, 1966.

Carrobello, Caridad, Martha Campos, Pelayo Terry, and Ariel Terrero, "¿Qué piensa el pueblo de su poder?" *Bohemia*, July 6, 1990, pp. 4–9.

Carrobello, Caridad, Susana Tesoro, Martha Campos, Pelayo Terry, and Ariel Terrero, "Debate público: Los caminos del poder," *Bohemia*, July 13, 1990, pp. 4–7.

Casals, Rodolfo, "Cuba Ratifies Its Socialist Option," *Granma Internacional*, March 1, 1998, URL: http://www.granma.cu/.

Castellanos, Benigno Pablo, *Quejas contra burocratismo: problemas actuales del perfeccionamiento de la democracia socialista en Cuba*, Havana: Política, 1988.

Castro, Fidel, *History Will Absolve Me!* New York: Lyle Stuart, 1961.

_____, speech given on September 28, 1967, *Granma Weekly Review*, October 8, 1967, pp. 8–12.

_____, speech given on May 20, 1970, *Granma Weekly Review*, May 31, 1970, pp. 7–12.

_____, speech given on July 26, 1970, *Granma Weekly Review*, August 2, 1970, pp. 2–6.

_____, speech given on August 23, 1970, *Granma Weekly Review*, August 30, 1970, pp. 2–6.

_____, speech given on September 3, 1970, *Granma Weekly Review*, September 20, 1970, pp. 2–6.

_____, speech given on September 28, 1970, *Granma Weekly Review*, October 4, 1970, p. 2–4.

_____, speech given on December 7, 1970, *Granma Weekly Review*, December 20, 1970, pp. 2–6.

_____, speech given on May 1, 1971, *Granma Weekly Review*, May 16, 1971, pp. 2–8.

_____, speech given on November 18, 1971, *Granma Weekly Review*, November 28, 1971, pp. 12–14.

_____, speech given on November 29, 1971, *Granma Weekly Review*, December 12, 1971, pp. 12–13.

_____, speech given on September 28, 1972, *Granma Weekly Review*, October 8, 1972, pp. 2–4.

_____, speech given on July 26, 1974, *Granma Weekly Review*, August 4, 1974, pp. 2–6.

_____, Press conference on August 21, 1975, *Granma Weekly Review*, August 31, 1975, pp. 7–9.

_____, speech given on September 28, 1976, *Granma Weekly Review*, October 10, 1976, pp. 2–5.

_____, speech given on December 2, 1978, *Granma Weekly Review*, December 17, 1978, pp. 6–9.

———, "Main Report to the Second Congress," *Cuba Update,* Vol. 2, No. 1 (March 1981), pp. 1–45.

———, speech given on April 27, 1959, in *El pensamiento de Fidel Castro: Selección temática,* Vol. 1, No. 2, Havana: Editores Política, 1983.

———, "Thirty Years of the Cuban Revolution," speech given on January 4, 1989, in Fidel Castro, *In Defense of Socialism: Four Speeches on the 30th Anniversary of the Cuban Revolution,* New York: Pathfinder Press, 1989.

———, speech given on February 20, 1990, *Granma Resumen Semanal,* March 4, 1990, pp. 2–3.

———, speech given on September 28, 1990, *Granma Weekly Review,* October 10, 1990.

———, *Granma International,* January 12, 1992, p. 2.

———, speech given on February 6, 1993, *Granma,* February 10, 1993, pp. 5–8.

———, television interview March 1, 1993, *Granma,* March 3, 1993, p. 3.

———, speech given on December 5, 1994, *Granma,* December 7, 1994, p. 3.

———, speech given on April 4, 1997, *Granma,* April 8, 1997.

———, speech given on December 13, 1997, *Granma,* December 18, 1997, pp. 5–12.

———, intervention in the National Assembly debate December 13, 1997, *Granma,* December 19, 1997, pp. 3–6.

———, speech given December 29, 1997, *Granma,* January 2, 1998, pp. 2–7.

———, interview on January 16, 1998, *Trabajadores* (Supplement), January 19, 1998, pp. 1–12.

Castro, Raúl, speech given on August 22, 1974, *Granma Weekly Review,* September 8, 1974, pp. 2–5.

Centeno, Miguel Angel, "Cuba's Search for Alternatives," in Miguel Angel Centeno and Mauricio Font (eds.), *Towards a New Cuba? Legacies of a Revolution,* Boulder: Lynne Rienner, 1997.

Centeno, Miguel Angel, and Mauricio Font (eds.), *Towards a New Cuba? Legacies of a Revolution,* Boulder: Lynne Rienner, 1997.

Centro de Estudios Sobre América, *Informe sobre el taller: los consejos populares la gestión del desarrollo y la participación popular en Cuba,* Havana: Centro de Estudios sobre América, 1995.

———, *Relatoria del taller: municipios, economía local y economía popular,* Havana: Centro de Estudios sobre América, 1996.

Cerroni, Umberto, *Teoría Poltica y Socialismo,* Mexico: Ediciones Era, 1976.

Chernov, B., "Organos locales de poder y administración del estado en la URSS," in M. Shafir et al. , *Los Soviets, organos del poder popular,* Moscow: Progreso, 1979.

Chitarin, Attilio, "Problemas de la transición del capitalismo al socialismo en la URSS," in Paul Sweezy et al. , *Teoría del proceso de transición,* Buenos Aires: Siglo XXI, 1973.

Churchward, L. G., "Public Participation in the USSR," in Everett M. Jacobs (ed.), *Soviet Local Politics and Government,* London: George Allen and Unwin, 1983.

Cole, G. D. H., *A History of Socialism,* Vol. 2, *Socialist Thought, Marxism and Anarchism, 1850–1890,* London: Macmillan, 1954.

Colletti, Lucio, *From Rousseau to Lenin: Studies in Ideology and Society,* London: New Left Books, 1972.

_____, "Introduction," in Karl Marx, *Early Writings*, New York: Vintage Books, 1975.

Concepción, Eloy, "Crear conciencia de rechazo a las ilegalidades, las indiciplinas sociales y el delito: Entrevista con Juan Contino, Coordinador Nacional de los CDR," *Trabajadores*, May 19, 1997.

_____, "Para aprobar una ley se necesita . . ." *Trabajadores*, July 20, 1998, p. 16.

"Constitución de la República de Cuba," *Granma Weekly Review*, September 22, 1992, pp. 3–10.

"Constitution of the Organs of People's Power," *Center for Cuban Studies Newsletter*, Vol. 2, No. 5–6 (October-December 1975), pp. 5–13.

"Constitution of the Republic of Cuba," *Granma Weekly Review*, March 7, 1976, pp. 1–12.

"Continuación del debate sobre formación y presentación de candidaturas," *Granma*, October 31, 1992, p. 3.

Cooney, John E., "'Popular Power': Cuban Province Takes Initial Steps in Test of Democratic Rule," *Wall Street Journal*, December 4, 1974, pp. 1, 39.

Coordinación Nacional de los CDR, "LLamamiento a todos los cederistas," *Granma*, May 13, 1995, p. 8.

"Cuban Parliament President Ricardo Alarcón Calls on Deputies and Delegates to Expand Their Work," *Radio Havana Cuba,* April 14, 1998, URL: http://www.radiohc.org.

"Cuba Weighs Castro Plan to Decentralize Power," *New York Times*, April 30, 1975, p. 3.

"Debate sobre el Proyecto de Ley del Sistema Tributario," *Granma*, August 5, 1994, p. 3.

"Debate sobre Proyecto de Ley para la Inversión Extranjera," *Granma*, September 5, 1995, p. 3

"Debates de la última jornada," *Granma*, August 6, 1994, p. 2.

"Declaraciones y aclaraciones," *Trabajadores*, June 29, 1998, p. 2.

"Decreto-Ley No. 149," *Granma*, May 5, 1994, p. 2.

"Decreto-Ley 150 de 1994," *Granma*, July 5, 1994, p. 1.

de Jesús, Ventura, "La propuesta de Rosa," *Granma*, September 10, 1997, p. 3.

de la Osa, José A., "Analizan presidentes de los Consejos Populares apoyo al programa de medicamentos," *Granma*, May 17, 1994, p. 1.

della Volpe, Galvano, *Rousseau and Marx and Other Writings*, London: Lawrence and Wishart, 1976.

"Demostración fehaciente de la confianza del pueblo en la Revolución y en sus instituciones," *Granma*, June 24, 1995, p. 8.

DePalma, Anthony, "It's Everything Castro Promised, on Lake Ontario," *New York Times*, June 11, 1998, p. A–4.

Dilla Alfonso, Haroldo, "Democracia y poder revolucionario en Cuba," *Cuadernos de Nuestra America*, Vol. 4, No. 7 (January-June 1987), pp. 55–75.

_____, "Participación popular y gobiernos locales en Cuba," paper presented at the Second Workshop of the Organizations of Community Power and Grassroots Democracy in Central America and the Caribbean, Havana, Cuba, November 28-December 2, 1988.

_____, "Notas sobre la relación centralización-decentralización en la transición socialista cubana," unpublished manuscript, 1989.

_____, "Cuba: ¿Cuál es la democracia deseable?" in Haroldo Dilla Alfonso (ed.), *La democracia en Cuba y el diferendo con los Estados Unidos*, Havana: Centro de Estudios sobre América, 1995.

_____, "Comunidad, participación y socialism: reinterpretando el dilema cubano," in Haroldo Dilla Alfonso (ed.), *La participación en Cuba y los retos del futuro*, Havana: Centro de Estudios sobre América, 1996.

_____, "Los municipios cubanos y los retos del futuro," in Haroldo Dilla Alfonso (ed.), *La participación en Cuba y los retos del futuro*, Havana: Centro de Estudios sobre América, 1996.

Dilla Alfonso, Haroldo, and Armando Fernández Soriano, "Las elecciones municipales en Cuba: un estudio de caso," *El Caribe Contemporaneo*, No. 23 (Julio-Diciembre 1991), pp. 75–90.

Dilla Alfonso, Haroldo, and Gerardo González Núñez, "Participación y desarrollo en los municipios cubanos," unpublished manuscript prepared for the Organizations of Community Power and Grassroots Democracy in Central America and the Caribbean, with assistance by the Centro Internacional de Investigaciones para el Desarrollo, Ottawa, Canada, 1991.

Dilla Alfonso, Haroldo, Gerardo González, and Ana T. Vincentelli, *Participación popular y desarrollo en los municipios cubanos*, Havana: Centro de Estudios sobre América, 1993.

_____, "Los Municipios en Cuba: una experiencia más allá de los paradigmas," paper presented at the annual meeting of the Latin American Studies Association, Washington, D.C., 1991.

Domínguez, Jorge I., *Cuba: Order and Revolution*, Cambridge: Harvard University Press, 1978.

_____, "Derechos políticos y el sistema político Cubano," *Revista Occidental*, No. 2 (January-April 1984), pp. 249–281.

dos Santos, Theotonio, "Socialism: Ideal and Historical Practice," in Milos Nicolic (ed.), *Socialism on the Threshold of the 21st Century*, London: Verson, 1985.

Draper, Hal, "The Death of the State in Marx and Engels," in Ralph Miliband and John Saville (eds.), *The Socialist Register 1970*, London: Merlin Press, 1970.

Hal Draper (ed.), *Karl Marx and Friedreich Engels: Writings on the Paris Commune*, New York: Monthly Review Press, 1971.

_____, *Karl Marx's Theory of Revolution*, Vol. 1, *State and Bureaucracy*, New York: Monthly Review Press, 1977.

_____, *Karl Marx's Theory of Revolution*, Vol. 3, *The "Dictatorship of the Proletariat"*, New York: Monthly Review Press, 1986.

"Encuesta de opinión: sí o no a los parlamentos," *Trabajadores*, March 14, 1994, p. 7.

Engels, Frederick, "Letter to Van Patten," in *Karl Marx and Frederick Engels, Selected Works*, New York: International Publishers, 1968.

_____, "Letter to A. Bebel, March 18–28, 1875," in Hal Draper, ed., *Karl Marx and Friedreich Engels: Writings on the Paris Commune*, New York: Monthly Review Press, 1971.

Evans, Michael, "Karl Marx and the Concept of Political Participation," in Geraint Parry (ed.), *Participation in Politics*, Totowa, N.J.: Rowman and Littlefield, 1972.

"La experiencia del arquitecto de la comunidad," *Granma*, October 22, 1994, p. 2.

Fagen, Richard, *The Transformation of Political Culture in Cuba*, Stanford: Stanford University Press, 1969.

Fernández Soriano, Armando, and Rubén Otazo Conde, "Comunidad, autogestión, participación y medio ambiente," in Haroldo Dilla Alfonso (ed.), *La participación en Cuba y los retos del futuro*, Havana: Centro de Estudios sobre América, 1996.

"Fidel con los estudiantes de 12 y Malecón," *Granma*, February 14, 1993, p. 3.

"Fidel sugiere que podría dejar el poder," *El Diario/La Prensa*, February 26, 1993, p. 11.

"Firmeza de pricipios y cambio de mentalidad," *Granma*, March 19, 1994, p. 3.

Fitzgerald, Frank T., "A Critique of the 'Sovietization of Cuba' Thesis," *Science and Society*, Vol. 92, No. 1 (Spring 1978), pp. 1–32.

Fralin, Richard, *Rousseau and Representation: A Study of the Development of His Concept of Political Institutions*, New York: Columbia University Press, 1978.

French, Howard W., "43,412 Stricken Cubans, and Not a Single Answer," *New York Times*, June 15, 1993, p. A–4.

Friedgut, Theodore H., *Political Participation in the USSR*, Princeton: Princeton University Press, 1979.

_____, "The Soviet Citizen's Perception of Local Government," in Everett M. Jacobs (ed.), *Soviet Local Politics and Government*, London: George Allen and Unwin, 1983.

Friedman, Thomas L., "Here Comes the Sun," *New York Times*, March 14, 1998, p. A–17.

Fuller, Linda, "The Politics of Workers' Control in Cuba, 1959–1983: The Work Center and the National Arena," Ph.D. dissertation, University of California, Berkeley, 1985.

Fundamental Law of Cuba 1959, Washington, D.C.: Pan American Union, 1959.

García Blanco, Reinaldo, "Queremos tanto a Guillermo!" *Pueblo*, Vol. 1, No. 4 (October 1987), pp. 14–16.

García Brigos, Jesús P., "Cinco tesis sobre los Consejos Populares," *Revista Cubana de Ciencias Sociales*, No. 31 (1966).

Garcia Cárdenas, Domingo, *State Organization in Cuba*, Havana: José Martí Publishing House, 1986.

Garcia Luis, Julio, "No es captar la 'onda,' sino pensar hondo," *Trabajadores*, February 21, 1994, p. 7.

_____, "¿Saldremos? La respuesta la tiene 'Holguín,'" *Trabajadores*, March 7, 1994, p. 6.

_____, "Tener mejores elecciones que nunca," *Trabajadores*, May 15, 1995, p 16.

_____, "Yo Participo: El pueblo dirá lo final de este proceso," *Trabajadores*, June 19, 1995, p. 16

_____, "Coordinación, comprensión y unidad como nunca antes," *Trabajadores*, September 16, 1996, p. 16.

_____, "Se trabaja con mucha seriedad para las elecciones," *Trabajadores*, August 18, 1997, p. 3.

_____, "La Lisa: una entre 169," *Trabajadores*, November 3, 1997, p. 16.

García Peyán, Carols, "Participación y decentralización en el planeamiento territorial," in Haroldo Dilla Alfonso (ed.), *La participación en Cuba y los retos del futuro*, Havana: Centro de Estudios sobre América, 1996.

Golden, Tim, "Cubans Get a Taste of Capitalism," *New York Times*, September 25, 1994, p. A–8.

_____, "A Year After Boat Exodus, Threat to Castro Dissipates," *New York Times*, August 15, 1995, pp. A–1, A–6.

Grogg, Patricia, "Rights-Cuba: Group accused of Sedition awaiting Verdict," *Inter-Press Service*, March 5, 1999.

Guevara, Ernesto "Che," "Notes on Man and Socialism in Cuba," in Ernesto "Che" Guevara, *Che Guevara Speaks*, New York: Merit, 1967.

Gumá, José Gabriel, "Desde el lunes rendición de cuenta," *Granma*, September 28, 1990, p. 1.

_____, "El Consejo Popular comenzará a actuar de inmediato y a adoptar las medidas oportunas," *Granma*, October 12, 1990, p. 3.

_____, "Rendición de cuenta: un verdadero intercambio de opiniones con la población," *Granma*, February 26, 1992, p. 1.

Gumá, José Gabriel, and Alberto Nuñez, "Consejos Populares en la capital: una bienvenida optimista," *Granma*, October 6, 1990, p. 3.

Hahn, Jeffrey W., *Soviet Grassroots: Citizen Participation in Local Soviet Government*, Princeton: Princeton University Press, 1988.

Hamberg, Jill, "The Dynamics of Cuban Housing Policy," in Rachel Bratt, Chester Hartman, and Ann Meyerson (eds.), *Critical Perspectives on Housing*, Philadelphia: Temple University Press, 1986.

Harding, Neil, *Lenin's Political Thought*, Vol. 2, *Theory and Practice in the Socialist Revolution*, London: Macmillan, 1981.

_____, "Socialism, Society, and the Organic Labour State," in Neil Harding (ed.), *The State in Socialist Society*, Albany: State University of New York Press, 1984.

Harnecker, Marta, *Cuba: Dictatorship or Democracy?* Westport, Conn.: Lawrence Hill, 1980.

Hart, Armando, speech on September 24, 1969, *Granma Weekly Review*, October 5, 1969, p. 4.

Hautrive, Iliana, "Discutir abiertament entre todos," *Trabajadores*, February 28, 1998, p. 6.

_____, "Modelo de resumen," *Trabajadores*, June 1, 1998, p. 2.

Hautrive, Iliana, and Julio García Luís, "Discutir abiertamente entre todos," *Trabajadores*, July 25, 1994, p. 3.

Hernández, Rafael, and Haroldo Dilla, "Political Culture and Popular Participation in Cuba," *Latin American Perspectives*, Issue 69, Vol. 18, No. 2 (Spring 1991), pp. 38–54.

Hernández Martinez, Lorenzo, "La rendición de cuenta: expresión práctica de la democrácia socialista," *El Militante Comunista* (April 1984), pp. 46–51.

Hill, Christopher, *Lenin and the Russian Revolution*, Harmondsworth, England: Penguin Books, 1971.

Hill, Ronald J., "Recent Developments in Soviet Local Government," *Community Development Journal*, Vol. 7 (1972), pp. 169–175.

_____, *Soviet Politics, Political Science and Reform*, New York: M. E. Sharpe, 1980.

_____, "The Development of Soviet Local Government Since Stalin's Death," in Everett M. Jacobs (ed.), *Soviet Local Politics and Government*, London: George Allen and Unwin, 1983.

_____, "The 'All-People's State' and 'Developed Socialism'," in Neil Harding (ed.), *The State in Socialist Society*, Albany: State University of New York Press, 1984.

Hobsbawm, Eric J., "Marx, Engels and Politics," in Eric J. Hobsbawm (ed.), *The History of Marxism*, Vol. 1, *Marxism in Marx's Day*, Bloomington: Indiana University Press, 1982.

_____, "Marx, Engels and Pre-Marxian Socialism," in Eric J. Hobsbawm (ed.), *The History of Marxism*, Vol. 1, *Marxism in Marx's Day*, Bloomington: Indiana University Press, 1982.

Hunt, Richard N., *The Political Ideas of Marx and Engels: Marxism and Totalitarian Democracy, 1850–1880*, Vol. 1, Pittsburgh: University of Pittsburgh Press, 1974.

"Información a la población," *Granma*, May 28, 1991, p. 2.

"Informe valorativo sobre el resultado del II Proceso asambleario de rendición de cuenta del delegado," Municipio de Cienfuegos, October 1987.

"Intervención de Fidel en el debate sobre Proyecto de Ley Tributaria," *Granma*, August 6, 1994, p. 3.

"Intervención de los delegados en la Asamblea Provincial," *Correo del Delegado*, No. 11 (January 1988), p. 3.

Johnstone, Monty, "The Paris Commune and Marx's Conception of the Dictatorship of the Proletariat," *Massachusetts Review*, Vol. 12, No. 3 (Summer 1971), pp. 447–462.

Jorgensen, Bard, "The Interrelationship Between Base and Superstructure in Cuba," *Ibero-Americana: Nordic Journal of Latin American Studies*, Vol. 13, No. 1 (1983), pp. 27–42.

Kagarlitsky, Boris, *The Thinking Reed: Intellectuals and the Soviet State 1917 to the Present*, New York: Verso, 1988.

Kenworthy, Eldon, "Institutionalizing Community Politics in Cuba: Cultural Proclivities and Revolutionary Dilemmas," paper presented at the annual meeting of the Latin American Studies Association, 1982.

Koldáiev, V., "Creación y desarrollo de los soviets," in M. Shafir et al., *Los Soviets, Organos del Podes Popular*, Moscow: Progreso, 1979.

Koppel, Martin, "Cuban Vote Registers Support for Revolution," *Militant*, November 10, 1997, p. 1.

Lafita Navarro, Caridad, "Salvar la seguridad social," *Trabajadores*, August 8, 1994, p. 3.

Lazo, Esteban, "El voto por la dignidad, por la soberanía, por la independencia de la Patria," *Trabajadores*, July 3, 1995, p. 4.

Lee, Susana, "Asistió Fidel a la sesión final de la IV Reunión de Presidentes Municipales," *Granma*, June 13, 1988, p. 8.

_____, "Acercar trámites, simplificar gestiones=menos viajes," *Granma*, September 2, 1992, p. 3.

_____, "El parlamento en los centros laborales," *Granma*, February 22, 1994, p. 3.

_____, "Parlamento en los centros laborales: no quede sólo en la reflexión colectiva," *Granma*, February 26, 1994, p. 3.

_____, "Ya se está actuando," *Granma*, May 12, 1994, p. 3.

_____, "Encaminar este proceso en función de las medidas que hay que adoptar," *Granma*, May 19, 1994, p. 8.

_____, "Acerca de la eliminación de gratuidades," *Granma*, July 9, 1994, p. 3.

_____, "Analizar lo bueno y lo malo," *Granma*, May 18, 1995, p. 1.

_____, "A las próximas elecciones del 9 de junio," *Granma*, June 27, 1995, p. 1.

_____, "Pensando en mi candidato," *Granma*, July 4, 1995, p 3.

_____, "¿Quién es el mejor y el más capaz?" *Granma*, July 5, 1995, p. 3

_____, "Las sociedades de consumo no son la fórmula, ni la democracía capitalista; nosotros podemos adoptar en lo económico algunas medidas pero en lo demás no vamos a apartarnos de lo hecho," *Granma*, July 10, 1995, p. 4.

_____, "Excepciones que confirman la regla," *Granma*, August 3, 1995, p. 2.

_____, "Convocan proceso de rendición de cuenta del delegado," *Granma*, October 17, 1995, p 3.

_____, "Comenzó la rendición de cuenta del delegado a sus electores," *Granma*, November 2, 1995, p. 1.

_____, "Rendición de cuenta en Camaguey: Se hace diálogo al andar," *Granma*, December 15, 1995, p. 3.

_____, "Para que las reuniones sean un diálogo abierto," *Granma*, November 9, 1995, p. 3.

_____, "Algún día la historia tendrá que consignar que hemos resistido en parte importante gracias a los Consejos Populares," *Granma*, November 14, 1995, p. 3.

_____, "Fructúferas jornadas de información, orientación e intercambio," *Granma*, September 17, 1996, pp. 4–5.

_____, "La batalla contra las ilegalidades y las indiciplinas sociales no se ganará sin los CDR," *Granma*, April 25, 1997, p. 3.

_____, "Determinadas 14,533 circunscripciones electorales para los próximos comicios," *Granma*, July 8, 1997, p. 8.

_____, "Examinan presidentes municipales temas relacionados con la Salud y la Educación," *Granma*, June 12, 1998. p. 3.

Lefebvre, Henri, "The Commune and the Nature of Revolution," in Jeffry Kaplow (ed.), *Western Civilization: Mainstream Readings and Radical Critiques*, Vol. 2, *From the French Revolution to the Present*, New York: Alfred A. Knopf, 1973.

Lenin, V. I., "Can the Bolsheviks Retain State Power?" in V. I. Lenin, *Selected Works*, Vol. 2, New York: International Publishers, 1967.

_____, "Declaration of Rights of the Working and Exploited People," in V. I. Lenin, *Selected Works*, Vol. 2, New York: International Publishers, 1967.

_____, "Draft Decree on the Dissolution of the Constituent Assembly," in V. I. Lenin, *Selected Works*, Vol. 2, New York: International Publishers, 1967.

_____, "Eighth All-Russian Congress of Soviets," in V. I. Lenin, *Selected Works*, Vol. 3, New York: International Publishers, 1967.

_____, "How to Organize Competition," in V. I. Lenin, *Selected Works*, Vol. 2, New York: International Publishers, 1967.

_____, "The Immediate Tasks of the Soviet Government," in V. I. Lenin, *Selected Works*, Vol. 2, New York: International Publishers, 1967.

_____, "Letter to American Workers," in V. I. Lenin, *Selected Works*, Vol. 3, New York: International Publishers, 1967.

_____, "Letter to the Bolshevik Comrades Attending the Congress of Soviets of the Northern Region," in V. I. Lenin, *Selected Works*, Vol. 2, New York: International Publishers, 1967.

_____, "Political Report of the Central Committee, Seventh Congress of the R.C.P.(B.)," in V. I. Lenin, *Selected Works*, Vol. 2, New York: International Publishers, 1967.

_____, "Political Report, Eleventh Congress of the R.C.P.(B.)," in V. I. Lenin, *Selected Works*, Vol. 3, New York: International Publishers, 1967.

_____, "Report on the Work of the Council of People's Commissars, Eighth All Russia Congress of Soviets," in V. I. Lenin, *Selected Works*, Vol. 3, New York: International Publishers, 1967.

_____, "The Seventh (April) All-Russia Conference of the R.S.D.L.P. (B.)," in V. I. Lenin, *Selected Works*, Vol. 2, New York: International Publishers, 1967.

_____, "The State and Revolution," in V. I. Lenin, *Selected Works*, Vol. 2, New York: International Publishers, 1967.

_____, "Theses on the Constituent Assembly," in V. I. Lenin, *Selected Works*, Vol. 2, New York: International Publishers, 1967.

_____, "To the Citizens of Russia," in V. I. Lenin, *Selected Works*, Vol. 2, New York: International Publishers, 1967.

_____, "To the Population," in V. I. Lenin, *Selected Works*, Vol. 2, New York: International Publishers, 1967.

_____, "What Is to Be Done?" in V. I. Lenin, *Selected Works*, Vol. 1, New York: International Publishers, 1967.

LeoGrande, William M., "Modes of Political Participation in Revolutionary Cuba," paper presented at the annual meeting of the Northeastern Political Science Association, November 10–12, 1977.

_____, "Participation in Cuban Municipal Government: From Local Power to People's Power," in Donald E. Schulz, and Jan S. Adams (eds.), *Political Participation in Communist Countries*, New York: Pergamon Press, 1981.

_____, "The Communist Party of Cuba Since the First Congress," in Stephen White and Daniel Nelson (eds.), *Communist Politics: A Reader*, New York: New York University Press, 1986.

Levinson, Sandra, "Gallup Poll in Cuba," *Cuba Update*, Vol. 16, No. 1 (February 1995), pp. 9.

Lewis, Gordon, "The Paris Commune Then and Now," *Monthly Review*, Vol. 28, No. 6 (November 1968), pp. 84–93.

"Ley Electoral," *Gaceta Oficial de la República de Cuba*, No. 9 (November 2, 1992), pp. 51–65.

Ley Electoral-Poder Popular, Havana: Ciencias Sociales, 1984.

Liebman, Marcel, "Lenin in 1905," *Monthly Review*, Vol. 21, No. 11 (April 1970), pp. 57–75.

_____, *The Russian Revolution*, New York: Random House, 1970.

_____, *Leninism Under Lenin*, London: Jonathan Cape, 1975.

Lindenberg, Gail, "The Labor Union in the Cuban Workplace," *Latin American Perspectives*, Issue 76, Vol. 20, No. 1, (Winter 1993), pp. 28–39.

Lutjens, Sheryl, "Democracy and Socialist Cuba," in Sandor Halebsky and John M. Kirk (eds.), *Cuba in Transition: Crisis and Transformation*, Boulder: Westview Press, 1992.

Machado Rodriguez, Dario L., "La lección del pueblo," *Granma*, October 25, 1997, p. 8.

Magdoff, Harry, "Socialism, Democracy and Planning: Remarks at a Conference," *Monthly Review*, Vol. 33, No. 2 (June 1981), pp. 22–30.

Mantilla Ramírez, Raúl, "El partido y la rendición de cuenta de los delegados a sus electores," *El Militante Comunista*, (April 1988), pp. 28–33.

Martín, José A., "Salud Pública en la agenda de los Consejos Populares," *Granma*, November 27, 1993, p. 2.

Martínez, Silvia, "A debate el palpitar de la sociedad," *Granma*, March 12, 1994, p. 3.

Marx, Karl, "Letter to Domela Nieuwenhuis, 22 February, 1881," in Karl Marx and Friedrich Engels, *Correspondence 1846–1895*, New York: International Publishers, 1935.

_____, "Critique of the Gotha Programme," in *Karl Marx and Frederick Engels, Selected Works*, New York: International Publishers, 1968..

_____, "The Civil War in France," in Hal Draper (ed.), *Karl Marx and Friedreich Engels: Writings on the Paris Commune*, New York: Monthly Review Press, 1971.

_____, "Letter to Liebnecht, April 6, 1871," in Hal Draper (ed.), *Karl Marx and Friedreich Engels: Writings on the Paris Commune*, New York: Monthly Review Press, 1971.

_____, "Letter to Kugelmann, April 12, 1871," in Hal Draper (ed.), *Karl Marx and Friedreich Engels: Writings on the Paris Commune*, New York: Monthly Review Press, 1971.

_____, speech at the International's anniversary banquet in London, September 24 or 25, 1871, in Hal Draper (ed.), *Karl Marx and Friedreich Engels: Writings on the Paris Commune*, New York: Monthly Review Press, 1971.

_____, "Conspectus of Bakunin's Statism and Anarchy," in David Fernbach (ed.), *Karl Marx, Political Writings*, Vol. 3, *The First International and After*, New York: Random House, 1974.

_____, "Critique of Hegel's Doctrine of the State," in Karl Marx, *Early Writings*, New York: Vintage Books, 1975.

Marx, Karl, and Frederick Engels, "Manifesto of the Communist Party," in *Karl Marx and Frederick Engels, Selected Works*, New York: International Publishers, 1968.

Mata Monfort, Nelson, "Los Gastos del Presupuesto de los OLPP," *Finanzas y Crédito*, No. 5 (January-May 1986), pp. 47–48.

Mayoral, María Julia, "Tratan Consejos Populares sobre lucha contra el delito," *Granma*, October 29, 1991, p. 2.

_____, "Concluyó rendición de cuenta en la capital," *Granma*, May 8, 1992, p. 1.

_____, "Armas de un Consejo," *Granma*, June 18, 1992, p. 2.

_____, "Indagación para bién de todos: Vivencias de la Presidenta de una Comisión de Candidaturas," *Granma*, January 22, 1993, p. 3.

_____, "585 diputados obtienen más de 90% de los votos," *Granma*, February 27, 1993, p. 8.

———, "Acción de los diputados en las rendiciones de cuenta," *Granma*, August 12, 1993, p. 1.

———, "Consejos Populares apoyan curso escolar," *Granma*, August 28, 1993, p. 3.

———, "Comenzará en octubre rendición de cuenta de los delegados," *Granma*, September 23, 1994, p. 1.

———, "Rendición de cuenta en la capital: Margarita con buenos jardineros," *Granma*, November 8, 1994, p. 2.

———, "Nuestras elecciones: limpias y justas," *Granma*, May 17, 1995, p. 1.

———, "Delegados; Con ser buenos no basta," *Granma*, May 23, 1995, p. 8.

———, "Ganar en calor humano," *Granma*, May 26, 1995, p. 2.

———, "Mucho más que un derecho democrático," *Granma*, June 9, 1995, p. 2.

———, "Entrarán en funciones las comisiones de candidaturas," *Granma*, June 10, 1995, p. 1.

———, "Democracía electoral, no sólo en las urnas," *Granma*, June 15, 1995, p. 5.

———, "Extraordinaria victoria revolucionaria en pleno período especial," *Granma*, July 11, 1995, p. 1.

———, "El número de vueltas no determina la elección de los delegados," *Granma*, July 18, 1995, p. 1.

———, "Después de las elecciones: Reordenan consejos populares," *Granma*, August 11, 1996, p. 1.

———, "Rendición de cuenta: Estamos hablando de cambios," *Granma*, August 22, 1996, p. 5.

———, "Este Consejo echa raíces," *Granma*, September 5, 1996, p. 5.

———, "Consultarán a los electores para conformar precandidaturas," *Granma*, June 27, 1997, p. 3.

———, "Alta participación del electorado en asambleas de rendición de cuenta," *Granma*, July 19, 1997, p. 2.

———, "Destaca secretario de la Comisión Electoral Nacional importancia de las asambleas de nominación," *Granma*, August 29, 1997, p. 8.

———, "Yamil, entre la alegría y el qué vendrá," *Granma*, September 12, 1997, p. 3.

———, "Por el mejor y con cabeza propia," *Granma*, September 19, 1997, p. 4.

———, "Tomarán mañana posesión de sus cargos los 14,533 delegados elegidos recientemente," *Granma*, November 1, 1997, p. 1.

———, "Buscando lo que la gente piensa," *Granma*, November 26, 1997, p. 3.

———, "Ni competencia ni figuras de relleno," *Granma*, January 8, 1998, p. 5.

———, "Proyecto de candidatura para preidencia de la Asamblea Nacional genera amplio análisis," *Granma*, February 20, 1998, p. 3.

———, "Relación deputados-electores: Con capacidad para mucho más," *Granma*, May 13, 1998, p. 3.

———, "Confusiones sobre los Consejos Populares," *Granma*, July 10, 1998, p. 4.

——— "Asambleas municipales: Una mirada a las debilidades," *Granma*, January 14, 1999. URL: http://www.granma.cubaweb.cu.

———, "Diez herramientas claves del Parlamento cubano," *Granma*, July 31, 1998, p. 3.

McGeary, Johanna, and Cathy Booth, "Cuba Alone," *Time*, Vol. 142, No. 24 (December 6, 1993), pp. 42–54.

McKinley, James C., Jr., "New York City Council Sees Little Upheaval in Elections," *New York Times*, August 19, 1993, p. A–1.

_____ "In Cuba's New Dual Economy, Have-Nots Far Exceed Haves," *New York Times*, January 11, 1999, pp. A–1, A–6.

"Medidas de precios, ingresos reales y estimulación," *Trabajadores*, June 13, 1994.

Meisel, James H., and Edward S. Kozera (eds.), *Materials for the Study of the Soviet System: State and Party Constitutions, Laws, Decrees, Decisions and Official Statements of the Leaders in Translation*, 2d edition, Ann Arbor: George Wahr, 1953.

Mesa-Lago, Carmelo, *Cuba in the 1970s*, Albuquerque: University of New Mexico Press, 1974.

Meyer, Alfred G., *Leninism*, New York: Praeger, 1971.

Miliband, Ralph, "Marx and the State," in Ralph Miliband and John Saville (eds.), *The Socialist Register*, New York: Monthly Review Press, 1965.

_____, *The State in Capitalist Society*, New York: Basic Books, 1969.

_____, *Marxism and Politics*, New York: Oxford University Press, 1977.

Miranda Pérez, Héctor, "El Partido controla y dirige no administra ni suplanta funciones," *Granma*, August 7, 1998, URL: http://www.granma.cubawd.cu.

"Miremos primero hacía dentro," *Trabajadores*, March 14, 1994, p. 2.

Morales, Isabel, "¿Puede haber consulta más exhaustiva y popular? Entrevista a Manuel Mendez Castellanos, presidente de la Comisión de Candidaturas Nacional, acerca de la marcha del proceso electoral," *Granma*, December 9, 1992, p. 3.

_____, "Distritos: algo más que una operación aritmática," *Granma*, January 21, 1993, p. 3.

Morales, Isabel, and Silvia Martínez, "Parlamento obrero: un desafio a enfrentar con trabajo," *Granma*, January 22, 1994, p. 3.

Mosak, Esther, "Democracy: Learning by Doing," *Cuba Update*, Vol. 12, Nos. 1–2 (Winter-Spring 1991), pp. 19–20, 22.

"La muralla del silencio," *Trabajadores*, July 17, 1995, p. 2.

Murray, Mary, and Marc Frank, "The Cuban Letter," *Cuban Action*, No. 7 (Spring 1994), p. 7.

Nafite Navarro, Caridad, "¿Quién es Teovaldo?" *Trabajadores*, January 9, 1998, p. 3.

Navarro, Vicente, "Workers and Community Participation and Democratic Control in Cuba," *International Journal of Health Services*, Vol. 10, No. 2 (1980), pp. 198–215.

Navarron, Mireya, "Cuba Passes Law to Attract Greater Foreign Investment," *New York Times*, September 7, 1995, p. A12

Núñez Betancourt, Alberto, "Resultan participación popular en el proceso de nominación de candidatos," *Granma*, October 1, 1997, p. 3.

Ojeda, Mireya, "Comentario a propósito de las asambleas de rendición de cuenta del delegado," *Cinco de Septiembre*, October 27, 1987, p. 2.

Ollman, Bertell, "Marx's Vision of Communism: A Reconstruction," *Critique*, No. 8 (Summer 1977), pp. 4–41.

"Opiniones de delegados," *Poder Popular*, Vol. 5 (1986), pp. 12–13.

Pagés, Raisa, and Isabel Morales, "Diputados abogan por mayor control de los recursos materiales y financieros," *Granma*, December 25, 1996, p. 3.

Partido Comunista de Cuba, "El trabajo del Partido en la actual conyuntura (V)," *Granma*, August 21, 1996, p. 3.

"Pasan revista a importantes asuntos en comisiones del Parlamento," *Granma*, December 24, 1996, p. 8.

Pérez Hechavarría, Agustín, "Afanza influencia de Consejos Populares," *Granma*, September 11, 1993, p. 2.

Pierson, Christopher, *Marxist Theory and Democratic Politics*, Cambridge: Polity Press, 1986.

Pita Astudillo, Felix, "Un mensaje insultante para los cubanos: Fariseísmo," *Granma*, May 26, 1996, p. 3.

Poder Popular: Boletín del Comité Ejecutivo Municipal de Cienfuegos, No. 2 (February 1989), pp. 9–12.

"Lo politico, la situación economicá y las finanzas," *Trabajadores,* January 17, 1994, p. 2.

Prada, Pedro, "Analizan distribución de productos agrícolas," *Granma*, April 11, 1992, p. 3.

Prado, José, "De nuestras elecciones: un caso singular en una asamblea normal," *Trabajadores*, April 4, 1989, p. 4.

Prieto González, Alfredo, and Haroldo Dilla Alfonso, "Para una reflexión sobre la democrácia en Cuba (a propósito de un artículo de Jorge Domínguez)," *El Caribe Contemporáneo*, Nos. 1, 2 (1988), pp. 36–52.

"Primer período ordinario de sesiones de la Cuarta Legislatura: Analizan gestión y experiencias de los Consejos Populares," *Granma*, July 1, 1993, p. 4.

"Primer período ordinario de sesiones de la Cuarta Legislatura: Reseña de los debates," *Granma*, June 29, 1993, pp. 2–4.

"El pueblo sabe," *Trabajadores*, July 3, 1995, p. 2.

"Quienes son los políticos de nuestra política," *Trabajadores*, January 10, 1994, p. 2.

Rabinowitch, Alexander, *The Bolsheviks Come to Power: The Revolution of 1917 in Petrograd*, New York: Norton, 1976.

Rabkin, Rhoda, "Cuba: The Aging of a Revolution," in Sergio Roca (ed.), *Socialist Cuba: Past Interpretations and Future Challenges*, Boulder: Westview Press, 1988.

Raluy, Antonio, "Una campaña electoral 'a la cubana,'" *El Diario/La Prensa*, February 7, 1993, p. 17.

Ramírez Manzano, Raul, "Por un diálogo directo," *Trabajadores*, November 13, 1995, p. 4.

Rass, Reynoldo, "Permutas laborales a partir del próximo lunes," *Granma*, January 31, 1992, p. 4.

"El reciente proceso de nominación de candidatos," *Granma*, June 24, 1995, p. 8.

Recio, Renato, "Cuba: integrar la democracia al patrimonio revolucionario," *Trabajadores*, July 7, 1993, p. 2.

Reed, Gail, "April 8: Election Day in Cuba," *Granma Weekly Review*, April 15, 1979, p. 4.

———, "Taking the Leap: Cuba's Fourth Party Congress," *Cuba Update*, Vol. 11, No. 4 (Fall 1990), pp. 19–20.

"Reseña de los debates de la última jornada," *Granma*, May 3, 1994, p. 4.

Resoluciones aprobadas por el III Congreso del Partido Comunista de Cuba, Havana: Editora Politica, 1986.

"La resolución sobre la división político-administrativa," *Primer Congreso del Partido Comunista de Cuba: Memorias*, Havana: Departmento de Orientación Revolucionaria del Comité Central del Partido Comunista de Cuba, 1976.

Rigby, T. H., "Introduction: Political Legitimacy, Weber and Communist Mono-organizational Systems," in T. H. Rigby and Ferenc Fehr (eds.), *Political Legitimation in Communist States*, New York: St. Martin's Press, 1982.

Ritter, Archibald R. M., "The Authenticity of Participatory Democracy in Cuba," in Archibald R. M. Ritter and David Pollock (eds.), *Latin American Prospects for the 1980's: Equity, Democratization and Development*, New York: Praeger 1983.

———, "People's Power and the Communist Party," in Sandor Halebsky and John M. Kirk (eds.), *Cuba: Twenty-five Years of Revolution, 1959–1984*, New York: Praeger, 1985.

Rodríguez, Grisell, "Elecciones en Cuba: un derecho ciudadano" (Interview with Ernesto Suárez), *Poder Popular*, Vol. 8, No. 3 (1989), p. 3.

Rodríguez, Javier, "Deputados Cubanos analizan producción y autoabasteciemiento," *Prensa Latina*, August 24, 1998, URL: http://www.prensa-latina.org.

Rodríguez Alemán, Lazara, "Crecen las relaciones económicas de Cuba, a pesar de Helms/Burton," *Prensa Latina*, December 20, 1998, URL: http://www.prensa-latina.org.

Rodríguez Cruz, Francisco, "Nominación de candidatos: no fué ejercicio acrítico," *Trabajadores*, December 1, 1997, p. 5.

———, "¿Cómo se planifica hoy en Cuba?" *Trabajadores*, December 8, 1997, p. 3.

———, "Prueba de conciencia patriótica, unidad y apoyo al sistema político," *Trabajadores*, December 15, 1997, p. 5.

Rodríguez Molina, Diego, "Rendición de cuenta de delegados: un diálogo de pueblo," *Granma*, November 18, 1995, p. 3.

Rodríguez Salas, Manolo, "Desde el Ministro hasta el bodeguero tienen que apoyar al delegado," *Granma*, November 10, 1995, p. 4.

Rojas Aguilera, Alexis, "El Consejo Popular de la Gallega," *Granma*, July 2, 1992, p. 3.

———, "Continúan encuentros de candidatos con los electores," *Granma*, December 16, 1997, p. 8.

Roman, Peter, "A Preliminary Report on the October 1986 Municipal Elections in Cuba," *Socialism and Democracy*, No. 5 (Fall-Winter 1987), pp. 89–102.

———, "Poder Popular en Cuba," *Pensamiento Crítico*, Vol. 11, No. 61 (October-December 1988), pp. 1–12.

———, "Representative Government in Socialist Cuba," *Latin American Perspectives*, Issue 76, Vol. 20, No. 1 (Winter 1993), pp. 7–27.

———, "The Cuban Municipal Assembly: Local Representative Government Under Socialism," Ph.D. dissertation, Princeton University,1994.

———, "Workers' Parliaments in Cuba," *Latin American Perspectives*, Issue 87, Vol. 22, No. 4 (Fall 1995) pp. 43–58.

Rosenberg, Arthur, *Democracy and Socialism*, Boston: Beacon Press, 1965.

Ross, Pedro, speech given on May 1, 1994, *Trabajadores*, May 2, 1994, pp. 8–9.

Rousseau, Jean-Jacques, "A Discourse on the Origin of Inequality," in Jean-Jacques Rousseau, *The Social Contract and Discourses*, New York: Dutton, 1950.

_____, "The Social Contract" in Jean-Jacques Rousseau, *The Social Contract and Discourses*, New York: Dutton, 1950.

_____, "Gouvernement de Pologne," in C. E. Vaughan, *The Political Writings of Jean Jacques Rousseau*, Vol. 2, New York: Wiley, 1962.

_____, "Letters Written from the Mountains," in *The Miscellaneous Works of Mr. J. J. Rousseau*, Vol. 4, New York: Burt Franklin, 1972.

R.S., "Asuntos del barrio," *Tribuna de la Habana*, May 19, 1996, p. 2.

Rubio, Vladia, "Sábado ejemplaizante en el Malecón," *Granma*, November 19, 1991, p. 2.

_____, "Unidad: arma principal en la lucha contra la indisciplina social," *Granma*, May 6, 1997, p. 2.

Rubio, Vladia, Isabel Morales, Iraida Calzadilla, Raisa Pagés, María Julia Mayoral, Sara Más, Silvia Martinez, Juan Varela Pérez, Emilio del Barrio, José Antonio de la Osa, José A. Martin, and Roger Ricardo Luis, "Sobre el Régimen Laboral en las Inversiones Extranjeras," *Granma*, September 6, 1995, p. 4.

Sanchez, Luis, "From Consumers to Producers: Work Experiences with Small Agricultural Groups to Improve the Food Self-Sufficiency Among the Members of a Community," unpublished manuscript.

Schulkind, Eugene, "Introduction," in Eugene Schulkind (ed.), *The Paris Commune of 1871: The View from the Left*, New York: Grove Press, 1974.

Schulz, Donald E. "Political Participation in Communist Systems: The Conceptual Approach," in Donald E. Schulz, and Jan S. Adams (eds.), *Political Participation in Communist Countries*, New York: Pergamon Press, 1981.

Shafir, M., and O. Kutafin, "La constitución de la URSS acerca de los soviets de diputados populares y las normas de su elección," in M. Shafir et al., *Los Soviets, Organos del Poder Popular*, Moscow: Progreso, 1979..

Shipler, David K., "The Politics of Neighborhood," *New Yorker*, June 3, 1991, pp. 45–77.

"Sobre precios y tarifas," *Trabajadores*, May 23, 1994, p. 2.

Sternheimer, Stephen, "Communications and Power in Soviet Urban Politics," in Everett M. Jacobs (ed.), *Soviet Local Politics and Government*, London: George Allen and Unwin, 1983.

Suárez Hernández, Georgina, "Protagonismo político en Cuba: antecedentes y proyección actual," paper presented at the Cuba Conference, Halifax, Nova Scotia, November 3, 1989.

Suárez Salazar, Luis, "Crisis, reestructuración y democracía en Cuba: apuntes para un debate," *Cuadernos de Nuestra America*, Vol. 10, No. 20 (July-December 1993), pp. 65–82.

_____, "The 1995 municipal elections: a different angle," *Cuban Review* (October 1995).

_____, "El sistema electoral cubano: apuntes para una crítica," in Haroldo Dilla alfonso (ed.), *La democracia en Cuba y el diferendo con los Estados Unidos*, Havana: Centro de Estudios sobre América, 1995.

"Synthesis Cuba," *Prensa Latina*, December 5, 1997, URL: http://www.prensa-latina.org.

"Synthesis Cuba," *Prensa Latina*, December 15, 1997, URL: http://www.prensa-latina.org.

Talmon, J. L., *The Origins of Totalitarian Democracy*, New York: Norton, 1970.

Tesoro, Susana, "Punto de vista: vale más precaver," *Bohemia*, February 17, 1989, p. 29.

_____, "A pecho descubierto: una conversación con el recién estrenado presidente de la Asamblea Nacional, Juan Escalona Reguera," *Bohemia*, July 20, 1990, pp. 50–55.

_____, "Elecciones 'Todo acto o voz genial viene del pueblo,'" *Bohemia*, December 5, 1997, p. B39.

Therborn, Goran, *What Does the Ruling Class Do When It Rules? State Apparatuses and State Power Under Feudalism, Capitalism and Socialism*, London: Verso, 1980.

Torrado, Fabio Raimundo, "Differences and Similarities," *Granma Internacional*, January 3, 1998, URL: http:www.granma.cu.

Treaster, Joseph B., "Cubans Arrested During Soviet Visit," *New York Times*, April 5, 1989, p. A–8.

"Un intercambio de opiniones," *Trabajadores*, March 16, 1991, p. 2.

Valdés, Teresa, "Crean secciones penales de los Tribunales Municipales a nivel de Consejo Popular," *Granma*, February 1, 1992, p. 2.

Valdés Paz, Juan, "Notas sobre el sistema político cubano," in Haroldo Dilla Alfonso (ed.), *La democracia en Cuba y el diferendo con los Estados Unidos*, Havana: Centro de Estudios sobre América, 1995.

_____, "Poder local y participación," in Haroldo Dilla Alfonso (ed.), *La participación en Cuba y los retos del futuro*, Havana: Centro de Estudios sobre América, 1996.

Vaughan, C. E., *The Political Writings of Jean Jacques Rousseau*, Vol. 2, New York: Wiley, 1962.

Vázquez Raña, Mario, "Entrevista de Raúl al periódico El Sol de Mexico," *Granma*, April 24, 1993.

"El voto unido: suprema unidad," *Trabajadores*, December 8, 1997, p. 2.

Waller, Michael, *Democratic Centralism: An Historical Commentary*, New York: St. Martin's Press, 1981.

White, Stephen, John Gardner, and George Schopflin, *Communist Political Systems: An Introduction*, 2d edition, London: Macmillan Education, 1987.

Wroe, Ann, "Heroic Illusions: A Survey of Cuba," *The Economist*, April 6, 1996, pp. survey 1–16.

Zaslavsky, Victor, and Robert J. Brym, "The Structure of Power and the Function of Soviet Local Elections," in Everett M. Jacobs (ed.), *Soviet Local Politics and Government*, London: George Allen and Unwin, 1983.

Zimbalist, Andrew, and Claes Brundenius, *The Cuban Economy: Measurement and Analysis of Socialist Performance*, Baltimore: Johns Hopkins University Press, 1989.

Index